Just The Facts About Jesus

Joanne,
It was great seeing you again!
Hope to see you again soon.
[signature]
Matthew 5:16

Lawrence B. Keffer

BIBLICAL RESEARCH CENTER
Tampa, FL 33687

Copyright © 2005 by Lawrence B. Keffer

BIBLICAL RESEARCH CENTER
P.O. Box 292576
Tampa, FL 33687
Phone: 813-376-8888

ISBN
Perfect Bound: 1-58374-117-8
Case Bound: 1-58374-119-4

Library of Congress Preassigned Card Number: 1583741178

Printed in the U.S.A.

10 9 8 7 6 5 4 3 2 1

It is the author's desire to reach as many people as possible with the Gospel of our Lord Jesus Christ. Therefore permission to reproduce portions of this book will likely be given to likeminded individuals or organizations who contact the publisher.

There are portions of this book the author obtained by permission and were to be used specifically for this printing. Therefore permission may have to be given by the originator. They are Bible believing, God loving Christians who desire the Gospel to be made known. So, I am sure they would likely agree also, if asked. They did so for me.

www.BiblicalResearchCenter.info

The scriptural text in this book is taken from
The Holy Bible, The King James Version, (Cambridge) 1769.

Acknowledgments

Writing the Book

Where to start? I would first need to acknowledge my God and Father of Jesus Christ, my Lord and Savior, for inviting me into His will and for giving me a sense of purpose while writing this book and providing me with direction and understanding. I give thanks to Him for teaching me the truth about His Word and bringing me from *believing* Jesus was the Lord to *knowing* He is my Lord and Savior. He has blessed me with a supportive wife and son who were very encouraging throughout the whole process. The Lord is good; I thank Him for creating in me a burden for the lost and providing me friends, like John Manibusan and Tony Granims who have helped me (more than they know) to write this book by giving me all their valuable insights and help. There has been many a day when I would ask their opinion on a particular subject and their ideas were the ones I used. Those two really love the Lord, and I am thankful to have them as friends and brothers in Christ.

Witnessing

I do not believe I had the confidence I needed to share the Gospel effectively until I read Ray Comfort's books and watched his videos. His video *"Hell's Best Kept Secret"* along with other excellent evangelistic information can be viewed for free on his website **www.LivingWaters.com**. Ray Comfort's video *"True and False Conversion"* helped me articulate my beliefs in a way that could be understood without difficulty. You can judge for yourself when you read the chapter "Is Jesus your Lord?" in this book. Most of the quotes in this book come from his books. When I was fumbling for words and requested permission to use his research and work for my book, he interrupted me and said, "Use whatever you want!" As I search out authors and ask permission to use their works my heart is warmed to know that there are men out there who are trusting God to be their sufficiency while helping people like me to serve God by allowing me to get the Gospel out by using their words. Ray Comfort is one of those men.

Understanding Biblical Prophecy

Herbert Lockyer was an accomplished author until his death in 1984. I learned a great deal from his book *All the Messianic Prophecies of the Bible*. I highly recommend it. He wrote dozens of books, and his style is easy to read and understand. I would recommend doing a name search on the internet and checking out all of his work.

3

Names, Titles and Descriptions of Jesus Christ

Dr. Steve Harmon, a Pastor for Maineville Baptist Church in Ohio, put the list together for the descriptions of Jesus. When I called him to ask permission to use it he said, "You don't need my permission its the Word of God!" I am very thankful for his love of God's Word and his diligence in putting the list together. I only changed the format; all the credit for such a great list goes to him.

Understanding Faith

The chapter in this book, "The Just Shall Live by Faith," is quoted from *It's Who You Know* by Morris Venden, published by The Concerned Group, Inc. (800-447-4332). Mr. Venden has a gift: communicating his thoughts to paper in a way that can be easily understood. I highly recommend reading his books. Permission to use the chapter has been obtained by both the author and publisher.

Understanding the King James Bible

There is a terrific website called **www.biblebelievers.com** which has all the information you need to understand the battle going on over God's Word. There are links to teachings from Samuel Gipp, whom I like because he doesn't pull any punches. He tells it like he sees it, and I respect that. James Knox is also a very passionate speaker with a gift for explaining biblical truths. Gail Riplinger has many books out that were a great help to me in regard to this subject. The book *New Age Bible Versions* is an exhaustive research on the deceptions of the modern versions. Mrs. Riplinger also graciously gave me her permission to use her research in my book. You can purchase her books on the website **www.avpublications.com**.

These are some of the websites that can help you with this subject as well as other topics:
http://jesus-is-lord.com/kinginde.htm
www.thebelieversorganization.org

Understanding Creation and Evolution

Another man I would like to acknowledge is Kent Hovind. Dr. Hovind intentionally does not copyright his work so that others like myself can use his material to spread the Gospel. He has a great website at **www.drdino.com**. Dr. Hovind was a science teacher for around 15 years and became an evangelist, exposing the lies of evolution in our school textbooks and teaching how real science proves the Bible is truth. I encourage you to investigate his videos and books; they will help you to draw closer to the Lord, as they did for me. This subject should not be ignored, as it is a great avenue for sharing the Gospel, starting with the natural (science) and working toward the spiritual (God's Word).

Dedication

I dedicate this book to my son Adam.
His kind heart, gentle spirit, and love for God inspires me
to try harder to be a better servant of my Lord Jesus Christ.

~

"Jesus answered and said unto her, Whosoever drinketh of this water shall thirst again: But whosoever drinketh of the water that I shall give him shall never thirst; but the water that I shall give him shall be in him a well of water springing up into everlasting life."

John 4:13-14

Table of Contents

Acknowledgments...Page 3

Forward..Page 8

Who is Jesus? ....Page 15

Jesus Christ's Names, Titles, and Descriptions....................Page 27

FACT: Jesus Represents Spiritual Israel........................Page 82

The Twelve Tribes..Page 84

Messages from Israel...Page 85

Introduction to Prophecy.......................................Page 87

Messianic Prophecy Fulfillment.................................Page 95

The Just Shall Live by His Faith.......................... ....Page 217

FACT: Jesus Christ Is the Word................................Page 227

Is Jesus Your Lord? ....Page 255

Last Word ....Page 269

Index ....Page 272

FORWARD

I was sitting in my office looking out the window wondering how I could share the Gospel more effectively. I had the desire, but which direction to go puzzled me. Years earlier, I had purchased a sailboat with the intentions of doing missionary work with it when I "semi-retired." I had dreams of taking my wife and son with me and going to third world countries and ministering to the people who were in need. I dreamed of living off the ocean and using the wind to direct my path. It seemed perfect in my mind. My dreams of the adventures my family and I would have helped me through the times of discouragement while refitting the boat.

After three and a half years and a zillion dollars I was ready for the maiden voyage of *The Messenger*, a name that fit the boat and the purpose it was given. There was one problem: My wife had lost interest in sailing! My son was initially excited about the idea of long term sailing and loved the water, but he had become "burnt out" with the boat from the years of dealing with my frustration while refitting it. *The Messenger* was no longer a relaxing enjoyable experience for him, but a place of work, tension, and arguing. He had been my biggest help in restoring the boat and now he didn't want anything to do with it. All my dreams, all my plans, all my hard work, all my money, had not brought what I thought God's will was in my life. I was very frustrated; I had lost my direction and didn't know what to do…I decided to go sailing anyway.

I asked my good friend John to go sailing with me and he agreed. I had been sharing my dreams of missionary work with him and he seemed to be getting hooked, so we stocked up the boat and set off to find those people hungry for the Gospel of our Lord Jesus Christ.

One thing I forgot to mention: when I bought the boat I didn't know anything about sailing! I quickly took a sailing class, but the boats were much smaller than mine and meant for day sailing. Though I had a basic knowledge of how to sail, I had never captained my sailboat for more than a few hours. My friend John knew even less than me and because of that, he thought I knew more than I did, so that is why he agreed to come along.

We set sail from Tampa and headed south, to where the wind does not blow and the heat hurts. We made many mistakes on our trip, but we survived and wound up docking at South Seas Plantation, a beautiful resort located on Sanibel Island, for the majority of our trip. This was the opposite of what I had envisioned. Instead of living off the ocean we were ordering fries from the poolside waitresses while looking for someone to share Christ with. Instead of helping a needy person, we were having dinner on a million dollar yacht. Though we were able to talk with some people, the opportunities were sparse and it seemed they were more interested in having fun than hearing about Christ. We stayed for 3 days before we realized our efforts were best served somewhere else. Also, the fish were not biting there and we really wanted to catch something!

Our return trip was more exciting than we could ever have hoped for. When we experienced some engine problems I decided to sail back (we had been motoring most of the way because of lack of wind). There we sat, floating at about 500 feet an hour, when all of a sudden the wind came! And boy did it come, 25 to 45 knot winds that heeled the boat over on its side. I think our mast even touched the water, but I don't know for sure because it was pitch black. It was scary for about 30 seconds, but once I regained control over *The Messenger,* it was the most exhilarating experience I've ever had. I felt like a rock leaving a sling shot. We were heeled over at about a 30 degree angle. The water sprayed over the bow and the little dinghy tied to the stern skimmed back and forth and looked like a power boat in our wake. John was wide eyed but seemed to be OK until I asked for my life vest, and then he seemed to hold on to the lifelines a little tighter. That wind brought us all the way home and we were better sailors because of it.

You might be asking yourself, "What does *his* sailing trip have to do with writing a book?" After the maiden voyage, I reflected on the whole sailboat experience from beginning to end. It took me a while, but I realized what I had done. I had imposed my will and labeled it God's will! I never asked God if it was His will that I buy a sailboat, or if I should use it for missionary purposes. I had kept God out of the picture. The Lord is good and kind and loving; God's Word says, **"And we know that all things work together for good to them that love God, to them who are the called according to His purpose." Romans 8:28**

This brings me back to my office, wondering how I could share the Gospel more effectively. I had never written a book before, just like sailing. I didn't know how to write a book, just like sailing. Publishing a book is expensive, just like sailing. One big difference: I asked God first in prayer! I wasn't going to make that mistake twice! It started out as an idea and then grew into a passion. I purchased one of those software programs that let you speak the words into your computer because I type with two fingers at about ten words a minute with five mistakes. Then I found out that the program made more mistakes than me, so I went back to my hunt-and-peck method.

I started researching Old Testament prophecies. I wanted to list all of them and show where and when they were fulfilled. I thought that would be helpful in showing people that God's Word was divine and the only source of truth in this world. I found some in Ralph Muncaster's book *A Skeptic's Search for God.* He was an atheist who came to Christ by trying to prove evolution. But my attention shifted to prophecies of Jesus, and then it happened--it became crystal clear what I was supposed to write about! "Just the facts about Jesus." It became so easy, resources appeared, authors gave permission to use their work, and I could see God's blessing on this work that I had not seen with the sailboat. I was receiving blessing after blessing while studying and researching for my book. My faith increased and God showed me new truths, as well as made me aware of a few deceptions I had accepted.

These studies shaped my understanding of the Lord and how I should walk in His precepts. I figured if they worked for me, they might work for someone else. In this work I did not try to reinvent the wheel. Instead, I drew heavily from scripture and learned from the insights and conclusions of Christian scholars.

9

I have been involved with many different religious denominations over the years and have come to agree with Catherine Booth's conclusion: **"I do not believe in any religion apart from doing the will of God."** I also have come to believe that the will of God is found in the Holy Bible. The Jesus who saves is the one found in the Holy Bible--not the one made up in the minds of people who have no knowledge of God's Word and think that by accepting Jesus as their Lord they receive a "sin credit card" and can do whatever they want because He paid the price for their sins.

My religion is striving to love God with all my heart, soul, mind, and strength and loving my neighbor as I love myself. Although I fall short in my attempts to do the will of my Father, it comforts me to know that my salvation has been assured by the blood of my Lord and Savior Jesus Christ. I trust Him to accomplish that which He has promised. I wait for His return with the hope of eternal fellowship with my God. What a joy it is to be a Christian and to have this hope! I thank God for preserving me so that I might come to know His Son.

My testimony is best understood in the parable of the Sower and the Seeds.

Matthew 13:3-8
"And he spake many things unto them in parables, saying, Behold, a sower went forth to sow; And when he sowed, some *seeds* fell by the way side, and the fowls came and devoured them up: Some fell upon stony places, where they had not much earth: and forthwith they sprung up, because they had no deepness of earth: And when the sun was up, they were scorched; and because they had no root, they withered away. And some fell among thorns; and the thorns sprung up, and choked them: But other fell into good ground, and brought forth fruit, some an hundredfold, some sixty fold, some thirtyfold."

Matthew 13:18-23
"Hear ye therefore the parable of the sower.
When any one heareth the word of the kingdom, and understandeth *it* not, then cometh the wicked *one*, and catcheth away that which was sown in his heart. This is he which received seed by the way side. But he that received the seed into stony places, the same is he that heareth the word, and anon with joy receiveth it; Yet hath he not root in himself, but dureth for a while: for when tribulation or persecution ariseth because of the word, by and by he is offended. He also that received seed among the thorns is he that heareth the word; and the care of this world, and the deceitfulness of riches, choke the word, and he becometh unfruitful. But he that received seed into the good ground is he that heareth the word, and understandeth *it*; which also beareth fruit, and bringeth forth, some an hundredfold, some sixty, some thirty."

I was every one of those seeds! I was the seed thrown by the wayside; when I heard the Word I did not understand it. I was blinded by my selfishness and greed. When I was young I thought I was a Christian because I went to church, but my life was my testimony. I had no relationship with my Lord. I had made a god of my own understanding. I worshipped the god of self. I had no idea who the living God was because I did not read the *Bible,* and as a result I was deceived! The worst part was that I didn't even know what I was doing to myself.

I was the seed thrown on rocky ground. When I was in the Army I borrowed my friend's Bible and read the book of Matthew and finally had a picture of Jesus I could believe in. I received the Word with joy. I can still remember crying and asking Jesus into my life. After that I studied the Bible, but mostly interpretations of it by others. As a result, when temptation came I fell; when tribulation came I reverted back to my old ways. I had no depth. I believed in Jesus but I didn't love Him. I had not yet made Him my Lord.

I was the seed sown among thorns. I professed to being a Christian. I could quote the Bible and argue with you about it over cocktails. That only meant that I had a "superficial head-knowledge" of the Bible but the good book was not in my heart. I believed that Jesus was God's Son, and I thought I was a pretty good guy compared to most people. But, the facts of my daily life proved me a liar - I loved money more than God. I put myself before everyone, even my wife and son at times, and for that I am ashamed. I cared more about things than I did about God, my family, and my friends. Though I had attained a level of success in business and finance, I had done nothing for the Lord. I was like a branch on a fruit tree with no fruit. I was still missing the mark; deceived, yet unaware. But my Lord was faithful, preserving me until I would come unto Him and repent, acknowledge Him as my Savior, and receive him as my Lord.

Finally, I was a seed thrown in good soil. I came to understand God's message of love. I experienced a pure faith when I came to know His Word was His Will. The truth became real to me! I learned about the prophecies in the Bible and realized that God had done a mighty work. Only God knows the future, and only the Bible has a 100 percent accuracy rate on prophecies.

He showed me other truths such as,
"But wilt thou know, O vain man, that faith without works is dead?" **James 2:20**

The one truth in His Word that really woke me up was,
"And hereby we do know that we know him, if we keep his commandments. He that saith, I know him, and keepeth not his commandments, is a liar, and the truth is not in him." **1 John 2:3, 4**

When I responded to my Lord's call I knew that I must take action to help others. I believe the works we do when we are born again not only express our love for God, but also confirm to ourselves our relationship with Jesus. My Lord showed me that love is an action, not a feeling; the feeling comes from the action. The most loving thing I could do was share the Gospel with every living person. This was the last command Jesus gave us while on earth.

"And Jesus came and spake unto them, saying, All power is given unto me in heaven and in earth. Go ye therefore, and teach all nations, baptizing them in the name of the Father, and of the Son, and of the Holy Ghost: Teaching them to observe all things whatsoever I have commanded you: and, lo, I am with you alway, *even* unto the end of the world. Amen." **Matthew 28:18-20**

If you're a Christian wondering what God's will is for you, I can help you right now, **"SHARE THE GOSPEL OF CHRIST!"** It is that simple. We have been given the ministry of reconciliation. Do something for the Lord. Remember - love is an action.

If you are not a Christian and have a desire to know if Jesus is the Lord, you can receive a copy of this book for free. Just write to:

Lawrence B. Keffer
P.O. Box 292576
Tampa, FL 33687

Ask for a free copy, and I will send one to you!
My hope is that this book will lead you to the Truth.

"Jesus saith unto him, I am the way, **the truth**, and the life: no man cometh unto the Father, but by me."
John 14:6

The scriptural text in this book is taken from
The Holy Bible, The King James Version, (Cambridge) 1769.

12

"Ask, and it shall be given you; seek, and ye shall find; knock, and it shall be opened unto you."

Matthew 7:7

14

Who is Jesus?

1 Timothy 3:16
And without controversy great is the mystery of godliness: **God was manifest in the flesh**, justified in the Spirit, seen of angels, preached unto the Gentiles, believed on in the world, received up into glory.

What did He say about Himself?

John 6:35
And Jesus said unto them, **I am the bread of life**: he that cometh to me shall never hunger; and he that believeth on me shall never thirst.

John 6:40
And this is the will of him that sent me, that **every one which seeth the Son, and believeth on him, may have everlasting life: and I will raise him up at the last day.**

John 6:47
Verily, verily, I say unto you, **He that believeth on me hath everlasting life.**

John 6:48
I am the bread of life.

John 8:12
Then spake Jesus again unto them, saying, **I am the light of the world**: he that followeth me shall not walk in darkness, but shall have the light of life.

John 8:28-29
Then said Jesus unto them, **when ye have lifted up the Son of man, then shall ye know that I am he, and that I do nothing of myself**; but as my Father hath taught me, I speak these things. And he that sent me is with me: **the Father hath not left me alone; for I do always those things that please him.**

John 8:42
Jesus said unto them, If God were your Father, ye would love me: **for I proceeded forth and came from God**; neither came I of myself, but **he sent me.**

Quotes..."The author of a quote, even though they may not be a Christian, shows how God's Word cuts through the fabric of every man's soul."
Unknown   **"See Genesis 1:27"**

John 8:58

Jesus said unto them, Verily, verily, I say unto you, **before Abraham was, I am.**

John 9:35-38

Jesus heard that they had cast him out; and when he had found him, he said unto him, **Dost thou believe on the Son of God?** He answered and said, **Who is he, Lord,** that I might believe on him? And Jesus said unto him, **Thou hast both seen him, and it is he that talketh with thee.** And he said, Lord, I believe. **And he worshipped him.**

John 10:7, 9

Then said Jesus unto them again, Verily, verily, I say unto you, **I am the door** of the sheep... **I am the door: by me if any man enter in, he shall be saved,** and shall go in and out, and find pasture.

John 10:11

I am the good shepherd: the good shepherd giveth his life for the sheep.

John 10:17, 18

Therefore doth my Father love me, because **I lay down my life, that I might take it again.** No man taketh it from me, **but I lay it down of myself. I have power to lay it down, and I have power to take it again.** This commandment have I received of my Father.

John 10:28-30

And I give unto them eternal life; and they shall never perish, neither shall any man pluck them out of my hand. My Father, which gave them me, is greater than all; and no man is able to pluck them out of my Father's hand. **I and my Father are one.**

"A man who was merely a man and said the sort of things Jesus said wouldn't be a great moral teacher. He'd be a lunatic – on the level with a man who says he's a poached egg, or else he'd be the devil of Hell. You must make your choice. Either this man was, and is, the Son of God: or else a madman or something worse. You can shut Him up for a fool, you can spit at Him and kill Him as a demon; or you can fall at His feet and call Him Lord and God. But don't let us come with any patronizing nonsense about His being a great human teacher. He hasn't left that open to us. He didn't intend to."

C. S. Lewis, *The Case for Christianity*   **"See Mark 14:61-62"**

16

John 10:36
Say ye of him, whom the Father hath sanctified, and sent into the world, Thou blasphemest; because I said, **I am the Son of God?**

John 11:25-26
Jesus said unto her, **I am the resurrection, and the life**: he that believeth in me, though he were dead, yet shall he live: And whosoever liveth and believeth in me shall never die. Believest thou this?

John 12:31-32
Now is the judgment of this world: now shall the prince of this world be cast out. **And I, if I be lifted up from the earth, will draw all men unto me.**

John 14:6
Jesus saith unto him, **I am the way, the truth, and the life**: no man cometh unto the Father, but by me.

John 15: 1, 2
I am the true vine and my Father is the husbandman. Every branch in me that beareth not fruit he taketh away: and every branch that beareth fruit, he purgeth it, that it may bring forth more fruit.

John 16:16
A little while, and ye shall not see me: and again, a little while, and ye shall see me, because I go to the Father.

John 17:5
And now, O Father, **glorify thou me with thine own self with the glory which I had with thee before the world was.**

"When we share our faith, we are in the win/win situation. If people accept what we say we win. If we plant the seed of God's word, we win; and even if we are rejected, we win. This is because the Bible says that when that happens, the Spirit of glory and of God rests upon us. When we contend for the faith and are rejected, we are to rejoice and leap for joy, for great is our reward in heaven (Luke 6:22, 23). It is a winning situation every single time that you share your faith!"

Mark Cahill   **"See 1 Peter 4:14"**

17

John 18:36-37

Jesus answered, My kingdom is not of this world: if my kingdom were of this world, then would my servants fight, that I should not be delivered to the Jews: but now is my kingdom not from hence. Pilate therefore said unto him, **Art thou a king then?** Jesus answered, **Thou sayest that I am a king. To this end was I born, and for this cause came I into the world,** that I should bear witness unto the truth. **Every one that is of the truth heareth my voice.**

John 6:48-51

I am that bread of life. Your fathers did eat manna in the wilderness, and are dead. This is the bread which cometh down from heaven, that a man may eat thereof, and not die. **I am the living bread** which came down from heaven: **if any man eat of this bread, he shall live for ever: and the bread that I will give is my flesh, which I will give for the life of the world.**

Matthew 11:27

All things are delivered unto me of my Father: and no man knoweth the Son, but the Father; neither knoweth any man the Father, save the Son, and he to whomsoever the Son will reveal him.

Matthew 24:27-30

For as the lightning cometh out of the east, and shineth even unto the west; **so shall also the coming of the Son of man be.** For wheresoever the carcass is, there will the eagles be gathered together. Immediately after the tribulation of those days shall the sun be darkened, and the moon shall not give her light, and the stars shall fall from heaven, and the powers of the heavens shall be shaken: **And then shall appear the sign of the Son of man in heaven**: and then shall all the tribes of the earth mourn, and **they shall see the Son of man coming in the clouds of heaven with power and great glory.**

Matthew 25:31-32

When the Son of man shall come in his glory, and all the holy angels with him, **then shall he sit upon the throne of his glory**: And before him shall be gathered all nations: and he shall separate them one from another, **as a shepherd divideth his sheep from the goats.**

"I really only love God as much as I love the person I love the least."

Dorothy Day   **"See 1 John 4:20"**

Mark 14:61-62

But he held his peace, and answered nothing. Again the high priest asked him, and said unto him, Art thou the Christ, the Son of the Blessed? And Jesus said, **I am: and ye shall see the Son of man sitting on the right hand of power, and coming in the clouds of heaven.**

Luke 18:31-33

Then he took unto him the twelve, and said unto them, Behold, we go up to Jerusalem, and all things that are written by the prophets concerning the Son of man shall be accomplished. For **he shall be delivered unto the Gentiles**, and shall be **mocked**, and **spitefully entreated**, and **spitted on**: And **they shall scourge** him, and **put him to death: and the third day he shall rise again.**

Luke 22:69-70

Hereafter shall the Son of man sit on the right hand of the power of God. Then said they all, Art thou then the **Son of God?** And he said unto them, **Ye say that I am.**

Luke 23:1-3

And the whole multitude of them arose, and led him unto Pilate. And they began to accuse him, saying, We found this fellow perverting the nation, and forbidding to give tribute to Caesar, **saying that he himself is Christ a King**. And Pilate asked him, saying, **Art thou the King of the Jews**? And he answered him and said, **Thou sayest it.**

"**I charge** *thee* **therefore before God, and the Lord Jesus Christ**, who shall judge the quick and the dead at his appearing and his kingdom; **Preach the word**; be instant in season, out of season; **reprove, rebuke, exhort** with all longsuffering and doctrine. For the time will come when they will not endure sound doctrine; but after their own lusts shall they heap to themselves teachers, having itching ears; And they shall turn away *their* ears from the truth, and shall be turned unto fables. But watch thou in all things, endure afflictions, **do the work of an evangelist, make full proof of thy ministry.**"

2 Timothy 4:1-5

What did others say about Jesus?

God the Father said:

Matthew 3:17
And lo **a voice from heaven**, saying, **This is my beloved Son, in whom I am well pleased.**

Mark 1:11
And there came a voice from heaven, saying, **Thou art my beloved Son, in whom I am well pleased.**

Luke 3:22
And the Holy Ghost descended in a bodily shape like a dove upon him, and a voice came from heaven, which said, **Thou art my beloved Son; in thee I am well pleased.**

John 5:37
And the Father himself, which hath sent me, hath borne witness of me. Ye have neither heard his voice at any time, nor seen his shape.

An angel said:

Matthew 1:20b-21
But while he thought on these things, behold, the angel of the Lord appeared unto him in a dream, saying, Joseph, thou son of David, fear not to take unto thee Mary thy wife: for that which is conceived in her is of the Holy Ghost. **And she shall bring forth a son, and thou shalt call his name JESUS: for he shall save his people from their sins.**

Luke 1:30-33
And the angel said unto her, Fear not, Mary: for thou hast found favour with God. **And, behold, thou shalt conceive in thy womb, and bring forth a son, and shalt call his name JESUS. He shall be great, and shall be called the Son of the Highest: and the Lord God shall give unto him the throne of his father David: And he shall reign over the house of Jacob for ever; and of his kingdom there shall be no end.**

"Perhaps the number one fruit of salvation will be that Jesus will become precious to the believer."

Unknown   **"See 1 Peter 2:7"**

20

Luke 1:35

And the **angel answered** and said unto her, The Holy Ghost shall come upon thee, and the power of the Highest shall overshadow thee: therefore also **that holy thing which shall be born of thee shall be called the Son of God.**

Luke 2:10-11

And the angel said unto them, Fear not: for, behold, I bring you good tidings of great joy, which shall be to all people. **For unto you is born this day in the city of David a Saviour, which is Christ the Lord.**

Simeon, a devout and just man, said:

Luke 2:25-32

And, behold, there was a man in Jerusalem, whose name was **Simeon; and the same man was just and devout,** waiting for the consolation of Israel: and the Holy Ghost was upon him. **And it was revealed unto him by the Holy Ghost, that he should not see death, before he had seen the Lord's Christ.** And he came by the Spirit into the temple: and when the parents brought in the child Jesus, to do for him after the custom of the law, Then took he him up in his arms, and blessed God, and said, Lord, now lettest thou thy servant depart in peace, according to thy word: **For mine eyes have seen thy salvation, Which thou hast prepared before the face of all people; A light to lighten the Gentiles, and the glory of thy people Israel.**

John the Baptist said:

John 1:29, 34-36

The next day John seeth Jesus coming unto him, and saith, **Behold the Lamb of God, which taketh away the sin of the world**…And I saw, and bare record that **this is the Son of God.** Again the next day after John stood, and two of his disciples; And looking upon Jesus as he walked, he saith, **Behold the Lamb of God!**

"If any man's life at home is unworthy, he should go several miles away before he stands up to preach. When he stands up, he should say nothing."

Charles Spurgeon   **"See 2 Timothy 4:5b"**

21

John, an apostle, said:

John 1:11-12
He came unto his own, and his own received him not. **But as many as received him, to them gave he power to become the sons of God, even to them that believe on his name.**

John 20:30-31
And many other signs truly did Jesus in the presence of his disciples, which are not written in this book: **But these are written, that ye might believe that Jesus is the Christ, the Son of God;** and that believing ye might have life through his name.

Peter, an apostle, said:

John 6:68-69
Then **Simon Peter** answered him, Lord, to whom shall we go? thou hast the words of eternal life. And we believe and are sure that **thou art that Christ, the Son of the living God.**

Matthew 16:16
And **Simon Peter** answered and said, **Thou art the Christ, the Son of the living God.**

Luke 9:20
He said unto them, **But whom say ye that I am?** Peter answering said, **The Christ of God.**

Paul, an apostle, said:

Philippians 2:5-11
Let this mind be in you, which was also in Christ Jesus: **Who, being in the form of God, thought it not robbery to be equal with God: But made himself of no reputation, and took upon him the form of a servant, and was made in the likeness of men: And being found in fashion as a man, he humbled himself, and became obedient unto death, even the death of the cross. Wherefore God also hath highly exalted him, and given him a name which is above every name: That at the name of Jesus every knee should bow, of things in heaven, and things in earth, and things under the earth; And that every tongue should confess that Jesus Christ is Lord, to the glory of God the Father.**

"If you wouldn't say it in prayer, don't say it at all."

Anonymous   **"See James 5:16"**

Thomas, an apostle, said:

John 20:28
And **Thomas** answered and said unto him, **My Lord and my God.**

His disciples said:

Matthew 14:33
And when they were come into the ship, the wind ceased. Then they that were in the ship came and worshipped him, saying, **Of a truth thou art the Son of God.**

John 16:30
His disciples said unto him, Lo, now speakest thou plainly, and speakest no proverb. Now are we sure that thou knowest all things, and needest not that any man should ask thee: **by this we believe that thou camest forth from God.**

Martha said:

John 11:24-27
Martha saith unto him, I know that he shall rise again in the resurrection at the last day. Jesus said unto her, I am the resurrection, and the life: he that believeth in me, though he were dead, yet shall he live: And whosoever liveth and believeth in me shall never die. Believest thou this? She saith unto him, **Yea, Lord: I believe that thou art the Christ, the Son of God, which should come into the world.**

Nathaniel said:

John 1:47-49
Jesus saw Nathanael coming to him, and saith of him, Behold an Israelite indeed, in whom is no guile! Nathanael saith unto him, Whence knowest thou me? Jesus answered and said unto him, Before that Philip called thee, when thou wast under the fig tree, I saw thee. Nathanael answered and saith unto him, **Rabbi, thou art the Son of God; thou art the King of Israel.**

"Man is never so tall as when he kneels before God - never so great as when he humbles himself before God. And the man who kneels to God can stand up to anything."

Lewis H. Evans   **"See Philippians 3:13"**

A Roman Centurion said:

Matthew 27:54
Now when the **centurion, and they that were with him**, watching Jesus, saw the earthquake, and those things that were done, they feared greatly, saying, **Truly this was the Son of God.**

Mark 15:39
And when the **centurion**, which stood over against him, saw that he so cried out, and gave up the ghost, he said, **Truly this man was the Son of God.**

The works He did said:

John 5:36
But I have greater witness than that of John: for the works which the Father hath given me to finish, **the same works that I do, bear witness of me, that the Father hath sent me.**

John 10:38
But if I do, though ye believe not me, **believe the works: that ye may know, and believe, that the Father is in me, and I in him.**

satan said:

Matthew 4:3-11
And when the tempter came to him, he said, **If thou be the Son of God**, command that these stones be made bread. But he answered and said, It is written, Man shall not live by bread alone, but by every word that proceedeth out of the mouth of God. Then the devil taketh him up into the holy city, and setteth him on a pinnacle of the temple, And saith unto him, **If thou be the Son of God**, cast thyself down: for it is written, He shall give his angels charge concerning thee: and in their hands they shall bear thee up, lest at any time thou dash thy foot against a stone. Jesus said unto him, It is written again, Thou shalt not tempt the Lord thy God. Again, the devil taketh him up into an exceeding high mountain, and sheweth him all the kingdoms of the world, and the glory of them; And saith unto him, All these things will I give thee, if thou wilt fall down and worship me. Then saith Jesus unto him, Get thee hence, Satan: for it is written, Thou shalt worship the Lord thy God, and him only shalt thou serve. Then the devil leaveth him, and, behold, angels came and ministered unto him.

"We all can do something for the Lord. The worst of us can serve as bad examples!"

Kent Hovind   **"See 2 Timothy 4:5"**

24

Luke 4:3-13

And the devil said unto him, **If thou be the Son of God,** command this stone that it be made bread. And Jesus answered him, saying, It is written, That man shall not live by bread alone, but by every word of God. And the devil, taking him up into an high mountain, shewed unto him all the kingdoms of the world in a moment of time. And the devil said unto him, All this power will I give thee, and the glory of them: for that is delivered unto me; and to whomsoever I will I give it. If thou therefore wilt worship me, all shall be thine. And Jesus answered and said unto him, Get thee behind me, Satan: for it is written, Thou shalt worship the Lord thy God, and him only shalt thou serve. And he brought him to Jerusalem, and set him on a pinnacle of the temple, and said unto him, **If thou be the Son of God**, cast thyself down from hence: For it is written, He shall give his angels charge over thee, to keep thee: And in their hands they shall bear thee up, lest at any time thou dash thy foot against a stone. And Jesus answering said unto him, It is said, Thou shalt not tempt the Lord thy God. And when the devil had ended all the temptation, he departed from him for a season.

The unclean spirit said:

Mark 1:23-24

And there was in their synagogue **a man with an unclean spirit**; and he cried out, Saying, Let us alone; what have we to do with thee, **thou Jesus of Nazareth**? art thou come to destroy us? **I know thee who thou art, the Holy One of God.**

Mark 3:11

And **unclean spirits**, when they saw him, fell down before him, and cried, saying, **Thou art the Son of God.**

Mark 5:6-8

But when he saw Jesus afar off, he ran and worshipped him, And cried with a loud voice, and said, What have I to do with thee, **Jesus, thou Son of the most high God**? I adjure thee by God, that thou torment me not. For he said unto him, Come out of the man, thou **unclean spirit.**

Luke 4:33, 34

And in the synagogue there was a man, which had a spirit of an **unclean devil**, and cried out with a loud voice, Saying, Let us alone; what have we to do with thee, thou **Jesus of Nazareth**? art thou come to destroy us? **I know thee who thou art; the Holy One of God.**

Luke 4:41

And **devils** also came out of many, crying out, and saying, **Thou art Christ the Son of God**. And he rebuking them suffered them not to speak: for they knew that he was Christ.

"He (**Jesus**) saith unto them, But **whom say ye that I am?**"

Matthew 16:15

25

Jesus saith unto him, "I am the way, the truth, and the life: no man cometh unto the Father, but by me."

John 14:6

Jesus Christ's
Names, Titles, and Descriptions

1. Advocate.   **1 John 2:1**

My little children, these things write I unto you, that ye sin not. And if any man sin, we have an **advocate** with the Father, Jesus Christ the righteous.

2. An Alien.   **Psalms 69:8**

I am become a stranger unto my brethren, and an **alien** unto my mother's children.

3. Alive for Evermore.   **Revelation 1:18**

I am he that liveth, and was dead; and, behold, I am **alive for evermore**, Amen; and have the keys of hell and of death.

4. The All, and in All.   **Colossians 3:11**

Where there is neither Greek nor Jew, circumcision nor uncircumcision, Barbarian, Scythian, bond nor free: but **Christ is all, and in all.**

5. The Almighty.   **Revelation 1:8**

I am Alpha and Omega, the beginning and the ending, saith the Lord, which is, and which was, and which is to come, **the Almighty.**

6. The Alpha and Omega.   **Revelation 1:8**

I am **Alpha and Omega**, the beginning and the ending, saith the Lord, which is, and which was, and which is to come, the Almighty.

7. An Altar.   **Hebrews 13:10**

We have **an altar**, whereof they have no right to eat which serve the tabernacle.

8. The Altogether Lovely.   **Song of Solomon 5:16**

His mouth is most sweet: yea, he is **altogether lovely.** This is my beloved, and this is my friend, O daughters of Jerusalem.

What is it?

**What is greater than God,
More evil than the devil,
The poor have it,
The rich need it,
And if you eat it, you'll die?**

(GNIHTON)

27

9. The Amen.   **Revelation 3:14**

And unto the angel of the church of the Laodiceans write; These things saith **the Amen**, the faithful and true witness, the beginning of the creation of God.

10. The Angel of God.   **Genesis 21:17**

And God heard the voice of the lad; and **the angel of God** called to Hagar out of heaven, and said unto her, What aileth thee, Hagar? fear not; for God hath heard the voice of the lad where he is.

11. The Angel of His Presence.   **Isaiah 63:9**

In all their affliction he was afflicted, and **the angel of his presence** saved them: in his love and in his pity he redeemed them; and he bare them, and carried them all the days of old.

12. The Angel of the Lord.   **Genesis 16:7**

And **the angel of the LORD** found her by a fountain of water in the wilderness, by the fountain in the way to Shur.

13. The Anointed.   **1 Samuel 2:35**

And I will raise me up a faithful priest, that shall do according to that which is in mine heart and in my mind: and I will build him a sure house; and he shall walk before mine **anointed** for ever.

                                                                 Psalms 2:2

The kings of the earth set themselves, and the rulers take counsel together, against the LORD, and against his **anointed...**

14. Another king.   **Acts 17:7**

Whom Jason hath received: and these all do contrary to the decrees of Caesar, saying that there is **another king**, one Jesus.

15. The Apostle of our Profession.   **Hebrews 3:1**

Wherefore, holy brethren, partakers of the heavenly calling, consider **the Apostle and High Priest of our profession**, Christ Jesus.

16. The Ark of the Covenant.   **Joshua 3:3**

And they commanded the people, saying, When ye see **the ark of the covenant** of the LORD your God, and the priests the Levites bearing it, then ye shall remove from your place, and go after it.

17. The Arm of the Lord.   **Isaiah 53:1**

Who hath believed our report? and to whom is **the arm of the LORD** revealed?

18. The Author of Eternal Salvation.   **Hebrews 5:9**

And being made perfect, he became **the author of eternal salvation** unto all them that obey him.

19. The Author of our Faith.   **Hebrews 12:2**

Looking unto Jesus the **author and finisher of our faith**; who for the joy that was set before him endured the cross, despising the shame, and is set down at the right hand of the throne of God.

"Conscience is the internal perception of God's moral Law."

Oswald Chambers   **"See Romans 2:15"**

28

20. The Balm of Gilead. Jeremiah 8:22

Is there no **balm in Gilead**; is there no physician there? why then is not the health of the daughter of my people recovered?

21. A Banner to Them that Fear Thee. Psalms 60:4

Thou hast given **a banner to them that fear thee**, that it may be displayed because of the truth. Selah.

22. The Bearer of Glory. Zechariah 6:13

Even he shall build the temple of the LORD; and he shall **bear the glory**, and shall sit and rule upon his throne; and he shall be a priest upon his throne: and the counsel of peace shall be between them both.

23. The Bearer of Sin. Hebrews 9:28

So Christ was once offered to **bear the sins** of many; and unto them that look for him shall he appear the second time without sin unto salvation.

24. Before All Things. Colossians 1:17

And he is **before all things**, and by him all things consist.

25. The Beginning. Colossians 1:18

And he is the head of the body, the church: who is **the beginning**, the firstborn from the dead; that in all things he might have the preeminence.

26. The Beginning of the Creation of God. Revelation 3:14

And unto the angel of the church of the Laodiceans write; These things saith the Amen, the faithful and true witness, **the beginning of the creation of God.**

27. The Beginning and Ending. Revelation 1:8

I am Alpha and Omega, **the beginning and the ending,** saith the Lord, which is, and which was, and which is to come, the Almighty.

28. The Beloved. Ephesians 1:6

To the praise of the glory of his grace, wherein he hath made us accepted in **the beloved.**

29. My Beloved Son. Matthew 3:17

And lo a voice from heaven, saying, This is **my beloved Son**, in whom I am well pleased.

30. The Bishop of Your Souls. 1 Peter 2:25

For ye were as sheep going astray; but are now returned unto the Shepherd and **Bishop of your souls.**

31. The Blessed and Only Potentate. 1 Timothy 6:15

Which in his times he shall show, who is **the blessed and only Potentate**, the King of kings, and Lord of lords.

"If Jesus Christ be God and died for me, no sacrifice I can make can be too great for Him."

C. T. Studd **"See Romans 12:1"**

32. The Blessed for Evermore. 2 Corinthians 11:31
The God and Father of our Lord Jesus Christ, which is **blessed for evermore**, knoweth that I lie not.

33. The Blessed Hope. Titus 2:13
Looking for that **blessed hope**, and the glorious appearing of the great God and our Saviour Jesus Christ.

34. The Branch. Zechariah 3:8
Hear now, O Joshua the high priest, thou, and thy fellows that sit before thee: for they are men wondered at: for, behold, I will bring forth my servant **the BRANCH.**

Zechariah 6:12

And speak unto him, saying, Thus speaketh the LORD of hosts, saying, Behold the man whose name is **The BRANCH**; and he shall grow up out of his place, and he shall build the temple of the LORD.

35. The Branch of the Lord. Isaiah 4:2
In that day shall **the branch of the LORD** be beautiful and glorious, and the fruit of the earth shall be excellent and comely for them that are escaped of Israel.

36. The Branch of Righteousness. Jeremiah 33:15
In those days, and at that time, will I cause **the Branch of righteousness** to grow up unto David; and he shall execute judgment and righteousness in the land.

37. The Bread of God. John 6:33
For **the bread of God** is he which cometh down from heaven, and giveth life unto the world.

38. The Bread of Life. John 6:35
And Jesus said unto them, I am **the bread of life**: he that cometh to me shall never hunger; and he that believeth on me shall never thirst.

39. The Bridegroom. John 3:29
He that hath the bride is **the bridegroom**: but the friend of the bridegroom, which standeth and heareth him, rejoiceth greatly because of the bridegroom's voice: this my joy therefore is fulfilled.

40. The Bright and Morning Star. Revelation 22:16
I Jesus have sent mine angel to testify unto you these things in the churches. I am the root and the offspring of David, and **the bright and morning star.**

41. The Brightness of His Glory. Hebrews 1:3
Who being **the brightness of his glory**, and the express image of his person, and upholding all things by the word of his power, when he had by himself purged our sins, sat down on the right hand of the Majesty on high…

42. The Brightness of thy Rising. Isaiah 60:3
And the Gentiles shall come to thy light, and kings to **the brightness of thy rising.**

"We must thrust the sword of the spirit into the hearts of men."

Charles's Spurgeon **"See Ephesians 6:10"**

43. Our Brother.   Matthew 12:50

For whosoever shall do the will of my Father which is in heaven, the same is **my brother**, and sister, and mother.

44. A Buckler.   Psalms 18:30

As for God, his way is perfect: the word of the LORD is tried: he is **a buckler** to all those that trust in him.

45. The Builder of the Temple.   Zechariah 6:12-13

And speak unto him, saying, Thus speaketh the LORD of hosts saying, Behold the man whose name is The BRANCH; and he shall grow up out of his place, and **he shall build the temple of the LORD: Even he shall build the temple of the LORD**; and he shall bear the glory, and shall sit and rule upon his throne; and he shall be a priest upon his throne: and the counsel of peace shall be between them both.

46. A Bundle of Myrrh.   Song of Solomon 1:13

A bundle of myrrh is my well beloved unto me; he shall lie all night betwixt my breasts.

47. The Captain of the Host of the Lord.   Joshua 5:14-15

And he said, Nay; but as **captain of the host of the LORD** am I now come. And Joshua fell on his face to the earth, and did worship, and said unto him, What saith my lord unto his servant? And **the captain of the LORD'S host** said unto Joshua, Loose thy shoe from off thy foot; for the place whereon thou standest is holy. And Joshua did so.

48. The Captain of Their Salvation.   Hebrews 2:10

For it became him, for whom are all things, and by whom are all things, in bringing many sons unto glory, to make **the captain of their salvation** perfect through sufferings.

49. The Carpenter.   Mark 6:3

Is not this **the carpenter**, the son of Mary, the brother of James, and Joses, and of Judah, and Simon? and are not his sisters here with us? And they were offended at him.

50. The Carpenter's Son.   Matthew 13:55

Is not this **the carpenter's son**? Is not his mother called Mary? And his brethren, James, and Joses, and Simon, and Judas?

51. A Certain Nobleman.   Luke 19:12

He said therefore, **a certain nobleman** went into a far country to receive for himself a kingdom, and to return.

52. A Certain Samaritan.   Luke 10:33

But **a certain Samaritan**, as he journeyed, came where he was: and when he saw him, he had compassion on him.

"Why call you me, Lord, Lord, and do not the things which I say?"

Luke 6:46

53. The Chief Cornerstone. Ephesians 2:20

And are built upon the foundation of the apostles and prophets, Jesus Christ himself being **the chief corner stone.**

1 Peter 2:6

Wherefore also it is contained in the scripture, Behold, I lay in Sion a **chief corner stone**, elect, precious: and he that believeth on him shall not be confounded.

54. The Chief Shepherd. 1 Peter 5:4

And when **the chief Shepherd** shall appear, ye shall receive a crown of glory that fadeth not away.

55. The Chiefest Among Ten Thousand. Song of Solomon 5:10

My beloved is white and ruddy, **the Chiefest among ten thousand.**

56. A Child Born. Isaiah 9:6

For unto us **a child is born**, unto us a son is given: and the government shall be upon his shoulder: and his name shall be called Wonderful, Counsellor, The mighty God, The everlasting Father, The Prince of Peace.

57. Child of the Holy Ghost. Matthew 1:18

Now the birth of Jesus Christ was on this wise: When as his mother Mary was espoused to Joseph, before they came together, she was found with **child of the Holy Ghost.**

58. The Child Jesus. Luke 2:27

And he came by the Spirit into the temple: and when the parents brought in **the child Jesus**, to do for him after the custom of the law…

Luke 2:43

And when they had fulfilled the days, as they returned, **the child Jesus** tarried behind in Jerusalem; and Joseph and his mother knew not of it.

59. The Chosen of God. 1 Peter 2:4

To whom coming, as unto a living stone, disallowed indeed of men, but **chosen of God**, and precious.

60. Chosen out of the People. Psalms 89:19

Then thou spakest in vision to thy holy one, and saidst, I have laid help upon one that is mighty; I have exalted one **chosen out of the people.**

61. Christ. Matthew 1:16

And Jacob begat Joseph the husband of Mary, of whom was born Jesus, who is called **Christ.**

62. The Christ. 1 John 5:1

Whosoever believeth that Jesus is **the Christ** is born of God: and every one that loveth him that begat loveth him also that is begotten of him.

"Your one business in life is to lead men to believe in Jesus Christ by the power of the Holy Spirit. Every other thing should be made subservient to this one objective."

Charles Spurgeon **"See Ephesians 3:9"**

63. Christ Come in the Flesh.   **1 John 4:2**

Hereby know ye the Spirit of God: Every spirit that confesseth that Jesus **Christ is come in the flesh** is of God.

64. Christ Crucified.   **1 Corinthians 1:23**

But we preach **Christ crucified**, unto the Jews a stumblingblock, and unto the Greeks foolishness.

65. The Christ of God.   **Luke 9:20**

He said unto them, But whom say ye that I am? Peter answering said, **The Christ of God.**

66. Christ Jesus.   **Acts 19:4**

Then said Paul, John verily baptized with the baptism of repentance, saying unto the people, that they should believe on him which should come after him, that is, on **Christ Jesus.**

67. Christ Jesus the Lord.   **2 Corinthians 4:5**

For we preach not ourselves, but **Christ Jesus the Lord**; and ourselves your servants for Jesus' sake.

68. Christ a King.   **Luke 23:2**

And they began to accuse him, saying, We found this fellow perverting the nation, and forbidding to give tribute to Caesar, saying that he himself is **Christ a King.**

69. Christ the Lord.   **Luke 2:11**

For unto you is born this day in the city of David a Saviour, which is **Christ the Lord.**

70. Christ our Passover.   **1 Corinthians 5:7**

Purge out therefore the old leaven, that ye may be a new lump, as ye are unleavened. For even **Christ our passover** is sacrificed for us.

71. Christ Risen from the Dead.   **1 Corinthians 15:20**

But now is **Christ risen from the dead**, and become the first fruits of them that slept.

72. A Cleft of the Rock.   **Exodus 33:22**

And it shall come to pass, while my glory passeth by, that I will put thee in **a cleft of the rock**, and will cover thee with my hand while I pass by.

73. A Cluster of Camphire.   **Song of Solomon 1:14**

My beloved is unto me as **a cluster of camphire** in the vineyards of Engedi.

74. The Comforter.   **John 14:16-18**

And I will pray the Father, and he shall give you another **Comforter,** that he may abide with you for ever; Even the Spirit of truth; whom the world cannot receive, because it seeth him not, neither knoweth him: but ye know him; for he dwelleth with you, and shall be in you. I will not leave you comfortless: I will come to you.

"I don't believe in any religion apart from doing the will of God."

Catherine Booth   **"See Hebrews 5:9"**

75. A Commander to the People. Isaiah 55:4

Behold, I have given him for a witness to the people, a leader and **commander to the people.**

76. Conceived of the Holy Ghost. Matthew 1:20

But while he thought on these things, behold, the angel of the Lord appeared unto him in a dream, saying, Joseph, thou son of David, fear not to take unto thee Mary thy wife: for that which is **conceived in her is of the Holy Ghost.**

77. The Consolation of Israel. Luke 2:25

And, behold, there was a man in Jerusalem, whose name was Simeon; and the same man was just and devout, waiting for **the consolation of Israel**: and the Holy Ghost was upon him.

78. The Corn of Wheat. John 12:24

Verily, verily, I say unto you, Except a **corn of wheat** fall into the ground and die, it abideth alone: but if it die, it bringeth forth much fruit.

79. Counselor. Isaiah 9:6

For unto us a child is born, unto us a son is given: and the government shall be upon his shoulder: and his name shall be called Wonderful, **Counselor**, The mighty God, The everlasting Father, The Prince of Peace.

80. The Covenant of the People. Isaiah 42:6

I the LORD have called thee in righteousness, and will hold thine hand, and will keep thee, and give thee for a **covenant of the people**, for a light of the Gentiles.

Isaiah 49:8

Thus saith the LORD, In an acceptable time have I heard thee, and in a day of salvation have I helped thee: and I will preserve thee, and give thee for a **covenant of the people**, to establish the earth, to cause to inherit the desolate heritages.

81. The Covert from the Tempest. Isaiah 32:2

And a man shall be as an hiding place from the wind, and **a covert from the tempest**; as rivers of water in a dry place, as the shadow of a great rock in a weary land.

82. The Covert of Thy Wings. Psalms 61:4

I will abide in thy tabernacle for ever: I will trust in **the covert of thy wings**. Selah.

83. The Creator. Romans 1:25

Who changed the truth of God into a lie, and worshipped and served the creature more than **the Creator**, who is blessed for ever. Amen.

84. The Creator of the Ends of the Earth. Isaiah 40:28

Hast thou not known? hast thou not heard, that the everlasting God, the LORD, **the Creator of the ends of the earth**, fainteth not, neither is weary? there is no searching of his understanding.

"You are more sinful than you ever dared to believe, but you are more loved than you ever dared to hope."

Mark Liederbach **"See 1 John 3:16"**

34

85. A Crown of Glory.   **Isaiah 28:5**

In that day shall the LORD of hosts be for **a crown of glory**, and for a diadem of beauty, unto the residue of his people.

86. My Darling.   **Psalms 22:20**

Deliver my soul from the sword; **my darling** from the power of the dog.

87. The Day.   **2 Peter 1:19**

We have also a more sure word of prophecy; whereunto ye do well that ye take heed, as unto a light that shineth in a dark place, until **the day** dawn, and the day star arise in your hearts.

88. The Daysman.   **Job 9:33**

Neither is there any **daysman** betwixt us, that might lay his hand upon us both.

89. The Day Spring from on High.   **Luke 1:78**

Through the tender mercy of our God; whereby **the dayspring from on high** hath visited us…

90. The Daystar to Arise.   **2 Peter 1:19**

We have also a more sure word of prophecy; whereunto ye do well that ye take heed, as unto a light that shineth in a dark place, until the day dawn, and **the day star arise** in your hearts.

91. His Dear Son.   **Colossians 1:13**

Who hath delivered us from the power of darkness, and hath translated us into the kingdom of **his dear Son.**

92. That Deceiver.   **Matthew 27:63**

Saying, Sir, we remember that **that deceiver** said, while he was yet alive, After three days I will rise again.

93. My Defense.   **Psalms 94:22**

But the LORD is **my defense**; and my God is the rock of my refuge.

94. My Deliverer.   **Psalms 40:17**

But I am poor and needy; yet the Lord thinketh upon me: thou art my help and **my deliverer**; make no tarrying, O my God.

95. The Desire of all Nations.   **Haggai 2:7**

And I will shake all nations, and **the desire of all nations** shall come: and I will fill this house with glory, saith the LORD of hosts.

96. Despised of the People.   **Psalms 22:6**

But I am a worm, and no man; a reproach of men, and **despised of the people.**

"Love will find a way. Indifference will find an excuse."

Anonymous   **"See Matthew 5:43-48"**

97. A Diadem of Beauty.   **Isaiah 28:5**

In that day shall the LORD of hosts be for a crown of glory, and for **a diadem of beauty**, unto the residue of his people.

98. The Door of the Sheep.   **John 10:7**

Then said Jesus unto them again, Verily, verily, I say unto you, I am **the door of the sheep.**

99. Dwelling Place.   **Psalms 90:1**

LORD, thou hast been our **dwelling place** in all generations.

100. Mine Elect.   **Isaiah 42:1**

Behold my servant, whom I uphold; **mine elect**, in whom my soul delighteth; I have put my spirit upon him: he shall bring forth judgment to the Gentiles.

101. Elijah.   **Matthew 16:14**

And they said, Some say that thou art John the Baptist: some, **Elias**; and others, Jeremias, or one of the prophets.

102. Emmanuel.   **Matthew 1:23**

Behold, a virgin shall be with child, and shall bring forth a son, and they shall call his name **Emmanuel**, which being interpreted is, God with us.

103. The End of the Law.   **Romans 10:4**

For Christ is **the end of the law** for righteousness to every one that believeth.

104. The Ensign of the People.   **Isaiah 11:10**

And in that day there shall be a root of Jesse, which shall stand for an **ensign of the people**; to it shall the Gentiles seek: and his rest shall be glorious.

105. Equal with God.   **Philippians 2:6**

Who, being in the form of God, thought it not robbery to be **equal with God.**

106. The Eternal God.   **Deuteronomy 33:27**

The eternal God is thy refuge, and underneath are the everlasting arms: and he shall thrust out the enemy from before thee; and shall say, Destroy them.

107. That Eternal Life.   **1 John 1:2**

For the life was manifested, and we have seen it, and bear witness, and show unto you **that eternal life**, which was with the Father, and was manifested unto us.

108. The Everlasting Father.   **Isaiah 9:6**

For unto us a child is born, unto us a son is given: and the government shall be upon his shoulder: and his name shall be called Wonderful, Counselor, The mighty God, **The everlasting Father**, The Prince of Peace.

"Courage is not the lack of fear. It is acting in spite of it."

Mark Twain   **"See Psalm 31:23-24"**

109. An Everlasting Light. Isaiah 60:19-20

The sun shall be no more thy light by day; neither for brightness shall the moon give light unto thee: but the LORD shall be unto thee **an everlasting light**, and thy God thy glory. Thy sun shall no more go down; neither shall thy moon withdraw itself: for the LORD shall be thine everlasting light, and the days of thy mourning shall be ended.

110. An Everlasting Name. Isaiah 63:12

That led them by the right hand of Moses with his glorious arm, dividing the water before them, to make himself **an everlasting name?**

111. Thy Exceeding Great Reward. Genesis 15:1

After these things the word of the LORD came unto Abram in a vision, saying, Fear not, Abram: I am thy shield, and **thy exceeding great reward.**

112. His Excellency. Job 13:11

Shall not **his excellency** make you afraid? and his dread fall upon you?

113. The Excellency of Our God. Isaiah 35:2

It shall blossom abundantly, and rejoice even with joy and singing: the glory of Lebanon shall be given unto it, the excellency of Carmel and Sharon, they shall see the glory of the LORD, and **the excellency of our God.**

114. Excellent. Psalms 8:1

O LORD our Lord, how **excellent** is thy name in all the earth! who hast set thy glory above the heavens.

Psalms 8:9

O LORD our Lord, how **excellent** is thy name in all the earth!

115. The Express Image of His Person. Hebrews 1:3

Who being the brightness of his glory, and **the express image of his person**, and upholding all things by the word of his power, when he had by himself purged our sins, sat down on the right hand of the Majesty on high.

116. The Face of the Lord. Luke 1:76

And thou, child, shalt be called the prophet of the Highest: for thou shalt go before **the face of the Lord** to prepare his ways.

117. Fairer than the Children of Men. Psalms 45:2

Thou art **fairer than the children of men**: grace is poured into thy lips: therefore God hath blessed thee for ever.

118. Faithful. 1 Thessalonians 5:24

Faithful is he that calleth you, who also will do it.

"Have you no wish for others to be saved Then you're not saved yourself. Be sure that."

Charles Spurgeon **"See 1 John 4:20-21"**

37

119. Faithful and True. — Revelation 19:11

And I saw heaven opened, and behold a white horse; and he that sat upon him was called **Faithful and True**, and in righteousness he doth judge and make war.

120. The Faithful and True Witness. — Revelation 3:14

And unto the angel of the church of the Laodiceans write; These things saith the Amen, **the faithful and true witness**, the beginning of the creation of God.

121. A Faithful Creator. — 1 Peter 4:19

Wherefore let them that suffer according to the will of God commit the keeping of their souls to him in well doing, as unto **a faithful Creator.**

122. A Faithful High Priest. — Hebrews 2:17

Wherefore in all things it behoved him to be made like unto his brethren, that he might be a merciful and **faithful high priest** in things pertaining to God, to make reconciliation for the sins of the people.

123. A Faithful Priest. — 1 Samuel 2:35

And I will raise me up **a faithful priest**, that shall do according to that which is in mine heart and in my mind: and I will build him a sure house; and he shall walk before mine anointed for ever.

124. The Faithful Witness. — Revelation 1:5

And from Jesus Christ, who is the **faithful witness,** and the first begotten of the dead, and the prince of the kings of the earth. Unto him that loved us, and washed us from our sins in his own blood…

125. A Faithful Witness Between Us. — Jeremiah 42:5

Then they said to Jeremiah, The LORD be a true and **faithful witness between us**, if we do not even according to all things for the which the LORD thy God shall send thee to us.

126. A Faithful Witness in Heaven. — Psalms 89:37

It shall be established for ever as the moon, and as **a faithful witness in heaven**. Selah.

127. My Fellow. — Zechariah 13:7

Awake, O sword, against my shepherd, and against the man that is **my fellow**, saith the LORD of hosts: smite the shepherd, and the sheep shall be scattered: and I will   turn mine hand upon the little ones.

128. The Finisher of the Faith. — Hebrews 12:2

Looking unto Jesus the author and **finisher of our faith**; who for the joy that was set before him endured the cross, despising the shame, and is set down at the right hand of the throne of God.

129. The First Begotten. — Hebrews 1:6

And again, when he bringeth in **the first begotten** into the world, he saith, And let all the angels of God worship him.

"No man is worth his salt who is not ready at all times to risk his body, to risk his well-being, to risk his life to a great cause."

Theodore Roosevelt   **"See 1 John 3:16"**

38

130. The First Begotten of the Dead. Revelation 1:5

And from Jesus Christ, who is the faithful witness, **and the first begotten of the dead**, and the prince of the kings of the earth. Unto him that loved us, and washed us from our sins in his own blood...

131. The Firstborn. Hebrews 12:23

To the general assembly and church of **the firstborn**, which are written in heaven, and to God the Judge of all, and to the spirits of just men made perfect...

132. The Firstborn Among Many Brethern. Romans 8:29

For whom he did foreknow, he also did predestinate to be conformed to the image of his Son, that he might be **the firstborn among many brethren.**

133. The Firstborn from the Dead. Colossians 1:18

And he is the head of the body, the church: who is the beginning, **the firstborn from the dead**; that in all things he might have the preeminence.

134. The Firstborn of Every Creature. Colossians 1:15

Who is the image of the invisible God, **the firstborn of every creature.**

135. Her Firstborn Son. Luke 2:7

And she brought forth **her firstborn son**, and wrapped him in swaddling clothes, and laid him in a manger; because there was no room for them in the inn.

136. The First Fruit. Romans 11:16

For if **the first fruit** be holy, the lump is also holy: and if the root be holy, so are the branches.

137. The First Fruits of Them That Slept. 1 Corinthians 15:20

But now is Christ risen from the dead, and become **the first fruits of them that slept.**

138. Flesh. John 1:14

And the Word was made **flesh**, and dwelt among us, (and we beheld his glory, the glory as of the only begotten of the Father,) full of grace and truth.

139. Foreordained Before the Foundation of the World. 1 Peter 1:20

Who verily was **foreordained before the foundation of the world**, but was manifest in these last times for you.

140. The Forerunner. Hebrews 6:20

Whither **the forerunner** is for us entered, even Jesus, made an high priest for ever after the order of Melchisedec.

"It was not the volume of sin that sent Christ to the cross; it was the fact of sin."

Ravi Zacharias **"See 1 Corinthians 15:3"**

141. Fortress. Psalms 18:2

The LORD is my rock, and my **fortress**, and my deliverer; my God, my strength, in whom I will trust; my buckler, and the horn of my salvation, and my high tower.

142. The Foundation which is Laid. 1 Corinthians 3:11

For other **foundation can no man lay than that is laid**, which is Jesus Christ.

143. The Fountain of Life. Psalms 36:9

For with thee is **the fountain of life**: in thy light shall we see light.

144. The Fountain of Living Waters. Jeremiah 17:13

O LORD, the hope of Israel, all that forsake thee shall be ashamed, and they that depart from me shall be written in the earth, because they have forsaken the LORD, **the fountain of living waters.**

145. The Friend of Publicans and Sinners. Luke 7:34

The Son of man is come eating and drinking; and ye say, Behold a gluttonous man, and a winebibber, **a friend of publicans and sinners!**

146. A Friend that Sticketh Closer than a Brother. Proverbs 18:24

A man that hath friends must show himself friendly: and there is **a friend that sticketh closer than a brother.**

147. The Fruit of the Earth. Isaiah 4:2

In that day shall the branch of the LORD be beautiful and glorious, and **the fruit of the earth** shall be excellent and comely for them that are escaped of Israel.

148. The Fruit of Thy Womb. Luke 1:42

And she spake out with a loud voice, and said, Blessed art thou among women, and blessed is **the fruit of thy womb.**

149. Fullers' Soap. Malachi 3:2

But who may abide the day of his coming? And who shall stand when he appeareth? For he is like a refiner's fire, and like **fullers' soap.**

150. The Gift of God. John 4:10

Jesus answered and said unto her, If thou knewest **the gift of God**, and who it is that saith to thee, Give me to drink; thou wouldest have asked of him, and he would have given thee living water.

"Receive every inward and outward trouble, every disappointment, pain, uneasiness, temptation, darkness and desolation with both hands, as to a true opportunity and blessed occasion of dying to self and entering into a fuller fellowship with the thy self-denying, suffering savior."

John Wesley **"See 2 Corinthians 7:4"**

151. A Gin. (A trap for Birds)   Isaiah 8:14
And he shall be for a sanctuary; but for a stone of stumbling and for a rock of offence to both the houses of Israel, for **a gin** and for a snare to the inhabitants of Jerusalem.

152. A Glorious High Throne from the Beginning.   Jeremiah 17:12
A glorious high throne from the beginning is the place of our sanctuary.

153. A Glorious name.   Isaiah 63:14
As a beast goeth down into the valley, the Spirit of the LORD caused him to rest: so didst thou lead thy people, to make thyself **a glorious name.**

154. Glory.   Haggai 2:7
And I will shake all nations, and the desire of all nations shall come: and I will fill this house with **glory**, saith the LORD of hosts.

155. My Glory.   Psalms 3:3
But thou, O LORD, art a shield for me; **my glory**, and the lifter up of mine head.

156. The Glory as of the Only Begotten of the Father.   John 1:14
And the Word was made flesh, and dwelt among us, (and we beheld his glory, the glory as of **the only begotten of the Father**,) full of grace and truth.

157. The Glory of God.   Romans 3:23
For all have sinned, and come short of **the glory of God.**

158. The Glory of His Father.   Matthew 16:27
For the Son of man shall come in **the glory of his Father** with his angels; and then he shall reward every man according to his works.

                                        Mark 8:38
Whosoever therefore shall be ashamed of me and of my words in this adulterous and sinful generation; of him also shall the Son of man be ashamed, when he cometh in **the glory of his Father** with the holy angels.

159. God.   Revelation 21:7
He that overcometh shall inherit all things; and I will be his **God**, and he shall be my son.

160. God Who Avengeth Me.   Psalms 18:47
It is **God that avengeth me**, and subdueth the people under me.

"God, send me anywhere, only go with me. Lay any burden on me, only sustain me. And sever any tie in my heart except the tie that binds my heart to yours."

David Livingstone   **"See Psalm 55:22"**

161. God Blessed Forever.   Romans 9:5

Whose are the fathers, and of whom as concerning the flesh Christ came, who is over all, **God blessed for ever.** Amen.

162. God Who Forgavest Them.   Psalms 99:8

Thou answeredst them, O LORD our God: thou wast a **God that forgavest them**, though thou tookest vengeance of their inventions.

163. Our God For Ever and Ever.   Psalms 48:14

For this God is **our God for ever and ever**: he will be our guide even unto death.

164. The God of Glory.   Psalms 29:3

The voice of the LORD is upon the waters: **the God of glory** thundereth: the LORD is upon many waters.

165. The God of My Life.   Psalms 42:8

Yet the LORD will command his loving-kindness in the daytime, and in the night his song shall be with me, and my prayer unto **the God of my life.**

166. God in the Midst of Her.   Psalms 46:5

God is in the midst of her; she shall not be moved: God shall help her, and that right early.

167. God Manifest in the Flesh.   1 Timothy 3:16

And without controversy great is the mystery of godliness: **God was manifest in the flesh**, justified in the Spirit, seen of angels, preached unto the Gentiles, believed on in the world, received up into glory.

168. God of My Righteousness.   Psalms 4:1

Hear me when I call, O **God of my righteousness**: thou hast enlarged me when I was in distress; have mercy upon me, and hear my prayer.

169. God of My Salvation.   Psalms 18:46

The LORD liveth; and blessed be my rock; and let the **God of my salvation** be exalted.

                                                Psalms 24:5

He shall receive the blessing from the LORD, and righteousness from the **God of his salvation.**

170. God of My Strength.   Psalms 43:2

For thou art the **God of my strength**: why dost thou cast me off? why go I mourning because of the oppression of the enemy?

171. God with Us.   Matthew 1:23

Behold, a virgin shall be with child, and shall bring forth a son, and they shall call his name Emmanuel, which being interpreted is, **God with us.**

"I would sooner bring one sinner to Jesus than unravel all the mysteries of the World, for salvation is the thing we live for."

Charles Spurgeon   **"See James 5:20"**

172. A Good Man. John 7:12

And there was much murmuring among the people concerning him: for some said, He is **a good man**: others said, Nay; but he deceiveth the people.

173. Good Master. Matthew 19:16

And, behold, one came and said unto him, **Good Master**, what good thing shall I do, that I may have eternal life?

174. The Good Shepherd. John 10:11

I am the good shepherd: **the good shepherd** giveth his life for the sheep.

175. The Govenor Among Nations. Psalms 22:28

For the kingdom is the LORD'S: and he is **the governor among the nations.**

176. Great. Jeremiah 32:18

Thou showest loving kindness unto thousands, and recompensest the iniquity of the fathers into the bosom of their children after them: the **Great**, the Mighty God, the LORD of hosts, is his name.

177. The Great God. Titus 2:13

Looking for that blessed hope, and the glorious appearing of **the great God** and our Saviour Jesus Christ.

178. A Great High Priest. Hebrews 4:14

Seeing then that we have **a great high priest**, that is passed into the heavens, Jesus the Son of God, let us hold fast our profession.

179. A Great Light. Isaiah 9:2

The people that walked in darkness have seen **a great light**: they that dwell in the land of the shadow of death, upon them hath the light shined.

180. A Great prophet. Luke 7:16

And there came a fear on all: and they glorified God, saying, That **a great prophet** is risen up among us; and, That God hath visited his people.

181. That Great Shepherd of the Sheep. Hebrews 13:20

Now the God of peace, that brought again from the dead our Lord Jesus, **that great shepherd of the sheep**, through the blood of the everlasting covenant.

"Which shew the work of the law written in their hearts, their conscience also bearing witness, and *their* thoughts the mean while accusing or else excusing one another."

Romans 2:15

182. Greater. 1 John 4:4

Ye are of God, little children, and have over-come them: because **greater** is he that is in you, than he that is in the world.

183. A Greater and More Perfect Tabernacle. Hebrews 9:11

But Christ being come an high priest of good things to come, by **a greater and more perfect tabernacle**, not made with hands, that is to say, not of this building.

184. Greater Than Our Father Abraham. John 8:53

Art thou **greater than our father Abraham**, which is dead? and the prophets are dead: whom makest thou thyself?

John 8:57-58

Then said the Jews unto him, Thou art not yet fifty years old, and hast thou seen Abraham? Jesus said unto them, Verily, verily, I say unto you, **Before Abraham was, I am.**

185. Greater Than Our Father Jacob. John 4:12

Art thou **greater than our father Jacob**, which gave us the well, and drank thereof himself, and his children, and his cattle?

186. Greater Than Jonas. Matthew 12:41

The men of Nineveh shall rise in judgement with this generation, and shall condemn it: because they repented at the preaching of Jonas; and, behold, a **greater than Jonas** is here.

187. Greater Than Solomon. Matthew 12:42

The queen of the south shall rise up in the judgment with this generation, and shall condemn it: for she came from the uttermost parts of the earth to hear the wisdom of Solomon; and, behold, a **greater than Solomon** is here.

188. Greater Than the Temple. Matthew 12:6

But I say unto you, That in this place is one **greater than the temple.**

189. Guest. Luke 19:7

And when they saw it, they all murmured, saying, That he was gone to be **guest** with a man that is a sinner.

190. Our Guide Even Unto Death. Psalms 48:14

For this God is our God for ever and ever: he will be **our guide even unto death.**

191. The Guiltless. Matthew 12:7

But if ye had known what this meaneth, I will have mercy, and not sacrifice, ye would not have condemned **the guiltless.**

192. The Habitation of Justice. Jeremiah 50:7

All that found them have devoured them: and their adversaries said, We offend not, because they have sinned against the LORD, **the habitation of justice**, even the LORD, the hope of their fathers.

"All that I have seen teaches me to trust the Creator for all I have not seen."

Ralph Waldo Emerson **"See Colossians 1:12-18"**

44

193. Harmless. Hebrews 7:26

For such an high priest became us, who is holy, **harmless**, undefiled, separate from sinners, and made higher than the heavens.

194. An He Goat. Proverbs 30:31

A greyhound; **an he goat** also; and a king, against whom there is no rising up.

195. The Head of all Principality and Power. Colossians 2:10

And ye are complete in him, which is **the head of all principality and power.**

196. The Head of Every Man. 1 Corinthians 11:3

But I would have you know, that **the head of every man** is Christ; and the head of the woman is the man; and the head of Christ is God.

197. The Head of the Body, the Church. Colossians 1:18

And he is **the head of the body, the church**: who is the beginning, the firstborn from the dead; that in all things he might have the preeminence.

198. The Head of the Corner. 1 Peter 2:7

Unto you therefore which believe he is precious: but unto them which be disobedient, the stone which the builders disallowed, the same is made **the head of the corner.**

199. The Heir. Mark 12:7

But those husbandmen said among themselves, This is **the heir**; come, let us kill him, and the inheritance shall be ours.

200. Heir of All Things. Hebrews 1:2

Hath in these last days spoken unto us by his Son, whom he hath appointed **heir of all things**, by whom also he made the worlds.

201. My Helper. Hebrews 13:6

So that we may boldly say, The Lord is **my helper**, and I will not fear what man shall do unto me.

202. The Helper of the Fatherless. Psalms 10:14

Thou hast seen it: for thou beholdest mischief and spite, to requite it with thy hand: the poor committeth himself unto thee; thou art **the helper of the fatherless.**

203. A Hen. Matthew 23:37

O Jerusalem, Jerusalem, thou that killest the prophets, and stonest them which are sent unto thee, how often would I have gathered thy children together, even as **a hen** gathereth her chickens under her wings, and ye would not!

"Consider as sin any minute of life spent on something other than saving souls for eternity from this world doomed to destruction."

Richard Wurmbrand **"See Romans 15:16"**

204. The Hidden Manna. **Revelation 2:17**

He that hath an ear, let him hear what the Spirit saith unto the churches; To him that overcometh will I give to eat of **the hidden manna,** and will give him a white stone, and in the stone a new name written, which no man knoweth saving he that receiveth it.

205. My Hiding Place. **Psalms 32:7**

Thou art **my hiding place**; thou shalt preserve me from trouble; thou shalt compass me about with songs of deliverance. Selah.

206. A Hiding Place from the Wind. **Isaiah 32:2**

And a man shall be as **an hiding place from the wind**, and a covert from the tempest; as rivers of water in a dry place, as the shadow of a great rock in a weary land.

207. The High and Lofty One Who Inhabiteth Eternity. **Isaiah 57:15**

For thus saith **the high and lofty One that inhabiteth eternity**, whose name is Holy; I dwell in the high and holy place, with him also that is of a contrite and humble spirit, to revive the spirit of the humble, and to revive the heart of the contrite ones.

208. An High Priest. **Hebrews 5:5**

So also Christ glorified not himself to be made **an high priest**; but he that said unto him, Thou art my Son, to day have I begotten thee.

209. An High Priest after the Order of Melchisedec. **Hebrews 5:10**

Called of God **an high priest after the order of Melchisedec.**

210. An High Priest Forever. **Hebrews 6:20**

Whither the forerunner is for us entered, even Jesus, made **an high priest for ever** after the order of Melchisedec.

211. My High Tower. **Psalms 18:2**

The LORD is my rock, and my fortress, and my deliverer; my God, my strength, in whom I will trust; my buckler, and the horn of my salvation, and **my high tower.**

212. The Highest Himself. **Psalms 87:5**

And of Zion it shall be said, This and that man was born in her: and **the highest himself** shall establish her.

"Here's the picture: 1600 years, 60 generations, the 40 plus authors, different walks of life, different places, different times, different moods, different continents, three languages, writing on hundreds of controversial subjects and yet when they're all brought together, there is absolute harmony from beginning to end... there is no other book in history to even compare with the uniqueness of this continuity."

Josh McDowell **"See 2 Timothy 3:16"**

213. Holy.   **Isaiah 57:15**

For thus saith the high and lofty One that inhabiteth eternity, whose name is **Holy**; I dwell in the high and holy place, with him also that is of a contrite and humble spirit, to revive the spirit of the humble, and to revive the heart of the contrite ones.

214. Thy Holy Child Jesus.   **Acts 4:27**

For of a truth against **thy holy child Jesus**, whom thou hast anointed, both Herod, and Pontius Pilate, with the Gentiles, and the people of Israel, were gathered together.

215. Thine Holy One.   **Acts 2:27**

Because thou wilt not leave my soul in hell, neither wilt thou suffer **thine Holy One** to see corruption.

216. The Holy One and Just.   **Acts 3:14**

But ye denied **the Holy One and the Just**, and desired a murderer to be granted unto you.

217. The Holy One of Israel.   **Psalms 89:18**

For the LORD is our defence; and **the Holy One of Israel** is our king.

218. That Holy Thing Which Shall be Born of Thee.   **Luke 1:35**

And the angel answered and said unto her, The Holy Ghost shall come upon thee, and the power of the Highest shall overshadow thee: therefore also **that holy thing which shall be born of thee** shall be called the Son of God.

219. Holy to the Lord.   **Luke 2:23**

As it is written in the law of the Lord, Every male that openeth the womb shall be called **holy to the Lord.**

220. Our Hope.   **1 Timothy 1:1**

Paul, an apostle of Jesus Christ by the commandment of God our Saviour, and Lord Jesus Christ, which is **our hope.**

221. The Hope of Glory.   **Colossians 1:27**

To whom God would make known what is the riches of the glory of this mystery among the Gentiles; which is Christ in you, **the hope of glory.**

222. The Hope of His People.   **Joel 3:16**

The LORD also shall roar out of Zion, and utter his voice from Jerusalem; and the heavens and the earth shall shake: but the LORD will be **the hope of his people**, and the strength of the children of Israel.

223. The Hope of Israel.   **Acts 28:20**

For this cause therefore have I called for you, to see you, and to speak with you: because that for **the hope of Israel** I am bound with this chain.

"There is not enough darkness in the world to extinguish the light of one small candle."

Spanish proverb   **"See 1 John 1:5-7"**

224. The Hope of Their Fathers.   **Jeremiah 50:7**

All that found them have devoured them: and their adversaries said, We offend not, because they have sinned against the LORD, the habitation of justice, even the LORD, **the hope of their fathers.**

225. The Horn of David.   **Psalms 132:17**

There will I make **the horn of David** to bud: I have ordained a lamp for mine anointed.

226. The Horn of the House of Israel.   **Ezekiel 29:21**

In that day will I cause **the horn of the house of Israel** to bud forth, and I will give thee the opening of the mouth in the midst of them; and they shall know that I am the LORD.

227. An Horn of Salvation.   **Luke 1:69**

And hath raised up **an horn of salvation** for us in the house of his servant David.

228. An House of Defense.   **Psalms 31:2**

Bow down thine ear to me; deliver me speedily: be thou my strong rock, for **an house of defense** to save me.

229. An Householder.   **Matthew 20:1**

For the kingdom of heaven is like unto a man that is **an householder**, which went out early in the morning to hire labourers into his vineyard.

230. Her Husband.   **Revelation 21:2**

And I John saw the holy city, new Jerusalem, coming down from God out of heaven, prepared as a bride adorned for **her husband.**

231. I Am.   **John 18:6**

As soon then as he had said unto them, **I am** he, they went backward, and fell to the ground.

232. The Image of the Invisible God.   **Colossians 1:15**

Who is **the image of the invisible God**, the firstborn of every creature.

233. Immanuel.   **Isaiah 7:14**

Therefore the Lord himself shall give you a sign; Behold, a virgin shall conceive, and bear a son, and shall call his name **Immanuel.**

234. Innocent Blood.   **Matthew 27:4**

Saying, I have sinned in that I have betrayed the **innocent blood.** And they said, What is that to us? See thou to that.

235. Isaac.   **Hebrews 11:17-18**

By faith Abraham, when he was tried, offered up **Isaac**: and he that had received the promises offered up his only begotten son. Of whom it was said, That in **Isaac** shall thy seed be called.

"Though you can give without loving, you can't love without giving."

Tom Drout   **"See James 2:5-10"**

236. The Jasper Stone.   **Revelation 4:3**

And he that sat was to look upon like a **jasper and a sardine stone**: and there was a rainbow round about the throne, in sight like unto an emerald.

237. Jeremiah.   **Matthew 16:14**

And they said, Some say that thou art John the Baptist: some, Elias; and others, **Jeremias**, or one of the prophets.

238. Jesus.   **Matthew 1:21**

And she shall bring forth a son, and thou shalt call his name **JESUS**: for he shall save his people from their sins.

239. Jesus Christ.   **Hebrews 13:8**

Jesus Christ the same yesterday, and to day, and forever.

240. Jesus Christ Our Lord.   **Romans 7:25**

I thank God through **Jesus Christ our Lord**. So then with the mind I myself serve the law of God; but with the flesh the law of sin.

241. Jesus Christ, the Son of God.   **John 20:31**

But these are written, that ye might believe that **Jesus is the Christ, the Son of God;** and that believing ye might have life through his name.

242. Jesus of Galilee.   **Matthew 26:69**

Now Peter sat without in the palace: and a damsel came unto him, saying, Thou also wast with **Jesus of Galilee.**

243. Jesus of Nazareth.   **John 1:45**

Philip findeth Nathanael, and saith unto him, We have found him, of whom Moses in the law, and the prophets, did write, **Jesus of Nazareth**, the son of Joseph.

244. Jesus of Nazareth, the King of the Jews.   **John 19:19**

And Pilate wrote a title, and put it on the cross. And the writing was, **JESUS OF NAZARETH THE KING OF THE JEWS.**

245. A Jew.   **John 4:9**

Then saith the woman of Samaria unto him, How is it that thou, being **a Jew,** askest drink of me, which am a woman of Samaria? for the Jews have no dealings with the Samaritans.

246. John the Baptist.   **Matthew 16:14**

And they said, Some say that thou art **John the Baptist**: some, Elias; and others, Jeremias, or one of the prophets.

247. Joseph's Son.   **Luke 4:22**

And all bare him witness, and wondered at the gracious words which proceeded out of his mouth. And they said, Is not this **Joseph's son?**

"Salvation comes through trusting Jesus Christ in the same way you trust a parachute. You don't just 'believe' in it, you put it on."
Ray Comfort   **"See Romans 13:14, Galatians 3:27"**

248. The Judge of All the Earth.   Genesis 18:25

That be far from thee to do after this manner, to slay the righteous with the wicked: and that the righteous should be as the wicked, that be far from thee: Shall not **the Judge of all the earth** do right?

249. The Judge of the Quick and the Dead.   Acts 10:42

And he commanded us to preach unto the people, and to testify that it is he which was ordained of God to be **the Judge of quick and dead.**

250. The Just One.   Acts 7:52

Which of the prophets have not your fathers persecuted? and they have slain them which showed before of the coming of **the Just One**; of whom ye have been now the betrayers and murderers.

251. This Just Person.   Matthew 27:24

When Pilate saw that he could prevail nothing, but that rather a tumult was made, he took water, and washed his hands before the multitude, saying, I am innocent of the blood of **this just person**: see ye to it.

252. Thy Keeper.   Psalms 121:5

The LORD is **thy keeper**: the LORD is thy shade upon thy right hand.

253. The Kindness and Love of God.   Titus 3:4

But after that **the kindness and love of God** our Saviour toward man appeared.

254. The King Eternal.   1 Timothy 1:17

Now unto **the King eternal**, immortal, invisible, the only wise God, be honour and glory for ever and ever. Amen.

255. The King Immortal.   1 Timothy 1:17

Now unto **the King eternal, immortal**, invisible, the only wise God, be honour and glory for ever and ever. Amen.

256. The King in His Beauty.   Isaiah 33:17

Thine eyes shall see **the king in his beauty**: they shall behold the land that is very far off.

257. The King Forever and Ever.   Psalms 10:16

The LORD is **King for ever and ever**: the heathen are perished out of his land.

258. The King Invisible.   1 Timothy 1:17

Now unto **the King eternal, immortal, invisible**, the only wise God, be honour and glory for ever and ever. Amen.

259. The King of All the Earth.   Psalms 47:7

For God is **the King of all the earth**: sing ye praises with understanding.

"Some people make things happen, some watch things happen, while others wonder what has happened."

Author Unknown   **"See 2 Timothy 4:5"**

50

260. The King of Glory.   Psalms 24:7-8

Lift up your heads, O ye gates; and be ye lift up, ye everlasting doors; and **the King of glory** shall come in. Who is this King of glory? The LORD strong and mighty, the LORD mighty in battle.

261. The King of Heaven.   Daniel 4:37

Now I Nebuchadnezzar praise and extol and honour **the King of heaven**, all whose works are truth, and his ways judgment: and those that walk in pride he is able to abase.

262. The King of Israel.   John 1:49

Nathanael answered and saith unto him, Rabbi, thou art the Son of God; thou art **the King of Israel.**

263. King of Kings.   Revelation 19:16

And he hath on his vesture and on his thigh a name written, **KING OF KINGS,** AND LORD OF LORDS.

264. The King of Peace.   Hebrews 7:2

To whom also Abraham gave a tenth part of all; first being by interpretation King of righteousness, and after that also King of Salem, which is, **King of peace.**

265. The King of Righteousness.   Hebrews 7:2

To whom also Abraham gave a tenth part of all; first being by interpretation **King of righteousness**, and after that also King of Salem, which is, King of peace.

266. King of Saints.   Revelation 15:3

And they sing the song of Moses the servant of God, and the song of the Lamb, saying, Great and marvellous are thy works, Lord God Almighty; just and true are thy ways, thou **King of saints.**

267. The King of Salem.   Hebrews 7:2

To whom also Abraham gave a tenth part of all; first being by interpretation King of righteousness, and after that also **King of Salem**, which is, King of peace.

268. King of the Jews.   Matthew 2:2

Saying, Where is he that is born **King of the Jews?** for we have seen his star in the east, and are come to worship him.

269. The King Who Cometh in the Name of the Lord.   Luke 19:38

Saying, Blessed be **the King that cometh in the name of the Lord**: peace in heaven, and glory in the highest.

270. The Kinsman.   Ruth 4:14

And the women said unto Naomi, Blessed be the LORD, which hath not left thee this day without **a kinsman**, that his name may be famous in Israel.

271. The Lamb.   Revelation 17:14

These shall make war with **the Lamb**, and the Lamb shall overcome them: for he is Lord of lords, and King of kings: and they that are with him are called, and chosen, and faithful.

"Go ye into all the world, and preach the gospel to every creature."

Mark 16:15

51

272. The Lamb of God.   **John 1:29**

The next day John seeth Jesus coming unto him, and saith, Behold **the Lamb of God**, which taketh away the sin of the world.

273. The Lamb Slain from the Foundation of the World.   **Revelation 13:8**

And all that dwell upon the earth shall worship him, whose names are not written in the book of life of **the Lamb slain from the foundation of the world.**

274. The Lamb that Was Slain.   **Revelation 5:12**

Saying with a loud voice, Worthy is **the Lamb that was slain** to receive power, and riches, and wisdom, and strength, and honour, and glory, and blessing.

275. The Lamb Who Is in the Midst of the Throne.   **Revelation 7:17**

For **the Lamb which is in the midst of the throne** shall feed them, and shall lead them unto living fountains of waters: and God shall wipe away all tears from their eyes.

276. The Last.   **Isaiah 44:6**

Thus saith the LORD the King of Israel, and his redeemer the LORD of hosts; I am the first, and I am **the last**; and beside me there is no God.

277. The Last Adam.   **1 Corinthians 15:45**

And so it is written, The first man Adam was made a living soul; **the last Adam** was made a quickening spirit.

278. The Lawgiver.   **James 4:12**

There is one **lawgiver,** who is able to save and to destroy: who art thou that judgest another?

279. A Leader.   **Isaiah 55:4**

Behold, I have given him for a witness to the people, **a leader** and commander to the people.

280. The Life.   **John 14:6**

Jesus saith unto him, I am the way, the truth, and **the life**: no man cometh unto the Father, but by me.

281. The Lifter-Up of Mine Head.   **Psalms 3:3**

But thou, O LORD, art a shield for me; my glory, and **the lifter up of mine head.**

282. The Light.   **John 1:7**

The same came for a witness, to bear witness of **the Light** that all men through him might believe.

283. The Light of Men.   **John 1:4**

In him was life; and the life was **the light of men.**

"I believe in preaching without compromise against sin."

Leonard Ravenhill   **"See 2 Corinthians 4:2"**

284. The Light of the City. Revelation 21:23
And **the city had no need of the sun**, neither of the moon, to shine in it: for the glory of **God did lighten it**, and the **Lamb is the light thereof.**

285. The Light of the Glorious Gospel of Christ. 2 Corinthians 4:4
In whom the god of this world hath blinded the minds of them which believe not, lest **the light of the glorious gospel of Christ**, who is the image of God, should shine unto them.

286. The Light of the Knowledge of the Glory of God. 2 Corinthians 4:6
For God, who commanded the light to shine out of darkness, hath shined in our hearts, to give **the light of the knowledge of the glory of God** in the face of Jesus Christ.

287. The Light of the Morning. 2 Samuel 23:3-4
The God of Israel said, the Rock of Israel spake to me, He that ruleth over men must be just, ruling in the fear of God. And He shall be as **the light of the morning**, when the sun riseth, even a morning without clouds; as the tender grass springing out of the earth by clear shining after rain.

288. The Light of the World. John 8:12
Then spake Jesus again unto them, saying, I am **the light of the world**: he that followeth me shall not walk in darkness, but shall have the light of life.

289. A Light to Lighten the Gentiles. Luke 2:32
A light to lighten the Gentiles, and the glory of thy people Israel.

290. A Light to the Gentiles. Isaiah 49:6
And he said, It is a light thing that thou shouldest be my servant to raise up the tribes of Jacob, and to restore the preserved of Israel: I will also give thee for **a light to the Gentiles**, that thou mayest be my salvation unto the end of the earth.

291. The Lily Among Thorns. Song of Solomon 2:2
As **the lily among thorns**, so is my love among the daughters.

292. The Lily of the Valleys. Song of Solomon 2:1
I am the rose of Sharon, and **the lily of the valleys.**

293. The Lion of the Tribe of Juda. Revelation 5:5
And one of the elders saith unto me, Weep not: behold**, the Lion of the tribe of Juda**, the Root of David, hath prevailed to open the book, and to loose the seven seals thereof.

"He that hath my commandments, and keepeth them, he it is that loveth me: and he that loveth me shall be loved of my Father, and **I will love him, and will manifest myself to him.**"

John 14:21

Jesus promises that He and the Father will reveal themselves to all who love and obey Him.

53

294. The Living Bread. John 6:51

I am **the living bread** which came down from heaven: if any man eat of this bread, he shall live for ever: and the bread that I will give is my flesh, which I will give for the life of the world.

295. The Living God. Psalms 42:2

My soul thirsteth for God, for **the living God:** when shall I come and appear before God?

296. Lord. John 13:13

Ye call me Master and **Lord**: and ye say well; for so I am.

297. Lord also of the Sabbath. Mark 2:28

Therefore the Son of man is **Lord also of the sabbath.**

298. My Lord and My God. John 20:28

And Thomas answered and said unto him, **My Lord and my God.**

299. The Lord and Saviour. 2 Peter 1:11

For so an entrance shall be ministered unto you abundantly into the everlasting kingdom of **our Lord and Saviour** Jesus Christ.

300. Lord Both of the Dead and the Living. Romans 14:9

For to this end Christ both died, and rose, and revived, that he might be **Lord both of the dead and living.**

301. The Lord from Heaven. 1 Corinthians 15:47

The first man is of the earth, earthy: the second man is **the Lord from heaven.**

302. Lord God Almighty. Revelation 16:7

And I heard another out of the altar say, Even so, **Lord God Almighty**, true and righteous are thy judgments.

303. The Lord God of the Holy Prophets. Revelation 22:6

And he said unto me, These sayings are faithful and true: and **the Lord God of the holy prophets** sent his angel to show unto his servants the things which must shortly be done.

304. Lord God of Truth. Psalms 31:5

Into thine hand I commit my spirit: thou hast redeemed me, **O LORD God of truth.**

305. Lord God Omnipotent. Revelation 19:6

And I heard as it were the voice of a great multitude, and as the voice of many waters, and as the voice of mighty thunderings, saying, Alleluia: for the **Lord God omnipotent** reigneth.

"False converts have 'crept in unawares' and sit amid God's people. They think that salvation and sin are compatible. They are actually workers of iniquity."

Unknown **"See Matthew 7:21-23"**

306. The Lord God Who Judgeth Her.   Revelation 18:8
Therefore shall her plagues come in one day, death, and mourning, and famine; and she shall be utterly burned with fire: for strong is **the Lord God who judgeth her.**

307. The Lord, Holy and True.   Revelation 6:10
And they cried with a loud voice, saying, How long, **O Lord, holy and true**, dost thou not judge and avenge our blood on them that dwell on the earth?

308. Lord Jesus.   Romans 10:9
That if thou shalt confess with thy mouth the **Lord Jesus**, and shalt believe in thine heart that God hath raised him from the dead, thou shalt be saved.

309. Lord Jesus Christ.   James 2:1
My brethren, have not the faith of our **Lord Jesus Christ**, the Lord of glory, with respect of persons.

310. The Lord of Glory.   1 Corinthians 2:8
Which none of the princes of this world knew: for had they known it, they would not have crucified **the Lord of glory.**

311. The Lord of the Harvest.   Matthew 9:38
Pray ye therefore **the Lord of the harvest**, that he will send forth labourers into his harvest.

312. Lord of Lords.   1 Timothy 6:15
Which in his times he shall show, who is the blessed and only Potentate, the King of kings, and **Lord of lords.**

313. Lord of Peace.   2 Thessalonians 3:16
Now the **Lord of peace** himself give you peace always by all means. The Lord be with you all.

314. The Lord of the Vineyard.   Matthew 20:8
So when even was come**, the lord of the vineyard** saith unto his steward, Call the labourers, and give them their hire, beginning from the last unto the first.

315. The Lord of the Whole Earth.   Psalms 97:5
The hills melted like wax at the presence of the LORD, at the presence of **the Lord of the whole earth.**

316. The Lord's Christ.   Revelation 11:15
And the seventh angel sounded; and there were great voices in heaven, saying, The kingdoms of this world are become the kingdoms of **our Lord, and of his Christ**; and he shall reign for ever and ever.

317. The Lord's Doing.   Matthew 21:42
Jesus saith unto them, Did ye never read in the scriptures, The stone which the builders rejected, the same is become the head of the corner: this is **the Lord's doing**, and it is marvellous in our eyes?

"Those who don't read have no advantage over those who can't read."

Mark Twain   **"See 2 Timothy 2:15"**

55

318. Lowly in Heart. Matthew 11:29

Take my yoke upon you, and learn of me; for I am meek and **lowly in heart**: and ye shall find rest unto your souls.

319. Magnified. Psalms 40:16

Let all those that seek thee rejoice and be glad in thee: let such as love thy salvation say continually, The LORD be **magnified.**

320. Our Maker. Psalms 95:6

O come, let us worship and bow down: let us kneel before the LORD **our maker.**

321. A Malefactor. John 18:30

They answered and said unto him, If he were not **a malefactor**, we would not have delivered him up unto thee.

322. The Man. John 19:5

Then came Jesus forth, wearing the crown of thorns, and the purple robe. And Pilate saith unto them, Behold **the man!**

323. A Man Approved of God. Acts 2:22

Ye men of Israel, hear these words; Jesus of Nazareth, **a man approved of God** among you by miracles and wonders and signs, which God did by him in the midst of you, as ye yourselves also know.

324. A Man Child. Revelation 12:5

And she brought forth **a man child**, who was to rule all nations with a rod of iron: and her child was caught up unto God, and to his throne.

325. The Man Christ Jesus. 1 Timothy 2:5

For there is one God, and one mediator between God and men, **the man Christ Jesus.**

326. A Man Gluttonous. Matthew 11:19

The Son of man came eating and drinking, and they say, Behold **a man gluttonous**, and a winebibber, a friend of publicans and sinners. But wisdom is justified of her children.

327. The Man Whose Name is the Branch. Zechariah 6:12

And speak unto him, saying, Thus speaketh the LORD of hosts, saying, Behold **the man whose name is The BRANCH**; and he shall grow up out of his place, and he shall build the temple of the LORD.

328. The Man of Sorrows. Isaiah 53:3

He is despised and rejected of men; **a man of sorrows**, and acquainted with grief: and we hid as it were our faces from him; he was despised, and we esteemed him not.

"Unless we see our shortcomings in the light of the Law and holiness of God, we do not see them as sin at all."

J.I. Packer **"See Proverbs 6:23"**

329. The Man Whom He Hath Ordained.   Acts 17:31

Because he hath appointed a day, in the which he will judge the world in righteousness by **that man whom he hath ordained**; whereof he hath given assurance unto all men, in that he hath raised him from the dead.

330. Manna.   Exodus 16:15

And when the children of Israel saw it, they said one to another, It is **manna**: for they wist not what it was. And Moses said unto them, This is the bread which the LORD hath given you to eat.

331. Marvelous in Our Eyes.   Matthew 21:42

Jesus saith unto them, Did ye never read in the scriptures, The stone which the builders rejected, the same is become the head of the corner: this is the Lord's doing, and it is **marvellous in our eyes?**

332. Your Master.   Matthew 23:10

Neither be ye called masters: for one is **your Master**, even Christ.

333. The Mediator.   1 Timothy 2:5

For there is one God, and one **mediator** between God and men, the man Christ Jesus.

334. The Mediator of a Better Covenant.   Hebrews 8:6

But now hath he obtained a more excellent ministry, by how much also he is **the mediator of a better covenant**, which was established upon better promises.

335. The Mediator of the New Covenant.   Hebrews 12:24

And to Jesus **the mediator of the new covenant**, and to the blood of sprinkling, that speaketh better things than that of Abel.

336. The Mediator of the New Testament.   Hebrews 9:15

And for this cause he is **the mediator of the new testament**, that by means of death, for the redemption of the transgressions that were under the first testament, they which are called might receive the promise of eternal inheritance.

337. Meek.   Matthew 11:29

Take my yoke upon you, and learn of me; for I am **meek** and lowly in heart: and ye shall find rest unto your souls.

338. Melchizedek.   Genesis 14:18

And **Melchizedek** king of Salem brought forth bread and wine and he was the priest of the most high God.

339. A Merciful and Faithful High Priest.   Hebrews 2:17

Wherefore in all things it behoved him to be made like unto his brethren, that he might be **a merciful and faithful high priest** in things pertaining to God, to make reconciliation for the sins of the people.

"But the wisdom that is from above is first pure, then peaceable, gentle, and easy to be entreated, full of mercy and good fruits, without partiality, and without hypocrisy."

James 3:17

340. His Mercy and His Truth.   **Psalms 57:3**

He shall send from heaven, and save me from the reproach of him that would swallow me up. Selah. God shall send forth **his mercy and his truth.**

341. The Messenger of the Covenant.   **Malachi 3:1**

Behold, I will send my messenger, and he shall prepare the way before me: and the Lord, whom ye seek, shall suddenly come to his temple, even **the messenger of the covenant**, whom ye delight in: behold, he shall come, saith the LORD of hosts.

342. Messiah.   **Daniel 9:26**

And after threescore and two weeks shall **Messiah** be cut off, but not for himself: and the people of the prince that shall come shall destroy the city and the sanctuary; and the end thereof shall be with a flood, and unto the end of the war desolations are determined.

343. Messiah the Prince.   **Daniel 9:25**

Know therefore and understand, that from the going forth of the commandment to restore and to build Jerusalem unto the **Messiah the Prince** shall be seven weeks, and threescore and two weeks: the street shall be built again, and the wall, even in troublous times.

344. Mighty.   **Psalms 89:19**

Then thou spakest in vision to thy holy one, and saidst, I have laid help upon one that is **mighty**; I have exalted one chosen out of the people.

345. The Mighty God.   **Isaiah 9:6**

For unto us a child is born, unto us a son is given: and the government shall be upon his shoulder: and his name shall be called Wonderful, Counsellor, **The mighty God**, The everlasting Father, The Prince of Peace.

346. The Mighty One of Jacob.   **Isaiah 60:16**

Thou shalt also suck the milk of the Gentiles, and shalt suck the breast of kings: and thou shalt know that I the LORD am thy Saviour and thy Redeemer, **the mighty One of Jacob.**

347. The Minister of Sin.   **Galatians 2:17**

But if, while we seek to be justified by Christ, we ourselves also are found sinners, is therefore Christ **the minister of sin?** God forbid.

348. A Minister of the Circumcision.   **Romans 15:8**

Now I say that Jesus Christ was **a minister of the circumcision** for the truth of God, to confirm the promises made unto the fathers.

349. The Minister of the Sanctuary.   **Hebrews 8:1-3**

Now of the things which we have spoken this is the sum: We have such an high priest, who is set on the right hand of the throne of the Majesty in the heavens; **A minister of the sanctuary**, and of the true tabernacle, which the Lord pitched, and not man. For every high priest is ordained to offer gifts and sacrifices: wherefore it is of necessity that this man have somewhat also to offer.

"When in doubt, tell the truth."

Mark Twain   **"See Proverbs 12:17, 19"**

350. A More Excellent Name. Hebrews 1:4

Being made so much better than the angels, as he hath by inheritance obtained **a more excellent name** than they.

351. The Morning Star. Revelation 2:28

And I will give him the **morning star.**

352. The Mouth of God. Matthew 4:4

But he answered and said, It is written, Man shall not live by bread alone, but by every word that proceedeth out of **the mouth of God.**

353. The Mystery of God. Colossians 2:2

That their hearts might be comforted, being knit together in love, and unto all riches of the full assurance of understanding, to the acknowledgment of **the mystery of God**, and of the Father, and of Christ.

354. A Nail Fastened in a Sure Place. Isaiah 22:23

And I will fasten him as **a nail in a sure place**; and he shall be for a glorious throne to his father's house.

355. A Name Above Every Name. Philippians 2:9

Wherefore God also hath highly exalted him, and given him **a name which is above every name.**

356. A Nazarene. Matthew 2:23

And he came and dwelt in a city called Nazareth: that it might be fulfilled which was spoken by the prophets, He shall be called **a Nazarene.**

357. An Offering and a Sacrifice to God. Ephesians 5:2

And walk in love, as Christ also hath loved us, and hath given himself for us **an offering and a sacrifice to God** for a sweet smelling savour.

358. The Offspring of David. Revelation 22:16

I Jesus have sent mine angel to testify unto you these things in the churches. I am the root and **the offspring of David**, and the bright and morning star.

359. Ointment Poured Forth. Song of Solomon 1:3

Because of the savour of thy good ointments thy name is as **ointment poured forth**, therefore do the virgins love thee.

360. The Omega. Revelation 22:13

I am Alpha and **Omega**, the beginning and the end, the first and the last.

361. His Only Begotten Son. John 3:16

For God so loved the world, that he gave his **only begotten Son,** that whosoever believeth in him should not perish, but have everlasting life.

"What comes into our minds when we think about God is the most important thing about us."

A.W. Tozer **"See Psalm 33:21-22"**

362. The Only Begotten of the Father.   **John 1:14**

And the Word was made flesh, and dwelt among us, (and we beheld his glory, the glory as of **the only begotten of the Father**,) full of grace and truth.

363. Only Potentate.   **1 Timothy 6:15**

Which in his times he shall shew, who is the blessed and **only Potentate**, the King of kings, and Lord of lords.

364. The Only Wise God.   **1 Timothy 1:17**

Now unto the King eternal, immortal, invisible, **the only wise God**, be honour and glory for ever and ever. Amen.

365. An Owl of the Desert.   **Psalms 102:6**

I am like a pelican of the wilderness: I am like **an owl of the desert.**

366. Our Passover.   **1 Corinthians 5:7**

Purge out therefore the old leaven, that ye may be a new lump, as ye are unleavened. For even Christ **our passover** is sacrificed for us.

367. A Pavilion.   **Psalms 31:20**

Thou shalt hide them in the secret of thy presence from the pride of man: thou shalt keep them secretly in **a pavilion** from the strife of tongues.

368. Our Peace.   **Ephesians 2:14**

For he is **our peace**, who hath made both one, and hath broken down the middle wall of partition between us.

369. A Pelican of the Wilderness.   **Psalms 102:6**

I am like **a pelican of the wilderness**: I am like an owl of the desert.

370. A Perfect Man.   **James 3:2**

For in many things we offend all. If any man offend not in word, the same is **a perfect man**, and able also to bridle the whole body.

371. The Person of Christ.   **2 Corinthians 2:10**

To whom ye forgive any thing, I forgive also: for if I forgave any thing, to whom I forgave it, for your sakes forgave I it in **the person of Christ.**

"To ask that God's love should be content with us as we are is to ask that God should cease to be God: because He is what He is, His love must, in the nature of things, be impeded and repelled by certain stains in our present character, and because he already loves us He must labor to make us lovable."

C.S. Lewis   **"See 1 Peter 5:10-11"**

60

372. Physician.   Luke 4:23

And he said unto them, Ye will surely say unto me this proverb, **Physician**, heal thyself: whatsoever we have heard done in Capernaum, do also here in thy country.

373. A Place of Refuge.   Isaiah 4:6

And there shall be a tabernacle for a shadow in the daytime from the heat, and for a **place of refuge**, and for a covert from storm and from rain.

374. A Plant of Renown.   Ezekiel 34:29

And I will raise up for them **a plant of renown**, and they shall be no more consumed with hunger in the land, neither bear the shame of the heathen any more.

375. A Polished Staff.   Isaiah 49:2

And he hath made my mouth like a sharp sword; in the shadow of his hand hath he hid me, and made me **a polished shaft**; in his quiver hath he hid me.

376. Poor.   2 Corinthians 8:9

For ye know the grace of our Lord Jesus Christ, that, though he was rich, yet for your sakes he became **poor**, that ye through his poverty might be rich.

377. My Portion.   Psalms 119:57

Thou art **my portion**, O LORD: I have said that I would keep thy words.

378. The Portion of Jacob.   Jeremiah 51:19

The **portion of Jacob** is not like them; for he is the former of all things: and Israel is the rod of his inheritance: the LORD of hosts is his name.

379. The Portion of Mine Inheritance.   Psalms 16:5

The LORD is **the portion of mine inheritance** and of my cup: thou maintainest my lot.

380. The Potter.   Jeremiah 18:6

O house of Israel, cannot I do with you as this potter? Saith the LORD. Behold, as the clay is in **the potter's** hand, so are ye in mine hand, O house of Israel.

381. The Power of God.   1 Corinthians 1:24

But unto them which are called, both Jews and Greeks, Christ **the power of God**, and the wisdom of God.

382. Precious.   1 Peter 2:7

Unto you therefore which believe he is **precious:** but unto them which be disobedient, the stone which the builders disallowed, the same is made the head of the corner.

"Love is an action, not a feeling. Love is a choice. In fact, love is a commandment."

Mack Timberlake   **"See Matthew 22:36-40"**

383. Precious Corner Stone.   **Isaiah 28:16**

Therefore thus saith the Lord GOD, Behold, I lay in Zion for a foundation a stone, a tried stone, **a precious corner stone**, a sure foundation: he that believeth shall not make haste.

384. Preeminence.   **Colossians 1:18**

And he is the head of the body, the church: who is the beginning, the firstborn from the dead; that in all things he might have the **preeminence.**

385. A Price.   **1 Corinthians 6:20**

For ye are bought with **a price:** therefore glorify God in your body, and in your spirit, which are God's.

386. The Price of His Redemption.   **Leviticus 25:52**

And if there remain but few years unto the year of jubilee, then he shall count with him, and according unto his years shall he give him again **the price of his redemption.**

387. A Priest Forever.   **Psalms 110:4**

The LORD hath sworn, and will not repent, Thou art **a priest for ever** after the order of Melchizedek.

388. The Priest of the Most High God.   **Hebrews 7:1**

For this Melchisedec, king of Salem, **priest of the most high God**, who met Abraham returning from the slaughter of the kings, and blessed him.

389. A Prince and Saviour.   **Acts 5:31**

Him hath God exalted with his right hand to be **a Prince and a Saviour**, for to give repentance to Israel, and forgiveness of sins.

390. The Prince of Life.   **Acts 3:15**

And killed **the Prince of life**, whom God hath raised from the dead; whereof we are witnesses.

391. The Prince of Peace.   **Isaiah 9:6**

For unto us a child is born, unto us a son is given: and the government shall be upon his shoulder: and his name shall be called Wonderful, Counsellor, The mighty God, The everlasting Father, **The Prince of Peace.**

392. Prince of Princes.   **Daniel 8:25**

And through his policy also he shall cause craft to prosper in his hand; and he shall magnify himself in his heart, and by peace shall destroy many: he shall also stand up against **the Prince of princes**; but he shall be broken without hand.

393. The Prince of the Kings of the Earth.   **Revelation 1:5**

And from Jesus Christ, who is the faithful witness, and the first begotten of the dead, and **the prince of the kings of the earth.** Unto him that loved us, and washed us from our sins in his own blood.

"The safest place to be is within the will of God."

Unknown   **"See Psalm 4:8"**

394. The Prophet. John 7:40

Many of the people therefore, when they heard this saying, said, Of a truth this is **the Prophet.**

395. A Prophet Mighty in Deed and Word. Luke 24:19

And he said unto them, What things? And they said unto him, Concerning Jesus of Nazareth, which was **a prophet mighty in deed** and word before God and all the people.

396. The Prophet of Nazareth. Matthew 21:11

And the multitude said, This is Jesus **the prophet of Nazareth** of Galilee.

397. A Prophet without Honour. Matthew 13:57

And they were offended in him. But Jesus said unto them, **A prophet is not without honour**, save in his own country, and in his own house.

398. One of the Prophets. Matthew 16:14

And they said, Some say that thou art John the Baptist: some, Elias; and others, Jeremias, or **one of the prophets.**

399. The Propitiation for Our Sins. 1 John 2:2

And he is **the propitiation for our sins:** and not for ours only, but also for the sins of the whole world.

400. Pure. 1 John 3:3

And every man that hath this hope in him purifieth himself, even as he is **pure.**

401. A Purifier of Silver. Malachi 3:3

And he shall sit as a refiner and **purifier of silver**: and he shall purify the sons of Levi, and purge them as gold and silver, that they may offer unto the LORD an offering in righteousness.

402. Of Quick Understanding. Isaiah 11:3

And shall make him **of quick understanding** in the fear of the LORD: and he shall not judge after the sight of his eyes, neither reprove after the hearing of his ears.

403. A Quickening Spirit. 1 Corinthians 15:45

And so it is written, The first man Adam was made a living soul; the last Adam was made **a quickening spirit.**

"And the servant of the Lord must not strive; but be gentle unto all men, apt to teach, patient, in meekness instructing those that oppose themselves; if God peradventure will give them repentance to the acknowledging of the truth."

2 Timothy 2:24, 25

This is the spirit in which we should share our faith!

63

404. Rabbi. John 3:2
The same came to Jesus by night, and said unto him, **Rabbi,** we know that thou art a teacher come from God: for no man can do these miracles that thou doest, except God be with him.

405. Rabboni. John 20:16
Jesus saith unto her, Mary. She turned herself, and saith unto him, **Rabboni**; which is to say, Master.

406. Rain Upon the Mown Grass. Psalms 72:6
He shall come down like **rain upon the mown grass:** as showers that water the earth.

407. A Ransom for All. 1 Timothy 2:6
Who gave himself **a ransom for all,** to be testified in due time.

408. A Ransom for Many. Matthew 20:28
Even as the Son of man came not to be ministered unto, but to minister, and to give his life **a ransom for many.**

409. My Redeemer. Job 19:25
For I know that **my redeemer** liveth, and that he shall stand at the latter day upon the earth.

410. Redemption. 1 Corinthians 1:30
But of him are ye in Christ Jesus, who of God is made unto us wisdom, and righteousness, and sanctification, and **redemption.**

Luke 21:28

And when these things begin to come to pass, then look up, and lift up your heads; for your **redemption** draweth nigh.

411. The Redemption of Their Soul. Psalms 49:8
(For **the redemption of their soul** is precious, and it ceaseth for ever).

412. A Refiner's Fire. Malachi 3:2
But who may abide the day of his coming? and who shall stand when he appeareth? for he is like **a refiner's fire**, and like fullers' soap.

413. Our Refuge. Psalms 46:1
God is **our refuge** and strength, a very present help in trouble.

414. A Refuge in Times of Trouble. Psalms 9:9
The LORD also will be a refuge for the oppressed, **a refuge in times of trouble.**

"The greatest proof of Christianity for others is not how far a man can logically analyze his reasons for believing, but how far in practice he will stake his life on his belief."

T.S. Eliot **"See Philippians 1:19-21"**

415. A Refuge for the Oppressed.   Psalms 9:9

The LORD also will be **a refuge for the oppressed**, a refuge in times of trouble.

416. A Refuge from the Storm.   Isaiah 25:4

For thou hast been a strength to the poor, a strength to the needy in his distress, **a refuge from the storm**, a shadow from the heat, when the blast of the terrible ones is as a storm against the wall.

417. Our Report.   Isaiah 53:1

Who hath believed **our report?** And to whom is the arm of the LORD revealed?

418. A Reproach of Men.   Psalms 22:6

But I am a worm, and no man; **a reproach of men,** and despised of the people.

419. Their Resting Place.   Jeremiah 50:6

My people hath been lost sheep: their shepherds have caused them to go astray, they have turned them away on the mountains: they have gone from mountain to hill, they have forgotten **their resting place.**

420. The Resurrection and the Life.   John 11:25

Jesus said unto her, I am **the resurrection, and the life:** he that believeth in me, though he were dead, yet shall he live.

421. Reverend.   Psalms 111:9

He sent redemption unto his people: he hath commanded his covenant for ever: holy and **reverend** is his name.

422. A Reward for the Righteous.   Psalms 58:11

So that a man shall say, Verily there is **a reward for the righteous**: verily he is a God that judgeth in the earth.

423. Rich.   Romans 10:12

For there is no difference between the Jew and the Greek: for the same Lord over all is **rich** unto all that call upon him.

424. The Riches of His Glory.   Romans 9:23

And that he might make known **the riches of his glory** on the vessels of mercy, which he had afore prepared unto glory.

425. The Riddle.   Judges 14:14

And he said unto them, Out of the eater came forth meat, and out of the strong came forth sweetness. And they could not in three days expound **the riddle.**

"There must be true and deep conviction of sin. This the preacher must labor to produce, for where this is not felt, the new birth has not taken place."

Charles Spurgeon   **"See 2 Timothy 2:24-26"**

426. Right.   Deuteronomy 32:4

He is the Rock, his work is perfect: for all his ways are judgment: a God of truth and without iniquity, just and **right** is he.

427. The Righteous.   1 John 2:1

My little children, these things write I unto you, that ye sin not. And if any man sin, we have an advocate with the Father, Jesus Christ **the righteous.**

428. A Righteous Branch.   Jeremiah 23:5

Behold, the days come, saith the LORD, that I will raise unto David **a righteous Branch**, and a King shall reign and prosper, and shall execute judgment and justice in the earth.

429. My Righteous Servant.   Isaiah 53:11

He shall see of the travail of his soul, and shall be satisfied: by his knowledge shall **my righteous servant** justify many; for he shall bear their iniquities.

430. The Righteous Judge.   2 Timothy 4:8

Henceforth there is laid up for me a crown of righteousness, which the Lord**, the righteous judge**, shall give me at that day: and not to me only, but unto all them also that love his appearing.

431. A Righteous Man.   Luke 23:47

Now when the centurion saw what was done, he glorified God, saying, Certainly this was **a righteous man.**

432. Righteousness.   1 Corinthians 1:30

But of him are ye in Christ Jesus, who of God is made unto us wisdom, and **righteousness**, and sanctification, and redemption.

433. The Righteousness of God.   Romans 10:3

For they being ignorant of God's righteousness, and going about to establish their own righteousness, have not submitted themselves unto **the righteousness of God.**

434. A River of Water in a Dry Place.   Isaiah 32:2

And a man shall be as an hiding place from the wind, and a covert from the tempest; as **rivers of water in a dry place**, as the shadow of a great rock in a weary land.

435. The Rock.   Matthew 16:18

And I say also unto thee, That thou art Peter, and upon this **rock** I will build my church; and the gates of hell shall not prevail against it.

"Then saith he unto his disciples, The harvest truly is plenteous, but the labourers are few; Pray ye therefore the Lord of the harvest, that he will send forth labourers into his harvest."

Matthew 9:37-38

436. The Rock that is Higher than I.   Psalms 61:2
From the end of the earth will I cry unto thee, when my heart is overwhelmed: lead me to **the rock that is higher than I.**

437. The Rock of Israel.   2 Samuel 23:3
The God of Israel said, **the Rock of Israel** spake to me, He that ruleth over men must be just, ruling in the fear of God.

438. A Rock of Offence.   Romans 9:33
As it is written, Behold, I lay in Sion a stumbling stone and **rock of offence:** and whosoever believeth on him shall not be ashamed.

439. The Rock of My Refuge.   Psalms 94:22
But the LORD is my defence; and my God is **the rock of my refuge.**

440. The Rock of His Salvation.   Deuteronomy 32:15
But Jeshurun waxed fat, and kicked: thou art waxen fat, thou art grown thick, thou art covered with fatness; then he forsook God which made him, and lightly esteemed **the Rock of his salvation.**

441. The Rock of Our Salvation.   Psalms 95:1
O come, let us sing unto the LORD: let us make a joyful noise to **the rock of our salvation.**

442. The Rock of Thy Strength.   Isaiah 17:10
Because thou hast forgotten the God of thy salvation, and hast not been mindful of **the rock of thy strength**, therefore shalt thou plant pleasant plants, and shalt set it with strange slips.

443. The Rod.   Micah 6:9
The LORD'S voice crieth unto the city, and the man of wisdom shall see thy name: hear ye **the rod**, and who hath appointed it.

444. A Rod out of the Stem of Jesse.   Isaiah 11:1
And there shall come forth **a rod out of the stem of Jesse**, and a Branch shall grow out of his roots.

445. The Root of David.   Revelation 5:5
And one of the elders saith unto me, Weep not: behold, the Lion of the tribe of Juda, **the Root of David**, hath prevailed to open the book, and to loose the seven seals thereof.

"People who risk nothing, have nothing!"

William A. Granims   **"See Matthew 25:14-30"**

446. A Root of Jesse. Romans 15:12

And again, Esaias saith, There shall be **a root of Jesse**, and he that shall rise to reign over the Gentiles; in him shall the Gentiles trust.

Isaiah 11:10

And in that day there shall be **a root of Jesse**, which shall stand for an ensign of the people; to it shall the Gentiles seek: and his rest shall be glorious.

447. A Root out of Dry Ground. Isaiah 53:2

For he shall grow up before him as a tender plant, and as **a root out of a dry ground**: he hath no form nor comeliness; and when we shall see him, there is no beauty that we should desire him.

448. The Root and Offspring of David. Revelation 22:16

I Jesus have sent mine angel to testify unto you these things in the churches. **I am the root and the offspring of David,** and the bright and morning star.

449. The Rose of Sharon. Song of Solomon 2:1

I am **the rose of Sharon**, and the lily of the valleys.

450. A Ruler. Micah 5:2

But thou, Bethlehem Ephratah, though thou be little among the thousands of Judah, yet out of thee shall he come forth unto me that is to be **ruler** in Israel; whose goings forth have been from of old, from everlasting.

451. The Sacrifice for Sins. Hebrews 10:12

But this man, after he had offered one **sacrifice for sins** for ever, sat down on the right hand of God.

452. A Sacrifice to God. Ephesians 5:2

And walk in love, as Christ also hath loved us, and hath given himself for us an offering and **a sacrifice to God** for a sweet smelling savour.

453. My Salvation. Psalms 27:1

The LORD is my light and **my salvation**; whom shall I fear? the LORD is the strength of my life; of whom shall I be afraid?

454. The Salvation of God. Luke 3:6

And all flesh shall see **the salvation of God.**

455. The Salvation of Israel. Jeremiah 3:23

Truly in vain is salvation hoped for from the hills, and from the multitude of mountains: truly in the LORD our God is **the salvation of Israel.**

"Depend on it. God's work done in God's way will never lack God's supply. He is too wise a God to frustrate His purposes for lack of funds, and He can just as easily supply them ahead of time as afterwards, and He much prefers doing so."

J. Hudson Taylor (China Inland Mission) **"See 2 Corinthians 3:4-5"**

456. A Samaritan. John 8:48

Then answered the Jews, and said unto him, Say we not well that thou art **a Samaritan**, and hast a devil?

457. The Same Yesterday, Today, and Forever. Hebrews 13:8

Jesus Christ **the same yesterday, and to day, and for ever.**

458. A Sanctuary. Isaiah 8:14

And he shall be for **a sanctuary**; but for a stone of stumbling and for a rock of offence to both the houses of Israel, for a gin and for a snare to the inhabitants of Jerusalem.

459. A Sardine Stone. Revelation 4:3

And he that sat was to look upon like a jasper and **a sardine stone**: and there was a rainbow round about the throne, in sight like unto an emerald.

460. The Saving Strength of His Anointed. Psalms 28:8

The LORD is their strength, and he is **the saving strength of his anointed.**

461. Saviour. Titus 2:13

Looking for that blessed hope, and the glorious appearing of the great God and our **Saviour** Jesus Christ.

462. The Saviour of All Men. 1 Timothy 4:10

For therefore we both labour and suffer reproach, because we trust in the living God, who is **the Saviour of all men,** specially of those that believe.

463. The Saviour of the Body. Ephesians 5:23

For the husband is the head of the wife, even as Christ is the head of the church: and he is **the Saviour of the body.**

464. The Saviour of the World. John 4:42

And said unto the woman, Now we believe, not because of thy saying: for we have heard him ourselves, and know that this is indeed the Christ, **the Saviour of the world.**

1 John 4:14

And we have seen and do testify that the Father sent the Son to be **the Saviour of the world.**

465. The Scapegoat. Leviticus 16:8

And Aaron shall cast lots upon the two goats; one lot for the LORD, and the other lot for **the scapegoat.**

John 11:49-52

And one of them, named Caiaphas, being the high priest that same year, said unto them, Ye know nothing at all, Nor consider that it is expedient for us, **that one man should die for the people,** and that the whole nation perish not. And this spake he not of himself: but being high priest that year, he prophesied that Jesus should die for that nation; And not for that nation only, but that also he should gather together in one the children of God that were scattered abroad.

"Never attribute to malice that which is adequately explained by stupidity."

Unknown **"See Romans 10:2-4"**

466. The Scepter of Israel. Numbers 24:17

I shall see him, but not now: I shall behold him, but not nigh: there shall come a Star out of Jacob, and **a Sceptre shall rise out of Israel,** and shall smite the corners of Moab, and destroy all the children of Sheth.

467. The Scepter of Thy Kingdom. Psalms 45:6

Thy throne, O God, is for ever and ever: **the sceptre of thy kingdom** is a right sceptre.

468. Secret. Judges 13:18

And the angel of the LORD said unto him, Why askest thou thus after my name, seeing it is **secret?**

469. The Secret of Thy Presence. Psalms 31:20

Thou shalt hide them in **the secret of thy presence** from the pride of man: thou shalt keep them secretly in a pavilion from the strife of tongues.

470. The Seed of Abraham. Galatians 3:16

Now to **Abraham and his seed** were the promises made. He saith not, And to seeds, as of many; but as of one, And to thy seed, which is Christ.

471. The Seed of David. Romans 1:3

Concerning his Son Jesus Christ our Lord, which was made of **the seed of David** according to the flesh.

2 Timothy 2:8

Remember that Jesus Christ of **the seed of David** was raised from the dead according to my gospel.

472. The Seed of the Woman. Genesis 3:15

And I will put enmity between thee and **the woman, and between thy seed and her seed**; it shall bruise thy head, and thou shalt bruise his heel.

473. The Sent One. John 9:4

I must work the works of **him that sent me**, while it is day: the night cometh, when no man can work.

474. Separate from His Brethern. Genesis 49:26

The blessings of thy father have prevailed above the blessings of my progenitors unto the utmost bound of the everlasting hills: they shall be on the head of Joseph, and on the crown of the head of him that was **separate from his brethren.**

475. Separate from Sinners. Hebrews 7:26

For such an high priest became us, who is holy, harmless, undefiled, **separate from sinners**, and made higher than the heavens.

476. The Serpent in the Wilderness. John 3:14

And as Moses lifted up **the serpent in the wilderness**, even so must the Son of man be lifted up.

"Going to church doesn't make you a Christian any more than going to the garage makes you a car."

Laurence J. Peter **"See John 3:3"**

70

477. My Servant.   **Isaiah 42:1**

Behold **my servant**, whom I uphold; mine elect, in whom my soul delighteth; I have put my spirit upon him: he shall bring forth judgment to the Gentiles.

478. A Servant of Rulers.   **Isaiah 49:7**

Thus saith the LORD, the Redeemer of Israel, and his Holy One, to him whom man despiseth, to him whom the nation abhorreth, to **a servant of rulers**, Kings shall see and arise, princes also shall worship, because of the LORD that is faithful, and the Holy One of Israel, and he shall choose thee.

479. My Servant the Branch.   **Zechariah 3:8**

Hear now, O Joshua the high priest, thou, and thy fellows that sit before thee: for they are men wondered at: for, behold, I will bring forth **my servant the BRANCH.**

480. A Shadow from the Heat.   **Isaiah 25:4**

For thou hast been a strength to the poor, a strength to the needy in his distress, a refuge from the storm, **a shadow from the heat,** when the blast of the terrible ones is as a storm against the wall.

481. The Shadow of the Almighty.   **Psalms 91:1**

He that dwelleth in the secret place of the most High shall abide under **the shadow of the Almighty.**

482. The Shadow of a Great Rock.   **Isaiah 32:2**

And a man shall be as an hiding place from the wind, and a covert from the tempest; as rivers of water in a dry place, as **the shadow of a great rock** in a weary land.

483. A Shelter.   **Psalms 61:3**

For thou hast been **a shelter** for me, and a strong tower from the enemy.

484. My Shepherd.   **Psalms 23:1**

The LORD is **my shepherd**; I shall not want.

                                                                        Isaiah 40:11

He shall feed his flock like a **shepherd:** he shall gather the lambs with his arm, and carry them in his bosom, and shall gently lead those that are with young.

485. The Shepherd of Israel.   **Psalms 80:1**

Give ear, O **Shepherd of Israel**, thou that leadest Joseph like a flock; thou that dwellest between the cherubims, shine forth.

486. Our Shield.   **Psalms 84:9**

Behold, O God **our shield**, and look upon the face of thine anointed.

487. Shiloh.   **Genesis 49:10**

The sceptre shall not depart from Judah, nor a lawgiver from between his feet, until **Shiloh** come; and unto him shall the gathering of the people be.

"When you turn your back on God, any way you go is a wrong direction."

Ray Comfort   **"See Colossians 3:1-4"**

488. A Sign of the Lord.   **Isaiah 7:11**

Ask thee **a sign of the LORD** thy God; ask it either in the depth, or in the height above.

489. Siloam.   **John 9:7**

And said unto him, Go, wash in the pool of **Siloam,** (which is by interpretation, Sent.) He went his way therefore, and washed, and came seeing.

490. Sin.   **2 Corinthians 5:21**

For he hath made him to be **sin** for us, who knew no sin; that we might be made the righteousness of God in him.

491. A Snare to the Inhabitants of Jerusalem.   **Isaiah 8:14**

And he shall be for a sanctuary; but for a stone of stumbling and for a rock of offence to both the houses of Israel, for a gin and for **a snare to the inhabitants of Jerusalem.**

492. The Son.   **Matthew 11:27**

All things are delivered unto me of my Father: and no man knoweth the Son, but the Father; neither knoweth any man the Father, save **the Son**, and he to whomsoever the Son will reveal him.

493. His Son from Heaven.   **1 Thessalonians 1:10**

And to wait for **his Son from heaven**, whom he raised from the dead, even Jesus, which delivered us from the wrath to come.

494. A Son Given.   **Isaiah 9:6**

For unto us a child is born, unto us **a son is given**: and the government shall be upon his shoulder: and his name shall be called Wonderful, Counsellor, The mighty God, The everlasting Father, The Prince of Peace.

495. The Son of Abraham.   **Matthew 1:1**

The book of the generation of Jesus Christ, the son of David, **the son of Abraham.**

496. The Son of David.   **Matthew 1:1**

The book of the generation of Jesus Christ, **the son of David**, the son of Abraham.

497. The Son of God.   **John 1:49**

Nathanael answered and saith unto him, Rabbi, thou art **the Son of God**; thou art the King of Israel.

498. The Son of Joseph.   **John 1:45**

Philip findeth Nathanael, and saith unto him, We have found him, of whom Moses in the law, and the prophets, did write, Jesus of Nazareth, **the son of Joseph.**

"God, grant me the serenity to accept the things I cannot change, the courage to change the things I can, and the wisdom to know the difference."

Reinhold Niebuhr   **"See Proverbs 9:10"**

499. The Son of Man.   **John 1:51**

And he saith unto him, Verily, verily, I say unto you, Hereafter ye shall see heaven open, and the angels of God ascending and descending upon **the Son of man.**

500. The Son of Mary.   **Mark 6:3**

Is not this the carpenter, **the son of Mary**, the brother of James, and Joses, and of Juda, and Simon? And are not his sisters here with us? And they were offended at him.

501. The Son of the Blessed.   **Mark 14:61**

But he held his peace, and answered nothing. Again the high priest asked him, and said unto him, Art thou the Christ, **the Son of the Blessed?**

502. The Son of the Father.   **2 John 1:3**

Grace be with you, mercy, and peace, from God the Father, and from the Lord Jesus Christ, **the Son of the Father**, in truth and love.

503. The Son of the Free Woman.   **Galatians 4:30**

Nevertheless what saith the scripture? Cast out the bondwoman and her son: for the son of the bondwoman shall not be heir with **the son of the freewoman.**

504. The Son of the Highest.   **Luke 1:32**

He shall be great, and shall be called **the Son of the Highest**: and the Lord God shall give unto him the throne of his father David.

505. The Son of the Living God.   **Matthew 16:16**

And Simon Peter answered and said, Thou art the Christ, **the Son of the living God.**

506. The Son of the Most High God.   **Mark 5:7**

And cried with a loud voice, and said, What have I to do with thee, Jesus, thou **Son of the most high God**? I adjure thee by God, that thou torment me not.

507. A Son over His own House.   **Hebrews 3:6**

But Christ as **a son over his own house**; whose house are we, if we hold fast the confidence and the rejoicing of the hope firm unto the end.

508. The Son who is Consecrated for Evermore.   **Hebrews 7:28**

For the law maketh men high priests which have infirmity; but the word of the oath, which was since the law, maketh **the Son, who is consecrated for evermore.**

509. My Song.   **Isaiah 12:2**

Behold, God is my salvation; I will trust, and not be afraid: for the LORD JEHOVAH is my strength and **my song;** he also is become my salvation.

"Kindness: a language the deaf can hear and the blind can see."

Unknown   **"See Psalm 117:1"**

510. A Sower.   **Matthew 13:4**
And when **he sowed**, some seeds fell by the way side, and the fowls came and devoured them up.

Matthew 13:37
He answered and said unto them, **He that soweth** the good seed is the Son of man.

511. A Sparrow Alone upon the Housetop.   **Psalms 102:7**
I watch, and am as **a sparrow alone upon the house top.**

512. That Spiritual Rock.   **1 Corinthians 10:4**
And did all drink the same spiritual drink: for they drank of **that spiritual Rock** that followed them: and that Rock was Christ.

513. A Star out of Jacob.   **Numbers 24:1**
I shall see him, but not now: I shall behold him, but not nigh: there shall come a **Star out of Jacob,** and a Sceptre shall rise out of Israel, and shall smite the corners of Moab, and destroy all the children of Sheth.

514. My Stay.   **Psalms 18:18**
They prevented me in the day of my calamity: but the LORD was **my stay.**

515. A Stone Cut out of the Mountain.   **Daniel 2:45**
Forasmuch as thou sawest that the **stone was cut out of the mountain** without hands, and that it brake in pieces the iron, the brass, the clay, the silver, and the gold; the great God hath made known to the king what shall come to pass hereafter: and the dream is certain, and the interpretation thereof sure.

516. A Stone Cut witout Hands.   **Daniel 2:34**
Thou sawest till that **a stone was cut out without hands**, which smote the image upon his feet that were of iron and clay, and brake them to pieces.

517. The Stone of Israel.   **Genesis 49:24**
But his bow abode in strength, and the arms of his hands were made strong by the hands of the mighty God of Jacob; (from thence is the shepherd, **the stone of Israel).**

518. A Stone of Stumbling.   **1 Peter 2:8**
And **a stone of stumbling**, and a rock of offence, even to them which stumble at the word, being disobedient: whereunto also they were appointed.

519. The Stone which the Builders Refused.   **Psalms 118:22**
The stone which the builders refused is become the head stone of the corner.

520. The Stone which the Builders Rejected.   **Matthew 21:42**
Jesus saith unto them, Did ye never read in the scriptures, **The stone which the builders rejected**, the same is become the head of the corner: this is the Lord's doing, and it is marvellous in our eyes?

"Kindness is the ability to love someone more than they deserve."

Anonymous   **"See Titus 3:4-6"**

521. The Stone which was set at Nought.   **Acts 4:11**

This is **the stone which was set at nought** of you builders, which is become the head of the corner.

522. A Stranger.   **Matthew 25:35**

For I was an hungered, and ye gave me meat; I was thirsty, and ye gave me drink; I was **a stranger**, and ye took me in.

523. My Strength.   **Isaiah 12:2**

Behold, God is my salvation; I will trust, and not be afraid: for the LORD JEHOVAH is **my strength** and my song; he also is become my salvation.

524. The Strength of Israel.   **1 Samuel 15:29**

And also **the Strength of Israel** will not lie nor repent: for he is not a man, that he should repent.

525. The Strength of My Life.   **Psalms 27:1**

The LORD is my light and my salvation; whom shall I fear? the LORD is **the strength of my life**; of whom shall I be afraid?

526. A Strength to the Needy in Distress.   **Isaiah 25:4**

For thou hast been a strength to the poor, **a strength to the needy in his distress**, a refuge from the storm, a shadow from the heat, when the blast of the terrible ones is as a storm against the wall.

527. A Strength to the Poor.   **Isaiah 25:4**

For thou hast been **a strength to the poor**, a strength to the needy in his distress, a refuge from the storm, a shadow from the heat, when the blast of the terrible ones is as a storm against the wall.

528. A Strong Consolation.   **Hebrews 6:18**

That by two immutable things, in which it was impossible for God to lie, we might have **a strong consolation**, who have fled for refuge to lay hold upon the hope set before us.

529. A Stronghold in the Day of Trouble.   **Nahum 1:7**

The LORD is good, **a strong hold in the day of trouble**; and he knoweth them that trust in him.

530. A Strong Tower.   **Proverbs 18:10**

The name of the LORD is **a strong tower**: the righteous runneth into it, and is safe.

531. A Strong Tower from the Enemy.   **Psalms 61:3**

For thou hast been a shelter for me, and **a strong tower from the enemy.**

"I expect to pass through this world but once. Any good therefore that I can do, or any kindness or abilities that I can show to any fellow creature, let me do it now. Let me not defer it or neglect it, for I shall not pass this way again."

William Penn   **"See 1 Corinthians 9:19-23"**

532. A Stronger than He. Luke 11:22

But when **a stronger than he** shall come upon him, and overcome him, he taketh from him all his armour wherein he trusted, and divideth his spoils.

533. A Stumbling Block. 1 Corinthians 1:23

But we preach Christ crucified, unto the Jews **a stumbling block**, and unto the Greeks foolishness.

534. The Sun of Righteousness. Malachi 4:2

But unto you that fear my name shall **the Sun of righteousness** arise with healing in his wings; and ye shall go forth, and grow up as calves of the stall.

535. A Sure Foundation. Isaiah 28:16

Therefore thus saith the Lord GOD, Behold, I lay in Zion for a foundation a stone, a tried stone, a precious corner stone, **a sure foundation**: he that believeth shall not make haste.

536. The Sure Mercies of David. Isaiah 55:3

Incline your ear, and come unto me: hear, and your soul shall live; and I will make an everlasting covenant with you, even **the sure mercies of David.**

Acts 13:34

And as concerning that he raised him up from the dead, now no more to return to corruption, he said on this wise, I will give you **the sure mercies of David.**

537. A Surety of a Better Testament. Hebrews 7:22

By so much was Jesus made **a surety of a better testament.**

538. A Sweet Smelling Savour. Ephesians 5:2

And walk in love, as Christ also hath loved us, and hath given himself for us an offering and a sacrifice to God for **a sweet smelling savour.**

539. A Tabernacle for a Shadow. Isaiah 4:6

And there shall be **a tabernacle for a shadow** in the daytime from the heat, and for a place of refuge, and for a covert from storm and from rain.

540. The Tabernacle of God. Revelation 21:3

And I heard a great voice out of heaven saying, Behold, **the tabernacle of God** is with men, and he will dwell with them, and they shall be his people, and God himself shall be with them, and be their God.

541. A Teacher Come from God. John 3:2

The same came to Jesus by night, and said unto him, Rabbi, we know that thou art **a teacher come from God**: for no man can do these miracles that thou doest, except God be with him.

542. The Temple. John 2:19

Jesus answered and said unto them, Destroy **this temple**, and in three days I will raise it up.

"Darkness cannot drive out darkness; only light can do that. Hate cannot drive out hate; only love can do that."

Martin Luther King, Jr. **"See 1 John 1:5-7"**

76

543. A Tender Plant.   **Isaiah 53:2**

For he shall grow up before him as **a tender plant**, and as a root out of a dry ground: he hath no form nor comeliness; and when we shall see him, there is no beauty that we should desire him.

544. The Tender Mercy of God.   **Luke 1:78**

Through **the tender mercy of our God**; whereby the dayspring from on high hath visited us.

545. The Testator.   **Hebrews 9:16**

For where a testament is, there must also of necessity be the death of **the testator.**

         Hebrews 9:17

For a testament is of force after men are dead: otherwise it is of no strength at all while **the testator** liveth.

546. The Testimony of God.   **1 Corinthians 2:1**

And I, brethren, when I came to you, came not with excellency of speech or of wisdom, declaring unto you **the testimony of God.**

547. This Treasure.   **2 Corinthians 4:7**

But we have **this treasure** in earthen vessels, that the excellency of the power may be of God, and not of us.

548. A Tried Stone.   **Isaiah 28:16**

Therefore thus saith the Lord GOD, Behold, I lay in Zion for a foundation a stone, **a tried stone,** a precious corner stone, a sure foundation: he that believeth shall not make haste.

549. The True Bread from Heaven.   **John 6:32**

Then Jesus said unto them, Verily, verily, I say unto you, Moses gave you not that bread from heaven; but my Father giveth you **the true bread from heaven.**

550. The True Light.   **John 1:9**

That was **the true Light**, which lighteth every man that cometh into the world.

551. The True Vine.   **John 15:1**

I am **the true vine**, and my Father is the husbandman.

552. The True Witness.   **Proverbs 14:25**

A true witness delivereth souls: but a deceitful witness speaketh lies.

553. The Truth.   **John 14:6**

Jesus saith unto him, I am the way, **the truth**, and the life: no man cometh unto the Father, but by me.

554. Undefiled.   **Hebrews 7:26**

For such an high priest became us, who is holy, harmless, **undefiled**, separate from sinners, and made higher than the heavens.

"The measure of a truly great man is the courtesy with which he treats lesser men."

Anonymous   **"See Acts 10:34"**

555. Understanding. Proverbs 3:19

The LORD by wisdom hath founded the earth; by **understanding** hath he established the heavens.

556. The Unknown God. Acts 17:23

For as I passed by, and beheld your devotions, I found an altar with this inscription, TO **THE UNKNOWN GOD.** Whom therefore ye ignorantly worship, him declare I unto you.

557. The Unspeakable Gift. 2 Corinthians 9:15

Thanks be unto God for his **unspeakable gift.**

558. The Upholder of All things. Hebrews 1:3

Who being the brightness of his glory, and the express image of his person, and **upholding all things** by the word of his power, when he had by himself purged our sins, sat down on the right hand of the Majesty on high.

559. Upright. Psalms 92:15

To show that the LORD is **upright**: he is my rock, and there is no unrighteousness in him.

560. The Veil. Hebrews 10:20

By a new and living way, which he hath consecrated for us, through **the veil,** that is to say, his flesh…

561. The Very God of Peace. 1 Thessalonians 5:23

And **the very God of peace** sanctify you wholly; and I pray God your whole spirit and soul and body be preserved blameless unto the coming of our Lord Jesus Christ.

562. Very Great. Psalms 104:1

Bless the LORD, O my soul. O LORD my God, thou art **very great;** thou art clothed with honour and majesty.

563. A Very Present Help in Trouble. Psalms 46:1

God is our refuge and strength, **a very present help in trouble.**

564. The Victory. 1 Corinthians 15:54

So when this corruptible shall have put on incorruption, and this mortal shall have put on immortality, then shall be brought to pass the saying that is written, Death is swallowed up in **victory.**

565. The Vine. John 15:5

I am **the vine**, ye are the branches: He that abideth in me, and I in him, the same bringeth forth much fruit: for without me ye can do nothing.

"Let him know, that he which converteth the sinner from the error of his way shall save a soul and shall hide a multitude of sins."

James 5:20

566. The Voice. Revelation 1:12

And I turned to see **the voice** that spake with me. And being turned, I saw seven golden candlesticks…

567. A Wall of Fire. Zechariah 2:5

For I, saith the LORD, will be unto her **a wall of fire** round about, and will be the glory in the midst of her.

568. The Wave Offering. Leviticus 7:30

His own hands shall bring the offerings of the LORD made by fire, the fat with the breast, it shall he bring, that the breast may be waved for **a wave offering** before the LORD.

569. The Way. John 14:6

Jesus saith unto him, I am **the way**, the truth, and the life: no man cometh unto the Father, but by me.

570. The Weakness of God. 1 Corinthians 1:25

Because the foolishness of God is wiser than men; and **the weakness of God** is stronger than men.

571. A Wedding Garment. Matthew 22:12

And he saith unto him, Friend, how camest thou in hither not having **a wedding garment?** And he was speechless.

572. The Well of Living Waters. John 4:14

But whosoever drinketh of the water that I shall give him shall never thirst; but the water that I shall give him shall be in him **a well of water springing up into everlasting life.**

573. The Well of Salvation. Isaiah 12:3

Therefore with joy shall ye draw water out of **the wells of salvation.**

574. Wiser. 1 Corinthians 1:25

Because the foolishness of God is **wiser** than men; and the weakness of God is stronger than men.

575. The Wisdom of God. 1 Corinthians 1:24

But unto them which are called, both Jews and Greeks, Christ the power of God and **the wisdom of God.**

576. A Wise Master Builder. 1 Corinthians 3:10

According to the grace of God which is given unto me, as **a wise master builder,** I have laid the foundation, and another buildeth thereon. But let every man take heed how he buildeth thereupon.

577. My Witness. Job 16:19

Also now, behold, **my witness** is in heaven, and my record is on high.

"I think a good rule of thumb to follow would be to presume the Lord wants you to share the gospel with everyone unless he leads you not to."

Danny Lehmann **"See Mark 16:15-16"**

79

578. A Witness of God.   1 John 5:9

If we receive the witness of men, the witness of God is greater: for this is the **witness of God** which he hath testified of his Son.

579. A Witness to the People.   Isaiah 55:4

Behold, I have given him for **a witness to the people,** a leader and commander to the people.

580. Wonderful.   Isaiah 9:6

For unto us a child is born, unto us a son is given: and the government shall be upon his shoulder: and his name shall be called **Wonderful,** Counsellor, The mighty God, The everlasting Father, The Prince of Peace.

581. The Word.   John 1:1

In the beginning was **the Word**, and **the Word** was with God, and **the Word** was God.

582. The Word of God.   Revelation 19:13

And he was clothed with a vesture dipped in blood: and his name is called **The Word of God.**

583. The Word of Life.   1 John 1:1

That which was from the beginning, which we have heard, which we have seen with our eyes, which we have looked upon, and our hands have handled, of **the Word of life.**

584. A Worm and No Man.   Psalms 22:6

But I am **a worm, and no man;** a reproach of men, and despised of the people.

585. Worthy.   Revelation 4:11

Thou art **worthy**, O Lord, to receive glory and honour and power: for thou hast created all things, and for thy pleasure they are and were created.

                                       Revelation 5:12

Saying with a loud voice, **Worthy** is the Lamb that was slain to receive power, and riches, and wisdom, and strength, and honour, and glory, and blessing.

586. That Worthy Name.   James 2:7

Do not they blaspheme **that worthy name** by the which ye are called?

587. Worthy to be Praised.   Psalms 18:3

I will call upon the LORD, who is **worthy to be praised**: so shall I be saved from mine enemies.

"For the weapons of our warfare *are* not carnal, but mighty through God to the pulling down of strong holds; Casting down imaginations, and every high thing that exalteth itself against the knowledge of God, and **bringing into captivity every thought to the obedience of Christ."**

II Corinthians 10:4, 5

588. The Yokefellow.   **Matthew 11:29-30**

Take my yoke upon you, and learn of me; for I am meek and lowly in heart: and ye shall find rest unto your souls. **For my yoke is easy**, and my burden is light.

589. The Young Child.   **Matthew 2:11**

And when they were come into the house, they saw **the young child** with Mary his mother, and fell down, and worshipped him: and when they had opened their treasures, they presented unto him gifts; gold, and frankincense, and myrrh.

590. The Zeal of the Lord of Hosts   **Isaiah 37:32**

For out of Jerusalem shall go forth a remnant, and they that escape out of mount Zion: **the zeal of the LORD of hosts** shall do this.

591. The Zeal of Thine House.   **John 2:17**

And his disciples remembered that it was written, **The zeal of thine house** hath eaten me up.

                                                  Psalms 69:9

For **the zeal of thine house** hath eaten me up; and the reproaches of them that reproached thee are fallen upon me.

The Function of the Law

"Sinners that think they need no physician will not endure the healer's hand. The Law is therefore necessary to give knowledge of sin, so that proud man, who thought he was whole, may be humbled by the discovery of his own great wickedness, and sigh and pant after the grace that is set forth in Christ."

Martin Luther   **"See Matthew 9:12"**

FACT: Jesus Represents Spiritual Israel
Here are some similarities between the two Israel's

1. **Israel had a Joseph**   **Genesis 30:24**
   And she called his name **Joseph**; and said, The LORD shall add to me another son.
   COMPARE
   Jesus had a Joseph   **Matthew 1:16**
   And Jacob begat **Joseph** the husband of Mary, of whom was born Jesus, who is called Christ.

2. **Israel's Joseph had dreams**   **Genesis 37:5**
   And Joseph **dreamed a dream**, and he told *it* his brethren: and they hated him yet the more.
   COMPARE
   Jesus' Joseph had dreams   **Matthew 2:13**
   Behold, the angel of the Lord appeareth to Joseph **in a dream...**

3. **Israel went into Egypt**   **Genesis 46:5-6**
   And the sons of Israel carried Jacob their father, and their little ones, and their wives...and **came into Egypt.**
   COMPARE
   Jesus went into Egypt   **Matthew 2:14**
   When he arose, he took the young child and his mother by night, and **departed into Egypt.**

4. **Israel came out of Egypt**   **Exodus 12:51**
   The LORD did bring the children of Israel out of the land of Egypt by their armies.
   COMPARE
   Jesus came out of Egypt   **Matthew 2:15**
   And was there until the death of Herod: that it might be fulfilled which was spoken of the Lord by the prophet, saying, **Out of Egypt have I called my son.**

5. **Israel was baptized (Red Sea)**   **1 Corinthians 10:2**
   And were all **baptized** unto Moses in the cloud and in the sea.
   COMPARE
   Jesus was Baptized   **Matthew 3:16**
   And Jesus, when he was **baptized**, went up straightway out of the water.

6. **Israel is called God's son**   **Hosea 11:1**
   When Israel *was* a child, then I loved him, and **called my son** out of Egypt.
   COMPARE
   Jesus is called God's Son   **Matthew 3:17**
   And lo a voice from heaven, saying, **This is my beloved Son**, in whom I am well pleased.

7. **Israel is called God's firstborn**   **Exodus 4:22**
   And thou shalt say unto Pharaoh, Thus saith the LORD, **Israel *is* my son, *even* my firstborn.**
   COMPARE
   Jesus is called God's firstborn   **Romans 8:29**
   For whom he did foreknow, he also did predestinate *to be* conformed to the image of his Son, that he might be the **firstborn** among many brethren.

8. **Israel was in the wilderness for 40 years**   **Hebrews 3:17**

But with whom was **he grieved forty years?** was it not with them that had sinned, **whose carcases fell in the wilderness?**

COMPARE

Jesus was in the wilderness 40 days   **Matthew 4:1-2**

Then was Jesus **led up of the Spirit into the wilderness** to be tempted of the devil. And when **he had fasted forty days and forty nights…**

9. **Deuteronomy given in the wilderness**   **Exodus 24:12**

And the LORD said unto Moses, Come up to me into the mount, and be there: and **I will give thee tables of stone**, and a **law, and commandments which I have written**; that thou mayest teach them.

COMPARE

Jesus uses Deuteronomy to resist temptation   **Matthew 4:4-10**

But he answered and said, **It is written,** Man shall not live by bread alone, but by every word that proceedeth out of the mouth of God…**It is written** again, Thou shalt not tempt the Lord thy God…for **it is written**, Thou shalt worship the Lord thy God, and him only shalt thou serve.

10. **The Law was taught on Mount Sinai**   **Exodus 24:12**

And the LORD said unto Moses, **Come up to me into the mount,** and be there: and I will give thee tables of stone, and a law, and commandments which I have written; **that thou mayest teach them.**

COMPARE

Sermon on the Mount teaches the Law   **Matthew 5-7**

And seeing the multitudes, he went **up into a mountain**: and when he was set, his disciples came unto him: And he opened his mouth, **and taught them**.

11. **God made a blood covenant with the 12 tribes**   **Exodus 24:8**

And Moses took the blood, and sprinkled *it* on the people, and said, **Behold the blood of the covenant**, which the LORD hath made with you concerning all these words.

COMPARE

Jesus made a blood covenant with His 12 apostles   **Matthew 26:28**

For this is my **blood of the new testament**, which is shed for many for the remission of sins.

12. **Israel is called God's vine**   **Psalm 80:8**

Thou hast brought **a vine out of Egypt**: thou hast cast out the heathen, and planted it.

COMPARE

Jesus is called God's vine   **John 15:1**

I am the true vine, and my Father is the husbandman.

13. **Israel was called the seed of Abraham**   **Isaiah 41:8**

But thou, Israel, *art* my servant, Jacob whom I have chosen, the **seed of Abraham** my friend.

COMPARE

Jesus is called the seed of Abraham   **Galatians 3:16**

Now to Abraham and his seed were the promises made. He saith not, And to seeds, as of many; but as of one, **And to thy seed, which is Christ.**

14. **Israel started a person and became a people**

Example: Israel (Jacob) grew into the **12 tribes of Israel.**

COMPARE

Jesus started as a person and became a people

Example: The church is referred to as the **body of Christ.**

The Twelve Tribes

1.   Ruben   **Genesis 29:32**
And Leah conceived, and bare a son, and she called his name **Reuben**: for she said, Surely the **LORD hath looked upon my affliction**; now therefore my husband will love me.

2.   Simean   **Genesis 29:33**
And she conceived again, and bare a son; and said, Because **the LORD hath heard** that I *was* hated, he hath therefore given me this *son* also: and she called his name **Simeon.**

3.   Levi   **Genesis 29:34**
And she conceived again, and bare a son; and said, Now this time will my husband **be joined unto me**, because I have born him three sons: therefore was his name called **Levi.**

4.   Judah   **Genesis 29:35**
And she conceived again, and bare a son: and she said, **Now will I praise the LORD:** therefore she called his name **Judah**; and left bearing.

5.   Dan   **Genesis 30:6**
And Rachel said, **God hath judged me, and hath also heard my voice**, and hath given me a son: therefore called she his name **Dan**.

6.   Naphtali   **Genesis 30:8**
And Rachel said, **With great wrestlings** have I wrestled with my sister, and I have prevailed: and she called his name **Naphtali.**

7.   Gad   **Genesis 30:11**
And Leah said, **A troop cometh**: and she called his name **Gad**.

8.   Asher   **Genesis 30:12**
And Zilpah, Leah's maid, bare Jacob a second son. And Leah said, **Happy am I**, for the daughters will call me blessed: and she called his name **Asher**.

9.   Issachar   **Genesis 30:18**
And Leah said, God hath **given me my hire**, because I have given my maiden to my husband: and she called his name **Issachar**.

10.   Zebulun   **Genesis 30:20**
And Leah said, God hath endued me *with* a good dowry; now will my husband **dwell with me**, because I have born him six sons: and she called his name **Zebulun.**

11.   Joseph   **Genesis 30:24**
And she called his name Joseph; and said, **The LORD shall add to me** another son.

12.   Benjamin   **Deuteronomy 33:12**
And of **Benjamin** he said, **The beloved of the LORD** shall dwell in safety by him; *and the LORD* shall cover him all the day long, and he shall dwell between his shoulders.

Messages from Israel

Old Testament
The tribes are listed in order of their births

1.	Ruben	(Gen. 29:32)	-	The LORD hath looked upon my affliction
2.	Simean	(Gen. 29:33)	-	The LORD hath heard
3.	Levi	(Gen. 29:34)	-	Be joined unto me
4.	Judah	(Gen. 29:35)	-	Now will I praise the LORD
5.	Dan	(Gen. 30:6)	-	God hath judged me
6.	Naphatali	(Gen. 30:8)	-	With great wrestling's
7.	Gad	(Gen. 30:11)	-	A troop cometh (Given good fortune)
8.	Asher	(Gen. 30:13)	-	Happy am I
9.	Issachar	(Gen. 30:18)	-	Given me my hire
10.	Zebulun	(Gen. 30:20)	-	Dwell with me
11.	Joseph	(Gen. 30:24)	-	The LORD shall add to me
12.	Benjamin	(Deut.33:12)	-	Beloved of the LORD

Message:

The Lord hath looked upon my affliction; the Lord hath heard me, be joined unto me. Now will I praise the Lord. God hath judged me. With great wrestling's, a troop cometh (I have been given good fortune). Happy am I for He has given me hire. Dwell with me and the Lord shall add unto me the beloved of the Lord.

New Testament
The tribes are in the order listed in Revelation 7:5-8

1.	Judah	(Gen. 29:35)	-	Now will I praise the LORD
2.	Ruben	(Gen. 29:32)	-	The LORD hath looked upon my affliction
3.	Gad	(Gen. 30:11)	-	A troop cometh (Given good fortune)
4.	Asher	(Gen. 30:13)	-	Happy am I
5.	Naphatali	(Gen. 30:8)	-	With great wrestling's
6.	Manasseh	(Gen. 41:51)	-	For God, hath made me to forget all my toil
7.	Simean	(Gen. 29:33)	-	The LORD hath heard
8.	Levi	(Gen. 29:34)	-	Be joined unto me
9.	Issachar	(Gen. 30:18)	-	Given me my hire
10.	Zebulun	(Gen. 30:20)	-	Dwell with me
11.	Joseph	(Gen. 30:24)	-	The LORD shall add to me
12.	Benjamin	(Deut.33:12)	-	Beloved of the LORD

Fact: In the book of Revelation there is a message revealed in the names of the twelve tribes. Notice that Dan is not mentioned and they are *not* listed in order of their births. This is the message given when using the biblical definitions for their names and placing those definitions in the order they are listed in the scriptures.

Message:

Now will I praise the Lord for the Lord hath looked upon my affliction and a troop cometh (I have been given good fortune), happy am I. With great wrestlings God hath made me to forget all my toil. The Lord hath heard me and will be joined unto me. He has given me my hire and will dwell with me. The Lord will add to me the beloved of the Lord.

"Search the scriptures; for in them ye think ye have eternal life: and they are they which testify of me."

John 5:39

INTRODUCTION TO PROPHECY

Jesus' fulfillment of prophecy is by far the most compelling evidence that His claims are true! Over and over again, Jesus pointed to the prophecies of the Old Testament to back up His claim that He was the Messiah. It is God's perfect way of proving His Word to be True.

Luke 24:27
And beginning at Moses and all the prophets, he expounded unto them in all the scriptures the things concerning himself.

Luke 24:44
And he said unto them, These *are* the words which I spake unto you, while I was yet with you, that all things must be fulfilled, which were written in the law of Moses, and *in* the prophets, and *in* the psalms, concerning me.

John 5:46
For had ye believed Moses, ye would have believed me: for he wrote of me.

John 8:56
Your father Abraham rejoiced to see my day: and he saw *it*, and was glad.

New Testament writers constantly appealed to fulfilled prophecy to support the claims of Jesus as the Son of God and the Messiah.

Acts 17:2-3
And Paul, as his manner was, went in unto them, and three sabbath days reasoned with them out of the scriptures, Opening and alleging, that Christ must needs have suffered, and risen again from the dead; and that this Jesus, whom I preach unto you, is Christ.

Acts 3:18
But those things, which God before had shewed by the mouth of all his prophets, that Christ should suffer, he hath so fulfilled.

"I know men and I tell you that Jesus Christ is no mere man. Between Him and every other person in the world there is no possible term of comparison. Alexander, Caesar, Charlemagne, and I have founded empires. But on what did we rest the creations of our genius? Upon force. Jesus Christ founded His Empire upon love; and at this hour millions of men would die for Him."

Napoleon Bonaparte   **"See John 7:46"**

God announced the coming of His Son, the Messiah and our Savior, throughout the Old-Testament, written thousands of years ago, He provided us with hundreds of prophecies that are so exact they cannot be denied. From the time of His arrival through how He would die, there is no room for doubt. No one except Jesus could have fulfilled these prophecies. Only the true Messiah, under the guidance of the Holy Spirit, could have fulfilled all the prophecies that are pointed out in the Old Testament not leaving even one unfinished.

He rose from the dead just as prophesied! No one else in all of man's history has made that claim!

The Resurrection of Christ is Proven by:

The Empty Tomb

John 20:1-9
The first *day* of the week cometh Mary Magdalene early, when it was yet dark, unto the sepulchre, and **seeth the stone taken away from the sepulchre**. Then she runneth, and cometh to Simon Peter, and to the other disciple, whom Jesus loved, and saith unto them, They have taken away the Lord out of the sepulchre, and we know not where they have laid him. Peter therefore went forth, and that other disciple, and came to the sepulchre. So they ran both together: and the other disciple did outrun Peter, and came first to the sepulchre. And he stooping down, *and looking in*, saw the linen clothes lying; yet went he not in. Then cometh Simon Peter following him, and went into the sepulchre, and seeth the linen clothes lie, And the napkin, that was about his head, not lying with the linen clothes, but wrapped together in a place by itself. Then went in also that other disciple, which came first to the sepulchre, and he saw, and believed. **For as yet they knew not the scripture, that he must rise again from the dead.**

The Angel's Testimony

Matthew 28:5-7
And the **angel answered** and said unto the women, **Fear not ye: for I know that ye seek Jesus, which was crucified. He is not here: for he is risen,** as he said. Come, see the place where the Lord lay. **And go quickly, and tell his disciples that he is risen from the dead;** and, behold, he goeth before you into Galilee; there shall ye see him: lo, I have told you.

"It takes no brains to be an atheist. Any stupid person can deny the existence of a supernatural power because man's physical senses cannot detect it. But there cannot be ignored the influence of conscience, the respect we feel for the Moral Law, the mystery of life… or the marvelous order in which the universe moves about us on this earth. All these evidence the handiwork of the beneficent Deity…That Deity is the God of the Bible and Jesus Christ, His Son."

Dwight Eisenhower   **"See Psalm 53:1"**

His Enemy's Response

Matthew 28:11-15

Now when they were going, behold, some of **the watch came into the city, and shewed unto the chief priests all the things that were done.** And when they were assembled with the elders, and had taken counsel, **they gave large money unto the soldiers, Saying, Say ye, His disciples came by night, and stole him** *away* **while we slept. And if this come to the governor's ears, we will persuade him, and secure you.** So they took the money, and did as they were taught: and this saying is commonly reported among the Jews until this day.

The Numerous Witnesses

Luke 24:46-48

And said unto them, Thus it is written, and thus it behoved Christ to suffer, and to rise from the dead the third day: And that repentance and remission of sins should be preached in his name among all nations, beginning at Jerusalem. **And ye are witnesses of these things.**

Acts 13:30-32

But God raised him from the dead: **And he was seen many days of them which came up with him from Galilee to Jerusalem, who are his witnesses unto the people.** And we declare unto you glad tidings, how that the promise which was made unto the fathers.

Acts 10:39-41

And we are witnesses of all things which he did both in the land of the Jews, and in Jerusalem; whom **they slew and hanged on a tree: Him God raised up the third day, and shewed him openly; Not to all the people, but unto witnesses chosen before of God,** *even* **to us, who did eat and drink with him after he rose from the dead.**

Acts 5:32

And we are his witnesses of these things; and *so is* **also the Holy Ghost**, whom God hath given to them that obey him.

Acts 3:14-15

But ye denied the Holy One and the Just, and desired a murderer to be granted unto you; And killed the Prince of life, whom God hath raised from the dead; **whereof we are witnesses**

"We may deceive all the people sometimes; we may deceive some of the people all the time, but not all the people all the time and not God at any time."

Abraham Lincoln   **"See John 2:24, 25"**

89

Many Infallible Proofs

John 20:20, 27
And when he had so said, he shewed unto them *his* hands and his side. Then were the disciples glad, when they saw the Lord… Then saith he to Thomas, **Reach hither thy finger, and behold my hands; and reach hither thy hand, and thrust *it* into my side: and be not faithless, but believing.**

Acts 1:3
To whom also **he shewed himself alive after his passion by many infallible proofs**, being seen of them forty days, and speaking of the things pertaining to the kingdom of God.

The Apostles' Teaching

Acts 1:22
Beginning from the baptism of John, unto that same day that he was taken up from us, must one be ordained to be a witness with us of his resurrection.

Acts 4:33
And with great power gave the apostles witness of the resurrection of the Lord Jesus: and great grace was upon them all.

A prophecy is the future told in advance by God through a prophet.

Isaiah 48:2-5
For they call themselves of the holy city, and stay themselves upon the God of Israel; The LORD of hosts *is* his name. **I have declared the former things from the beginning; and they went forth out of my mouth**, and I shewed them; I did *them* suddenly, and they came to pass. Because I knew that thou *art* obstinate, and thy neck *is* an iron sinew, and thy brow brass; I have **even from the beginning declared *it* to thee; before it came to pass I shewed *it* thee**: lest thou shouldest say, Mine idol hath done them, and my graven image, and my molten image, hath commanded them.

2 Peter 1:19-21
We have also a more sure word of prophecy; whereunto ye do well that ye take heed, as unto a light that shineth in a dark place, until the day dawn, and the day star arise in your hearts: **Knowing this first, that no prophecy of the scripture is of any private interpretation.** For the prophecy came not in old time by the will of man: **but holy men of God spake *as they were* moved by the Holy Ghost.**

God gave us a reasoning mind; let us reason together with God's Holy Word and come to know with an exact certainty that Jesus is the Christ. A study of the prophecies compiled in this book should prove beyond a doubt that His Word is true. When studying prophecy, if you take a few sentences here and a part of a sentence there and come up with your own interpretation that doesn't prove anything. But if we take all the prophecies collectively it becomes very clear that they are not just someone's interpretation or a coincidence; they are evidence, **FACTS** of the divine announcement of our Lord. There is no other logical explanation.

You might think some of these prophecies are unclear, and you might not understand them right away and have to do a little studying of the scriptures before you understand them. But there are many prophecies about our Lord that are so clear and exact that there is no denying that He fulfilled them. Many scriptures in the New Testament explain that a particular event occurred so that a prophecy would be fulfilled.

Matthew 13:34-35
All these things spake Jesus unto the multitude in parables; and without a parable spake he not unto them: **That it might be fulfilled which was spoken by the prophet, saying, I will open my mouth in parables; I will utter things which have been kept secret from the foundation of the world.**

As we study the prophecies of the Bible, we start to see that only Jesus Christ could have fulfilled these prophecies (30 on the day of his crucifixion alone!). This proves not only that he is the Messiah, but also that there is a God who foresaw these events and inspired them to be written down hundreds or thousands of years prior.

The mathematical odds of Jesus fulfilling just the prophecies on the day of His crucifixion are astronomical and could easily be called impossible.

satan tries to counterfeit God's miracle of prophecy so that he might deceive the world. But he is limited; only God knows the future. This can be explained by people like Nostradamus, mediums, psychics, and other fortune tellers; they only have a small percentage of accuracy. If they were true seers, they would put Las Vegas out of business. The same people would be winning the lottery, and horse racing would shut down. Gambling would not be part of our society because the same people would be winning all the money.

The Bible tells us that if a Prophet predicts something and it does not come to pass, he should be considered a false prophet and killed.

Deuteronomy 18:20-22
But the prophet, which shall presume to speak a word in my name, which I have not commanded him to speak, or that shall speak in the name of other gods, even **that prophet shall die.** And if thou say in thine heart, How shall we know the word which the LORD hath not spoken? **When a prophet speaketh in the name of the LORD, if the thing follow not, nor come to pass, that is the thing which the LORD hath not spoken,** but the prophet hath spoken it presumptuously: thou shalt not be afraid of him.

In this portion of my book, we are focusing on approximately **320** prophecies concerning the identity of the Messiah taken from the Old Testament. In my research, I have read there are as many as 425 messianic prophecies concerning our Lord Jesus Christ, I chose the prophecies I could understand and agree with to put in this book. There are also some prophecies that repeat; I have found several prophecies in one single verse. Therefore, I have combined some of these prophecies together for easier understanding.

I pray that God will reveal to you knowledge of the Truth which is Christ Jesus our Lord through His Word, I pray that if the Holy Spirit is drawing you to Him, you will respond with "Here I am Lord!" I pray that you are already a child of God, and you will answer the call to do His Will by sharing the Gospel with every living creature. For truly the time is short and our Lord is coming back soon! Let us seek first the Kingdom of God and all His Righteousness. Eternal fellowship with our God is our prize! Let us run to win!

The Passover Plot
A mathematical impossibility

"It is estimated that there were 250 million people alive in the world the year Jesus died. This means that one male out of the 250 million people would have had to die that year by crucifixion, be of Jewish descent from King David, be born in Bethlehem, have been a teacher using parables, healed others and performed miracles. He would have had to ride into Jerusalem on a donkey, been rejected by the leaders and then died four days later with no broken bones but with pierced feet, hands and side during absolute darkness. This individual would have had to die during one unique predicted week. The probability of all of this happening to one single male, is 1 out of 2.54×10^{28}.

By using the modern science of probability in reference to eight prophecies, we find that the chance that any man might have lived down to the present time and fulfilled all eight prophecies is 1 in 10^{17}.
That would be 1 in 100,000,000,000,000,000. That is the equivalent of covering the state of Texas with specially marked silver dollars 2 feet deep and having a blindfolded man finding 1 special coin.

The chance that any one man fulfilled all 48 prophecies is 1 in 10^{157}, or 1 in 100,000,000,000,000,000,000,000,000,000,000,000,000,000,000,000,000,000,000, 000,000,000,000,000,000,000,000,000,000,000,000,000,000,000,000,000,000, 000,000,000,000,000,000,000,000,000,000,000,000,000,000,000,000.

If the estimated number of electrons in the universe is around 10^{79} then Jesus was a mathematical impossibility. He was a miracle! He <u>is</u> the Messiah."

From the book, *Science Speaks* by mathematician and scientist, Peter Stoner

92

"And ye shall seek me, <u>and find</u> *me*, when ye shall search for me with all your heart."

Jeremiah 29:13

93

"Behold, what manner of love the Father hath bestowed upon us, that we should be called the sons of God: therefore the world knoweth us not, because it knew him not. Beloved, now are we the sons of God, and it doth not yet appear what we shall be: but we know that, when he shall appear, we shall be like him; for we shall see him as he is."

1 John 3:1-2

MESSIANIC PROPHECY FULFILLMENT

GENESIS

The first book of Moses, written approximately 1450 B.C. – 1400 B.C. Genesis covers from the beginning to about 1620 B.C. It was written in the wilderness and has 50 chapters.

1.   **He would come from the seed of a woman (virgin birth)**   **Genesis3:15**
And I will put enmity **between thee and the woman, and between thy seed
and her seed;** it shall bruise thy head, and thou shalt bruise his heel.
    Fulfillment: Matthew 1:18
Now the birth of Jesus Christ was on this wise: When as his mother Mary was espoused to Joseph, before they came together, **she was found with child of the Holy Ghost.** Then Joseph her husband, being a just *man*, and not willing to make her a publick example, was minded to put her away privily. But while he thought on these things, behold, the angel of the Lord appeared unto him in a dream, saying, Joseph, thou son of David, fear not to take unto thee Mary thy wife: **for that which is conceived in her is of the Holy Ghost.**
    Fulfillment: Luke 1:35
And the angel answered and said unto her, **The Holy Ghost shall come upon thee**, and the power of the Highest shall overshadow thee: therefore also **that holy thing which shall be born of thee shall be called the Son of God.**
    Fulfillment: Galatians 4:4
But when the fulness of the time was come, **God sent forth his Son, made of a woman**, made under the law.

2.   **He will bruise satan's head**   **Genesis 3:15**
And I will put enmity between thee and the woman, and between thy seed and her seed; **it shall bruise thy head**, and thou shalt bruise his heel.
    Fulfillment: Hebrews 2:14
Forasmuch then as the children are partakers of flesh and blood, he also himself likewise took part of the same; that **through death he might destroy him that had the power of death, that is, the devil.**

"I tell you that there is no greater joy than leading someone to faith in Jesus Christ. Even if they reject your message, it still feels great to obey Christ. Yet regardless of how we feel, we need to remember this is what He has commanded."

D. James Kennedy   **"See Mark 16:15-16"**

95

3.   **Shem would be an ancestor**   **Genesis 9:26-27**

And he said, **Blessed be the LORD God of Shem**; and Canaan shall be his servant. God shall enlarge Japheth, and he shall dwell in the tents of Shem; and Canaan shall be his servant.

Fulfillment: Luke 3:23-38

And Jesus himself began to be about thirty years of age, being (as was supposed) the son of Joseph, which was *the son* of Heli, [24]Which was *the son* of Matthat, which was *the son* of Levi, which was *the son* of Melchi, which was *the son* of Janna, which was *the son* of Joseph, [25]Which was *the son* of Mattathias, which was *the son* of Amos, which was *the son* of Naum, which was *the son* of Esli, which was *the son* of Nagge, [26]Which was *the son* of Maath, which was *the son* of Mattathias, which was *the son* of Semei, which was *the son* of Joseph, which was *the son* of Juda, [27]Which was *the son* of Joanna, which was *the son* of Rhesa, which was *the son* of Zorobabel, which was *the son* of Salathiel, which was *the son* of Neri, [28]Which was *the son* of Melchi, which was *the son* of Addi, which was *the son* of Cosam, which was *the son* of Elmodam, which was *the son* of Er, [29]Which was *the son* of Jose, which was *the son* of Eliezer, which was *the son* of Jorim, which was *the son* of Matthat, which was *the son* of Levi, [30]Which was *the son* of Simeon, which was *the son* of Juda, which was *the son* of Joseph, which was *the son* of Jonan, which was *the son* of Eliakim, [31]Which was *the son* of Melea, which was *the son* of Menan, which was *the son* of Mattatha, which was *the son* of Nathan, which was *the son* of David, [32]Which was *the son* of Jesse, which was *the son* of Obed, which was *the son* of Booz, which was *the son* of Salmon, which was *the son* of Naasson, [33]Which was *the son* of Aminadab, which was *the son* of Aram, which was *the son* of Esrom, which was *the son* of Phares, which was *the son* of Juda, [34]Which was *the son* of Jacob, which was *the son* of Isaac, which was *the son* of Abraham, which was *the son* of Thara, which was *the son* of Nachor, [35]Which was *the son* of Saruch, which was *the son* of Ragau, which was *the son* of Phalec, which was *the son* of Heber, which was *the son* of Sala,[36]Which was *the son* of

Cainan, which was *the son* of Arphaxad, which was *the son* of **Sem**, which was *the son* of Noe, which was *the son* of Lamech, [37]Which was *the son* of Mathusala, which was *the son* of Enoch, which was *the son* of Jared, which was *the son* of Maleleel, which was *the son* of Cainan, [38]Which was *the son* of Enos, which was *the son* of Seth, which was *the son* of Adam, which was *the son* of God.

4.   **As Abraham's seed, He will bless all nations**   **Genesis 12:2-3**

And I will make of thee a great nation, and I will bless thee, and make thy name great; and thou shalt be a blessing: And I will bless them that bless thee, and curse him that curseth thee: **and in thee shall all families of the earth be blessed.**

Fulfillment: Genesis 22:18

And in thy seed shall all the nations of the earth be blessed; because thou hast obeyed my voice.

Fulfillment: Acts 3:25-26

Ye are the children of the prophets, and of the covenant which God made with our fathers, saying unto Abraham, **And in thy seed shall all the kindreds of the earth be blessed.** Unto you first **God, having raised up his Son Jesus, sent him to bless you**, in turning away every one of you from his iniquities.

"There are many who speak only of the forgiveness of sin, but who say little or nothing about repentance. If there is nevertheless no forgiveness of sins without repentance, so also forgiveness of sins cannot be understood without repentance. Therefore, if forgiveness of sins is preached without repentance, it follows that the people imagine they have already received the forgiveness of sins, and thereby they become cocksure and fearless, which is then greater error and sin than all the error that preceded our time."

Melanchthon   **"See Luke 24:47"**

5.   **A priest after Melchizedek**   **Genesis 14:18-19**

And **Melchizedek** king of Salem brought forth bread and wine: and **he was the priest of the most high God**. And he blessed him, and said, Blessed be Abram of the most high God, possessor of heaven and earth: Then Melchizedek king of Salem brought out bread and wine; he was the priest of God Most High. And he blessed him and said: "Blessed be Abram of God Most High, Possessor of heaven and earth.

        Fulfillment: Hebrews 6:20

Whither the forerunner is for us entered, even **Jesus, made an high priest for ever after the order of Melchisedec.**

6.   **He would be a King also**   **Genesis 14:18-19**

And Melchizedek king of Salem brought forth bread and wine: and he was the priest of the most high God. And he blessed him, and said, Blessed be Abram of the most high God, possessor of heaven and earth.

        Fulfillment: Hebrews 7:1-3

For this **Melchisedec, king of Salem**, priest of the most high God, who met Abraham returning from the slaughter of the kings, and blessed him; To whom also Abraham gave a tenth part of all; first being by interpretation **King of righteousness**, and after that also King of Salem, which is, **King of peace**; Without father, without mother, without descent, having neither beginning of days, nor end of life; but **made like unto the Son of God**; abideth a priest continually.

7.   **The Last Supper foreshadowed**   **Genesis 14:18-19**

And Melchizedek king of Salem **brought forth bread and wine**: **and he was the priest of the most high God.** And he blessed him, and said, Blessed be Abram of the most high God, possessor of heaven and earth.

        Fulfillment: Matthew 26:26-28

And as they were eating, **Jesus took bread, and blessed it, and brake it, and gave it to the disciples, and said, Take, eat; this is my body. And he took the cup, and gave thanks, and gave it to them, saying, Drink ye all of it; For this is my blood of the new testament, which is shed for many for the remission of sins.**

The Function of the Law

"Just as the world was not ready for the New Testament before it received the Old, just as the Jews were not prepared for the ministry of Christ until John the Baptist had gone before Him with his claimant call to repentance, so the unsaved are in no condition today for the gospel till the Law be applied to their hearts, for 'by the Law is the knowledge of sin.' It is a waste of time to sow seed on ground which has never been ploughed or spaded! To present vicarious sacrifice of Christ to those who's dominant passion is to take fill of sin, is to give that which is holy to the dogs."

A.W. Pink   **"See Matthew 7:6"**

8.   **He would come from the seed of Isaac**   **Genesis 17:19**
And God said, Sarah thy wife shall bear thee a son indeed; and thou shalt call his name **Isaac: and I will establish my covenant with him for an everlasting covenant, and with his seed after him.**
        Fulfillment: Matthew 1:1-2
The book of **the generation of Jesus Christ, the son of David, the son of Abraham. Abraham begat Isaac;** and Isaac begat Jacob; and Jacob begat Judas and his brethren.
        Fulfillment: Romans 9:7
Neither, because they are the seed of Abraham, are they all children: but, **In Isaac shall thy seed be called.**

9.   **He would make intercession for us**   **Genesis 18:23-33**
And **Abraham drew near, and said, Wilt thou also destroy the righteous with the wicked? Peradventure there be fifty righteous within the city: wilt thou also destroy and not spare the place for the fifty righteous that** *are* **therein?** That be far from thee to do after this manner, to slay the righteous with the wicked: and that the righteous should be as the wicked, that be far from thee: Shall not the Judge of all the earth do right? **And the LORD said, If I find in Sodom fifty righteous within the city, then I will spare all the place for their sakes.** And Abraham answered and said, Behold now, I have taken upon me to speak unto the Lord, which *am but* dust and ashes: **Peradventure there shall lack five of the fifty righteous: wilt thou destroy all the city for** *lack of* **five?** And he said, If I find there forty and five, I will not destroy *it*. And he spake unto him yet again, and said, **Peradventure there shall be forty found there.** And he said, I will not do *it* for forty's sake. And he said *unto him*, **Oh let not the Lord be angry, and I will speak: Peradventure there shall thirty be found there**. And he said, I will not do *it*, if I find thirty there. And he said, Behold now, I have taken upon me to speak unto the Lord: **Peradventure there shall be twenty found there.** And he said, I will not destroy *it* for twenty's sake. And he said, Oh let not the Lord be angry, and I will speak yet but this once: **Peradventure ten shall be found there.** And he said, **I will not destroy** *it* **for ten's sake. And the LORD went his way, as soon as he had left communing with Abraham**: and Abraham returned unto his place.
        Fulfillment: Hebrews 7:25
Wherefore he is able also to save them to the uttermost that come unto God by him, **seeing he ever liveth to make intercession for them.**
        Fulfillment: 1 John 2:1
My little children, these things write I unto you, that ye sin not. And if any man sin, **we have an advocate with the Father, Jesus Christ the righteous.**

"All heaven is interested in the cross of Christ, all hell terribly afraid of it, while men are the only beings who more or less ignore its meaning."

Oswald Chambers   **"See Philippians 2:9"**

10.   **Identifying the place of his crucifixion**   **Genesis 22:1-4**
And it came to pass after these things, that God did tempt Abraham, and said unto him, Abraham: and he said, Behold, here I am. And he said, Take now thy son, thine only son Isaac, whom thou lovest, and get thee into the **land of Moriah**; and offer him there for a burnt offering **upon one of the mountains** which I will tell thee of. And Abraham rose up early in the morning, and saddled his ass, and took two of his young men with him, and Isaac his son, and clave the wood for the burnt offering, and rose up, and went unto the place of which God had told him. **Then on the third day Abraham lifted up his eyes, and saw the place afar off.**
            Fulfillment: Mark 15:15-25
And so Pilate, willing to content the people, released Barabbas unto them, and delivered Jesus, when he had scourged him, to be crucified. And the soldiers led him away into the hall, called Praetorium; and they call together the whole band. And they clothed him with purple, and platted a crown of thorns, and put it about his head, 18And began to salute him, Hail, King of the Jews! And they smote him on the head with a reed, and did spit upon him, and bowing their knees worshipped him. And when they had mocked him, they took off the purple from him, and put his own clothes on him, and led him out to crucify him. And they compel one Simon a Cyrenian, who passed by, coming out of the country, the father of Alexander and Rufus, to bear his cross. **And they bring him unto the place Golgotha, which is, being interpreted, the place of a skull**. And they gave him to drink wine mingled with myrrh: but he received it not. And when they had crucified him, they parted his garments, casting lots upon them, what every man should take. And it was the third hour, **and they crucified him.**

Why Doesn't Everyone Accept The Gospel?

"The same sunlight that melts wax also hardens clay. As God's light shines on man, the sinner's heart determines his response. One whose heart is tender will respond to God; one whose heart is bent on evil will harden his heart further against God and will remain in darkness.

And this is the condemnation, that light is come into the world, and men loved darkness rather than light, because their deeds were evil. For every one that doeth evil hateth the light, neither cometh to the light, lest his deeds should be reproved."

John 3:19-20

99

11. **He would be the only son** Genesis 22:2

And he said, **Take now thy son, thine only** *son* **Isaac**, whom thou lovest, and get thee into the land of Moriah; and offer him there for a burnt offering upon one of the mountains which I will tell thee of.

Fulfillment: John 3:16-18

For God so loved the world, that **he gave his only begotten Son**, that whosoever believeth in him should not perish, but have everlasting life. For God sent not his Son into the world to condemn the world; but that the world through him might be saved. He that believeth on him is not condemned: but he that believeth not is condemned already, because he hath not believed in the name of **the only begotten Son of God.**

12. **He would bear the burden of carrying His cross to His death** Genesis 22:6

And **Abraham took the wood of the burnt offering, and laid** *it* **upon Isaac his son**; and he took the fire in his hand, and a knife; and they went both of them together.

Fulfillment: John 19:17-18

And he **bearing his cross** went forth into a place called *the place* of a skull, which is called in the Hebrew Golgotha: Where they crucified him and two other with him, on either side one, and Jesus in the midst.

13. **The Lamb of God promised** Genesis 22:8

And Abraham said, My son, **God will provide himself a lamb** for a burnt offering: so they went both of them together.

Fulfillment: John 1:29

The next day John seeth Jesus coming unto him, and saith, **Behold the Lamb of God, which taketh away the sin of the world.**

14. **He would wear a crown of thorns** Genesis 22:13

And Abraham lifted up his eyes, and looked, and behold **behind** *him* **a ram caught in a thicket by his horns.**

Fulfillment: Matthew 27:28

And when **they had platted a crown of thorns, they put** *it* **upon his head**, and a reed in his right hand: and they bowed the knee before him, and mocked him, saying, Hail, King of the Jews!

Fulfillment: Mark 15:17

And they clothed him with purple, and **platted a crown of thorns, and put it about his** *head*.

"The gospel alone is sufficient to rule the lives of Christians everywhere...any additional rules made to govern men's conduct added nothing to the perfection already found in the Gospel of Jesus Christ."

John Wycliffe **"See Proverbs 30:5-6"**

100

15.   **As Isaac's seed, all nations will be blessed**   **Genesis 22:16-18**
And said, **By myself have I sworn, saith the LORD, for because thou hast done this thing, and hast not withheld thy son, thine only son:** That in blessing I will bless thee, and in multiplying I will multiply thy seed as the stars of the heaven, and as the sand which is upon the sea shore; and thy seed shall possess the gate of his enemies; And **in thy seed shall all the nations of the earth be blessed; because thou hast obeyed my voice.**
          Fulfillment: Galations 3:16
Now to Abraham and his seed were the promises made. He saith not, And to seeds, as of many; but as of one, And to thy seed, which is Christ.
          Fulfillment: Galatians 4:28
Now we, brethren, **as Isaac was, are the children of promise.**
          Fulfillment: Matthew 22:32
I am the God of Abraham, and **the God of Isaac**, and the God of Jacob? God is not the God of the dead, but of the living.

16.   **As Isaac's seed, He will bless all nations as the Redeemer**   **Genesis 26:1-5**
And there was a famine in the land, beside the first famine that was in the days of Abraham. And Isaac went unto Abimelech king of the Philistines unto Gerar. And the LORD appeared unto him, and said, Go not down into Egypt; dwell in the land which I shall tell thee of: Sojourn in this land, and I will be with thee, and will bless thee; **for unto thee, and unto thy seed, I will give all these countries, and I will perform the oath which I sware unto Abraham thy father**; And I will make thy seed to multiply as the stars of heaven, and will give unto thy seed all these countries; **and in thy seed shall all the nations of the earth be blessed;** Because that Abraham obeyed my voice, and kept my charge, my commandments, my statutes, and my laws.
          Fulfillment: Galatians 3:16
Now to Abraham and **his seed were the promises made**. He saith not, And to seeds, as of many; but as of one, And to thy seed, which is Christ.
          Fulfillment: Hebrews 11:18
Of whom it was said, **That in Isaac shall thy seed be called.**

HUMILITY?

"If the sinless Christ, who is literally God in human flesh and Lord of all, would so humble Himself for us, we dare not denigrate humility or aspire to self-esteem instead of lowliness...Do you want to be blessed? Develop a servant's heart. If Jesus can step down from His glorious equality with God to become a man, and then further humble Himself to be a servant and wash the feet of twelve undeserving sinners-then humble Himself to die so horribly on our behalf, surely we ought to be willing to suffer any indignity to serve Him."

John Macarthur, "Humility," *Moody Magazine*   **"See Matthew 20:28"**

17. **He would come from the seed of Jacob**   **Genesis 28:10-15**

And **Jacob** went out from Beersheba, and went toward Haran. And he lighted upon a certain place, and tarried there all night, because the sun was set; and he took of the stones of that place, and put *them for* his pillows, and lay down in that place to sleep. And he dreamed, and behold a ladder set up on the earth, and the top of it reached to heaven: and behold the angels of God ascending and descending on it. And, behold, the LORD stood above it, and said, I *am* the LORD God of Abraham thy father, and the God of Isaac: the land whereon thou liest, **to thee will I give it, and to thy seed**; And thy seed shall be as the dust of the earth, and thou shalt spread abroad to the west, and to the east, and to the north, and to the south: and in thee and in thy seed shall all the families of the earth be blessed. And, behold, I *am* with thee, and will keep thee in all *places* whither thou goest, and will bring thee again into this land; for I will not leave thee, until I have done *that* which I have spoken to thee of.

Fulfillment: Luke 3:23-38

And Jesus himself began to be about thirty years of age, being (as was supposed) the son of Joseph, which was *the son* of Heli, [24]Which was *the son* of Matthat, which was *the son* of Levi, which was *the son* of Melchi, which was *the son* of Janna, which was *the son* of Joseph, [25]Which was *the son* of Mattathias, which was *the son* of Amos, which was *the son* of Naum, which was *the son* of Esli, which was *the son* of Nagge, [26]Which was *the son* of Maath, which was *the son* of Mattathias, which was *the son* of Semei, which was *the son* of Joseph, which was *the son* of Juda, [27]Which was *the son* of Joanna, which was *the son* of Rhesa, which was *the son* of Zorobabel, which was *the son* of Salathiel, which was *the son* of Neri, [28]Which was *the son* of Melchi, which was *the son* of Addi, which was *the son* of Cosam, which was *the son* of Elmodam, which was *the son* of Er, [29]Which was *the son* of Jose, which was *the son* of Eliezer, which was *the son* of Jorim, which was *the son* of Matthat, which was *the son* of Levi, [30]Which was *the son* of Simeon, which was *the son* of Juda, which was *the son* of Joseph, which was *the son* of Jonan, which was *the son* of Eliakim, [31]Which was *the son* of Melea, which was *the son* of Menan, which was *the son* of Mattatha, which was *the son* of Nathan, which was *the son* of David, [32]Which was *the son* of Jesse, which was *the son* of Obed, which was *the son* of Booz, which was *the son* of Salmon, which was *the son* of Naasson, [33]Which was *the son* of Aminadab, which was *the son* of Aram, which was *the son*

of Esrom, which was *the son* of Phares, which was *the son* of Juda, [34]Which was *the son* of **Jacob**, which was *the son* of Isaac, which was *the son* of Abraham, which was *the son* of Thara, which was *the son* of Nachor, [35]Which was *the son* of Saruch, which was *the son* of Ragau, which was *the son* of Phalec, which was *the son* of Heber, which was *the son* of Sala, [36]Which was *the son* of Cainan, which was *the son* of Arphaxad, which was *the son* of Sem, which was *the son* of Noe, which was *the son* of Lamech, [37]Which was *the son* of Mathusala, which was *the son* of Enoch, which was *the son* of Jared, which was *the son* of Maleleel, which was *the son* of Cainan, [38]Which was *the son* of Enos, which was *the son* of Seth, which was *the son* of Adam, which was *the son* of God.

The Uniqueness of Jesus

"This Jesus of Nazareth, without money and arms, conquered more millions than Alexander, Caesar, Mohammed, and Napoleon; without science and learning, He shed more light on things human and divine than all philosophers and scholars combined; without the eloquence of schools, He spoke such words of life as were never spoken before or since, and produced effects which lie beyond the reach of orator or poet; without writing a single line, He set more pens in motion, and furnished themes for more sermons, orations, discussions, learned volumes, works of art, and songs of praise than the whole army of great men of ancient and modern times."

Philip Schaff, *The Person of Christ*   **"See John 6:68"**

18. **Jesus would come from the seed of Judah** Genesis 49:10

The sceptre shall not depart from Judah, nor a lawgiver from between his feet, **until Shiloh come**; and unto him shall the gathering of the people be.

Fulfillment: Luke 3:23-38

And Jesus himself began to be about thirty years of age, being (as was supposed) the son of Joseph, which was *the son* of was *he* son of Joseph, [25]Which was *the son* of Mattathias, which was *the son* of Amos, which was *the son* of Naum, which was *the son* of Esli, which was *the son* of Nagge, [26]Which was *the son* of Maath, which was *the son* of Mattathias, which was *the son* of Semei, which was *the son* of Joseph, which was *the son* of Juda, [27]Which was *the son* of Joanna, which was *the son* of Rhesa, which was *the son* of Zorobabel, which was *the son* of Salathiel, which was *the son* of Neri, [28]Which was *the son* of Melchi, which was *the son* of Addi, which was *the son* of Cosam, which was *the son* of Elmodam, which was *the son* of Er, [29]Which was *the son* of Jose, which was *the son* of Eliezer, which was *the son* of Jorim, which was *the son* of Matthat, which was *the son* of Levi, [30]Which was *the son* of Simeon, which was *the son* of Juda, which was *the son* of Joseph, which was *the son* of Jonan, which was *the son* of Eliakim, [31]Which was *the son* of Melea, which was *the son* of Menan, which was *the son* of Mattatha, which was *the son* of Nathan, which was *the son* of David, [32]Which was *the son* of Jesse, which was *the son* of Obed, which was *the son* of Booz, which was *the son* of Salmon, which was *the son* of Naasson, [33]Which was *the son* of Aminadab, which was *the son* of Aram, which was *the son*

of Esrom, which was *the son* of Phares, which was *the son* of **Juda**, [34]Which was *the son* of Jacob, which was *the son* of Isaac, which was *the son* of Abraham, which was *the son* of Thara, which was *the son* of Nachor, [35]Which was *the son* of Saruch, which was *the son* of Ragau, which was *the son* of Phalec, which was *the son* of Heber, which was *the son* of Sala, [36]Which was *the son* of Cainan, which was *the son* of Arphaxad, which was *the son* of Sem, which was *the son* of Noe, which was *the son* of Lamech, [37]Which was *the son* of Mathusala, which was *the son* of Enoch, which was *the son* of Jared, which was *the son* of Maleleel, which was *the son* of Cainan, [38]Which was *the son* of Enos, which was *the son* of Seth, which was *the son* of Adam, which was *the son* of God.

Fulfillment: Galatians 4:4

But when the fullness of the time was come, **God sent forth his Son**, made of a woman, made under the law.

19. **He would come before Judah lost its identity, He is called Shiloh**

Genesis 49:10

The sceptre shall not depart from Judah, nor a lawgiver from between his feet, **until Shiloh come**; and unto him shall the gathering of the people be.

Fulfillment: John 11:47-52, 17:3

Then gathered the chief priests and the Pharisees a council, and said, What do we? For this man doeth many miracles. If we let him thus alone, all men will believe on him: and the Romans shall come and take away both our place and nation. And one of them, named Caiaphas, being the high priest that same year, said unto them, Ye know nothing at all, Nor consider that it is expedient for us, that **one man should die for the people, and that the whole nation perish not.** And this spake he not of himself: but being high priest that year, he prophesied that Jesus should die for that nation; And not for that nation only, but that also he should gather together in one the children of God that were scattered abroad… And this is life eternal, that they might know thee the only true God, and Jesus Christ, whom thou hast sent.

"If we abide by the principles taught in the Bible, our country will go on prospering and to prosper; but if we and our posterity neglect its instructions and authority, no man can tell how sudden a catastrophe may overwhelm us and bury all our glory in profound obscurity."

Daniel Webster **"See Psalms 33:12"**

20. **He shall gather the people unto Him**   **Genesis 49:10**
The sceptre shall not depart from Judah, nor a lawgiver from between his feet, until Shiloh come; **and unto him shall the gathering of the people be.**
        Fulfillment: John 10:16
And other sheep I have, which are not of this fold: them also I must bring, **and they shall hear my voice**; and there shall be one fold, and one shepherd.

21. **He is the stone of Israel**   **Genesis 49:24**
But his bow abode in strength, and the arms of his hands were made strong by the hands of the mighty *God* of Jacob; (from thence *is* the shepherd, **the stone of Israel).**
        Fulfillment: Matthew 21:44
And whosoever shall fall on **this stone** shall be broken: but on whomsoever it shall fall, it will grind him to powder.
        Fulfillment: Acts 4:11-12
This is the stone which was set at nought of you builders, which is become the head of the corner. Neither is there salvation in any other: for there is none other name under heaven given among men, **whereby we must be saved.**
        Fulfillment: Ephesians 2:20
And are built upon the foundation of the apostles and prophets, **Jesus Christ himself being the chief corner *stone.***
        Fulfillment: 1 Peter 2:6
Wherefore also it is contained in the scripture, **Behold, I lay in Sion a chief corner stone,** elect, precious: and he that believeth on him shall not be confounded.

How to prove God's existence.

"When we look at a building, how do we know that there was a builder? We can't see him, hear him, touch, taste, or smell him. Of course, **the building is proof that there was a builder**. In fact, we couldn't want better evidence that there was a builder than to have the building in front of us. We don't need "faith" to know that there was a builder. All we need are eyes that can see and a brain that works. Likewise, when we look at a painting, how can we know that there was a painter? Again, **the painting is proof positive that there was a painter**. We don't need "faith" to believe in a painter because we can see the clear evidence. The same principle applies with the existence of God. When we look at creation, how can we know that there was a creator? We can't see him, hear him, touch him, taste him, or smell him. How can we know that he exists? Why, **creation shows us that there is a Creator**. We couldn't want better proof that a creator exists than to have the creation in front of us. **We don't need faith to believe in a creator-all we need are eyes that can see and a brain that works.**"

Ray Comfort   **"See Romans 1:20"**

104

EXODUS

The second book of Moses, written approximately 1580 B.C. – 1230 B.C. Exodus covers from about 1677 B.C. –1450 B.C. It was written in the wilderness and has 40 chapters.

22. **The Great "I Am"** Exodus 3:13–14

And Moses said unto God, Behold, when I come unto the children of Israel, and shall say unto them, The God of your fathers hath sent me unto you; and they shall say to me, What is his name? what shall I say unto them? And God said unto Moses, **I AM THAT I AM**: and he said, Thus shalt thou say unto the children of Israel, **I AM** hath sent me unto you.

Fulfillment: Mark 14:61-62

Art thou the Christ, the Son of the Blessed? **And Jesus said, I am:** and ye shall see the Son of man sitting on the right hand of power, and coming in the clouds of heaven.

Fulfillment: John 8:58

Jesus said unto them, Verily, verily, I say unto you, Before Abraham was, **I am.**

Fulfillment: John 6:35

And Jesus said unto them, **I am** the bread of life: he that cometh to me shall never hunger; and he that believeth on me shall never thirst.

Fulfillment: John 8:12

Then spake Jesus again unto them, saying, **I am** the light of the world: he that followeth me shall not walk in darkness, but shall have the light of life.

Fulfillment: John 11:25

esus said unto her, **I am** the resurrection, and the life: he that believeth in me, though he were dead, yet shall he live.

23. **The Lord called Israel His Son** Exodus 4:22

And thou shalt say unto Pharaoh, Thus saith the LORD, **Israel is my son, even my firstborn.**

Fulfillment: Matthew 3:17

And lo a voice from heaven, saying, **This is my beloved Son, in whom I am well pleased.**

Fulfillment: Romans 8:29

For whom he did foreknow, he also did predestinate to be conformed to the image of his Son, that he might be **the firstborn among many brethren.**

24. **A Lamb without blemish** Exodus 12:5

Your lamb shall be without blemish, a male of the first year: ye shall take it out from the sheep, or from the goats.

Fulfillment: 1 Peter 1:19

But with the precious blood of **Christ**, as of **a lamb without blemish and without spot.**

"The devil can cite Scripture for his purpose."

William Shakespeare **"See Luke 4:9-13"**

105

25. **He would be Holy** **Exodus 15:11**

Who *is* like unto thee, O LORD, among the gods? who *is* like thee, **glorious in holiness**, fearful *in* praises, doing wonders?

Fulfillment: Acts 4:27

For of a truth against **thy holy child Jesus**, whom thou hast anointed, both Herod, and Pontius Pilate, with the Gentiles, and the people of Israel, were gathered together.

Fulfillment: Revelations 3:7

And to the angel of the church in Philadelphia write; **These things saith he that is holy,** he that is true, he that hath the key of David, he that openeth, and no man shutteth; and shutteth, and no man openeth.

26. **The blood of the Lamb saves us from the wrath, Christ is our Passover**
Exodus 12:13, 21-27

And **the blood shall be to you for a token** upon the houses where ye are: **and when I see the blood, I will pass over you,** and the plague shall not be upon you to destroy you, when I smite the land of Egypt… Then Moses called for all the elders of Israel, and said unto them, Draw out and take you a lamb according to your families, and kill the passover. And ye shall take a bunch of hyssop, and dip it in the blood that is in the bason, and strike the lintel and the two side posts with the blood that is in the bason; and none of you shall go out at the door of his house until the morning. **For the LORD will pass through to smite the Egyptians; and when he seeth the blood upon the lintel, and on the two side posts, the LORD will pass over the door, and will not suffer the destroyer to come in unto your houses to smite you.** And ye shall observe this thing for an ordinance to thee and to thy sons for ever. And it shall come to pass, when ye be come to the land which the LORD will give you, according as he hath promised, that ye shall keep this service. And it shall come to pass, when your children shall say unto you, What mean ye by this service? That ye shall say, It is the sacrifice of the LORD'S passover, who passed over the houses of the children of Israel in Egypt, when he smote the Egyptians, and delivered our houses. And the people bowed their head and worshipped.

Fulfillment: Romans 5:8-9

But God commendeth his love toward us, in that, while we were yet sinners, Christ died for us. Much more then, being now **justified by his blood**, we shall be saved from wrath through him.

Fulfillment: 1 Corinthians 5:7

Purge out therefore the old leaven, that ye may be a new lump, as ye are unleavened. **For even Christ our passover is sacrificed for us.**

"God doesn't think as we do. He is omniscient – He knows all things. That means he never has an idea. If a concept suddenly came to him, then He would be ignorant of the thought before it formed in His mind. However, God doesn't have thoughts "come to His mind." Because He is omniscient, His mind has all thoughs resident."

"Known unto God are all his works from the beginning of the world."

Acts15:18

106

27. **Not a bone of the Lamb would be broken**   **Exodus 12:43-46**
And the LORD said unto Moses and Aaron, This is the ordinance of the passover: There shall no stranger eat thereof: But every man's servant that is bought for money, when thou hast circumcised him, then shall he eat thereof. A foreigner and an hired servant shall not eat thereof. In one house shall it be eaten; thou shalt not carry forth ought of the flesh abroad out of the house; **neither shall ye break a bone thereof.**
          Fulfillment: John 19:31-37
The Jews therefore, because it was the preparation, that the bodies should not remain upon the cross on the sabbath day, (for that sabbath day was an high day,) besought Pilate that their legs might be broken, and that they might be taken away. Then came the soldiers, and brake the legs of the first, and of the other which was crucified with him. But when they came to Jesus, and saw that he was dead already, **they brake not his legs**: But one of the soldiers with a spear pierced his side, and forthwith came there out blood and water. And he that saw it bare record, and his record is true: and he knoweth that he saith true, that ye might believe. **For these things were done, that the scripture should be fulfilled, A bone of him shall not be broken**. And again another scripture saith, They shall look on him whom they pierced.

28. **The Spiritual Rock of Israel**   **Exodus 17:6**
Behold, I will stand before thee there upon the rock in Horeb; and **thou shalt smite the rock, and there shall come water out of it, that the people may drink.** And Moses did so in the sight of the elders of Israel.
          Fulfillment: 1 Corinthians 10:4
And did all drink the same spiritual drink: **for they drank of that spiritual Rock that followed them: and that Rock was Christ.**

"If I had my way, I would declare a moratorium on public preaching of 'the plan of salvation' in America for one to two years. Then I would call on everyone who has use of the airwaves and the pulpits to preach the holiness of God, the righteousness of God, and the law of God, until sinners would cry out, 'What must we do to be saved?' Then I would take them off in a corner and whisper the gospel to them. Don't use John 3:16. Such drastic action is needed because we have gospel hardened a generation of sinners by telling them how to be saved before they have any understanding why they need to be saved."

Paris Reid   **"See John 3:16"**

29. **His Merciful Character** **Exodus 33:19**

And he said, I will make all my goodness pass before thee, and I will proclaim the name of the LORD before thee; and will be gracious to whom **I will be gracious, and will shew mercy on whom I will shew mercy.**

Fulfillment: Luke 1:72-79

To perform the mercy promised to our fathers, and to remember his holy covenant; The oath which he sware to our father Abraham, That he would grant unto us, that we being delivered out of the hand of our enemies might serve him without fear, In holiness and righteousness before him, all the days of our life. And thou, child, shalt be called the prophet of the Highest: for thou shalt go before the face of the Lord to prepare his ways; To give knowledge of salvation unto his people by the remission of their sins, Through **the tender mercy of our God**; whereby the dayspring from on high hath visited us, To give light to them that sit in darkness and in the shadow of death, to guide our feet into the way of peace.

The Parable of the Fishless Fishermen

They were surrounded by streams and lakes full of hungry fish. They met regularly to discuss the call to fish, the abundance of fish, and the thrill of catching fish. They got excited about fishing!

Someone suggested that they needed a philosophy of fishing, so they carefully defined and redefined fishing, and the purpose of fishing. They developed fishing strategies and tactics. Then they realized that they had been going at it backwards. They had approached fishing from the point of view of the fisherman, and not for the point of view of the fish. How do fish view the world? How does the fisherman appear to the fish? What do fish eat, and when? These are all good things to know. So they began research studies and attended conferences on fishing. Some traveled to faraway places to study different kinds of fish with different habits. Some got doctorates in fishology. But no one had yet gone fishing.

So a committee was formed to send out fisherman. As prospective fishing places outnumbered fishermen, the committee needed to determine priorities. A priority list of fishing places was posted on bulletin boards in all of the Fellowship halls. But still, no one was fishing. A survey was launched to find out why. Most did not answer the survey, but from those who did, it was discovered that some felt called to study fish, a few to furnish fishing equipment, and several to go around encouraging the fisherman. What with meetings, conferences, and seminars, they just simply didn't have time to fish.

Now, Jake was a newcomer to the fisherman's club. After one stirring meeting of Fellowship, he went fishing and caught a large fish. At the next meeting he told his story and was honored for his catch. He was told that he had a special "gift of fishing." He was then scheduled to speak at the Fellowship chapters and tell how he did it.

With all the speaking invitations and his election to the Board of Directors of the fishermen's Fellowship, Jake no longer had time to go fishing. But soon he began to feel restless and empty. He longed to feel the tug on the line once again. So he cut the speaking, he resigned from the board, and he said to a friend, "Let's go fishing." They did, just the two of them, and they caught fish. The members of the fisherman's Fellowship were many, the fish were plentiful, but the fishers were few!

Anonymous **"See Mark 1:35"**

LEVITICUS

The third book written by Moses, written approximately 1450 B.C. – 1400 B.C. Leviticus covers from about 1461 B.C. to 1423 B.C. It was written in the wilderness and has 27 chapters.

30.   **The Leper cleansed – Sign of Priesthood**   **Leviticus 14:11**
And **the priest that maketh him clean** shall present the man that is to be made clean, and those things, before the LORD, at the door of the tabernacle of the congregation.
          Fulfillment: Luke 5:12-14
And it came to pass, when he was in a certain city, behold a **man full of leprosy: who seeing Jesus** fell on his face, and besought him, **saying, Lord, if thou wilt, thou canst make me clean. And he put forth his hand, and touched him, saying, I will: be thou clean. And immediately the leprosy departed from him**. And he charged him to tell no man: **but go, and shew thyself to the priest, and offer for thy cleansing, according as Moses commanded, for a testimony unto them.**

31.   **He would be poor**   **Leviticus 14:21-22**
And if he *be* **poor,** and cannot get so much; then he shall take one lamb *for* a trespass offering to be waved, to make an atonement for him, and one tenth deal of fine flour mingled with oil for a meat offering, and a log of oil; **And two turtledoves, or two young pigeons, such as he is able to get; and the one shall be a sin offering, and the other a burnt offering.**
          Fulfillment: Luke 2:21-24
And when eight days were accomplished for the circumcising of the child, **his name was called JESUS**, which was so named of the angel before he was conceived in the womb. And when the days of her purification according to the law of Moses were accomplished, they brought him to Jerusalem, to present *him* to the Lord; (As it is written in the law of the Lord, Every male that openeth the womb shall be called holy to the Lord;) **And to offer a sacrifice according to that which is said in the law of the Lord, A pair of turtledoves, or two young pigeons.**

"A barracks is meant to be a place where real soldiers were to be fed and equipped for war, not a place to settle down in or as a comfortable snuggery in which to enjoy ourselves. I hope that if ever they, our soldiers, do settle down God will burn their barracks over their heads."

Catherine Booth   **"See Ephesians 6:11-20"**

32. **Prefigures Christ's once and for all death**   **Leviticus 16:15-19**

Then shall he kill **the goat of the sin offering,** that is for the people, and bring his blood within the vail, and do with that blood as he did with the blood of the bullock, and sprinkle it upon the mercy seat, and before the mercy seat: **And he shall make an atonement for the holy place, because of the uncleanness of the children of Israel, and because of their transgressions in all their sins**: and so shall he do for the tabernacle of the congregation, that remaineth among them in the midst of their uncleanness. And there shall be no man in the tabernacle of the congregation when he goeth in to make an atonement in the holy place, until he come out, and have made an atonement for himself, and for his household, and for all the congregation of Israel. And he shall go out unto the altar that is before the LORD, and make an atonement for it; and shall take of the blood of the bullock, and of the blood of the goat, and put it upon the horns of the altar round about. And he shall sprinkle of the blood upon it with his finger seven times, and cleanse it, and hallow it from the uncleanness of the children of Israel.

Fulfillment: Hebrews 13:11-12

For the bodies of those **beasts, whose blood is brought into the sanctuary by the high priest for sin,** are burned without the camp. Wherefore **Jesus also, that he might sanctify the people with his own blood, suffered without the gate.**

33. **Suffering Outside the camp**   **Leviticus 16:27**

And the bullock for the sin offering, and the goat for the sin offering, whose blood was brought in to make atonement in the holy place, **shall one carry forth without the camp;** and they shall burn in the fire their skins, and their flesh, and their dung.

Fulfillment: Hebrews 13:11, 12

For the bodies of those beasts, whose blood is brought into the sanctuary by the high priest for sin, are burned without the camp. **Wherefore Jesus also, that he might sanctify the people with his own blood, suffered without the gate.**

Fulfillment: Matthew 27:33-37

And when they were come unto **a place called Go**lgotha, that is to say, **a place of a skull,** They gave him vinegar to drink mingled with gall: and when he had tasted *thereof,* he would not drink. **And they crucified him**, and parted his garments, casting lots: that it might be fulfilled which was spoken by the prophet, They parted my garments among them, and upon my vesture did they cast lots. And sitting down they watched him there.

"Genuine outrage is not just a permissible reaction to the hard-pressed Christian; God himself feels it, and so should the Christian in the presence of pain, cruelty, violence, and injustice. God, who is the Father of Jesus Christ, is neither impersonal nor beyond good and evil. By the absolute immutability of His character, He is implacably opposed to evil and outraged by it."

Os Guinness   **"See Matthew 21:12-13"**

34. **The Blood is the life of the flesh, it is the Blood that makes an atonement**

Leviticus 17:11

For the life of the flesh is in the blood: and I have given it to you upon the altar to make an atonement **for your souls: for it is the blood that maketh an atonement for the soul.**

   Fulfillment: Matthew 26:28

For this is **my blood of the new testament, which is shed for many for the remission of sins.**

   Fulfillment: Mark 10:45

For even the Son of man came not to be ministered unto, but to minister, and **to give his life a ransom for many.**

35. **Drink Offering, "If any man thirst"**   **Leviticus 23:36-37**

Seven days ye shall offer an offering made by fire unto the LORD: on the eighth day shall be an holy convocation unto you; and ye shall offer an offering made by fire unto the LORD: it is a solemn assembly; and ye shall do no servile work therein. These are the feasts of the LORD, which ye shall proclaim to be holy convocations, to offer an offering made by fire unto the LORD, a burnt offering, and a meat offering, a sacrifice, and **drink offerings**, every thing upon his day.

   Fulfillment: John 7:37-38

In the last day, that great day of the feast, Jesus stood and cried, saying, **If any man thirst, let him come unto me, and drink. He that believeth on me, as the scripture hath said, out of his belly shall flow rivers of living water.**

36. **The Messiah would walk among His people**   **Leviticus 26:12**

And I will walk among you, and will be your God, and ye shall be my people.

   Fulfillment: John 7:1

After these things **Jesus walked in Galilee**: for he would not walk in Jewry, because the Jews sought to kill him.

   Fulfillment: John 10:22-25

And it was at Jerusalem the feast of the dedication, and it was winter. **And Jesus walked in the temple in Solomon's porch. Then came the Jews round about him,** and said unto him, How long dost thou make us to doubt? If thou be the Christ, tell us plainly. Jesus answered them, I told you, and ye believed not: the works that I do in my Father's name, they bear witness of me.

"It is common sense to take a method and try it; if it fails, admit it frankly and try another. But above all, try something!"

Franklin D. Roosevelt   **"See 2 Timothy 4:1-2"**

NUMBERS

The fourth book written by Moses, written approximately 1450 B.C. – 1400 B.C. Numbers covers from about 1461 B.C. – 1421 B.C. It was written in the wilderness and has 36 chapters. Chapters 1-21 are the wilderness years, 26-36 are a new generation, this book covers 39 years.

37.   **Not a bone of Him would be broken**   **Numbers 9:12**

They shall leave none of it unto the morning, **nor break any bone** of it: according to all the ordinances of the passover they shall keep it.

       Fulfillment: John 19:31-36

The Jews therefore, because it was the preparation, that the bodies should not remain upon the cross on the sabbath day, (for that sabbath day was an high day,) besought Pilate that their legs might be broken, and that they might be taken away. Then came the soldiers, and brake the legs of the first, and of the other which was crucified with him. But when they came to Jesus, and saw that he was dead already, **they brake not his legs:** But one of the soldiers with a spear pierced his side, and forthwith came there out blood and water. And he that saw it bare record, and his record is true: and he knoweth that he saith true, that ye might believe. **For these things were done, that the scripture should be fulfilled, A bone of him shall not be broken.**

38.   **His ministry would include miracles**   **Numbers 14:22**

Because all those men which have seen my glory, and my miracles, which I did in Egypt and in the wilderness, and have tempted me now these ten times, and have not hearkened to my voice.

       Fulfillment: John 2:11, 23

This beginning of miracles did Jesus in Cana of Galilee, and manifested forth his glory; and his disciples believed on him… Now when he was in Jerusalem at the passover, in the feast *day*, many believed in his name, **when they saw the miracles which he did.**

       Fulfillment: John 3:2

The same came to Jesus by night, and said unto him, Rabbi, we know that thou art a teacher come from God: **for no man can do these miracles that thou doest**, except God be with him.

       Fulfillment: John 7:31

And many of the people believed on him, and said, **When Christ cometh, will he do more miracles than these which this *man* hath done?**

       Fulfillment: John 11:47

Then gathered the chief priests and the Pharisees a council, and said, **What do we? for this man doeth many miracles.**

       Fulfillment: John 12:37

But though **he had done so many miracles before them, yet they believed not on him.**

"To be a Christian without prayer is no more possible than to be alive without breathing."

Martin Luther   **"See Luke 18:1"**

39. **The serpent on a pole – Christ must be lifted up** Numbers 21:9
And Moses made **a serpent of brass, and put it upon a pole**, and it came to pass, that if a serpent had bitten any man, when he beheld the serpent of brass, he lived.
  Fulfillment: John 3:14-18
And as Moses lifted up the serpent in the wilderness, even so must the Son of man be lifted up: That whosoever believeth in him should not perish, but have eternal life. For God so loved the world, that he gave his only begotten Son, that whosoever believeth in him should not perish, but have everlasting life. For God sent not his Son into the world to condemn the world; but that the world through him might be saved. He that believeth on him is not condemned: but he that believeth not is condemned already, because he hath not believed in the name of the only begotten Son of God.

40. **His Kingdom shall be exalted** Numbers 24:7
He shall pour the water out of his buckets, and his seed shall be in many waters, and his king shall be higher than Agag, **and his kingdom shall be exalted.**
  Fulfillment: Revelations 19:16
And he hath on his vesture and on his thigh a name written, **KING OF KINGS, AND LORD OF LORDS.**

41. **He would come out of Egypt** Numbers 24:8
God brought him forth out of Egypt; he hath as it were the strength of an unicorn: he shall eat up the nations his enemies, and shall break their bones, and pierce *them* through with his arrows.
  Fulfillment: Matthew 2:14-15
When he arose, he took the young child and his mother by night, and departed into Egypt: And was there until the death of Herod: that it might be fulfilled which was spoken of the Lord by the prophet, saying, **Out of Egypt have I called my son.**

42. **I shall see Him, but not now** Numbers 24:17
I shall see him, but not now: I shall behold him, but not nigh: there shall come a Star out of Jacob, and a Sceptre shall rise out of Israel, and shall smite the corners of Moab, and destroy all the children of Sheth.
  Fulfillment: Galatians 4:4
But when the fullness of the time was come, God sent forth his Son, made of a woman, made under the law.

43. **A star, connected with His birth** Numbers 24:17
I shall see him, but not now: I shall behold him, but not nigh: there shall come **a Star out of Jacob,** and a Sceptre shall rise out of Israel, and shall smite the corners of Moab, and destroy all the children of Sheth.
  Fulfillment: Matthew 2:2
Saying, Where is he that is born King of the Jews? **For we have seen his star in the east,** and are come to worship him.

"Common sense is not so common"

Voltaire **"See Psalm 19:7"**

113

DEUTERONOMY

This is the fifth book of Moses, written approximately 1450 B.C. – 1400 B.C. Deuteronomy covers from 1423 B.C. to 1422 B.C. It was written in the wilderness, on the banks of Jordan, it has 34 chapters.

44.   **He would suffer hunger**   Deuteronomy 8:2-3
And thou shalt remember all the way which the LORD thy God led thee these forty years in the wilderness, to humble thee, *and* to prove thee, to know what *was* in thine heart, whether thou wouldest keep his commandments, or no. **And he humbled thee, and suffered thee to hunger,** and fed thee with manna, which thou knewest not, neither did thy fathers know; that he might make thee know that man doth not live by bread only, but by every *word* that proceedeth out of the mouth of the LORD doth man live.
     Fulfillment: Matthew 4:2,
And when he had fasted forty days and forty nights, **he was afterward an hungred.**
     Fulfillment: Matthew 25:42
For **I was an hungred, and ye gave me no meat**: I was thirsty, and ye gave me no drink.

45.   **God would raise Him up a prophet**   Deuteronomy 18:15
The LORD thy God will raise up unto thee a Prophet from the midst of thee, of thy brethren, like unto me; unto him ye shall hearken.
     Fulfillment: John 6:14
Then those men, when they had seen the miracle that Jesus did, said, **This is of a truth that prophet that should come into the world.**
     Fulfillment: Matthew 13:57
And they were offended in him. But Jesus said unto them, **A prophet is not without honour, save in his own country, and in his own house.**
     Fulfillment: Matthew 21:11
And the multitude said, **This is Jesus the prophet of Nazareth of Galilee.**
     Fulfillment: Luke 7:16
And there came a fear on all: and they glorified God, saying, **That a great prophet is risen up among us**; and, That God hath visited his people.
     Fulfillment: John 7:40
Many of the people therefore, when they heard this saying, said, **Of a truth this is the Prophet.**

"Dietrich Bonhoeffer wrote that 'only he who believes is obedient, and only he who is obedient believes.' Neither proposition can stand alone. Christians often think we are doing the Lord's work when we are not. Jesus Himself warned us about this. We cannot serve two masters. The one we choose will determine whether at our death we hear, 'Well done, good and faithful servant,' or 'I never knew you.' "

Daniel Weiss   **"See Luke 19:17"**

46. **"Had ye believed Moses, Ye would have believed me"** Deuteronomy 18:15-16 **The LORD thy God will raise up unto thee a Prophet from the midst of thee, of thy brethren, like unto me; unto him ye shall hearken**; According to all that thou desiredst of the LORD thy God in Horeb in the day of the assembly, saying, Let me not hear again the voice of the LORD my God, neither let me see this great fire any more, that I die not.

       Fulfillment: John 5:45-47

Do not think that I will accuse you to the Father: there is one that accuseth you, even Moses, in whom ye trust. **For had ye believed Moses, ye would have believed me**: for he wrote of me. But if ye believe not his writings, how shall ye believe my words?

47. **He was sent by the Father to speak His Word** Deuteronomy 18:18 I will raise them up a Prophet from among their brethren, like unto thee, **and will put my words in his mouth; and he shall speak unto them all that I shall command him.**

       Fulfillment: John 8:28-29

Then said Jesus unto them, When ye have lifted up the Son of man, then shall ye know that I am he, and that I do nothing of myself; **but as my Father hath taught me, I speak these things.** And he that sent me is with me: the Father hath not left me alone; for **I do always those things that please him.**

48. **Whoever will not hear must bear his own sin** Deuteronomy 18:19 And it shall come to pass, **that whosoever will not hearken unto my words which he shall speak in my name, I will require it of him.**

       Fulfillment: Hebrews 3:7-19

Wherefore (as the Holy Ghost saith, To day if ye will hear his voice, **Harden not your hearts, as in the provocation**, in the day of temptation in the wilderness: When your fathers tempted me, proved me, and saw my works forty years. Wherefore I was grieved with that generation, and said, They do I err in their heart; and **they have not known my ways.** So I sware in my wrath, They shall not enter into my rest.) Take heed, brethren, lest there be in any of you an evil heart of unbelief, in departing from the living God. But exhort one another daily, while it is called To day; lest any of you be hardened through the deceitfulness of sin. For we are made partakers of Christ, if we hold the beginning of our confidence stedfast unto the end; While it is said, **To day if ye will hear his voice, harden not your hearts, as in the provocation.** For some, when they had heard, did provoke: howbeit not all that came out of Egypt by Moses. But with whom was he grieved forty years? **Was it not with them that had sinned, whose carcases fell in the wilderness? And to whom sware he that they should not enter into his rest, but to them that believed not? So we see that they could not enter in because of unbelief.**

"For the invisible things of Him from the creation of the world are clearly seen, being understood by the things that are made, even his eternal power and Godhead; so that they are without excuse."

Romans 1:20

115

49.   **He would be cursed and die hanging on a tree**   **Deuteronomy 21:23**
His body shall not remain all night upon the tree, but thou shalt in any wise bury him that day (**for he that is hanged is accursed of God**) that thy land be not defiled, which the LORD thy God giveth thee for an inheritance.

Fulfillment: Galatians 3:10-13

For as many as are of the works of the law are under the curse: for it is written, Cursed is every one that continueth not in all things which are written in the book of the law to do them. But that no man is justified by the law in the sight of God, it is evident: for, The just shall live by faith. And the law is not of faith: but, The man that doeth them shall live in them. Christ hath redeemed us from the curse of the law, being made a curse for us: for it is written, **Cursed is every one that hangeth on a tree.**

Fulfillment: Acts 5:30

The God of our fathers raised up Jesus, whom **ye slew and hanged on a tree.**

Christ's Resurrection Appearances

1.   **Mary**   **John 20:10-18**

2.   **Mary and women**   **Matthew 28:1-10**

3.   **Peter**   **1 Corinthians 15:5**

4.   **Two disciples**   **Luke 24:13-35**

5.   **Ten apostles**   **Luke 24:36-49; John 20:19-23**

6.   **Eleven apostles**   **John 20:24-31**

7.   **Seven apostles**   **John 21**

8.   **All apostles**   **Matthew28:16-20; Mark 16:14-18**

9.   **500 brethren**   **1 Corinthians 15:6**

10.   **James**   **1 Corinthians 15:7**

11.   **All apostles**   **Acts 1:4-8**

12.   **Paul**   **Acts 9:1-9; 1 Corinthians 15:8**

SAMUEL

These are the ninth & tenth books of the Bible, written approximately 1070 B.C. – 850 B.C. 1st & 2nd Samuel cover between about 1126 B.C. to 988 B.C. It is unknown where it was written or who wrote them. 1st Samuel has 31 chapters & 2nd Samuel has 24 chapters.

50.   **He shall be an anointed King to the Lord**   **1 Samuel 2:10**
The adversaries of the LORD shall be broken to pieces; out of heaven shall he thunder upon them: the LORD shall judge the ends of the earth; and **he shall give strength unto his king, and exalt the horn of his anointed.**
        Fulfillment: Matthew 28:18
And Jesus came and spake unto them, saying, **All power is given unto me in heaven and in earth.**

51.   **King David would be Christ's ancestor**   **2 Samuel 7:11-16**
And as since the time that I commanded judges to be over my people Israel, and have caused thee to rest from all thine enemies. Also the LORD telleth thee that he will make thee an house. And when thy days be fulfilled, and thou shalt sleep with thy fathers, I will set up thy seed after thee, which shall proceed out of thy bowels, and **I will establish his kingdom. He shall build an house for my name, and I will stablish the throne of his kingdom for ever.** I will be his father, and he shall be my son. If he commit iniquity, I will chasten him with the rod of men, and with the stripes of the children of men: But my mercy shall not depart away from him, as I took it from Saul, whom I put away before thee. **And thine house and thy kingdom shall be established for ever before thee: thy throne shall be established for ever.**
        Fulfillment: 1 Chronicles 17:11-13a
And it shall come to pass, when thy days be expired that thou must go to be with thy fathers, that **I will raise up thy seed after thee**, which shall be of thy sons; and I will establish his kingdom. He shall build me an house, and I will stablish his throne for ever. I will be his father, and he shall be my son: and I will not take my mercy away from him, as I took it from him that was before thee.
        Fulfillment: Matthew 1:1
The book of the **generation of Jesus Christ, the son of David**, the son of Abraham.
        Fulfillment: Matthew 9:27
And when Jesus departed thence, two blind men followed him, crying, and saying, **Thou Son of David, have mercy on us.**
        Fulfillment: Luke 3:23-38
And Jesus himself began to be about thirty years of age, being (as was supposed) the son of Joseph...**which was the son of David...**

"What we love to do we find time to do."

John L. Spalding   **"See 2 Timothy 4:1-5"**

52. **He will be "The Son of God"** 2 Samuel 7:14a
I will be his father, and he shall be my son.
Fulfillment: Luke 1:32
He shall be great, and shall be **called the Son of the Highest**: and the Lord God shall give unto him the throne of his father David.
Fulfillment: Hebrews 1:5
For unto which of the angels said he at any time, **Thou art my Son**, this day have I begotten thee? And again, **I will be to him a Father, and he shall be to me a Son?**

53. **David's house would be established forever** 2 Samuel 7:16
And thine house and thy kingdom shall be established for ever before thee: **thy throne shall be established forever.**
Fulfillment: Luke 1:32, 33
He shall be great, and shall be called the **Son of the Highest**: and the Lord God shall give unto him the throne of his father David: 33And he shall reign over the house of Jacob for ever; and of **his kingdom there shall be no end.**
Fulfillment: Revelations 22:16
I Jesus have sent mine angel to testify unto you these things in the churches. **I am the Root and the Offspring of David, and the bright and morning Star.**

Psalm 23

The LORD *is* my shepherd; I shall not want.
He maketh me to lie down in green pastures;
He leadeth me beside the still waters.
He restoreth my soul;
He leadeth me in the paths of righteousness for his name's sake.
Yea, though I walk through the valley of the shadow of death,
I will fear no evil: for thou *art* with me;
Thy rod and thy staff they comfort me.
Thou preparest a table before me
in the presence of mine enemies.
Thou anointest my head with oil; my cup runneth over.
Surely goodness and mercy shall follow me all the days of my life.
And I will dwell in the house of the LORD forever.

KINGS

These are the 11th & 12th books of the Bible, written approximately 971 B.C. – 536 B.C. 1st & 2nd Kings cover between 1025 B.C. to 561 B.C. They were written perhaps in the Babylonian area, but it is unknown. The writer is unknown also, but is traditionally said to be Jeremiah. 1st Kings has 22 chapters and 2nd Kings has 25 chapters.

54.   **The bodily ascension to heaven illustrated**   **2 Kings 2:11**
And it came to pass, as they still went on, and talked, that, behold, there appeared a chariot of fire, and horses of fire, and parted them both asunder; **and Elijah went up by a whirlwind into heaven.**
         Fulfillment: Luke 24:51
And it came to pass, while he blessed them, **he was parted from them, and carried up into heaven.**

CHRONICLES

These are the 13th & 14th books of the Bible, written approximately 500 B.C. – 450 B.C. 1st & 2nd Chronicles cover between 1699 B.C. to 444 B.C. It is unknown where they were written. Tradition holds that Ezra wrote the books. 1st Chronicles has 29 chapters and 2nd Chronicles has 36 chapters.

55.   **He will be "The Son of God"**   **1 Chronicles 17:13a**
I will be his father, and he shall be my son
         Fulfillment: Hebrews 1:5
For unto which of the angels said he at any time, **Thou art my Son**, this day have I begotten thee? And again, **I will be to him a Father, and he shall be to me a Son?**

NEHEMIAH

This is the 16th book of the Bible, written approximately 445 B.C. – 420 B.C... Nehemiah covers between about 445 B.C. to 425 B.C. It is unknown where it was written, perhaps; Jerusalem. Nehemiah has 13 chapters.

56.   **God provided water out of a rock for thirst**   **Nehemiah 9:15**
And gavest them bread from heaven for their hunger, **and broughtest forth water for them out of the rock for their thirst**, and promisedst them that they should go in to possess the land which thou hadst sworn to give them.
         Fulfillment: John 7:37-38
In the last day, that great day of the feast, Jesus stood and cried, saying, **if any man thirst, let him come unto me, and drink.** He that believeth on me, as the scripture hath said, out of his belly shall flow rivers of living water.

"Before we pray 'Thy Kingdom come,' we must be willing to pray 'my kingdom go.'"

Alan Redpath   **"See Matthew 19:29"**

JOB

This is the 18th book of the Bible, it is unknown when it was written, by whom it was written, and where it was written. It is believed that Job lived in the time of the patriarchs before the Law of Moses because Job offers sacrifices as the head of his family (Job 1.5) as the patriarchs did before the Law.   Job has 42 chapters.

57.   **The resurrection predicted**   Job19:23-27

Oh that my words were now written! Oh that they were printed in a book! That they were graven with an iron pen and lead in the rock forever! **For I know that my redeemer liveth, and that he shall stand at the latter day upon the earth**: And though after my skin worms destroy this body, yet in my flesh shall I see God: Whom I shall see for myself, and mine eyes shall behold, and not another; though my reins be consumed within me.

Fulfillment: John 5:24-29

Verily, verily, I say unto you, He that heareth my word, and believeth on him that sent me, hath everlasting life, and shall not come into condemnation; but is passed from death unto life. **Verily, verily, I say unto you, The hour is coming, and now is, when the dead shall hear the voice of the Son of God: and they that hear shall live.** For as the Father hath life in himself; so hath he given to the Son to have life in himself; And hath given him authority to execute judgment also, because he is the Son of man. Marvel not at this: for the hour is coming, in the which all that are in the graves shall hear his voice, and shall come forth; they that have done good, unto the resurrection of life; and they that have done evil, unto the resurrection of damnation.

58.   **He would come as a teacher**   Job 36:22

Behold, **God exalteth** by his power: **who teacheth like him**?

Fulfillment: Matthew 26:55

In that same hour said Jesus to the multitudes, Are ye come out as against a thief with swords and staves for to take me? **I sat daily with you teaching in the temple**, and ye laid no hold on me.

Fulfillment: Mark 6:34

And Jesus, when he came out, saw much people, and was moved with compassion toward them, because they were as sheep not having a shepherd: and **he began to teach them many things.**

Fulfillment: John 3:2

The same came to Jesus by night, and said unto him, Rabbi, **we know that thou art a teacher come from God**: for no man can do these miracles that thou doest, except God be with him.

Fulfillment: John 8: 1-2

Jesus went unto the mount of Olives. [2]And early in the morning he came again into the temple, and all the people came unto him; **and he sat down, and taught them.**

Fulfillment: John 18:20

Jesus answered him, I spake openly to the world; **I ever taught in the synagogue**, and in the temple, whither the Jews always resort; and in secret have I said nothing.

It is not "anti-choice" and "pro-choice" it is "pro-life" and "pro-death."

L.B.K.   **"See Deuteronomy 27:25"**

120

59.   **He is worthy of the name Wonderful**   **Job 42.3**
Who *is* he that hideth counsel without knowledge? therefore have **I uttered that I understood not; things too wonderful for me**, which I knew not.

       Fulfillment: Matthew 21:15
And when the chief priests and scribes **saw the wonderful things that he did**, and the children crying in the temple, and saying, Hosanna to the Son of David; they were sore displeased.

       Fulfillment: Luke 4:22
And all bare him witness, **and wondered at the gracious words which proceeded out of his mouth.** And they said, Is not this Joseph's son?

God does the "follow up."

"The exciting thing about true conversion is that there will be little need for what is commonly called "follow up." A true convert will not need to be followed. He will put his hand to the plow and not look back (**Luke 9:62**). Of course, he will have to be fed, discipled, and nurtured. These things are Biblical and most necessary. This can be done simply by encouraging him to read the Bible daily, answering questions he may have, and teaching him principles of fellowship, prayer, evangelism, etc. Sometimes there is confusion between "follow up" (we need to follow the new convert because he will fall away if we don't) and discipleship (instructing him to continue in the word of Christ, **John 8:31**). Look what happened after the Ethiopian eunuch was saved he was left with out follow up. The spirit of God transported Phillip away and left the new convert in the wilderness. This is because his salvation wasn't dependent on Phillip, but upon his relationship with the indwelling Lord. Those whom God saves, He keeps. If He is the author of our faith, He will be the finisher. If He has begun a work in them, He will complete it. He is able to keep them from falling and present them faultless before the presence of His glory with exceeding joy."

Ray Comfort   **"See Acts 8:39"**

PSALMS

This is the 19th book of the Bible. It is unknown when it was written and unknown what dates it covers, possibly 1423 B.C. to 444 B.C. Psalms was written by David, Asaph, sons of Korah, Solomon, Ethan, and Moses. All but 34 bear some title as anonymous. It was written in many places and has 150 chapters.

60.   **The enmity of Kings foretold against the Lord**   **Psalm 2:1-3**
Why do the heathen rage, and the people imagine a vain thing? **The kings of the earth set themselves, and the rulers take counsel together, against the LORD, and against his anointed**, saying, Let us break their bands asunder, and cast away their cords from us.
     Fulfillment: Acts 4:25-28
Who by the mouth of thy servant David hast said, Why did the heathen rage, and the people imagine vain things? **The kings of the earth stood up, and the rulers were gathered together against the Lord, and against his Christ**. For of a truth against thy holy child Jesus, whom thou hast anointed, both Herod, and Pontius Pilate, with the Gentiles, and the people of Israel, were gathered together, For to do whatsoever thy hand and thy counsel determined before to be done.

61.   **To own the title, Anointed "Christ"**   **Psalm 2:2**
The kings of the earth set themselves, and the rulers take counsel together, against the LORD, and against **his anointed.**
     Fulfillment: Acts 2:36
Therefore let all the house of Israel know assuredly, **that God hath made that same Jesus, whom ye have crucified, both Lord and Christ.**

62.   **He owns the title King**   **Psalm 2:6**
Yet have I set **my king** upon my holy hill of Zion.
     Fulfillment: Matthew 2:2
Saying, Where is he that is born **King of the Jews**? For we have seen his star in the east, and are come to worship him.
     Fulfillment: Matthew 27:36
And set up over his head his accusation written, **THIS IS JESUS THE KING OF THE JEWS.**
     Fulfillment: Timothy 6:14
That thou keep *this* commandment without spot, unrebukeable, until the appearing of our Lord Jesus Christ: **Which in his times he shall shew**, *who is* the blessed and only Potentate, **the King of kings**, and Lord of lords.

"I believe that lack of efficient personal work is one of the failures of the Church today. The people of the Church are like squirrels in a cage. Lots of activity, but accomplishing nothing. It doesn't require a Christian life to sell oyster soup or run a bazaar or a rummage sale…"

Billy Sunday   **"See 2 Timothy 4:1-5"**

63. **He is declared the "Beloved Son"** Psalm 2:7

I will declare the decree: the LORD hath said unto me, **Thou art my Son; this day have I begotten thee.**

Fulfillment: Matthew 3:17

And lo a voice from heaven, saying, **This is my beloved Son**, in whom I am well pleased.

64. **Life comes through faith in Him** Psalm 2:12

Kiss the Son, lest he be angry, and ye perish from the way, when his wrath is kindled but a little. **Blessed are all they that put their trust in him.**

Fulfillment: John 20:31

But these are written, that ye might believe that Jesus is the Christ, the Son of God; and that **believing ye might have life through his name.**

65. **The children praise would praise Him** Psalm 8:2

Out of the mouth of babes and sucklings hast thou ordained strength because of thine enemies, that thou mightest still the enemy and the avenger.

Fulfillment: Matthew 21:16

And said unto him, **Hearest thou what these say**? And Jesus saith unto them, Yea; have ye never read, **Out of the mouth of babes and sucklings thou hast perfected praise?**

66. **He would be humbled and made a little lower than the angels** Psalm 8:5

For thou hast made him a little lower than the angels, and hast crowned him with glory and honour.

Fulfillment: Matthew 11:29

Take my yoke upon you, and learn of me; **for I am meek and lowly in heart**: and ye shall find rest unto your souls.

Fulfillment: Matthew 21:5

Tell ye the daughter of Sion, Behold, **thy King cometh unto thee, meek**, and sitting upon an ass, and a colt the foal of an ass.

Fulfillment: Hebrews 2:9

But we see **Jesus, who was made a little lower than the angels** for the suffering of death, crowned with glory and honour; that he by the grace of God should taste death for every man.

"Neither Mary nor Caesar nor the Roman tax collectors did the *timing*, nor were they in charge of affairs; but the God who rules the world behind the scenes had His hand on the wheel, and He literally "moved the peoples of the world" and timed everything to the very day, so that Mary and Joseph got to Bethlehem in *the nick of time*, that Jesus, the chosen Messiah, might be born in the right place, the place designated by the infallible finger of prophecy."

Dr. F. J. Meldau **"See Luke 2:1-7"**

123

67. **He has put all things under Him** **Psalm 8:5-6**
For thou hast made him a little lower than the angels, and hast crowned him with glory and honour. **Thou madest him to have dominion over the works of thy hands; thou hast put all things under his feet.**
Fulfillment: Luke 24:50-53
And he led them out as far as to Bethany, and **he lifted up his hands, and blessed them. And it came to pass, while he blessed them, he was parted from them, and carried up into heaven.** And they worshipped him, and returned to Jerusalem with great joy: And were continually in the temple, praising and blessing God. Amen.
Fulfillment: 1 Corinthians 15:27
For he hath put all things under his feet. But when he saith all things are put under him, it is manifest that he is excepted, **which did put all things under him.**

68. **He was not to see corruption** **Psalm 16:10**
For thou wilt not leave my soul in hell; **neither wilt thou suffer thine Holy One to see corruption.**
Fulfillment: Acts 2:31
He seeing this before spake of the resurrection of Christ, **that his soul was not left in hell, neither his flesh did see corruption.**

69. **He would not remain in the grave** **Psalm 16:9-11**
Therefore my heart is glad, and my glory rejoiceth: my flesh also shall rest in hope. For **thou wilt not leave my soul in hell**; neither wilt thou suffer thine Holy One to see corruption. **Thou wilt shew me the path of life**: in thy presence is fulness of joy; at thy right hand there are pleasures for evermore.
Fulfillment: John 20:9
For as yet they knew not the scripture, that **he must rise again from the dead.**

70. **The resurrection predicted** **Psalm 17:15**
As for me, I will behold thy face in righteousness: **I shall be satisfied, when I awake, with thy likeness.**
Fulfillment: Luke 24:6-7
He is not here, but is risen: remember how he spake unto you when he was yet in Galilee, Saying, **The Son of man must be delivered into the hands of sinful men, and be crucified, and the third day rise again.**

Jesus' Three-Fold Title

"The Lord Jesus Christ"

Lord – This shows His Sovereign Diety
Jesus – This Shows His Humanity
Christ – This Declares him to be God's Annointed

71.   **He would be forsaken because of the sins of others**   **Psalm 22:1**
My God, my God, why hast thou forsaken me? Why art thou so far from helping me, and from the words of my roaring?
        Fulfillment: 2 Corinthians 5:21
For he hath made him to be sin for us, who knew no sin; that we might be made the righteousness of God in him.
        Fulfillment: Matthew 27:46
And about the ninth hour Jesus cried with a loud voice, saying, Eli, Eli, lama sabachthani? That is to say, **My God, my God, why hast thou forsaken me?**

72.   **Darkness upon Calvary**   **Psalm 22:2**
O my God, I cry in the daytime, but thou hearest not; and in the night season, and am not silent.
        Fulfillment: Matthew 27:45
Now from the sixth hour **there was darkness over all the land unto the ninth hour.**

73.   **They revile Him and shake their heads**   **Psalm 22:7**
All they that see me laugh me to scorn: **they shoot out the lip, they shake the head**.
        Fulfillment: Matthew 27:39-44
And they that passed by **reviled him, wagging their heads,** And saying, Thou that destroyest the temple, and buildest *it* in three days, save thyself. If thou be the Son of God, come down from the cross. **Likewise also the chief priests mocking *him*, with the scribes and elders**, said, He saved others; himself he cannot save. If he be the King of Israel, let him now come down from the cross, and we will believe him. He trusted in God; let him deliver him now, if he will have him: for he said, I am the Son of God. **The thieves also, which were crucified with him, cast the same in his teeth.**

74.   **"He trusted in God, let Him deliver Him"**   **Psalm 22:8**
He trusted on the LORD that he would deliver him: let him deliver him, seeing he delighted in him.
        Fulfillment: Matthew 27:43
He trusted in God; let him deliver him now, if he will have him: for he said, I am the Son of God.

75.   **He was born the Saviour**   **Psalm 22:9, 10**
But thou art he that **took me out of the womb**: thou didst make me hope when I was upon my mother's breasts. I was cast upon thee from the womb: **thou art my God from my mother's belly.**
        Fulfillment: Luke 2:7
And she **brought forth her firstborn son**, and wrapped him in swaddling clothes, and laid him in a manger; because there was no room for them in the inn.

"Scientists were rated as great heretics by the church, but they were truly religious men because of their faith in the orderliness of the universe."

Albert Einstein   **"See Romans 1:20"**

76. **He would be encircled by enemies mocking and reviling Him   Psalm 22:11-13**
Be not far from me; for trouble is near; for there is none to help. **Many bulls have compassed me: strong bulls of Bashan have beset me round. They gaped upon me with their mouths**, as a ravening and a roaring lion.
        Fulfillment: Matthew 27:41-44
Likewise also **the chief priests mocking him, with the scribes and elders**, said, He saved others; himself he cannot save. If he be the King of Israel, let him now come down from the cross, and we will believe him. He trusted in God; let him deliver him now, if he will have him: for he said, I am the Son of God. **The thieves also, which were crucified with him, cast the same in his teeth.**

77. **He died of a broken (ruptured) heart   Psalm 22:14**
I am poured out like water, and all my bones are out of joint: **my heart is like wax; it is melted in the midst of my bowels.**
        Fulfillment: John 19:34
But one of the soldiers with a **spear pierced his side, and forthwith came there out blood and water.**

78. **Suffering agony on Calvary   Psalm 22:14-15**
I am poured out like water, and **all my bones are out of joint**: my heart is like wax; it is melted in the midst of my bowels. **My strength is dried up like a potsherd; and my tongue cleaveth to my jaws;** and thou hast brought me into the dust of death.
        Fulfillment: Mark: 15:34-37
And at the ninth hour **Jesus cried with a loud voice, saying, Eloi, Eloi, lama sabachthani? Which is, being interpreted, My God, my God, why hast thou forsaken me?** And some of them that stood by, when they heard it, said, Behold, he calleth Elias. And one ran and filled a spunge full of vinegar, and put it on a reed, and gave him to drink, saying, Let alone; let us see whether Elias will come to take him down. And **Jesus cried with a loud voice**, and gave up the ghost.

79. **He would die by crucifixion   Psalm 22:14-16**
I am poured out like water, and all **my bones are out of joint**: my **heart is like wax**; it is melted in the midst of my bowels. My **strength is dried up** like a potsherd; and **my tongue cleaveth to my jaws;** and thou hast brought me into the dust of death. For dogs have compassed me: the assembly of the wicked have inclosed me: **they pierced my hands and my feet.**
        Fulfillment: Matthew 27:31
And after that they had mocked him, they took the robe off from him, and put his own raiment on him, and **led him away to crucify** *him.*
        Fulfillment: Mark 15:20, 25
And when they had mocked him, they took off the purple from him, and put his own clothes on him, and led him out to crucify him…And it was the third hour, and **they crucified him.**

"Beloved, we must win souls; we cannot live and see man damned."

Charles Spurgeon   **"See 2 Timothy 4:1-5"**

80.   **He thirsted**   **Psalm 22:15**
My strength is dried up like a potsherd; and **my tongue cleaveth to my jaws**; and thou
hast brought me into the dust of death.
         Fulfillment: John 19:28
After this, Jesus knowing that all things were now accomplished, **that the scripture
might be fulfilled, saith, I thirst.**

81.   **They pierced His hands and feet**   **Psalm 22:16**
For dogs have compassed me: the assembly of the wicked have enclosed me**: they
pierced my hands and my feet.**
         Fulfillment: John 19: 37
And again another scripture saith, **They shall look on him whom they pierced.**
         Fulfillment: John 20: 27
Then saith he to Thomas, **Reach hither thy finger, and behold my hands; and reach
hither thy hand, and thrust it into my side**: and be not faithless, but believing.

82.   **They stripped him before the stares of men**   **Psalm 22:17, 18**
I may tell all my bones: they look and stare upon me. They part my garments among
them, and cast lots upon my vesture.
         Fulfillment: Luke 23:34-35
Then said Jesus, Father, forgive them; for they know not what they do. **And they
parted his raiment, and cast lots. And the people stood beholding.** And the rulers
also with them derided him, saying, He saved others; let him save himself, if he be
Christ, the chosen of God.

83.   **They parted his Garments and cast lots upon His vesture**   **Psalm 22:18**
They part my garments among them, and cast lots upon my vesture.
         Fulfillment: John 19:23-24
Then the soldiers, when they had crucified Jesus, took his garments, and made four
parts, to every soldier a part; and also his coat: now the coat was without seam, woven
from the top throughout. They said therefore among themselves, Let us not rend it, but
cast lots for it, whose it shall be: that the scripture might be fulfilled, which saith, **They
parted my raiment among them, and for my vesture they did cast lots.** These things
therefore the soldiers did.

84.   **He committed Himself to God**   **Psalm 22:19-21**
But be not thou far from me, O LORD: **O my strength, haste thee to help me.** Deliver
my soul from the sword; my darling from the power of the dog. Save me from the lion's
mouth: for thou hast heard me from the horns of the unicorns.
         Fulfillment: Luke 23:46
And when Jesus had cried with a loud voice, he said, **Father, into thy hands I
commend my spirit:** and having said thus, he gave up the ghost.

"The root of joy is gratefulness…It is not joy that makes us grateful; it is gratitude
that makes us joyful."
David Steindl-Rast   **"See Psalm 95:1-3"**

85. **Satanic power bruising the Redeemer's heel**   **Psalm 22:20-21**
Deliver my soul from the sword; my darling from the power of the dog. **Save me from the lion's mouth**: for thou hast heard me from the horns of the unicorns.
     Fulfillment: Hebrews 2:14
Forasmuch then as the children are partakers of flesh and blood, he also himself likewise took part of the same; **that through death he might destroy him that had the power of death, that is, the devil.**

86. **His resurrection declared**   **Psalm 22:22-27**
I will declare thy name unto my brethren: in the midst of the congregation will I praise thee. Ye that fear the LORD, praise him; all ye the seed of Jacob, glorify him; and fear him, all ye the seed of Israel. **For he hath not despised nor abhorred the affliction of the afflicted; neither hath he hid his face from him; but when he cried unto him, he heard.** My praise shall be of thee in the great congregation: I will pay my vows before them that fear him. The meek shall eat and be satisfied: they shall praise the LORD that seek him: your heart shall live for ever. **All the ends of the world shall remember and turn unto the LORD**: and all the kindreds of the nations shall worship before thee.
     Fulfillment: John 20:17
Jesus saith unto her, Touch me not; for I am not yet ascended to my Father: but go to my brethren, and say unto them, **I ascend unto my Father, and your Father; and to my God, and your God.**

87. **He shall rule the Nations**   **Psalm 22:27-28**
All the ends of the world shall remember and turn unto the LORD: and all the kindreds of the nations shall worship before thee. **For the kingdom is the LORD'S**: and he is the governor among the nations.
     Fulfillment: Colossians 1:16
For by him were all things created, that are in heaven, and that are **in earth**, visible and invisible, whether they be **thrones**, or **dominions**, or **principalities**, or **powers**: **all things were created by him, and for him.**

88. **"It is Finished"**   **Psalm 22:31**
They shall come, and shall declare his righteousness unto a people that shall be born, **that he hath done this.**
     Fulfillment: John 19:30
When Jesus therefore had received the vinegar, he said, **It is finished**: and he bowed his head, and **gave up the ghost.**

"Christ said, 'I came into this world for one reason – to reach and save lost souls!' Yet, this was not only Jesus' mission. He made it our mission as well: 'And he said unto them, Go ye into all the world, and preach the gospel to every creature.'"

David Wilkerson   **"See Luke 19:10 & Mark 16:15"**

89. **"I am the Good Shepherd"**   **Psalm 23**
The LORD is my shepherd; I shall not want. He maketh me to lie down in green pastures: he leadeth me beside the still waters. He restoreth my soul: he leadeth me in the paths of righteousness for his name's sake. Yea, though I walk through the valley of the shadow of death, I will fear no evil: for thou art with me; thy rod and thy staff they comfort me. Thou preparest a table before me in the presence of mine enemies: thou anointest my head with oil; my cup runneth over. **Surely goodness and mercy shall follow me all the days of my life: and I will dwell in the house of the LORD forever.**
          Fulfillment: John 10:11
I am the good shepherd: the good shepherd giveth his life for the sheep.

90. **His exaltation predicted**   **Psalm 24:3**
Who shall **ascend into the hill of the LORD?** Or who shall **stand in his holy place?**
          Fulfillment: Acts 1:11
Which also said, Ye men of Galilee, why stand ye gazing up into heaven? This same Jesus, which is **taken up from you into heaven**, shall so come in like manner as ye have seen him go into heaven.
          Fulfillment: Philippians 2:9
Therefore **God also has highly exalted Him** and given Him the name which is above every name.

91. **He is good and upright**   **Psalm 25:8**
Good and upright *is* **the LORD**: therefore will he teach sinners in the way.
          Fulfillment: Matthew 19:16-17
And, behold, one came and said unto him, **Good Master**, what good thing shall I do, that I may have eternal life? 17And he said unto him, Why callest thou me good**? there is none good but one, that is, God:** but if thou wilt enter into life, keep the commandments.
          Fulfillment: Acts 10:38
How God anointed Jesus of Nazareth with the Holy Ghost and with power: **who went about doing good**, and healing all that were oppressed of the devil; for God was with him.

92. **His resurrection predicted**   **Psalm 30:3**
O LORD, thou hast brought up my soul from the grave: thou hast kept me alive, that I should not go down to the pit.
          Fulfillment: Acts 2:32
This Jesus hath God raised up, whereof we all are witnesses.

"God's Word is our primary weapon in evangelism. It is not designed to destroy life, but to give it. It is not to be used to harm but like a surgeon's scalpel, to save. Just as a builder knows his tools and an artist knows his brushes and pens, we need to know the Bible."

Greg Laurie   **"See Psalms 119:16"**

129

93. **His friends fled from Him** **Psalm 31:11**

I was a reproach among all mine enemies, but especially among my neighbours, and a fear to mine acquaintance: **they that did see me without fled from me.**
      Fulfillment: Mark 14:48-50
And Jesus answered and said unto them, Are ye come out, as against a thief, with swords and with staves to take me? I was daily with you in the temple teaching, and ye took me not: but the scriptures must be fulfilled. **And they all forsook him, and fled.**

94. **They took counsel to put Him to death** **Psalm 31:13**

For I have heard the slander of many: fear was on every side: **while they took counsel together against me, they devised to take away my life.**
      Fulfillment: John 11:53
Then from that day forth **they took counsel together for to put him to death.**

95. **Into Thy hands I commit my spirit** **Psalm 31:15**

My times are in thy hand: deliver me from the hand of mine enemies, and from them that persecute me.
      Fulfillment: Luke 23: 46
And when Jesus had cried with a loud voice, he said, **Father, into thy hands I commend my spirit**: and having said thus, he gave up the ghost.

96. **He trusted the Lord and said, Thou *art* my God** **Psalm 31:14-15**

But **I trusted in thee, O LORD**: I said, **Thou art my God.** My times are in thy hand: deliver me from the hand of mine enemies, and from them that persecute me.
      Fulfillment: Matthew 27:43
He trusted in God; let him deliver him now, if he will have him: for he said, I am the Son of God.

97. **There would be no guile in him** **Psalm 32:2**

Blessed *is* the man unto whom the LORD imputeth not iniquity, **and in whose spirit *there is* no guile.**
      Fulfillment: 1 Peter 2:21-24
For even hereunto were ye called: because Christ also suffered for us, leaving us an example, that ye should follow his steps: Who did no sin, **neither was guile found in his mouth**: Who, when he was reviled, reviled not again; when he suffered, he threatened not; but committed *himself* to him that judgeth righteously: Who his own self bare our sins in his own body on the tree, that we, being dead to sins, should live unto righteousness: by whose stripes ye were healed.

"There is no doctrine which I would more willingly remove from Christianity than the doctrine of hell, if it lay in my power. But it has the full support of Scripture and, especially, of our Lord's own words; it has always been held by the Christian Church, and it has the support of reason."

C.S. Lewis **"See Matthew 10:28"**

130

98.   **Not a bone would be broken**   **Psalm 34:20**
He keepeth all his bones: **not one of them is broken.**
            Fulfillment: John 19:31-36
The Jews therefore, because it was the preparation, that the bodies should not remain upon the cross on the sabbath day, (for that sabbath day was an high day,) besought Pilate that their legs might be broken, and that they might be taken away. Then came the soldiers, and brake the legs of the first, and of the other which was crucified with him. But when they came to Jesus, and saw that he was dead already, **they brake not his legs**: But one of the soldiers with a spear pierced his side, and forthwith came there out blood and water. And he that saw it bare record, and his record is true: and he knoweth that he saith true, that ye might believe. **For these things were done, that the scripture should be fulfilled, A bone of him shall not be broken.**

99.   **False witness rose up against Him**   **Psalm 35:11**
False witnesses did rise up; they laid to my charge things that I knew not.
            Fulfillment: Matthew 26:59-60
Now the chief priests, and elders, and all the council, **sought false witness against Jesus, to put him to death.** But found none: yea, though many **false witnesses** came, *yet* found they none. At the last came two **false witnesses.**

100.   **He was hated without cause**   **Psalm 35:19**
Let not them that are mine enemies wrongfully rejoice over me: neither let them wink with the eye that **hate me without a cause.**
            Fulfillment: John 15:25
But this cometh to pass, that the word might be fulfilled that is written in their law, **They hated me without a cause.**

101.   **His friends stood afar off**   **Psalm 38:11**
My lovers and my friends stand aloof from my sore; and **my kinsmen stand afar off.**
            Fulfillment: Luke 23:49
And all his acquaintance, and the women that followed him from Galilee, **stood afar off, beholding these things.**

"Our Lord needs no secret agents! Those who are not willing to confess Christ publicly are not willing to confess Christ. Perhaps acceptance of Christ begins as a very personal and private experience, but it can never stay that way."

Guy Rice Doud, *Joy in the Journey*   **"See Luke 12:8"**

102. **He would be accused but say nothing in His defense** Psalm 38:12-14

They also that seek after my life lay snares *for me*: and **they that seek my hurt speak mischievous things, and imagine deceits** all the day long. But I, as a deaf *man*, heard not; and *I was* **as a dumb man** *that* **openeth not his mouth**. Thus I was as a man that heareth not, and **in whose mouth** *are* **no reproofs.**

Fulfillment: Matthew 27:12-14

And when he was accused of the chief priests and elders, **he answered nothing.** Then said Pilate unto him, Hearest thou not how many things they witness against thee? **And he answered him to never a word;** insomuch that the governor marvelled greatly.

Fulfillment: 1 Peter 2:23

Who, **when he was reviled, reviled not again;** when he suffered, he threatened not; but committed *himself* to him that judgeth righteously.

103. **The joy of His resurrection** Psalm 40:2-5

He brought me up also out of an horrible pit, out of the miry clay, and set my feet upon a rock, and established my goings. **And he hath put a new song in my mouth, even praise unto our God:** many shall see it, and fear, and shall trust in the LORD. Blessed is that man that maketh the LORD his trust, and respecteth not the proud, nor such as turn aside to lies. Many, **O LORD my God, are thy wonderful works which thou hast done,** and thy thoughts which are to us-ward: they cannot be reckoned up in order unto thee: if I would declare and speak of them, they are more than can be numbered.

Fulfillment: John 20:20

And when he had so said, he shewed unto them his hands and his side. **Then were the disciples glad, when they saw the Lord.**

104. **He will delight in the will of the Father** Psalm 40:6-8

Sacrifice and offering thou didst not desire; mine ears hast thou opened: burnt offering and sin offering hast thou not required. Then said I, Lo, I come: in the volume of the book it is written of me, **I delight to do thy will, O my God:** yea, thy law is within my heart.

Fulfillment: John 8:29

And He who sent Me is with Me. The Father has not left Me alone, **for I always do those things that please Him.**

Fulfillment: John 4:34

Jesus said to them, **"My food is to do the will of Him who sent Me,** and to finish His work.

"The vast majority of people who are members of churches in America today are not Christians. I say that without the slightest fear of contradiction. I base it on empirical evidence of twenty-four years of examining thousands of people."

Dr. D. James Kennedy **"See Matthew 25:12"**

105. **He was to preach the righteousness in Israel**   **Psalm 40:9-10**
I have preached righteousness in the great congregation: lo, I have not refrained my lips, O LORD, thou knowest. I have not hid thy righteousness within my heart; I have declared thy faithfulness and thy salvation: **I have not concealed thy loving kindness and thy truth from the great congregation.**
        Fulfillment: Matthew 4:17
From that time **Jesus began to preach, and to say, Repent: for the kingdom of heaven is at hand.**

106. **He was confronted by adversaries and drove them backwards**   **Psalm 40:14**
Let them be ashamed and confounded together **that seek after my soul to destroy it; let them be driven backward** and put to shame that wish me evil.
        Fulfillment: Matthew 26:47-56
And while he yet spake, lo, Judas, one of the twelve, **came, and with him a great multitude with swords and staves, from the chief priests and elders of the people.** Now he that betrayed him gave them a sign, saying, Whomsoever I shall kiss, that same is he: hold him fast. And forthwith he came to Jesus, and said, Hail, master; and kissed him. And Jesus said unto him, Friend, wherefore art thou come? Then came they, and laid hands on Jesus, and took him. And, behold, one of them which were with Jesus stretched out *his* hand, and drew his sword, and struck a servant of the high priest's, and smote off his ear. Then said Jesus unto him, Put up again thy sword into his place: for all they that take the sword shall perish with the sword. Thinkest thou that I cannot now pray to my Father, and he shall presently give me more than twelve legions of angels? But how then shall the scriptures be fulfilled, that thus it must be? In that same hour said Jesus to the multitudes, Are ye come out as against a thief with swords and staves for to take me? I sat daily with you teaching in the temple, and ye laid no hold on me. **But all this was done, that the scriptures of the prophets might be fulfilled.** Then all the disciples forsook him, and fled.
        Fulfillment: John 18:4-6
Jesus therefore, knowing all things that should come upon him, went forth, and said unto them, Whom seek ye? They answered him, Jesus of Nazareth. Jesus saith unto them, I am he. And Judas also, which betrayed him, stood with them. As soon then as he had said unto them, I am he, **they went backward, and fell to the ground.**

107. **He was betrayed by a friend**   **Psalm 41:9**
Yea, mine own familiar friend, in whom I trusted, which did eat of my bread, hath lifted up his heel against me.
        Fulfillment: John 13:18
I speak not of you all: I know whom I have chosen: but that the scripture may be fulfilled, **He that eateth bread with me hath lifted up his heel against me.**

"Heaven doesn't rejoice over those who make 'decisions.' It reserves its rejoicing for sinners who repent."

Ray Comfort   **"See Luke 15:10"**

133

108.   **Words of grace would come from His lips**   **Psalm 45:2**
Thou art fairer than the children of men: **grace is poured into thy lips**: therefore God hath blessed thee for ever.
        Fulfillment: Luke 4:22
And all bare him witness, and wondered at the **gracious words which proceeded out of his mouth.** And they said, Is not this Joseph's son?

109.   **To own the title, God or Elohim**   **Psalm 45:6**
Thy throne, O God, is for ever and ever: the sceptre of thy kingdom is a right sceptre.
        Fulfillment: Hebrews 1:8
But unto the Son he saith, **Thy throne, O God, is for ever and ever**: a sceptre of righteousness is the sceptre of thy kingdom.

110.   **A special anointing by the Holy Spirit**   **Psalm 45:7**
Thou lovest righteousness, and hatest wickedness: therefore God, **thy God, hath anointed thee** with the oil of gladness above thy fellows.
        Fulfillment: Matthew 3:16
And Jesus, when he was baptized, went up straightway out of the water: and, lo, **the heavens were opened unto him**, and he saw **the Spirit of God descending like a dove, and lighting upon him.**
        Fulfillment: Luke 4:18
The Spirit of the Lord *is* upon me, because **he hath anointed me** to preach the gospel to the poor; he hath sent me to heal the brokenhearted, to preach deliverance to the captives, and recovering of sight to the blind, to set at liberty them that are bruised.
        Fulfillment: Hebrews 1:9
Thou hast loved righteousness, and hated iniquity; therefore God, even thy **God, hath anointed thee** with the oil of gladness above thy fellows.

111.   **He would be betrayed by a Friend**   **Psalm 55:12-14**
For it was not an enemy that reproached me; then I could have borne it: neither was it he that hated me that did magnify himself against me; then I would have hid myself from him: **But it was thou, a man mine equal, my guide, and mine acquaintance. We took sweet counsel together, and walked unto the house of God in company.**
        Fulfillment: John 13:18
I speak not of you all: I know whom I have chosen: but that the scripture may be fulfilled, **He that eateth bread with me hath lifted up his heel against me.**

"Prayer is the open admission that without Christ we can do nothing. And prayer is the turning away from ourselves to God in the confidence that He will provide the help we need. Prayer humbles us as needy and exhalts God as all-sufficient."

John Piper   **"See Luke 11:2"**

134

112. **Death of the betrayer** Psalm 55:15

Let death seize upon them, and let them go down quick into hell: **for wickedness is in their dwellings, and among them.**

Fulfillment: Matthew 27:3-5

Then Judas, which had betrayed him, when he saw that he was condemned, repented himself, and brought again the thirty pieces of silver to the chief priests and elders, Saying, I have sinned in that I have betrayed the innocent blood. And they said, What is that to us? See thou to that. And he cast down the pieces of silver in the temple, and departed, **and went and hanged himself.**

Fulfillment: Acts 1:16-19

Men and brethren, this scripture must needs have been fulfilled, which the Holy Ghost by the mouth of David spake before concerning Judas, which was guide to them that took Jesus. For he was numbered with us, and had obtained part of this ministry. **Now this man purchased a field with the reward of iniquity; and falling headlong, he burst asunder in the midst, and all his bowels gushed out.** And it was known unto all the dwellers at Jerusalem; insomuch as that field is called in their proper tongue, Aceldama, that is to say, The field of blood.

113. **He would give gifts to men** Psalm 68:18

Thou hast ascended on high, thou hast led captivity captive: **thou hast received gifts for men;** yea, for the rebellious also, that the LORD God might dwell among them.

Fulfillment: Ephesians 4:7-16

But unto every one of us is given grace according to the measure of the gift of Christ. Wherefore he saith, When he ascended up on high, he led captivity captive, **and gave gifts unto men.** (Now that he ascended, what is it but that he also descended first into the lower parts of the earth? He that descended is the same also that ascended up far above all heavens, that he might fill all things.) **And he gave some, apostles; and some, prophets; and some, evangelists; and some, pastors and teachers; For the perfecting of the saints, for the work of the ministry,** for the edifying of the body of Christ: Till we all come in the unity of the faith, and of the knowledge of the Son of God, unto a perfect man, unto the measure of the stature of the fulness of Christ: That we henceforth be no more children, tossed to and fro, and carried about with every wind of doctrine, by the sleight of men, and cunning craftiness, whereby they lie in wait to deceive; But speaking the truth in love, may grow up into him in all things, which is the head, even Christ: From whom the whole body fitly joined together and compacted by that which every joint supplieth, according to the effectual working in the measure of every part, maketh increase of the body unto the edifying of itself in love.

"Preach with this object, that men may quit their sins and fly to Christ for pardon, that by the Blessed spirit they may be renovated and become as much in love with everything that is holy as they are now in love with everything that is sinful."

Charles Spurgeon **"See 2 Timothy 2:24-26"**

114. **He ascended into Heaven** Psalm 68:18

Thou hast ascended on high, thou hast led captivity captive: thou hast received gifts for men; yea, for the rebellious also, that the LORD God might dwell among them.

Fulfillment: **Luke 24:51**

And it came to pass, while he blessed them, he was parted from them, **and carried up into heaven.**

Fulfillment: **Acts 1:9**

And when he had spoken these things, while they beheld, **he was taken up; and a cloud received him out of their sight.**

115. **He was hated without cause** Psalm 69:4

They that hate me without a cause are more than the hairs of mine head: they that would destroy me, being mine enemies wrongfully, are mighty: then I restored that which I took not away.

Fulfillment: **John 15:24-25**

If I had not done among them the works which none other man did, they had not had sin: **but now have they both seen and hated both me and my Father**. But this cometh to pass, that the word might be fulfilled that is written in their law, **They hated me without a cause.**

116. **He was rejected by His own brothers** Psalm 69:8

I am become a stranger unto my brethren, and an alien unto my mother's children.

Fulfillment: **Luke 8:20-21**

And it was told him by certain which said, **Thy mother and thy brethren stand without,** desiring to see thee. And he answered and said unto them, **My mother and my brethren are these which hear the word of God, and do it.**

Fulfillment: **John 7:1-5**

After these things Jesus walked in Galilee: for he would not walk in Jewry, because the Jews sought to kill him. Now the Jews' feast of tabernacles was at hand. **His brethren therefore said unto him, Depart hence, and go into Judaea**, that thy disciples also may see the works that thou doest. For *there is* no man *that* doeth any thing in secret, and he himself seeketh to be known openly. If thou do these things, shew thyself to the world. **For neither did his brethren believe in him.**

"The idea that the service to God should have only to do with a church altar, singing, reading, sacrifice, and the like is without doubt but the worst trick of the devil. How could the devil have led us more effectively astray than by the narrow conception that service to God takes place only in a church and by the works done therein...The whole world could abound with the services to the Lord, Gottesdienste - not only in churches but also in the home, kitchen, workshop, field."

Martin Luther **"See Matthew 24:14"**

117.　**He would be zealous for the Lord's House**　　　　　　　　　　**Psalm 69:9**
For the zeal of thine house hath eaten me up; and the reproaches of them that reproached thee are fallen upon me.
　　　　Fulfillment:　John 2:13-17
And the Jews' passover was at hand, and Jesus went up to Jerusalem, And found in the temple those that sold oxen and sheep and doves, and the changers of money sitting: And when he had made a scourge of small cords, he drove them all out of the temple, and the sheep, and the oxen; and poured out the changers' money, and overthrew the tables; And said unto them that sold doves, Take these things hence; make not my Father's house an house of merchandise. And his disciples remembered that it was written, **The zeal of thine house hath eaten me up.**

118.　**The Messiah's anguish of soul before crucifixion**　　　　**Psalm 69:14-20**
Deliver me out of the mire, and let me not sink: let me be delivered from them that hate me, and out of the deep waters. Let not the water flood overflow me, neither let the deep swallow me up, and let not the pit shut her mouth upon me. Hear me, O LORD; for thy lovingkindness is good: turn unto me according to the multitude of thy tender mercies. And hide not thy face from thy servant; for I am in trouble: hear me speedily. Draw nigh unto my soul, and redeem it: deliver me because of mine enemies. Thou hast known my reproach, and my shame, and my dishonour: mine adversaries are all before thee. **Reproach hath broken my heart; and I am full of heaviness:** and I looked for some to take pity, but there was none; and for comforters, but I found none.
　　　　Fulfillment:　Matthew 26:36-45
Then cometh Jesus with them unto a place called Gethsemane, and saith unto the disciples, Sit ye here, while I go and pray yonder. And he took with him Peter and the two sons of Zebedee, **and began to be sorrowful and very heavy. Then saith he unto them, My soul is exceeding sorrowful, even unto death: tarry ye here, and watch with me.** And he went a little further, and fell on his face, and prayed, saying, **O my Father, if it be possible, let this cup pass from me: nevertheless not as I will, but as thou wilt.** And he cometh unto the disciples, and findeth them asleep, and saith unto Peter, What, could ye not watch with me one hour? Watch and pray, that ye enter not into temptation: the spirit indeed is willing, but the flesh is weak. He went away again the second time, and prayed, saying, **O my Father, if this cup may not pass away from me, except I drink it, thy will be done.** And he came and found them asleep again: for their eyes were heavy. And he left them, and went away again, and prayed the third time, saying the same words. Then cometh he to his disciples, and saith unto them, Sleep on now, and take your rest: behold, the hour is at hand, and the Son of man is betrayed into the hands of sinners.

"A watchful eye must be kept on ourselves lest, while we are building great monuments of renown and bliss here, we neglect to have our names enrolled in the annals of Heaven."

James Madison　　　　　　　　　　　　　　　　　　　　**"See Luke 9:25"**

119. **He was given vinegar and gall** Psalm 69:21
They gave me also gall for my meat; and in my thirst they gave me **vinegar to drink.**
        Fulfillment: Matthew 27:34
They gave him vinegar to drink mingled with gall: and when he had tasted thereof, he would not drink.
        Fulfillment: John 19:28-30
After this, Jesus knowing that all things were now accomplished, that the scripture might be fulfilled, saith, I thirst. Now there was set a vessel full of vinegar: and **they filled a spunge with vinegar, and put *it* upon hyssop, and put *it* to his mouth**. When Jesus therefore had received the vinegar, he said, It is finished: and he bowed his head, and gave up the ghost.

120. **The Saviour given and smitten by God** Psalm 69:26
For they **persecute him whom thou hast smitten; and they talk to the grief of those whom thou hast wounded.**
        Fulfillment: John 17:4
I have glorified thee on the earth: **I have finished the work which thou gavest me to do.**
        Fulfillment: John 18:11
Then said Jesus unto Peter, Put up thy sword into the sheath: **the cup which my Father hath given me, shall I not drink it?**

Weigh the Evidence

"Love God with the whole heart. Three children were watching a new television set their father had just purchased for them. When their dad arrived home, they didn't even get up and greet him at the door. Instead, they were watching TV. The father walked over to it, turned it off and said, "Kids, I purchased that television set because I love you and want you to be happy. But if it comes between you and your love for me, I am going to sell it, because you are loving the gift more than the giver. If we love anything more than God (our mother, father, brother, sister, spouse, children, job, sports, or even our own life), we are loving the gift more than the Giver. This is called 'inordinate affection.' **To love anything more than we love God is to transgress the First Commandment.**"

Ray Comfort **"See Luke 10:27"**

121. **His Kingdom would have dominion over all the earth**   **Psalm 72:8**
He shall have dominion also from sea to sea, and from the river **unto the ends of the earth.**
                Fulfillment: Luke 1:33
And he shall reign over the house of Jacob for ever; and of **his kingdom there shall be no end.**
                Fulfillment: Hebrews 1:8
But unto the Son *he saith*, **Thy throne, O God,** *is* **for ever and ever: a sceptre of righteousness** *is* **the sceptre of thy kingdom.**
                Fulfillment: Revelation 11:15, 17
And the seventh angel sounded; and there were great voices in heaven, saying, **The kingdoms of this world are become** *the kingdoms* **of our Lord, and of his Christ;** and he shall reign for ever and ever…Saying, We give thee thanks, O Lord God Almighty, which art, and wast, and art to come; **because thou hast taken to thee thy great power, and hast reigned.**

122. **Great persons were to visit Him and give Him gifts**   **Psalm 72:10-11**
The kings of Tarshish and of the isles **shall bring presents**: the kings of Sheba and Seba **shall offer gifts**. Yea, **all kings shall fall down before him: all nations shall serve him.**
                Fulfillment: Matthew 2:1-11
Now when Jesus was born in Bethlehem of Judaea in the days of Herod the king, behold, **there came wise men from the east to Jerusalem, Saying, Where is he that is born King of the Jews**? For we have seen his star in the east, and are come to worship him. When Herod the king had heard these things, he was troubled, and all Jerusalem with him. And when he had gathered all the chief priests and scribes of the people together, he demanded of them where Christ should be born. And they said unto him, In Bethlehem of Judaea: for thus it is written by the prophet, And thou Bethlehem, in the land of Juda, art not the least among the princes of Juda: for out of thee shall come a Governor, that shall rule my people Israel. Then Herod, when he had privily called the wise men, enquired of them diligently what time the star appeared. And he sent them to Bethlehem, and said, Go and search diligently for the young child; and when ye have found him, bring me word again, that I may come and worship him also. When they had heard the king, they departed; and, lo, the star, which they saw in the east, went before them, till it came and stood over where the young child was. When they saw the star, they rejoiced with exceeding great joy. And when they were come into the house, they saw the young child with Mary his mother, **and fell down, and worshipped him: and when they had opened their treasures, they presented unto him gifts; gold, and frankincense, and myrrh.**

"The greatest enemy to human souls is the self-righteous spirit which makes men look to themselves for salvation."

Charles Spurgeon   **"See Titus 2:11-14"**

123. **The corn and wheat shall flourish** Psalm 72:16

There shall be an handful of corn in the earth upon the top of the mountains; the fruit thereof shall shake like Lebanon: and **they of the city shall flourish like grass of the earth.**

   Fulfillment: John 12:24

Verily, verily, I say unto you, Except a corn of wheat fall into the ground and die, it abideth alone: but if it die, **it bringeth forth much fruit.** "Most assuredly, I say to you, unless a grain of wheat falls into the ground and dies, it remains alone; but if it dies, **it produces much grain.**

124. **His name shall endure and be called blessed** Psalm 72:19

And blessed be his glorious name for ever: and let the whole earth be filled with his glory.

   Fulfillment: Luke 1:48

For he hath regarded the low estate of his handmaiden: for, behold, from henceforth **all generations shall call me blessed.**

   Fulfillment: Philippians 2:9

Wherefore God also hath highly exalted him, and **given him a name which is above every name.**

125. **He would teach in parables** Psalm 78:1-2

Give ear, O my people, to my law: incline your ears to the words of my mouth. **I will open my mouth in a parable**: I will utter dark sayings of old.

   Fulfillment: Matthew 13:34-35

All these things spake Jesus unto the multitude in parables; and **without a parable spake he not unto them**: That it might be fulfilled which was spoken by the prophet, saying, I will open my mouth in parables; I will utter things which have been kept secret from the foundation of the world.

126. **He would speak the wisdom of God with authority** Psalm 78:1-4

Give ear, O my people, to my law: incline your ears to the words of my mouth. I will open my mouth in a parable: **I will utter dark sayings of old**: Which we have heard and known, and our fathers have told us. **We will not hide them from their children, shewing to the generation to come the praises of the LORD, and his strength, and his wonderful works that he hath done.**

   Fulfillment: Matthew 7:29

For he taught them as one **having authority**, and not as the scribes.

God's Law Does The Following:

1. Converts the soul **2.** Makes wise the simple **3.** Makes the heart rejoice **4.** Enlightens the eyes **5.** Produces the fear of the Lord **6.** Reveals God's true and righteous judgement **7.** Is more to be desired than gold **8.** Is sweeter than honey **9.** Warns us of God's wrath **10.** Provides a great reward

127.   **He would be full of compassion**   **Psalm 78:38**
But he, *being* **full of compassion**, forgave *their* iniquity, and destroyed *them* not: yea, many a time turned he his anger away, and did not stir up all his wrath.
          Fulfillment: Matthew 9:36
But when he saw the multitudes, **he was moved with compassion** on them, because they fainted, and were scattered abroad, as sheep having no shepherd.
          Fulfillment: Matthew 15:32
Then Jesus called his disciples *unto him*, and said, **I have compassion** on the multitude, because they continue with me now three days, and have nothing to eat: and I will not send them away fasting, lest they faint in the way.
          Fulfillment: Mark 5:19
Howbeit Jesus suffered him not, but saith unto him, Go home to thy friends, and tell them how great things the Lord hath done for thee, and hath **had compassion on thee.**

128.   **The Lord is good**   **Psalm 86:5**
          Fulfillment: Matthew 19:16-17
And, behold, one came and said unto him, Good Master, what good thing shall I do, that I may have eternal life? And he said unto him, **Why callest thou me good?** *there is* **none good but one,** *that is,* **God:** but if thou wilt enter into life, keep the commandments.
          Fulfillment: Acts 10:38
How God anointed Jesus of Nazareth with the Holy Ghost and with power: **who went about doing good,** and healing all that were oppressed of the devil; for God was with him.

129.   **They stood afar off and watched**   **Psalm 88:8**
Thou hast put away mine acquaintance far from me; thou hast made me an abomination unto them: I am shut up, and I cannot come forth.
          Fulfillment: Luke 23:49
And all his acquaintance, and the women that followed him from Galilee, **stood afar off, beholding these things.**

130.   **Emmanuel to be higher than earthly kings**   **Psalm 89:27**
Also I will make him my firstborn, **higher than the kings of the earth.**
          Fulfillment: Luke 1:32-33
He shall be great, and shall be **called the Son of the Highest**: and the Lord God shall give unto him the throne of his father David: And he shall reign over the house of Jacob for ever; **and of his kingdom there shall be no end.**

"The world tells you, you can't confront people with Jesus; you'll run them off. Where are you going to run them off too? Hell number two?"

Darrell Robinson   **"See Jude 23"**

131. **David's seed, throne, kingdom would endure forever**   **Psalm 89:35-37**
Once have I sworn by my holiness that I will not lie unto David. **His seed shall endure for ever**, and his throne as the sun before me. It shall be established for ever as the moon, and as a faithful witness in heaven. Selah.
    Fulfillment: Luke 1:32-33
He shall be great, and shall be called the Son of the Highest: and the Lord God shall give unto him the throne of his father David: And he shall reign over the house of Jacob for ever; **and of his kingdom there shall be no end.**

132.   **He is a Faithful witness**   **Psalm 89:36-37**
His seed shall endure for ever, and his throne as the sun before me. It shall be established for ever as the moon, **and as a faithful witness in heaven**. Selah.
    Fulfillment: Revelation 1:5
And from **Jesus Christ, who is the faithful witness**, and the first begotten of the dead, and the prince of the kings of the earth. Unto him that loved us, and washed us from our sins in his own blood.
    Fulfillment: Revelation 3:14
And unto the angel of the church of the Laodiceans write; These things saith the Amen, **the faithful and true witness**, the beginning of the creation of God.

The Pre-existence of Jesus

"For I came down from heaven, not to do mine own will, but the will of him that sent me."
John 6:38

"Jesus said unto them, If God were your Father, ye would love me: for **I proceeded forth and came from God**; neither came I of myself, but he sent me."
John 8:42

"And he said unto them, Ye are from beneath; **I am from above**:
ye are of this world; **I am not of this world."**
John 8:23

"And now, O Father, glorify thou me with thine own self with the glory **which I had with thee before the world was."**
John 17:5

142

133.   **He is from everlasting**   **Psalm 90:2**

Before the mountains were brought forth, or ever thou hadst formed the earth and the world, even **from everlasting to everlasting, thou art God.**

     Fulfillment: John 1:1-4

In the beginning was the Word, and the Word was with God, and the Word was God. The same was in the beginning with God. All things were made by him; and without him was not any thing made that was made. **In him was life; and the life was the light of men.**

134.   **Angels would have charge over Him used to tempt Christ**   **Psalm 91:11, 12**

For he shall give his angels charge over thee, to keep thee in all thy ways. They shall bear thee up in their hands, lest thou dash thy foot against a stone.

     Fulfillment: Luke 4:10-11

For it is written, **He shall give his angels charge over thee**, to keep thee: And in their hands they shall bear thee up, lest at any time thou dash thy foot against a stone.

134.   **His exaltation was predicted**   **Psalm 97:9**

For thou, LORD, art high above all the earth: thou art exalted far above all gods.

     Fulfillment: Acts 1:11

Which also said, Ye men of Galilee, why stand ye gazing up into heaven? **This same Jesus**, which is taken up from you into heaven, **shall so come in like manner as ye have seen him go into heaven.**

     Fulfillment: Ephesians 1:20

Which he wrought in Christ, when he raised him from the dead, **and set *him* at his own right hand in the heavenly *places*.**

135.   **His character is Goodness**   **Psalm 100:5**

For the LORD is good; his mercy is everlasting; and his truth endureth to all generations.

     Fulfillment: Matthew 19:16-17

And, behold, one came and said unto him, **Good Master**, what good thing shall I do, that I may have eternal life? And he said unto him, Why callest thou me good? **There is none good but one, that is, God:** but if thou wilt enter into life, keep the commandments.

"There must be true and deep conviction of sin. This the preacher must labor to produce, for where this is not felt, the new birth has not taken place."

Charles Spurgeon   **"See 2 Corinthians 7:9-10"**

136. **The Suffering and Reproach of Calvary**   Psalm 102:1-11

Hear my prayer, O LORD, and let my cry come unto thee. Hide not thy face from me in the day when I am in trouble; incline thine ear unto me: in the day when I call answer me speedily. For my days are consumed like smoke, and my bones are burned as an hearth. **My heart is smitten, and withered like grass;** so that I forget to eat my bread. **By reason of the voice of my groaning my bones cleave to my skin.** I am like a pelican of the wilderness: I am like an owl of the desert. I watch, and am as a sparrow alone upon the house top. **Mine enemies reproach me all the day;** and they that are mad against me are sworn against me. For I have eaten ashes like bread, and mingled my drink with weeping, Because of thine indignation and thy wrath: for thou hast lifted me up, and cast me down. My days are like a shadow that declineth; and I am withered like grass.

Fulfillment: John 19:16-30

Then delivered he him therefore unto them to be crucified. And they took Jesus, and led him away. And he bearing his cross went forth into a place called the place of a skull, which is called in the Hebrew Golgotha: Where they crucified him, and two other with him, on either side one, and Jesus in the midst. And Pilate wrote a title, and put it on the cross. And the writing was, **JESUS OF NAZARETH THE KING OF THE JEWS.** This title then read many of the Jews: for the place where Jesus was crucified was nigh to the city: and it was written in Hebrew, and Greek, and Latin. Then said the chief priests of the Jews to Pilate, Write not, The King of the Jews; but that he said, I am King of the Jews. Pilate answered, What I have written I have written. Then the soldiers, when they had crucified Jesus, took his garments, and made four parts, to every soldier a part; and also his coat: now the coat was without seam, woven from the top throughout. They said therefore among themselves, Let us not rend it, but cast lots for it, whose it shall be: that the scripture might be fulfilled, which saith, They parted my raiment among them, and for my vesture they did cast lots. These things therefore the soldiers did.

Now there stood by the cross of Jesus his mother, and his mother's sister, Mary the wife of Cleophas, and Mary Magdalene. When Jesus therefore saw his mother, and the disciple standing by, whom he loved, he saith unto his mother, Woman, behold thy son! Then saith he to the disciple, Behold thy mother! And from that hour that disciple took her unto his own home. After this, Jesus knowing that all things were now accomplished, that the scripture might be fulfilled, saith, I thirst. Now there was set a vessel full of vinegar: and they filled a spunge with vinegar, and put it upon hyssop, and put it to his mouth. When Jesus therefore had received the vinegar, he said, It is finished: and he bowed his head, and gave up the ghost.

"Tolerance is a virtue for those who have no convictions."

G.K. Chesterton   **"See Ephesians 6:11-20"**

137.   **The Messiah is the preexistent Son**   **Psalm 102:25-27**
Of old hast thou laid the foundation of the earth: and the heavens are the work of thy hands. They shall perish, but thou shalt endure: yea, all of them shall wax old like a garment; as a vesture shalt thou change them, and they shall be changed: **But thou art the same, and thy years shall have no end.**
        Fulfillment: Hebrews 1:10-12
And, Thou, Lord, in the beginning hast laid the foundation of the earth; and the heavens are the works of thine hands: They shall perish; but thou remainest; and they all shall wax old as doth a garment; And as a vesture shalt thou fold them up, and they shall be changed: but **thou art the same, and thy years shall not fail.**

138.   **He will send the Spirit of God**   **Psalm 104:30**
Thou sendest forth thy spirit, they are created: and thou renewest the face of the earth.
        Fulfillment: John 16:7
Nevertheless I tell you the truth; It is expedient for you that I go away: for if I go not away, the Comforter will not come unto you; but if I depart, **I will send him unto you.**

139.   **He would calm the storm**   **Psalm 107:29**
He maketh the storm a calm, so that the waves thereof are still.
        Fulfillment: Matthew 8:23-27
And when he was entered into a ship, his disciples followed him. And, behold, there arose a great tempest in the sea, insomuch that the ship was covered with the waves: but he was asleep. And his disciples came to him, and awoke him, saying, Lord, save us: we perish. And he saith unto them, Why are ye fearful, O ye of little faith? **Then he arose, and rebuked the winds and the sea; and there was a great calm.** But the men marvelled, saying, **What manner of man is this, that even the winds and the sea obey him!**

140.   **He would be accused by false witnesses**   **Psalm 109:2**
For the mouth of the wicked and the mouth of the deceitful are opened against me: they have spoken against me with a lying tongue.
        Fulfillment: Matthew 26:59-60
Now the chief priests, and elders, and all the council, **sought false witness against Jesus**, to put him to death; But found none: yea, though **many false witnesses came**, *yet* found they none. **At the last came two false witnesses.**

141.   **He would pray for His persecutors**   **Psalm 109:4**
For my love they are my adversaries: **but I *give myself unto* prayer.**
        Fulfillment: Luke 23:34
Then said Jesus, Father, forgive them; for they know not what they do. And they parted his raiment, and cast lots.

"The fool hath said in his heart, *There is* no God."

Psalm 53:1

142.   **He would be the object of ridicule**   **Psalm 109:25**
I became also a reproach unto them: when they looked upon me they shaked their heads.
        Fulfillment: Matthew 27:39
And they **that passed by reviled him,** wagging their heads.

143.   **He would be the Son of David and be called Lord**   **Psalm 110:1**
The LORD said unto my Lord, Sit thou at my right hand, until I make thine enemies thy footstool.
        Fulfillment: Matthew 22:43-45
He saith unto them, How then doth David in spirit call him Lord, saying, The LORD said unto my Lord, Sit thou on my right hand, till I make thine enemies thy footstool? **If David then call him Lord, how is he his son?**

144.   **He would ascend to the right-hand of the Father**   **Psalm 110:1**
The LORD said unto my Lord, **Sit thou at my right hand**, until I make thine enemies thy footstool.
        Fulfillment: Mark 16:19
So then after the Lord had spoken unto them, he was received up into heaven, and **sat on the right hand of God.**

145.   **A priest after Melchizedeks's order**   **Psalm 110:4**
The LORD hath sworn, and will not repent, **Thou art a priest for ever after the order of Melchizedek.**
        Fulfillment: Hebrews 6:20
Whither the forerunner is for us entered, even Jesus, **made an high priest for ever after the order of Melchisedec.**

146.   **His character is Compassionate**   **Psalm 112:4**
Unto the upright there ariseth light in the darkness: he is gracious, and **full of compassion**, and righteous.
        Fulfillment: Matthew 9:36
But when he saw the multitudes, he was **moved with compassion** on them, because they fainted, and were scattered abroad, as sheep having no shepherd.

"If you were given $1,000 every time you witnessed to someone, would you be more zealous in your evangelism? If so, you are serving money rather than God."

Ray Comfort   **"See Luke 16:13"**

146

147. **The Messiah's Resurrection is assured** Psalm 118:17-18

I shall not die, but live, and declare the works of the LORD. The LORD hath chastened me sore: **but he hath not given me over unto death.**

Fulfillment: Luke 24:5-7

And as they were afraid, and bowed down their faces to the earth, they said unto them, Why seek ye the living among the dead? He is not here, but is risen: remember how he spake unto you when he was yet in Galilee, Saying, **The Son of man must be delivered into the hands of sinful men, and be crucified, and the third day rise again.**

Fulfillment: 1 Corinthians 15:20

But now is Christ risen from the dead, and become the first fruits of them that slept.

God promised to preserve His Word

"The words of the LORD *are* pure words: *as* silver tried in a furnace of earth, purified seven times. Thou shalt keep them, O LORD, **thou shalt preserve them from this generation for ever."**

Psalm 12:6

"The grass withereth, the flower fadeth: but **the word of our God shall stand for ever."**

Isaiah 40:8

"Heaven and earth shall pass away: but **my words shall not pass away."**
Mark 13:31

"For verily I say unto you, Till heaven and earth pass, **one jot or one tittle shall in no wise pass from the law, till all be fulfilled."**
Matthew 5:18

"And it is easier for heaven and earth to pass, **than one tittle of the law to fail."**
Luke 16:17

"Being born again, not of corruptible seed, but of incorruptible, by **the word of God, which liveth and abideth for ever."**
1 Peter 1:23

The King James Bible is the perfect, pure Word that God promised to preserve. Don't be fooled by devilish counterfeits!
L.B.K.

147

148. **The rejected stone is the Head of the corner** **Psalm 118:22-23**
The stone which the builders refused is become the head stone of the corner. This is the LORD'S doing; it is marvellous in our eyes.
      Fulfillment: Matthew 21:42-43
Jesus saith unto them, Did ye never read in the scriptures, **The stone which the builders rejected, the same is become the head of the corner:** this is the Lord's doing, and it is marvellous in our eyes? Therefore say I unto you, The kingdom of God shall be taken from you, and given to a nation bringing forth the fruits thereof.

149. **The Blessed One presented to Israel** **Psalm 118:26a**
Blessed be he that cometh in the name of the LORD: we have blessed you out of the house of the LORD.
      Fulfillment: Matthew 21:9
And the multitudes that went before, and that followed, cried, saying, Hosanna to the Son of David: **Blessed is he that cometh in the name of the Lord;** Hosanna in the highest.

150. **He would come while the Temple was still standing** **Psalm 118:26b**
Blessed be he that cometh in the name of the LORD: **we have blessed you out of the house of the LORD.**
      Fulfillment: Matthew 21:12-15
And Jesus went into the temple of God, and **cast out all them that sold and bought in the temple,** and overthrew the tables of the moneychangers, and the seats of them that sold doves, And said unto them, It is written, **My house shall be called the house of prayer;** but ye have made it a den of thieves. And the blind and the lame came to him in the temple; and he healed them. And when the chief priests and scribes saw the wonderful things that he did, and the children crying in the temple, and saying, Hosanna to the Son of David; they were sore displeased.

151. **His testimony is wonderful** **Psalm 119:129**
Thy testimonies *are* wonderful: therefore doth my soul keep them.
      Psalm 139:6
Such knowledge *is* **too wonderful for me;** it is high, I cannot *attain* unto it.
      Fulfillment: Luke 4:22
And all bare him witness, and **wondered at the gracious words which proceeded out of his mouth.** And they said, Is not this Joseph's son?

152. **The Seed of David (the fruit of His body)** **Psalm 132:11**
The LORD hath sworn in truth unto David; he will not turn from it; **Of the fruit of thy body** will I set upon thy throne.
      Fulfillment: Luke 1:32
He shall be great, and shall be called the Son of the Highest: and **the Lord God shall give unto him the throne of his father David.**

"He who kneels the most stands best."
D.L. Moody **"See Matthew 23:12"**

153.   **The supremacy of David's Seed amazes kings**   **Psalm 138:1-6**
I will praise thee with my whole heart: before the gods will I sing praise unto thee. I will worship toward thy holy temple, and praise thy name for thy lovingkindness and for thy truth: for thou hast magnified thy word above all thy name. In the day when I cried thou answeredst me, and strengthenedst me with strength in my soul. **All the kings of the earth shall praise thee, O LORD,** when they hear the words of thy mouth. Yea, they shall sing in the ways of the LORD: for great is the glory of the LORD.

        Fulfillment: Matthew 2:2-6
Saying, **Where is he that is born King of the Jews? For we have seen his star in the east, and are come to worship him.** When Herod the king had heard these things, he was troubled, and all Jerusalem with him. And when he had gathered all the chief priests and scribes of the people together, he demanded of them where Christ should be born. And they said unto him, In Bethlehem of Judaea: for thus it is written by the prophet, And thou Bethlehem, in the land of Juda, art not the least among the princes of Juda: **for out of thee shall come a Governor, that shall rule my people Israel.**

154.   **The Lord is good to all**   **Psalm 145:9**
The LORD *is* **good to all**: and his tender mercies *are* over all his works.
        Fulfillment: Acts 10:38
How God anointed **Jesus of Nazareth** with the Holy Ghost and with power: **who went about doing good, and healing all that were oppressed of the devil**; for God was with him.

155.   **Christ's earthly ministry described**   **Psalm 147:3-6**
He healeth the broken in heart, and bindeth up their wounds…The LORD lifteth up the meek: he casteth the wicked down to the ground.
        Fulfillment: Luke 4:18-19
The Spirit of the Lord is upon me, because he hath anointed me to **preach the gospel to the poor;** he hath **sent me to heal the brokenhearted, to preach deliverance to the captives, and recovering of sight to the blind, to set at liberty them that are bruised, To preach the acceptable year of the Lord.**

"He who masters his passions is a king even while in chains. He who is ruled by his passions is a slave even while sitting on a throne."

Richard Wurmbrand   **"See Proverbs 16:32"**

PROVERBS

This is the 20th book of the Bible, written approximately 970 B.C. – 930 B.C. It was written in Jerusalem and Solomon is credited with 25 to 29 chapters. It has 31 chapters.

156.   **He will send the Spirit of God**   **Proverbs 1:23**

Turn you at my reproof: behold, **I will pour out my spirit unto you,** I will make known my words unto you.

Fulfillment: John 16:7-13

Nevertheless I tell you the truth; It is expedient for you that I go away: for if I go not away, the Comforter will not come unto you; but if I depart, **I will send him unto you.** And when he is come, he will reprove the world of sin, and of righteousness, and of judgment: Of sin, because they believe not on me; Of righteousness, because I go to my Father, and ye see me no more; Of judgment, because the prince of this world is judged. I have yet many things to say unto you, but ye cannot bear them now. Howbeit when he, **the Spirit of truth,** is come, he will guide you into all truth: for he shall not speak of himself; but whatsoever he shall hear, *that* shall he speak: and he will shew you things to come.

Fulfillment: Acts 2:4, 17-18

And they were all filled with the Holy Ghost, and began to speak with other tongues, as the Spirit gave them utterance. And it shall come to pass in the last days, saith God, **I will pour out of my Spirit upon all flesh:** and your sons and your daughters shall prophesy, and your young men shall see visions, and your old men shall dream dreams: And on my servants and on my handmaidens **I will pour out in those days of my Spirit;** and they shall prophesy.

SONG OF SOLOMON

This is the 22nd book of the Bible, written approximately 962 B.C. – 922 B.C. Song of Solomon covers 962 B.C. and was written in Jerusalem, probably by Solomon. It has 8 chapters.

156.   **The altogether lovely One**   **Song of Solomon 5:16**

His mouth *is* most sweet: yea, **he *is* altogether lovely.** This *is* my beloved, and this *is* my friend, O daughters of Jerusalem.

Fulfillment: John 1:17

For the law was given by Moses, ***but* grace and truth came by Jesus Christ.**

"Live as though Christ died yesterday, rose from the grave today, and is coming back tomorrow."

Theodore Epp   **"See Matthew 24:44"**

ISAIAH

This is the 23rd book of the Bible, written approximately 750 B.C. – 680 B.C. Isaiah covers between the fall of Lucifer and about 539 B.C. Isaiah was probably written in Jerusalem by Isaiah, who was eventually martyred by being sawed asunder. It has 66 chapters.

157.   **When Isaiah saw His glory, Parables fall on deaf ears**   **Isaiah 6:1, 9-10**

In the year that king Uzziah died I saw also **the Lord sitting upon a throne,** high and lifted up, and his train filled the temple…And he said, Go, and tell this people, Hear ye indeed, but understand not; and see ye indeed, but perceive not. Make the heart of this people fat, **and make their ears heavy,** and shut their eyes; lest they see with their eyes, and hear with their ears, and understand with their heart, and convert, and be healed.

            Fulfillment: John 12:40-41

He hath **blinded their eyes, and hardened their heart;** that they should not see with their eyes, nor understand with their heart, and be converted, and I should heal them. These things said Esaias, when he saw his glory, and spake of him.

"Forty" is the prominent probation number in Scripture. A Study of it can help our understanding as to why Christ would choose to spend "forty" days on earth after His resurrection and not more or less. These are just some of the examples of the use of "Forty days" in the Bible.

Forty days	Noah witnessed the flood destroying the fallen earth. **Genesis 7:12, 17**
Forty days	Moses was on the Mount after the sin of the people worshipping the Golden Calf. **Deuteronomy 9:18, 25**
Forty days	The spies of Israel were in the promised land, Israel's rejection resulted in 40 years (a year for a day) of wandering in the wilderness. **Numbers 13:25, 14:34**
Forty days	Elijah spent in Horeb **1 Kings 19:8**
Forty days	Jonah and Nineveh. **Jonah 3:4**
Forty days	Ezekial lay on his right side to symbolize the forty years of Judah's transgression. **Ezekial 4:6**
Forty days	Jesus was in the wilderness being temped of the devil. **Matthew 4:2**
Forty days	Jesus showed Himself alive and taught His disciples the things pertaining to the Kingdom of God. **Acts 1:3**

158. **They are blinded to Christ and deaf to His words** Isaiah 6:9-12

And he said, **Go, and tell this people, Hear ye indeed, but understand not; and see ye indeed, but perceive not. Make the heart of this people fat, and make their ears heavy, and shut their eyes; lest they see with their eyes, and hear with their ears, and understand with their heart,** and convert, and be healed. Then said I, Lord, how long? And he answered, Until the cities be wasted without inhabitant, and the houses without man, and the land be utterly desolate, And the LORD have removed men far away, and there be a great forsaking in the midst of the land.

Fulfillment: Acts 28:23-29

And when they had appointed him a day, there came many to him into his lodging; to whom he expounded and testified the kingdom of God, persuading them concerning Jesus, both out of the law of Moses, and out of the prophets, from morning till evening. And some believed the things which were spoken, and some believed not. And when **they agreed not among themselves,** they departed, after that Paul had spoken one word. Well spake the Holy Ghost by Esaias the prophet unto our fathers, Saying, Go unto this people, and say, **Hearing ye shall hear, and shall not understand; and seeing ye shall see, and not perceive: For the heart of this people is waxed gross, and their ears are dull of hearing, and their eyes have they closed;** lest they should see with their eyes, and hear with their ears, and understand with their heart, and should be converted, and I should heal them. Be it known therefore unto you, that the salvation of God is sent unto the Gentiles, and that they will hear it. And when he had said these words, the Jews departed, and had great reasoning among themselves.

Fulfillment: Matthew 13:14-15

And in them is fulfilled the prophecy of Esaias, which saith, **By hearing ye shall hear, and shall not understand; and seeing ye shall see, and shall not perceive**: **For this people's heart is waxed gross, and** *their* **ears are dull of hearing, and their eyes they have closed;** lest at any time they should see with *their* eyes, and hear with *their* ears, and should understand with *their* heart, and should be converted, and I should heal them.

159. **He would be born of a virgin** Isaiah 7:14

Therefore the Lord himself shall give you a sign; **Behold, a virgin shall conceive, and bear a son,** and shall call his name Immanuel.

Fulfillment: Matthew 1:22-23

Now all this was done, that it might be fulfilled which was spoken of the Lord by the prophet, saying, **Behold, a virgin shall be with child, and shall bring forth a son,** and they shall call his name Emmanuel, which being interpreted is, God with us.

Fulfillment: Luke 1:34-35

Then said Mary unto the angel, **How shall this be, seeing I know not a man?** And the angel answered and said unto her, The Holy Ghost shall come upon thee, and the power of the Highest shall overshadow thee: therefore also **that holy thing which shall be born of thee shall be called the Son of God.**

"The grass withereth, the flower fadeth: but the word of our God shall stand for ever."

Isaiah 40:8

160. **He would be Emmanuel-God with us** Isaiah 7:14

Therefore the Lord himself shall give you a sign; Behold, a virgin shall conceive, and bear a son, and shall **call his name Immanuel.**

Fulfillment: Matthew 1:18-23

Now the birth of Jesus Christ was on this wise: When as his mother Mary was espoused to Joseph, before they came together, **she was found with child of the Holy Ghost.** Then Joseph her husband, being a just man, and not willing to make her a publick example, was minded to put her away privily. But while he thought on these things, behold, the angel of the Lord appeared unto him in a dream, saying, Joseph, thou son of David, fear not to take unto thee Mary thy wife: for that which is conceived in her is of the Holy Ghost. And she shall bring forth a son, and thou shalt call his name JESUS: for he shall save his people from their sins. Now all this was done, that it might be fulfilled which was spoken of the Lord by the prophet, saying, **Behold, a virgin shall be with child, and shall bring forth a son, and they shall call his name Emmanuel, which being interpreted is, God with us.**

161. **He shall pass through Judah and reach all nations** Isaiah 8:8

And he shall pass through Judah; he shall overflow and go over, he shall reach even to the neck; and the stretching out of his wings **shall fill the breadth of thy land,** O Immanuel.

Fulfillment: Matthew 28:18-20

And Jesus came and spake unto them, saying, **All power is given unto me in heaven and in earth. Go ye therefore, and teach all nations, baptizing them in the name of the Father, and of the Son, and of the Holy Ghost:** Teaching them to observe all things whatsoever I have commanded you: and, lo, I am with you I, even unto the end of the world. Amen.

162. **He shall be a stumbling stone, a rock of offence, Israel would reject Him**

Isaiah 8:14

And he shall be for a sanctuary; **but for a stone of stumbling** and for a **rock of offence** to both the houses of Israel, for a gin and for a snare to the inhabitants of Jerusalem.

Fulfillment: 1 Peter 2:8

And **a stone of stumbling, and a rock of offence,** even to them which stumble at the word, being disobedient: whereunto also they were appointed.

He is the Way, the Truth, and the Life

Matthew says,	"Behold your king"
Mark says,	"Behold the man"
Luke says,	"Behold my servant"
John says,	"Behold your God"

163. **His ministry would begin in Galilee** Isaiah 9:1-2

Nevertheless the dimness shall not be such as was in her vexation, when at the first he lightly afflicted the land of **Zebulun and the land of Naphtali,** and afterward did more grievously afflict her by the way of the sea, beyond Jordan, **in Galilee of the nations**. **The people that walked in darkness have seen a great light:** they that dwell in the land of the shadow of death, upon them hath the light shined.

Fulfillment: Matthew 4:12-17

Now when Jesus had heard that John was cast into prison, he departed into Galilee; And leaving Nazareth, he came and dwelt in Capernaum, which is upon the sea coast, in the borders of **Zabulon and Nephthalim:** That it might be fulfilled which was spoken by Esaias the prophet, saying, **The land of Zabulon, and the land of Nephthalim,** by the way of the sea, beyond Jordan, **Galilee of the Gentiles;** The people which sat in darkness saw great light; and to them which sat in the region and shadow of death light is sprung up. **From that time Jesus began to preach, and to say, Repent: for the kingdom of heaven is at hand.**

164. **A child is born, given Humanity** Isaiah 9:6

For unto us a child is born, unto us a son is given: and the government shall be upon his shoulder: and **his name shall be called Wonderful, Counsellor, The mighty God, The everlasting Father, The Prince of Peace.**

Fulfillment: Luke 1:31

And, behold, thou shalt **conceive in thy womb, and bring forth a son,** and shalt call his name JESUS.

165. **A Son given – Deity** Isaiah 9:6

For unto us a child is born, unto us a son is given: and the government shall be upon his shoulder: and **his name shall be called Wonderful, Counsellor, The mighty God, The everlasting Father, The Prince of Peace.**

Fulfillment: Mark 1:1

The beginning of the gospel of **Jesus Christ, the Son of God.**

Fulfillment: Luke 1:32

He shall be great, and shall be called the Son of the Highest: and the Lord God shall give unto him the throne of his father David.

Fulfillment: Luke 2:7

And she brought forth her firstborn son, and wrapped him in swaddling clothes, and laid him in a manger; because there was no room for them in the inn.

Fulfillment: John 1:14

And the **Word was made flesh, and dwelt among us,** (and we beheld his glory, the glory as of the only begotten of the Father,) full of grace and truth.

Fulfillment: 1 Timothy 3:16

And without controversy great is the mystery of godliness: **God was manifest in the flesh,** justified in the Spirit, seen of angels, preached unto the Gentiles, believed on in the world, received up into glory.

"What health is to the heart, holiness is to the soul."

John Flavel **"See 3 John 2"**

166. **The Wonderful One** Isaiah 9:6
For unto us a child is born, unto us a son is given: and the government shall be upon his shoulder: **and his name shall be called Wonderful, Counsellor,** The mighty God, The everlasting Father, The Prince of Peace.
Fulfillment: Matthew 21:15
And when the chief priests and scribes saw **the wonderful things that he did,** and the children crying in the temple, and saying, Hosanna to the Son of David; they were sore displeased.
Fulfillment: Luke 4:22
And all bare him witness, and **wondered at the gracious words which proceeded out of his mouth.** And they said, Is not this Joseph's son?

167. **The Everlasting Father** Isaiah 9:6
For unto us a child is born, unto us a son is given: and the government shall be upon his shoulder: and his name shall be called Wonderful, Counsellor, The mighty God, **The everlasting Father,** The Prince of Peace.
Fulfillment: John 8:58
Jesus said unto them, Verily, verily, I say unto you, **Before Abraham was, I am.**

168. **The Prince of Peace** Isaiah 9:6
For unto us a child is born, unto us a son is given: and the government shall be upon his shoulder: **and his name shall be** called Wonderful, Counsellor, The mighty God, The everlasting Father, **The Prince of Peace.**
Fulfillment: John 16:33
These things I have spoken unto you, **that in me ye might have peace.** In the world ye shall have tribulation: but be of good cheer; I have overcome the world.

169. **He would be a Counselor manifesting perfect wisdom** Isaiah 9:6
For unto us a child is born, unto us a son is given: and the government shall be upon his shoulder: **and his name shall be called Wonderful, Counsellor,** The mighty God, The everlasting Father, The Prince of Peace.
Fulfillment: Matthew 13:54
And when he was come into his own country, **he taught them in their synagogue, insomuch that they were astonished, and said, Whence hath this *man* this wisdom,** and *these* mighty works?
Fulfillment: Ephesians 1:11
In whom also we have obtained an inheritance, **being predestinated according to the purpose of him who worketh all things after the counsel of his own will.**
Fulfillment: Hebrews 6:17
Wherein God, willing more abundantly to shew unto the heirs of promise **the immutability of his counsel,** confirmed *it* by an oath.

"Holy practice is the most decisive evidence of the reality of our repentance."

Jonathan Edwards **"See James 2:26"**

170. **He is the mighty God** Isaiah 9:6

For unto us a child is born, unto us a son is given: and the government shall be upon his shoulder: **and his name shall be** called Wonderful, Counsellor, **The mighty God,** The everlasting Father, The Prince of Peace.

Fulfillment: Matthew 3:11

I indeed baptize you with water unto repentance: **but he that cometh after me is mightier than I,** whose shoes I am not worthy to bear: he shall baptize you with the Holy Ghost, and *with* fire.

Fulfillment: Matthew 28:18

And Jesus came and spake unto them, saying, **All power is given unto me in heaven and in earth.**

Fulfillment: Luke 19:37

And when he was come nigh, even now at the descent of the mount of Olives, the whole multitude of **the disciples began to rejoice and praise God with a loud voice for all the mighty works that they had seen.**

171. **He will establish an everlasting Kingdom** Isaiah 9:7

Of the increase of **his government and peace there shall be no end**, **upon the throne of David, and upon his kingdom,** to order it, and to establish it with judgment and with justice from henceforth even for ever. The zeal of the LORD of hosts will perform this.

Fulfillment: Luke 1:32-33

He shall be great, and shall be called the Son of the Highest: and the Lord God shall give unto him the throne of his father David: And he shall reign over the house of Jacob for ever; and of **his kingdom there shall be no end.**

172. **His Character is Just** Isaiah 9:7

Of the increase of his government and peace there shall be no end, upon the throne of David, and upon his kingdom, to order it, and **to establish it with judgment and with justice from henceforth even for ever.** The zeal of the LORD of hosts will perform this.

Fulfillment: John 5:30

I can of mine own self do nothing: as I hear, **I judge: and my judgment is just;** because I seek not mine own will, but the will of the Father which hath sent me.

173. **There will be no end to His Government** Isaiah 9:7

Of the increase of his government and peace there shall be no end, upon the throne of David, and upon his kingdom, to order it, and to establish it with judgment and with justice from henceforth even for ever. The zeal of the LORD of hosts will perform this.

Fulfillment: Luke 1:32-33

He shall be great, and shall be called the Son of the Highest: and the Lord God shall give unto him the throne of his father David: And he shall reign over the house of Jacob for ever; and of **his kingdom there shall be no end.**

"Heaven and earth shall pass away: but my words shall not pass away."
Mark 13:31

174. **He is called a Nazarene – the Branch**   Isaiah 11:1

And there shall come forth a rod out of the stem of Jesse, and **a Branch shall grow out of his roots.**

> Fulfillment: Matthew 2:23

And he came and dwelt in a city called Nazareth: that **it might be fulfilled which was spoken by the prophets, He shall be called a Nazarene.**

175. **A rod out of Jesse - Son of Jesse**   Isaiah 11:1

And there shall come forth a **rod out of the stem of Jesse,** and a Branch shall grow out of his roots.

> Fulfillment: Luke 3:23-38

And Jesus himself began to be about thirty years of age, being (as was supposed) the son of Joseph, which was *the son* of Heli, [24] Which was *the son* of Matthat, which was *the son* of Levi, which was *the son* of Melchi, which was *the son* of Janna, which was *the son* of Joseph, [25] Which was *the son* of Mattathias, which was *the son* of Amos, which was *the son* of Naum, which was *the son* of Esli, which was *the son* of Nagge, [26] Which was *the son* of Maath, which was *the son* of Mattathias, which was *the son* of Semei, which was *the son* of Joseph, which was *the son* of Juda, [27] Which was *the son* of Joanna, which was *the son* of Rhesa, which was *the son* of Zorobabel, which was *the son* of Salathiel, which was *the son* of Neri, [28] Which was *the son* of Melchi, which was *the son* of Addi, which was *the son* of Cosam, which was *the son* of Elmodam, which was *the son* of Er, [29] Which was *the son* of Jose, which was *the son* of Eliezer, which was *the son* of Jorim, which was *the son* of Matthat, which was *the son* of Levi, [30] Which was *the son* of Simeon, which was *the son* of Juda, which was *the son* of Joseph, which was *the son* of Jonan, which was *the son* of Eliakim, [31] Which was *the son* of Melea, which was *the son* of Menan, which was *the son* of Mattatha, which was *the son* of Nathan,

which was *the son* of David, [32] Which was ***the son*** **of Jesse,** which was *the son* of Obed, which was *the son* of Booz, which was *the son* of Salmon, which was *the son* of Naasson, [33] Which was *the son* of Aminadab, which was *the son* of Aram, which was *the son* of Esrom, which was *the son* of Phares, which was *the son* of Juda, [34] Which was *the son* of Jacob, which was *the son* of Isaac, which was *the son* of Abraham, which was *the son* of Thara, which was *the son* of Nachor, [35] Which was *the son* of Saruch, which was *the son* of Ragau, which was *the son* of Phalec, which was *the son* of Heber, which was *the son* of Sala, [36] Which was *the son* of Cainan, which was *the son* of Arphaxad, which was *the son* of Sem, which was *the son* of Noe, which was *the son* of Lamech, [37] Which was *the son* of Mathusala, which was *the son* of Enoch, which was *the son* of Jared, which was *the son* of Maleleel, which was *the son* of Cainan, [38] Which was *the son* of Enos, which was *the son* of Seth, which was *the son* of Adam, which was *the son* of God.

176. **The Spirit of the Lord shall rest upon Him**   Isaiah 11:1-2

And there shall come forth a rod out of the stem of Jesse, and a Branch shall grow out of his roots: **And the spirit of the LORD shall rest upon him,** the spirit of wisdom and understanding, the spirit of counsel and might, the spirit of knowledge and of the fear of the LORD.

> Fulfillment: Matthew 3:16

And Jesus, when he was baptized, went up straightway out of the water: and, lo, the heavens were opened unto him, and **he saw the Spirit of God descending like a dove, and lighting upon him.**

> Fulfillment: Luke 4:18

The Spirit of the Lord is upon me, because he hath anointed me to preach the gospel to the poor; he hath sent me to heal the brokenhearted, to preach deliverance to the captives, and recovering of sight to the blind, to set at liberty them that are bruised.

"We have grasped the mystery of the atom and rejected the Sermon on the Mount...The world has achieved brilliance without conscience. Ours is a world of nuclear giants and ethical infants."

General Omar Bradley   **"See Matthew 5:1-12"**

157

177. **He is the anointed One by the Spirit**   **Isaiah 11:2**
And the spirit of the LORD shall rest upon him, the spirit of wisdom and understanding, the spirit of counsel and might, the spirit of knowledge and of the fear of the LORD.

Fulfillment: Luke 4:18-19
The Spirit of the Lord is upon me, because he hath anointed me to preach the gospel to the poor; he hath sent me to heal the brokenhearted, to preach deliverance to the captives, and recovering of sight to the blind, to set at liberty them that are bruised, To preach the acceptable year of the Lord.

178. **His Character is Wisdom and Understanding**   **Isaiah 11:2**
And the spirit of the LORD shall rest upon him, **the spirit of wisdom and understanding,** the spirit of counsel and might, the spirit of knowledge and of the fear of the LORD.

Fulfillment: John 4:4-26
And he must needs go through Samaria. Then cometh he to a city of Samaria, which is called Sychar, near to the parcel of ground that Jacob gave to his son Joseph. Now Jacob's well was there. Jesus therefore, being wearied with his journey, sat thus on the well: and it was about the sixth hour. There cometh a woman of Samaria to draw water: **Jesus saith unto her, Give me to drink**. (For his disciples were gone away unto the city to buy meat.) Then saith the woman of Samaria unto him, **How is it that thou, being a Jew, askest drink of me, which am a woman of Samaria? For the Jews have no dealings with the Samaritans. Jesus answered and said unto her, If thou knewest the gift of God, and who it is that saith to thee, Give me to drink; thou wouldest have asked of him, and he would have given thee living water. The woman saith unto him, Sir, thou hast nothing to draw with, and the well is deep: from whence then hast thou that living water?** Art thou greater than our father Jacob, which gave us the well, and drank thereof himself, and his children, and his cattle? **Jesus answered and said unto her, Whosoever drinketh of this water shall thirst again: But whosoever drinketh of the water that I shall give him shall never thirst; but the water that I shall give him shall be in him a well of water springing up into everlasting life.** The woman saith unto him, Sir, give me this water, that I thirst not, neither come hither to draw. Jesus saith unto her, Go, call thy husband, and come hither. **The woman answered and said, I have no husband. Jesus said unto her, Thou hast well said, I have no husband: For thou hast had five husbands; and he whom thou now hast is not thy husband: in that saidst thou truly. The woman saith unto him, Sir, I perceive that thou art a prophet.** Our fathers worshipped in this mountain; and ye say, that in Jerusalem is the place where men ought to worship. Jesus saith unto her, Woman, believe me, the hour cometh, when ye shall neither in this mountain, nor yet at Jerusalem, worship the Father. Ye worship ye know not what: we know what we worship: for salvation is of the Jews. But the hour cometh, and now is, when the true worshippers shall worship the Father in spirit and in truth: for the Father seeketh such to worship him. God is a Spirit: and they that worship him must worship him in spirit and in truth. **The woman saith unto him, I know that Messiah cometh, which is called Christ: when he is come, he will tell us all things. Jesus saith unto her, I that speak unto thee am he.**

179. **His Character is Truth** Isaiah 11:4

But **with righteousness shall he judge the poor,** and reprove with equity for the meek of the earth: and he shall smite the earth with the rod of his mouth, and with the breath of his lips shall he slay the wicked.

Fulfillment: John 14:6

Jesus saith unto him, I am the way, **the truth,** and the life: no man cometh unto the Father, but by me.

180. **He shall be faithful** Isaiah 11:5

And righteousness shall be the girdle of his loins, and **faithfulness the girdle of his reins.**

Fulfillment: 1 Thessalonians 5:23-24

And the very God of peace sanctify you wholly; and *I pray God* your whole spirit and soul and body be preserved blameless unto the coming of our Lord Jesus Christ. **Faithful *is* he that calleth you, who also will do *it*.**

Fulfillment: 2 Timothy 2:13

If we believe not, *yet* **he abideth faithful:** he cannot deny himself.

Fulfillment: Revelations 1:5

And from Jesus Christ, *who is* **the faithful witness,** *and* the first begotten of the dead, and the prince of the kings of the earth. Unto him that loved us, and washed us from our sins in his own blood.

181. **The Gentiles will seek Him** Isaiah 11:10

And in that day there shall be a root of Jesse, which shall stand for an ensign of the people; to it **shall the Gentiles seek:** and his rest shall be glorious.

Fulfillment: John 12:18-21

For this cause the people also met him, for that they heard that he had done this miracle. The Pharisees therefore said among themselves, Perceive ye how ye prevail nothing? Behold, the world is gone after him. And there were certain **Greeks among them that came up to worship** at the feast: The same came therefore to Philip, which was of Bethsaida of Galilee, and desired him, saying, Sir, we would see Jesus.

Fulfillment: Mathew 12:18-21

Behold my servant, whom I have chosen; my beloved, in whom my soul is well pleased: I will put my spirit upon him, and **he shall shew judgment to the Gentiles**. He shall not strive, nor cry; neither shall any man hear his voice in the streets. A bruised reed shall he not break, and smoking flax shall he not quench, till he send forth judgment unto victory. **And in his name shall the Gentiles trust.**

"The foundations of our society and our government rest so much on the teachings of the Bible that it would be difficult to support them if faith in these teachings would cease to be practically universal in our country."

Calvin Coolidge   **"See Psalms 67:4"**

182. **From the root and stump of Jesse**   Isaiah 11:1-5
And there shall come forth a rod out of the stem of Jesse, and a Branch shall grow out of his roots: And the spirit of the LORD shall rest upon him, the spirit of wisdom and understanding, the spirit of counsel and might, the spirit of knowledge and of the fear of the LORD; And shall make him of quick understanding in the fear of the LORD: and he shall not judge after the sight of his eyes, neither reprove after the hearing of his ears: But with righteousness shall he judge the poor, and reprove with equity for the meek of the earth: and he shall smite the earth with the rod of his mouth, and with the breath of his lips shall he slay the wicked. And righteousness shall be the girdle of his loins, and faithfulness the girdle of his reins.

                                                                            Isaiah 11:10
And in that day there shall be a root of Jesse, which shall stand for an ensign of the people; to it shall the Gentiles seek: and his rest shall be glorious.
      Fulfillment: Romans 15:12
And again, Esaias saith, **There shall be a root of Jesse,** and he that shall rise to reign over the Gentiles; in him shall the Gentiles trust.
      Fulfillment: Matthew 1:1-2a, 5-6, 16
The book of the generation of Jesus Christ, the **son of David,** the son of Abraham. Abraham begat Isaac; and Isaac begat Jacob; and Jacob begat Judas and his brethren... And Salmon begat Booz of Rachab; and Booz begat Obed of Ruth; and Obed begat Jesse; And **Jesse begat David** the king; and David the king begat Solomon of her that had been the wife of Urias... And Jacob begat Joseph the husband of Mary, of **whom was born Jesus, who is called Christ.**

183. **He would come from the house of David**   Isaiah 16:5
And in mercy shall the throne be established: **and he shall sit upon it in truth in the tabernacle of David,** judging, and seeking judgment, and hasting righteousness.
      Fulfillment: Matthew 1:1-2a, 5-6, 16
The book of the generation of Jesus Christ, the **son of David**, the son of Abraham. Abraham begat Isaac; and Isaac begat Jacob; and Jacob begat Judas and his brethren... And Salmon begat Booz of Rachab; and Booz begat Obed of Ruth; and Obed begat Jesse; **And Jesse begat David** the king; and David the king begat Solomon of her that had been the wife of Urias...And Jacob begat Joseph the husband of Mary, of **whom was born Jesus, who is called Christ.**

184. **The Resurrection predicted**   Isaiah 25:8
He will swallow up death in victory; and the Lord GOD will wipe away tears from off all faces; and the rebuke of his people shall he take away from off all the earth: for the LORD hath spoken it.
      Fulfillment: 1 Corinthians 15:54
So when **this corruptible shall have put on incorruption,** and this mortal shall have put on immortality, then shall be brought to pass the saying that is written, **Death is swallowed up in victory.**

We are born in iniquity, we have received a sin nature, that causes us to transgress the Commandments of God. And you ask, "Why do we need a Savior?"

L.B.K.   **"See 1 John 3:4"**

160

185. **His power of Resurrection predicted** Isaiah 26:19

Thy dead men shall live, together with my dead body shall they arise. Awake and sing, ye that dwell in dust: for thy dew is as the dew of herbs, **and the earth shall cast out the dead.**

Fulfillment: John 11:43-44

And when he thus had spoken, he cried with a loud voice, Lazarus, come forth. **And he that was dead came forth,** bound hand and foot with grave clothes: and his face was bound about with a napkin. Jesus saith unto them, Loose him, and let him go.

How to use the Ten Commandments in Witnessing
This should be done in the spirit of love and gentleness

"Do you think you have kept the Ten Commandments? Have you ever told a lie (including "white lies," half truths, exaggerations, etc.)? If you have, then you are a "liar,' and you cannot enter the kingdom of God. Have you ever stolen (the value is irrelevant)? Then you are a thief. Jesus said that if you look with lust, you have committed adultery in your heart. If you hate someone, then you have committed murder in your heart. God requires truth "in the inward parts" – He sees even the thought-life.

Have you loved God above all else? Has He always been first in your affections? Have you made a "god" to suit yourself (having your own beliefs about God)? That is called idolatry, and the Bible warns that no idolater will enter the kingdom of God. Have you ever used God's holy name to curse, or been greedy? Have you kept the Sabbath holy? Have you always implicitly honored your parents? Have you broken any of the Ten Commandments?

Knowing that God has seen your thought-life and every deed done in darkness, will you be innocent or guilty on Judgment Day? You know you will be guilty. So, will you end up in heaven or hell?

The Law brings individuals to a point of seeing that they have sinned against God, that His wrath abides on them. It causes them to see their mouth of justification (Romans 3:19), and prepares the heart for the good news of the gospel.

The only thing you can do to be saved from His wrath is to repent and put your faith in the Savior, Jesus Christ. When He died on the cross, He took the punishment for our sins. He, once and for all, stepped into the Courtroom and completely paid the fine for us. Then He rose from the dead, defeating death. If you want to be saved from God's wrath, confess and forsake your sins, put your faith in Jesus for your eternal salvation, and you will pass from death into life. Then read the Bible daily and obey what you read (see John 14:21). God will never let you down."

Ray Comfort **"See Psalms 51:6"**

161

186. **The Messiah is the precious corner stone** Isaiah 28:16
Therefore thus saith the Lord GOD, Behold, I lay in Zion for a foundation a stone, **a tried stone, a precious corner stone, a sure foundation:** he that believeth shall not make haste.
   Fulfillment: Acts 4:11-12
This is the stone which was set at nought of you builders, **which is become the head of the corner.** Neither is there salvation in any other: for there is none other name under heaven given among men, whereby we must be saved.

187. **He indicated hypocritical obedience to His Word** Isaiah 29:13
Wherefore the Lord said, **Forasmuch as this people draw near me with their mouth, and with their lips do honour me, but have removed their heart far from me,** and their fear toward me is taught by the precept of men.
   Fulfillment: Matthew 15:7-9
Ye hypocrites, well did Esaias prophesy of you, saying, This people draweth nigh unto me with their mouth, and **honoureth me with their lips; but their heart is far from me.** But in vain they do worship me, teaching for doctrines the commandments of men.

188. **The wise are confounded by the Word** Isaiah 29:14
 Therefore, behold, I will proceed to do a marvellous work among this people, even a marvellous work and a wonder: **for the wisdom of their wise men shall perish, and the understanding of their prudent men shall be hid.**
   Fulfillment: 1 Corinthians 1:18-31
For the preaching of the cross is to them that perish foolishness; but unto us which are saved it is the power of God. For it is written, **I will destroy the wisdom of the wise, and will bring to nothing the understanding of the prudent.** Where is the wise? Where is the scribe? Where is the disputer of this world? Hath not **God made foolish the wisdom of this world?** For after that in the wisdom of God the world by wisdom knew not God, it pleased God by the foolishness of preaching to save them that believe. For the Jews require a sign, and the Greeks seek after wisdom: But we preach Christ crucified, unto the Jews a stumbling block, and unto the Greeks foolishness; But unto them which are called, both Jews and Greeks, Christ the power of God, and the wisdom of God. **Because the foolishness of God is wiser than men;** and the weakness of God is stronger than men. For ye see your calling, brethren, how that not many wise men after the flesh, not many mighty, not many noble, are called: But God hath chosen the foolish things of the world to confound the wise; and **God hath chosen the weak things of the world to confound the things which are mighty;** And base things of the world, and things which are despised, hath God chosen, yea, and things which are not, to bring to nought things that are: That no flesh should glory in his presence. But of him are ye in Christ Jesus, who of God is made unto us wisdom, and righteousness, and sanctification, and redemption: That, according as it is written, He that glorieth, let him glory in the Lord.

"The impulse to pursue God originates with God."
A. W. Tozer **"See John 6:64"**

189. **His ministry would include miraculous healing**   **Isaiah 29:18**
And in that day shall the **deaf hear the words** of the book, and the **eyes of the blind shall see** out of obscurity, and out of darkness.
        Fulfillment: Luke 7:20-22
When the men were come unto him, they said, John Baptist hath sent us unto thee, saying, Art thou he that should come? Or look we for another? **And in that same hour he cured many of their infirmities and plagues, and of evil spirits; and unto many that were blind he gave sight.** Then Jesus answering said unto them, Go your way, and tell John what things ye have seen and heard; how that **the blind see, the lame walk, the lepers are cleansed, the deaf hear, the dead are raised, to the poor the gospel is preached.**

190.   **He would be a refuge – A man shall be a hiding place**   **Isaiah 32:2**
And a man shall be as an hiding place from the wind, and a covert from the tempest; as rivers of water in a dry place, as the shadow of a great rock in a weary land.
        Fulfillment: Matthew 23:37
O Jerusalem, Jerusalem, thou that killest the prophets, and stonest them which are sent unto thee, **how often would I have gathered thy children together, even as a hen gathereth her chickens under her wings, and ye would not!**

191.   **He will come and save you**   **Isaiah 35:4**
Say to them that are of a fearful heart, Be strong, fear not: behold, your God will come with vengeance, even God with a recompence; **he will come and save you.**
        Fulfillment: Matthew 1:21
And she shall bring forth a son, and thou shalt call his name JESUS: for **he shall save his people from their sins.**

192.   **He will have a ministry of miracles**   **Isaiah 35:5-6**
Then the eyes of the blind shall be opened, **and the ears of the deaf shall be unstopped**. Then shall **the lame man leap as an hart, and the tongue of the dumb sing:** for in the wilderness shall waters break out, and streams in the desert.
        Fulfillment: Matthew 11:4-6
Jesus answered and said unto them, Go and shew John again those things which ye do hear and see: **The blind receive their sight, and the lame walk, the lepers are cleansed, and the deaf hear, the dead are raised up,** and the poor have the gospel preached to them. And blessed is he, whosoever shall not be offended in me.

The Hope of the Promise of His Return

The truth of Christ's return dominates the New Testament, being mentioned more than any other fundamental doctrine. It is mentioned 318 times which makes about one in every twenty five verses in the New Testament refer to our Lord's return.

Three "I Wills"
"I will send my spirit." "I will build my church." "I will come again."

193.   **He would be preceded by a prophet who would announce Him**   Isaiah 40:1-4

Comfort ye, comfort ye my people, saith your God. Speak ye comfortably to Jerusalem, and cry unto her, that her warfare is accomplished, that her iniquity is pardoned: for she hath received of the LORD'S hand double for all her sins. **The voice of him that crieth in the wilderness, Prepare ye the way of the LORD,** make straight in the desert a highway for our God. Every valley shall be exalted, and every mountain and hill shall be made low: and the crooked shall be made straight, and the rough places plain.

   Fulfillment: John 1:19-23

And this is the **record of John**, when the Jews sent priests and Levites from Jerusalem to ask him, Who art thou? And he confessed, and denied not; but confessed, I am not the Christ. And they asked him, What then? Art thou Elias? And he saith, I am not. Art thou that prophet? And he answered, No. Then said they unto him, Who art thou? That we may give an answer to them that sent us. What sayest thou of thyself? **He said, I am the voice of one crying in the wilderness, Make straight the way of the Lord, as said the prophet Esaias.**

   Fulfillment: Matthew 3:1-3

In those days came John the Baptist, preaching in the wilderness of Judaea, And saying, Repent ye: for the kingdom of heaven is at hand. **For this is he that was spoken of by the prophet Esaias, saying, The voice of one crying in the wilderness, Prepare ye the way of the Lord, make his paths straight.**

Aim for Repentance rather than a decision

"As you witness, divorce yourself from the thought that you are merely seeking "decisions for Christ." What we should be seeking is repentance within the heart. This is the purpose of the law, to bring the knowledge of sin. How can a man repent if he doesn't know what sin is?   If there is no repentance, there is no salvation. Jesus said, "unless you repent, you shall all likewise perish" (Luke 13:3). God is not willing that any should perish, but that all should come to repentance (2 Peter 3:9). Many don't understand that the salvation of a soul is not a resolution to change the way of life, but "repentance towards God, and faith toward our Lord Jesus Christ." The modern concept of success in evangelism is to relate how many people were "saved" (that is, how many prayed the "sinner's prayer"). This produces a "no decisions, no success" mentality. This shouldn't be, because Christians who seek decisions in evangelism become discouraged after a time of witnessing if "no one came to the Lord." The Bible tells us that as we sow the good seed of the gospel, one sows and the other reaps. If you faithfully sow the seed, someone will reap. If you reap, it is because someone has sown in the past, but it is God who causes the seed to grow. If His hand is not on the person you are leading in a prayer of committal, if there is not God-given repentance, then you will end up with a stillborn on your hands, and that is nothing to rejoice about. We should measure our success by how faithfully we sowed the seed. In that way, we will avoid becoming discouraged."

Ray Comfort   **"See Acts 20:21"**

194.   **Behold your God!**   Isaiah 40:9

O Zion, that bringest good tidings, get thee up into the high mountain; O Jerusalem, that bringest good tidings, lift up thy voice with strength; lift it up, be not afraid; say unto the cities of Judah, **Behold your God!**

    Fulfillment: John 1:36

And looking upon Jesus as he walked, he saith, **Behold the Lamb of God!**

    Fulfillment: John 19:14

And it was the preparation of the passover, and about the sixth hour: and he saith unto the Jews, **Behold your King!**

195.   **He will be like a good shepherd, and give His life for them**   Isaiah 40:11

He shall feed his flock like a shepherd: he shall gather the lambs with his arm, and carry them in his bosom, and shall gently lead those that are with young.

    Fulfillment: John 10:10-18

The thief cometh not, but for to steal, and to kill, and to destroy: I am come that they might have life, and that they might have it more abundantly. **I am the good shepherd: the good shepherd giveth his life for the sheep.** But he that is an hireling, and not the shepherd, whose own the sheep are not, seeth the wolf coming, and leaveth the sheep, and fleeth: and the wolf catcheth them, and scattereth the sheep. The hireling fleeth, because he is an hireling, and careth not for the sheep. **I am the good shepherd, and know my sheep, and am known of mine.** As the Father knoweth me, even so know I the Father: and **I lay down my life for the sheep.** And other sheep I have, which are not of this fold: them also I must bring, and they shall hear my voice; and there shall be one fold, and one shepherd. Therefore doth my Father love me, because I lay down my life, that I might take it again. No man taketh it from me, but I lay it down of myself. I have power to lay it down, and I have power to take it again. This commandment have I received of my Father.

196.   **He would be tender and compassionate**   Isaiah 40:11

He shall feed his flock like a shepherd: he shall gather the lambs with his arm, and carry them in his bosom, and shall gently lead those that are with young.

    Fulfillment: Matthew 12:18-21

Behold my servant, whom I have chosen; my beloved, in whom my soul is well pleased: I will put my spirit upon him, and he shall shew judgment to the Gentiles. He shall not strive, nor cry; neither shall any man hear his voice in the streets. A bruised reed shall he not break, and smoking flax shall he not quench, till he send forth judgment unto victory. **And in his name shall the Gentiles trust.**

"If you will not have death unto sin, you shall have sin unto death. There is no alternative. If you do not die to sin, you shall die for sin. If you do not slay sin, sin will slay you."

Charles Spurgeon   **"See 1 John 1:5-10"**

197. **He would be as a faithful, patient redeemer, a servant**   Isaiah 42:1-4
Behold my servant, whom I uphold; mine elect, in whom my soul delighteth; **I have put my spirit upon him: he shall bring forth judgment to the Gentiles.** He shall not cry, nor lift up, nor cause his voice to be heard in the street. A bruised reed shall he not break, and the smoking flax shall he not quench: he shall bring forth judgment unto truth. He shall not fail nor be discouraged, till he have set judgment in the earth: and the isles shall wait for his law.
  Fulfillment: Matthew 12:18-21
Behold my servant, whom I have chosen; my beloved, in whom my soul is well pleased: **I will put my spirit upon him, and he shall shew judgment to the Gentiles.** He shall not strive, nor cry; neither shall any man hear his voice in the streets. A bruised reed shall he not break, and smoking flax shall he not quench, till he send forth judgment unto victory. **And in his name shall the Gentiles trust.**

198. **He is the Light (Salvation) to the Gentiles**   Isaiah 42:6
I the LORD have called thee in righteousness, and will hold thine hand, and will keep thee, and give thee for a covenant of the people, **for a light of the Gentiles.**
  Fulfillment: Luke 2:32
A light to lighten the Gentiles, and the glory of thy people Israel.

199. **He will uphold His elect unto the end of the world**   Isaiah 42:1, 6
Behold my servant, whom **I uphold; mine elect,** in whom my soul delighteth; **I have put my spirit upon him:** he shall bring forth judgment to the Gentiles… I the LORD have called thee in righteousness, **and will hold thine hand, and will keep thee,** and give thee for a covenant of the people, for a light of the Gentiles.
  Fulfillment: Matthew 28:18b-20
And Jesus came and spake unto them, saying, All power is given unto me in heaven and in earth. Go ye therefore, and teach all nations, baptizing them in the name of the Father, and of the Son, and of the Holy Ghost: Teaching them to observe all things whatsoever I have commanded you: and, lo, **I am with you I, even unto the end of the world.** Amen.

"The pain was absolutely unbearable. In fact, it was literally beyond words to describe; they had to invent a new word: excruciating. Literally, excruciating means 'out of the cross.'"

Alexander Metherell, M.D., Ph.D.   **"See Matthew 27:46"**

200. **Blind eyes opened**   Isaiah 42:7

To open the blind eyes, to bring out the prisoners from the prison, and them that sit in darkness out of the prison house.

   Fulfillment: John 9:25-38

He answered and said, Whether he be a sinner or no, I know not: one thing I know, that, whereas **I was blind, now I see.** Then said they to him again, What did he to thee? How opened he thine eyes? He answered them, I have told you already, and ye did not hear: wherefore would ye hear it again? Will ye also be his disciples? Then they reviled him, and said, Thou art his disciple; but we are Moses' disciples. We know that God spake unto Moses: as for this fellow, we know not from whence he is. The man answered and said unto them, Why herein is a marvellous thing, that ye know not from whence he is, and yet he hath opened mine eyes. Now we know that God heareth not sinners: but if any man be a worshipper of God, and doeth his will, him he heareth. Since the world began was it not heard that any man opened the eyes of one that was born blind. If this man were not of God, he could do nothing. They answered and said unto him, Thou wast altogether born in sins, and dost thou teach us? And they cast him out. Jesus heard that they had cast him out; and when he had found him, he said unto him, Dost thou believe on the Son of God? He answered and said, Who is he, Lord, that I might believe on him? And Jesus said unto him, Thou hast both seen him, and it is he that talketh with thee. And he said, Lord, I believe. And he worshipped him.

201. **He is the only Saviour**   Isaiah 43:11

I, even I, am the LORD; and beside me there is no saviour.

   Fulfillment: Acts 4:12

Neither is there salvation in any other: **for there is none other name under heaven given among men, whereby we must be saved.**

202. **He will send the Spirit of God**   Isaiah 44:3

For I will pour water upon him that is thirsty, and floods upon the dry ground: **I will pour my spirit upon thy seed,** and my blessing upon thine offspring.

   Fulfillment: John 16:7, 13

Nevertheless I tell you the truth; It is expedient for you that I go away: for if I go not away, **the Comforter will not come unto you;** but if I depart, **I will send him unto you…**Howbeit when he, the **Spirit of truth, is come, he will guide you into all truth:** for he shall not speak of himself; but whatsoever he shall hear, that shall he speak: and he will shew you things to come.

   Fulfillment: Matthew 12:17-18

That it might be fulfilled which was spoken by Esaias the prophet, saying, Behold my servant, whom I have chosen; my beloved, in whom my soul is well pleased: **I will put my spirit upon him,** and he shall shew judgment to the Gentiles.

"Christians who don't read their Bible are no better off than non-Christians who refuse to!"

Anonymous   **"See 2 Timothy 2:15"**

167

203. **He will be the Judge; every one will worship**   Isaiah 45:23
I have sworn by myself, **the word is gone out of my mouth in righteousness, and shall not return, That unto me every knee shall bow, every tongue shall swear.**
       Fulfillment: John 5:22
For the Father judgeth no man, but hath **committed all judgment unto the Son.**
       Fulfillment: Romans 14:11
For it is written, As I live, saith the Lord, **every knee shall bow to me, and every tongue shall confess to God.**

204. **He is the First and the Last**   Isaiah 48:12
Hearken unto me, O Jacob and Israel, my called; **I am he; I am the first, I also am the last.**
       Fulfillment: Revelations 1:8, 17
I am Alpha and Omega, the beginning and the ending, saith the Lord, which is, and which was, and which is to come, the Almighty... And when I saw him, I fell at his feet as dead. And he laid his right hand upon me, saying unto me, Fear not; I am the first and the last.

205. **He would come as a Teacher**   Isaiah 48:17
Thus saith the LORD, thy Redeemer, the Holy One of Israel; **I am the LORD thy God which teacheth thee** to profit, which leadeth thee by the way that thou shouldest go.
       Fulfillment: John 3:2
The same came to Jesus by night, and said unto him, Rabbi, **we know that thou art a teacher come from God:** for no man can do these miracles that thou doest, except God be with him.

206. **His Humanity, called from the womb**   Isaiah 49:1
Listen, O isles, unto me; and hearken, ye people, from far; **The LORD hath called me from the womb;** from the bowels of my mother hath he made mention of my name.
       Fulfillment: Matthew 1:18
Now the birth of Jesus Christ was on this wise: When as his mother Mary was espoused to Joseph, before they came together, **she was found with child of the Holy Ghost.**

207. **A Servant from the womb**   Isaiah 49:5
And now, saith the LORD that **formed me from the womb to be his servant,** to bring Jacob again to him, Though Israel be not gathered, yet shall I be glorious in the eyes of the LORD, and my God shall be my strength.
       Fulfillment: Luke 1:31
And, behold, thou shalt **conceive in thy womb,** and bring forth a son, and shalt call his name JESUS.
       Fulfillment: Philippians 2:7
But made himself of no reputation, and took upon him **the form of a servant,** and was made in the likeness of men.

"You gain by giving that which you can't buy with money."
Dr. Edwin Cole   **"See Luke 6:38"**

208. **He is Salvation for Israel** Isaiah 49:6

And he said, It is a light thing that thou shouldest be my servant to raise up the tribes of Jacob, **and to restore the preserved of Israel:** I will also give thee for a light to the Gentiles, that thou mayest be **my salvation unto the end of the earth.**

Fulfillment: Luke 2:29-32

Lord, now lettest thou thy servant depart in peace, according to thy word: **For mine eyes have seen thy salvation,** Which thou hast prepared before the face of all people; A light to lighten the Gentiles, **and the glory of thy people Israel.**

209. **He is the Light to the Gentiles** Isaiah 49:6

And he said, It is a light thing that thou shouldest be my servant to raise up the tribes of Jacob, and to restore the preserved of Israel: **I will also give thee for a light to the Gentiles, that thou mayest be my salvation unto the end of the earth.**

Fulfillment: Acts 13:47

For so hath the Lord commanded us, saying, I have set thee to be **a light of the Gentiles,** that thou shouldest be for salvation unto the ends of the earth.

210. **He is the Salvation unto the ends of the earth** Isaiah 49:6

And he said, It is a light thing that thou shouldest be my servant to raise up the tribes of Jacob, and to restore the preserved of Israel: I will also give thee for a light to the Gentiles, that **thou mayest be my salvation unto the end of the earth.**

Fulfillment: Acts 15:7-18

And when there had been much disputing, Peter rose up, and said unto them, Men and brethren, ye know how that a good while ago God made choice among us, **that the Gentiles by my mouth should hear the word of the gospel, and believe.** And God, which knoweth the hearts, bare them witness, giving them the Holy Ghost, even as he did unto us; **And put no difference between us and them, purifying their hearts by faith.** Now therefore why tempt ye God, to put a yoke upon the neck of the disciples, which neither our fathers nor we were able to bear? But we believe that through the grace of the Lord Jesus Christ we shall be saved, even as they. Then all the multitude kept silence, and gave audience to Barnabas and Paul, declaring what miracles and wonders God had wrought among the Gentiles by them. And after they had held their peace, James answered, saying, Men and brethren, hearken unto me: Simeon hath declared how God at the first did visit the Gentiles, to take out of them a people for his name. And to this agree the words of the prophets; as it is written, After this I will return, and will build again the tabernacle of David, which is fallen down; and I will build again the ruins thereof, and I will set it up: **That the residue of men might seek after the Lord, and all the Gentiles, upon whom my name is called, saith the Lord, who doeth all these things. Known unto God are all his works from the beginning of the world.**

"In every true searcher of nature there is a kind of religious reverence, for he finds it impossible to imagine that he is the first to have thought out the exceedingly delicate threads that connect his perceptions."

Albert Einstein **"See Romans 1:20"**

211. **He is despised of the Nation**   Isaiah 49:7
Thus saith the LORD, the Redeemer of Israel, and his Holy One, **to him whom man despiseth, to him whom the nation abhorreth,** to a servant of rulers, Kings shall see and arise, princes also shall worship, because of the LORD that is faithful, and the Holy One of Israel, and he shall choose thee.
        Fulfillment: John 8:48-49
Then answered the Jews, and said unto him, Say we not well that **thou art a Samaritan, and hast a devil?** Jesus answered, I have not a devil; but I honour my Father, and ye do dishonour me.
        Fulfillment: John 15: 24-25
If I had not done among them the works which none other man did, they had not had sin**: but now have they both seen and hated both me and my Father.** But this cometh to pass, that the word might be fulfilled that is written in their law, **They hated me without a cause.**

212. **Kings would bow down to Him**   Isaiah 49:23
And kings shall be thy nursing fathers, and their queens thy nursing mothers: **they shall bow down to thee with *their* face toward the earth,** and lick up the dust of thy feet; and thou shalt know that I *am* the LORD: for they shall not be ashamed that wait for me.
        Fulfillment: Matthew 2:11
And when they were come into the house, they saw the young child with Mary his mother, and **fell down, and worshipped him:** and when they had opened their treasures, they presented unto him gifts; gold, and frankincense, and myrrh.

213. **Heaven is clothed in black at His humiliation**   Isaiah 50:3
I **clothe the heavens with blackness,** and I make sackcloth their covering.
        Fulfillment: Luke 23:44-45
And it was about the sixth hour, and **there was a darkness over all the earth** until the ninth hour. And the sun was darkened, and the veil of the temple was rent in the midst.

214. **He is a learned counselor for the weary**   Isaiah 50:4
The Lord GOD hath given me the tongue of the learned, that I should know how to speak a word in season to him that is weary: he wakeneth morning by morning, he wakeneth mine ear to hear as the learned.
        Fulfillment: Matthew 11:28-29
Come unto me, all ye that labour and are heavy laden, and I will give you rest. Take my yoke upon you, and learn of me; for I am meek and lowly in heart: and ye shall find rest unto your souls.

This is the spirit in which we should share our faith:

"Love your enemies, do good to them which hate you, bless them that curse you, and pray for them which despitefully use you."

Luke 6:27-28

215.   He was a Servant bound willingly to obedience   **Isaiah 50:5**
The Lord GOD hath opened mine ear, **and I was not rebellious,** neither turned away back.
          Fulfillment: Matthew 26:39
And he went a little further, and fell on his face, and prayed, saying, O my Father, if it be possible, let this cup pass from me: nevertheless **not as I will, but as thou wilt.**

216.   He was beaten, His beard was pulled out and they spit upon His face
                                                                                        Isaiah 50:6
I gave my back to the smiters, **and my cheeks to them that plucked off the hair: I hid not my face from shame and spitting.**
          Fulfillment: Matthew 26:67
Then did they spit in his face, and buffeted him; and others smote him with the palms of their hands.
          Fulfillment: Matthew 27:26
Then released he Barabbas unto them: and when he had **scourged Jesus,** he **delivered him to be crucified.**
          Fulfillment: Matthew 27:30
And they spit upon him, and took the reed, and **smote him on the head.**
          Fulfillment: Mark 14:65
And some began to spit on him, and to cover his face, and to buffet him, and to say unto him, Prophesy: and the servants did strike him with the palms of their hands.

217.   He would bring good tidings of peace   **Isaiah 52:7**
How beautiful upon the mountains are the feet of him that **bringeth good tidings, that publisheth peace; that bringeth good tidings of good, that publisheth salvation;** that saith unto Zion, Thy God reigneth!
          Fulfillment: Luke 4:14-15
And Jesus returned in the **power of the Spirit** into Galilee: and there went out a fame of him through all the region round about. **And he taught in their synagogues, being glorified of all.**

218.   He will give gifts to men   **Isaiah 53:12**
For ye shall not go out with haste, nor go by flight: **for the LORD will go before you; and the God of Israel** *will be* **your rereward.**
          Fulfillment: Ephesians 4:7-16
But unto every one of us is given grace according to the measure of the gift of Christ. Wherefore he saith, When he ascended up on high, he led captivity captive, and **gave gifts unto men.**

"We must all mutually share in the knowledge that our existence only attains its true value when we have experienced in ourselves the truth of the declaration: 'He who loses his life shall find it.'"

Albert Schweitzer   **"See Matthew 16:25"**

171

219. **He shall be a highly exalted Servant and Son**   Isaiah 52:13
   Behold, my servant shall deal prudently, **he shall be exalted** and extolled, and be very high.
      Fulfillment: Ephesians 1:19-22
   And what is the exceeding greatness of his power to us-ward who believe, according to the working of **his mighty power, Which he wrought in Christ,** when he raised him from the dead, and set him at his own right hand in the heavenly places, Far above all principality, and power, and might, and dominion, and every name that is named, not only in this world, but also in that which is to come: **And hath put all things under his feet, and gave him to be the head over all things to the church.**
      Fulfillment: Matthew 17:5
   While he yet spake, behold, a bright cloud overshadowed them: and behold a voice out of the cloud, which said, **This is my beloved Son, in whom I am well pleased; hear ye him.**
      Fulfillment: Philippians 2:5-8
   Let this mind be in you, which was also in Christ Jesus: Who, being in the form of God, thought it not robbery to be equal with God: But made himself of no reputation, and **took upon him the form of a servant, and was made in the likeness of men:** And being found in fashion as a man, **he humbled himself, and became obedient unto death,** even the death of the cross.

Confessing Our Sins

"Whereas, it is the duty of nations as well as of men to own their dependence upon the overruling power of God, to confess their sins and transgressions in humble sorrow yet with assured hope that genuine repentance will lead to mercy and pardon, and to recognize the sublime truth, announced in the Holy Scriptures and proven by all history: that those nations only are blessed whose God is Lord..."We have been the recipients of the choicest bounties of Heaven. We have been preserved these many years in peace and prosperity. We have grown in numbers, wealth and power as no other nation has ever grown. But we have forgotten God. We have forgotten the gracious Hand which preserved us in peace, and multiplied and enriched and strengthened us; and we have vainly imagined, in the deceitfulness of our hearts, that all these blessings were produced by some superior wisdom and virtue of our own. Intoxicated with unbroken success, we have become too self sufficient to feel the necessity of redeeming and preserving grace, too proud to pray to the God that made us! It behooves us then to humble ourselves before the offended Power, to confess our national sins and to pray for clemency and forgiveness."

Abraham Lincoln   **"See Proverbs 28:13"**

   1863, in declaring a day of national fasting, prayer and humiliation

172

220. **People were shocked at the visage of Christ** Isaiah 52:14

As **many were astonished** at thee; **his visage was so marred more than any man, and his form more than the sons of men.**

Fulfillment: Matthew 26:66-68

What think ye? They answered and said, **He is guilty of death. Then did they spit in his face, and buffeted him;** and others smote him with the palms of their hands, Saying, Prophesy unto us, thou Christ, Who is he that smote thee?

Fulfillment: Matthew 27:26-30

Then released he Barabbas unto them: and when **he had scourged Jesus,** he delivered *him* to be crucified. Then the soldiers of the governor took Jesus into the common hall, and gathered unto him the whole band *of soldiers*. And they stripped him, and put on him a scarlet robe. And when they had platted a crown of thorns, they put *it* upon his head, and a reed in his right hand: and they bowed the knee before him, and mocked him, saying, Hail, King of the Jews! **And they spit upon him, and took the reed, and smote him on the head.**

Fulfillment: Mark 15:16-20

And the soldiers led him away into the hall, called Praetorium; and they call together the whole band. And they clothed him with purple, **and platted a crown of thorns, and put it about his *head*,** And began to salute him, Hail, King of the Jews! **And they smote him on the head with a reed, and did spit upon him,** and bowing *their* knees worshipped him. And when they had mocked him, they took off the purple from him, and put his own clothes on him, and **led him out to crucify him.**

Fulfillment: Luke 18:31-34

Then he took unto him the twelve, and said unto them, Behold, we go up to Jerusalem, and all things that are written by the prophets concerning the Son of man shall be accomplished. **For he shall be delivered unto the Gentiles, and shall be mocked, and spitefully entreated, and spitted on: And they shall scourge him, and put him to death:** and the third day he shall rise again. And they understood none of these things: and this saying was hid from them, neither knew they the things which were spoken.

221. **His blood was shed to make an atonement for all** Isaiah 52:15

So shall he sprinkle many nations; the kings shall shut their mouths at him: for that which had not been told them shall they see; and that which they had not heard shall they consider.

Fulfillment: Revelations 1:5

And from Jesus Christ, who is the faithful witness, and the first begotten of the dead, and **the prince of the kings of the earth.** Unto him that loved us, and **washed us from our sins in his own blood.**

"A little faith will bring your soul to heaven; A great faith will bring heaven to your soul."

Charles Spurgeon **"See 1 John 5:4"**

222.   **His people would not believe Him**   Isaiah 53:1
Who hath believed our report? And to whom is the arm of the LORD revealed?
          Fulfillment: John 12:37-38
But though he had done so many miracles before them, **yet they believed not on him:**
That the saying of Esaias the prophet might be fulfilled, which he spake, **Lord, who
hath believed our report?** And to whom hath the arm of the Lord been revealed?

223.   **He would grow up in a poor family, His appearance would be ordinary**
                                                                           Isaiah 53:2
  For he shall grow up before him as a tender plant, **and as a root out of a dry ground:
  he hath no form nor comeliness;** and when we shall see him, **there is no beauty that
  we should desire him.**
          Fulfillment: Luke 2:7
And she brought forth **her firstborn son, and wrapped him in swaddling clothes, and
laid him in a manger; because there was no room for them in the inn.**
          Fulfillment: Philippians 2:7-8
But made himself of no reputation, and took upon him the form of a servant, and was
made in the likeness of men: And being found in fashion as a man, he humbled himself,
and became obedient unto death, even the death of the cross.

224.   **He would be despised, rejected with great sorrow and grief**   Isaiah 53:3
He is despised and rejected of men; a man of sorrows, and acquainted with grief:
and we hid as it were our faces from him; **he was despised,** and we esteemed him not.
          Fulfillment: Matthew 27:21-23
The governor answered and said unto them, Whether of the twain will ye that I release
unto you? They said, Barabbas. Pilate saith unto them, What shall I do then with Jesus
which is called Christ? **They all say unto him, Let him be crucified.** And the governor
said, Why, what evil hath he done? **But they cried out the more, saying, Let him be
crucified.**
          Fulfillment: Luke 4:28-29
And all they in the synagogue, when they heard these things, **were filled with wrath,
And rose up, and thrust him out of the city,** and led him unto the brow of the hill
whereon their city was built, **that they might cast him down headlong.**
          Fulfillment: Luke 19:41-42
And when he was come near, he beheld the city, and wept over it, Saying, If thou
hadst known, even thou, at least in this thy day, the things which belong unto thy peace!
But now they are hid from thine eyes.

"If there is anything in my thoughts or style to commend, the credit is due to my
parents for instilling in me an early love of Scriptures."

Daniel Webster   **"See Psalms 119:97"**

225. **He was familiar with suffering** Isaiah 53:3

He is despised and rejected of men; **a man of sorrows, and acquainted with grief:** and we hid as it were our faces from him; he was despised, and we esteemed him not.

Fulfillment: Matthew 12:14

Then the Pharisees went out, and held a council against him, how they might destroy him.

Fulfillment: Mark 5:14-17

And they that fed the swine fled, and told it in the city, and in the country. And they went out to see what it was that was done. And they come to Jesus, and see him that was possessed with the devil, and had the legion, sitting, and clothed, and in his right mind: and they were afraid. And they that saw it told them how it befell to him that was possessed with the devil, and also concerning the swine. **And they began to pray him to depart out of their coasts.**

Fulfillment: John 7:1

After these things Jesus walked in Galilee: for he would not walk in Jewry, because **the Jews sought to kill him.**

Fulfillment: John 7:1- 5

After these things Jesus walked in Galilee: for he would not walk in Jewry, because **the Jews sought to kill him.** Now the Jews' feast of tabernacles was at hand. His brethren therefore said unto him, Depart hence, and go into Judaea, that thy disciples also may see the works that thou doest. For there is no man that doeth any thing in secret, and he himself seeketh to be known openly. If thou do these things, shew thyself to the world. **For neither did his brethren believe in him.**

Fulfillment: John 10:31-33

Then the Jews took up stones again to stone him. Jesus answered them, Many good works have I shewed you from my Father; for which of those works do ye stone me? The Jews answered him, saying, For a good work we stone thee not; but for blasphemy; and because that thou, being a man, makest thyself God.

226. **Men would hide from being associated with Him** Isaiah 53:3d

He is despised and rejected of men; a man of sorrows, and acquainted with grief: and we hid as it were our faces from him; he was despised, and we esteemed him not.

Fulfillment: Mark 14:50-52

And they all forsook him, and fled. And there followed him a certain young man, having a linen cloth cast about his naked body; and the young men laid hold on him: And he left the linen cloth, **and fled from them naked.**

"You cannot say, 'No Lord,' and mean both words; one annuls the other. If you say no to Him then He is not your Lord."

D. James Kennedy **"See Luke 6:46"**

175

227. **He would bear our grief and sorrows** Isaiah 53:4

Surely **he hath borne our griefs, and carried our sorrows:** yet we did esteem him stricken, smitten of God, and afflicted.

Fulfillment: Matthew 8:14-17

And when Jesus was come into Peter's house, he saw his wife's mother laid, and sick of a fever. And he touched her hand, and the fever left her: and she arose, and ministered unto them. When the even was come, they brought unto him many that were possessed with devils: and he cast out the spirits with *his* word, and healed all that were sick: **That it might be fulfilled which was spoken by Esaias the prophet, saying, Himself took our infirmities, and bare *our* sicknesses.**

228. **He would have a healing ministry** Isaiah 53:4-5

Surely he hath borne our griefs, and carried our sorrows: yet we did esteem him stricken, smitten of God, and afflicted. But he was wounded for our transgressions, he was bruised for our iniquities: the chastisement of our peace was upon him; and **with his stripes we are healed.**

Fulfillment: Luke 6:17-19

And he came down with them, and stood in the plain, and the company of his disciples, and a great multitude of people out of all Judaea and Jerusalem, and from the sea coast of Tyre and Sidon, **which came to hear him, and to be healed of their diseases;** And they that were vexed with unclean spirits: and they were healed. And the whole multitude sought to touch him: **for there went virtue out of him, and healed them all.**

The Beatitudes

"**Blessed are** the poor in spirit: for theirs is the Kingdom of Heaven.
Blessed are they that mourn: for they shall be comforted.
Blessed are the Meek: for they shall inherit the earth.
Blessed are they which hunger and thirst after righteousness:
for they shall be filled.
Blessed are the merciful: for they shall obtain mercy.
Blessed are the pure in heart: for they shall see God.
Blessed are the peacemakers:
for they shall be called the children of God.
Blessed are they which are persecuted for righteousness' sake:
for theirs is the Kingdom of Heaven.
Blessed are ye, when men shall revile you, and persecute you, and
shall say all manner of evil against you falsely, for my sake."

Matthew 5:3-11

229. **He would bear the sins of the world** Isaiah 53:4-5
Surely he hath borne our griefs, and carried our sorrows: yet we did esteem him stricken, smitten of God, and afflicted. But he was wounded for our transgressions, he was bruised for our iniquities: the chastisement of our peace was upon him; and with his stripes we are healed.
        Fulfillment: 1 Peter 2:24
Who his own self bare our sins in his own body on the tree, that we, being dead to sins, should live unto righteousness: by whose stripes ye were healed.

230. **Thought to be cursed by God** Isaiah 53:4-5
Surely he hath borne our griefs, and carried our sorrows: **yet we did esteem him stricken, smitten of God, and afflicted.** But he was wounded for our transgressions, he was bruised for our iniquities: the chastisement of our peace was upon him; and with his stripes we are healed.
        Fulfillment: Matthew 27:41-46
Likewise also **the chief priests mocking him, with the scribes and elders,** said, He saved others; himself he cannot save. If he be the King of Israel, let him now come down from the cross, and we will believe him. **He trusted in God; let him deliver him now, if he will have him: for he said, I am the Son of God. The thieves also, which were crucified with him, cast the same in his teeth.** Now from the sixth hour there was darkness over all the land unto the ninth hour. And about the ninth hour Jesus cried with a loud voice, saying, Eli, Eli, lama sabachthani? that is to say, **My God, my God, why hast thou forsaken me?**

231. **He bears the penalty for mankind** Isaiah 53:4-5
Surely he hath borne our griefs, and carried our sorrows: yet we did esteem him stricken, smitten of God, and afflicted. **But he was wounded for our transgressions, he was bruised for our iniquities:** the chastisement of our peace was upon him; and with his stripes we are healed.
        Fulfillment: Luke 23:33
And when they were come to the place, which is called Calvary, there **they crucified him,** and the malefactors, one on the right hand, and the other on the left.

232. **His sacrifice would provide peace between man and God** Isaiah 53:4-5
Surely he hath borne our griefs, and carried our sorrows: yet we did esteem him stricken, smitten of God, and afflicted. But he was wounded for our transgressions, he was bruised for our iniquities: **the chastisement of our peace was upon him;** and with his stripes we are healed.
        Fulfillment: Colossians 1:20
And, having made peace through the blood of his cross, by him to reconcile all things unto himself; by him, I say, whether they be things in earth, or things in heaven.

"Prayer doesn't get man's will done in Heaven; it gets God's will done on earth."
Ronald Dunn   **"See Luke 11:2"**

233. **His back would be whipped** Isaiah 53:4-5

Surely he hath borne our griefs, and carried our sorrows: yet we did esteem him stricken, smitten of God, and afflicted. But he was wounded for our transgressions, he was bruised for our iniquities: the chastisement of our peace was upon him; **and with his stripes we are healed.**

      Fulfillment: Matthew 27:26

Then released he Barabbas unto them: and when he had **scourged Jesus,** he delivered him to be crucified.

234. **It was God's Will that He be the sin-bearer for all mankind** Isaiah 53:6

All we like sheep have gone astray; we have turned every one to his own way; **and the LORD hath laid on him the iniquity of us all.**

      Fulfillment: Galatians 1:4

Who gave himself for our sins, that he might deliver us from this present evil world, according to the will of God and our Father.

      Fulfillment: 1 John 4:10

Herein is love, not that we loved God, but that he loved us, and **sent his Son to be the propitiation for our sins.**

235. **Oppressed and afflicted** Isaiah 53:7a

He was oppressed, and he was afflicted, yet he opened not his mouth: he is brought as a lamb to the slaughter, and as a sheep before her shearers is dumb, so he openeth not his mouth.

      Fulfillment: Matthew 27:27-31

Then the soldiers of the governor took Jesus into the common hall, and gathered unto him the whole band of soldiers. And **they stripped him,** and put on him a scarlet robe. And when they had platted a **crown of thorns,** they put it upon his head, and a reed in his right hand: and they bowed the knee before him, and mocked him, saying, Hail, King of the Jews! And **they spit upon him, and took the reed, and smote him on the head.** And after that they had mocked him, they took the robe off from him, and put his own raiment on him, and **led him away to crucify him.**

236. **He would be silent before His accusers** Isaiah 53:7b

He was oppressed, and he was afflicted, yet **he opened not his mouth:** he is broughtAs a lamb to the slaughter, and as a sheep before her shearers is dumb, so he openeth not his mouth.

      Fulfillment: Matthew 27:12-14

And when he was accused of the chief priests and elders, he answered nothing. Then said Pilate unto him, Hearest thou not how many things they witness against thee? **And he answered him to never a word;** insomuch that the governor marvelled greatly.

"If any man places his purse into his head, no one can take it from him."

Benjamin Franklin **"See Matthew 6:21"**

237. **He would be our sacrificial Lamb**   Isaiah 53:7c
He was oppressed, and he was afflicted, yet he opened not his mouth: **he is brought as a lamb to the slaughter,** and as a sheep before her shearers is dumb, so he openeth not his mouth.
                    Fulfillment: John 1:29
The next day John seeth Jesus coming unto him, and saith, **Behold the Lamb of God, which taketh away the sin of the world.**

Confidence in Witnessing

"When you represent the Lord Jesus Christ as His disciple, you can be assured that you are representing the One who possesses all power, wisdom, and authority. You have everything when you have Him. Jesus said: 'Verily, verily, I say unto you, He that believeth on me, the works that I do shall he do also; and greater *works* than these shall he do; because I go unto my Father.'
John 14:12
No power can resist you as you go in obedience and faith as His ambassador. "To wit, that God was in Christ, reconciling the world unto himself, not imputing their trespasses unto them; and hath committed unto us the word of reconciliation. Now then we are ambassadors for Christ, as though God did beseech *you* by us: we pray *you* in Christ's stead, be ye reconciled to God."
2 Corinthians 5:19, 20
You have the promise, 'Ye are of God, little children, and have overcome them: because greater is he that is in you, than he that is in the world.' **1 John 4:4**
Also, you are assured that even the gates of hell will not prevail against you, 'And I say also unto thee, That thou art Peter, and upon this rock (Jesus) I will build my church; and the gates of hell shall not prevail against it.'   **Matthew 16:18**
The more you understand who Christ is and all that He has done and will do for you and through you, the more completely you will want to trust, obey and serve Him."

Dr. Bill Bright   **"See 2 Timothy 4:10"**

238.   **Confined and persecuted**   Isaiah 53:8a

He was taken from prison and from judgment: and who shall declare his generation? For he was cut off out of the land of the living: for the transgression of my people was he stricken.

                Fulfillment: Matthew 26:47-27:31

And while he yet spake, lo, Judas, one of the twelve, came, and with him a great multitude with swords and staves, from the chief priests and elders of the people. Now he that betrayed him gave them a sign, saying, Whomsoever I shall kiss, that same is he: hold him fast. And forthwith he came to Jesus, and said, Hail, master; and kissed him. And Jesus said unto him, Friend, wherefore art thou come? **Then came they, and laid hands on Jesus, and took him.** And, behold, one of them which were with Jesus stretched out his hand, and drew his sword, and struck a servant of the high priest's, and smote off his ear. Then said Jesus unto him, Put up again thy sword into his place: for all they that take the sword shall perish with the sword. Thinkest thou that I cannot now pray to my Father, and he shall presently give me more than twelve legions of angels? But how then shall the scriptures be fulfilled, that thus it must be? In that same hour said Jesus to the multitudes, Are ye come out as against a thief with swords and staves for to take me? I sat daily with you teaching in the temple, and ye laid no hold on me. But all this was done, that the scriptures of the prophets might be fulfilled. **Then all the disciples forsook him, and fled. And they that had laid hold on Jesus led him away to Caiaphas the high priest, where the scribes and the elders were assembled.** But Peter followed him afar off unto the high priest's palace, and went in, and sat with the servants, to see the end. Now the chief priests, and elders, and all the council, sought false witness against Jesus, to put him to death; But found none: yea, though many false witnesses came, yet found they none. **At the last came two false witnesses,** And said, This fellow said, I am able to destroy the temple of God, and to build it in three days. And the high priest arose, and said unto him, Answerest thou nothing? What is it which these witness against thee? But Jesus held his peace. And the high priest answered and said unto him, I adjure thee by the living God, that thou tell us whether thou be the Christ, the Son of God. Jesus saith unto him, Thou hast said: nevertheless I say unto you, Hereafter shall ye see the Son of man sitting on the right hand of power, and coming in the clouds of heaven. Then the high priest rent his clothes, saying, He hath spoken blasphemy; what further need have we of witnesses? Behold, now ye have heard his blasphemy. What think ye? They answered and said, **He is guilty of death. Then did they spit in his face, and buffeted him; and others smote him with the palms of their hands,** Saying, Prophesy unto us, thou Christ, Who is he that smote thee?

"Indeed, I disagree very much with those who are unwilling that Holy Scripture, translated into the vulgar tongue, be read by the uneducated, as if Christ taught such intricate doctrines that they could scarcely be understood by very few theologians, or as if the strength of the Christian religion consisted in men's ignorance of it."

Desiderius Erasmus   **"See 1 Timothy 2:3-6"**

Chapter 27

When the morning was come, all the chief priests and elders of the people took counsel against Jesus to put him to death: And when they had bound him, they led *him* away, and delivered him to Pontius Pilate the governor. Then Judas, which had betrayed him, when he saw that he was condemned, repented himself, and brought again the thirty pieces of silver to the chief priests and elders, Saying, I have sinned in that I have betrayed the innocent blood. And they said, What *is that* to us? See thou *to that.* And he cast down the pieces of silver in the temple, and departed, and went and hanged himself. And the chief priests took the silver pieces, and said, It is not lawful for to put them into the treasury, because it is the price of blood. And they took counsel, and bought with them the potter's field, to bury strangers in. Wherefore that field was called, The field of blood, unto this day. Then was fulfilled that which was spoken by Jeremy the prophet, saying, And they took the thirty pieces of silver, the price of him that was valued, whom they of the children of Israel did value; And gave them for the potter's field, as the Lord appointed me. And Jesus stood before the governor: and the governor asked him, saying, Art thou the King of the Jews? And Jesus said unto him, Thou sayest. And when he was accused of the chief priests and elders, he answered nothing. Then said Pilate unto him, Hearest thou not how many things they witness against thee? And he answered him to never a word; insomuch that the governor marvelled greatly. Now at *that* feast the governor was wont to release unto the people a prisoner, whom they would. And they had then a notable prisoner, called Barabbas. Therefore when they were gathered together, Pilate said unto them, Whom will ye that I release unto you? Barabbas, or Jesus which is called Christ? For he knew that for envy they had delivered him. When he was set down on the judgment seat, his wife sent unto him, saying, Have thou nothing to do with that just man: for I have suffered many things this day in a dream because of him. But the chief priests and elders persuaded the multitude that they should ask Barabbas, and destroy Jesus. The governor answered and said unto them, Whether of the twain will ye that I release unto you? They said, Barabbas. Pilate saith unto them, What shall I do then with Jesus which is called Christ? *They* all say unto him, **Let him be crucified.** And the governor said, Why, what evil hath he done? But they cried out the more, saying, **Let him be crucified.** When Pilate saw that he could prevail nothing, but *that* rather a tumult was made, he took water, and washed *his* hands before the multitude, saying, I am innocent of the blood of this just person: see ye *to it.* Then answered all the people, and said, His blood *be* on us, and on our children. Then released he Barabbas unto them: and when he had **scourged Jesus,** he delivered *him* to be crucified. Then the soldiers of the governor took Jesus into the common hall, and gathered unto him the whole band *of soldiers.* **And they stripped him,** and put on him a scarlet robe. And when they had **platted a crown of thorns,** they put *it* upon his head, and a reed in his right hand: and they bowed the knee before him, and mocked him, saying, Hail, King of the Jews! **And they spit upon him, and took the reed, and smote him on the head.** And after that they had mocked him, they took the robe off from him, and put his own raiment on him, **and led him away to crucify** *him.*

"See what wickedness there is in the nature of man. How much are we beholden to the restraining grace of God! For, were it not for this, man, who was made a little lower than the angels, would make himself a great deal lower than the devils."

Matthew Henry   **"See Hebrews 2:9"**

239. **He would be judged** Isaiah 53:8b

He was taken from prison and from judgment: and who shall declare his generation? For he was cut off out of the land of the living: **for the transgression of my people was he stricken.**

Fulfillment: John 18:13-22

And led him away to Annas first; for he was father in law to Caiaphas, which was the high priest that same year. Now Caiaphas was he, which gave counsel to the Jews, that it was expedient that one man should die for the people. And Simon Peter followed Jesus, and so did another disciple: that disciple was known unto the high priest, and went in with Jesus into the palace of the high priest. But Peter stood at the door without. Then went out that other disciple, which was known unto the high priest, and spake unto her that kept the door, and brought in Peter. Then saith the damsel that kept the door unto Peter, Art not thou also one of this man's disciples? He saith, I am not. And the servants and officers stood there, who had made a fire of coals; for it was cold: and they warmed themselves: and Peter stood with them, and warmed himself. **The high priest then asked Jesus of his disciples, and of his doctrine.** Jesus answered him, I spake openly to the world; I ever taught in the synagogue, and in the temple, whither the Jews always resort; and in secret have I said nothing. Why askest thou me? Ask them which heard me, what I have said unto them: behold, they know what I said. **And when he had thus spoken, one of the officers which stood by struck Jesus with the palm of his hand, saying, Answerest thou the high priest so?**

240. **He would be killed and die for the sins of the world** Isaiah 53:8b

He was taken from prison and from judgment: and who shall declare his generation? **For he was cut off out of the land of the living:** for the transgression of my people was he stricken.

Fulfillment: Matthew 27:35

And they crucified him, and parted his garments, casting lots: that it might be fulfilled which was spoken by the prophet, They parted my garments among them, and upon my vesture did they cast lots.

Fulfillment: 1 John 2:2

And he is the propitiation for our sins: and not for ours only, **but also for the sins of the whole world.**

"If you wish to know God, you must know His Word. If you wish to perceive His power, you must see how He works by His Word. If you wish to know His purpose before it comes to pass, you can only discover it by His Word."

Charles Spurgeon **"See Luke 4:4"**

241. **He would be buried with the wicked in a rich man's grave even though He was innocent and had done no violence, no deceit was found in His mouth.**

Isaiah 53:9

And **he made his grave with the wicked, and with the rich in his death;** because he had done no violence, **neither was any deceit in his mouth.**

Fulfillment: Matthew 27:38, 57-60

Then were there **two thieves crucified with him,** one on the right hand, and another on the left.

Fulfillment: Mark 15:3

And the chief priests accused him of many things: but **he answered nothing.**

Fulfillment: John 18:38

Pilate saith unto him, What is truth? And when he had said this, he went out again unto the Jews, and saith unto them, **I find in him no fault at all.**

242. **It was God's will that He die for mankind, an offering for sin**   **Isaiah 53:10**

Yet it pleased the LORD to bruise him; he hath put him to grief: when thou shalt make his soul an offering for sin, he shall see his seed, he shall prolong his days, and the pleasure of the LORD shall prosper in his hand.

Fulfillment: John 18:11

Then said Jesus unto Peter, Put up thy sword into the sheath: **the cup which my Father hath given me, shall I not drink it?**

Fulfillment: Matthew 20:28

Even as the Son of man came not to be ministered unto, but to minister, **and to give his life a ransom for many.**

243. **He would prosper**   **Isaiah 53:10**

Yet it pleased the LORD to bruise him; he hath put him to grief: when thou shalt make his soul an offering for sin, he shall see his seed, he shall prolong his days, **and the pleasure of the LORD shall prosper in his hand.**

Fulfillment: John 17:1-5

These words spake Jesus, and lifted up his eyes to heaven, and said, Father, the hour is come; **glorify thy Son,** that thy Son also may glorify thee: **As thou hast given him power over all flesh, that he should give eternal life to as many as thou hast given him.** And this is life eternal, that they might know thee the only true God, and Jesus Christ, whom thou hast sent. I have glorified thee on the earth: I have finished the work which thou gavest me to do. And now, **O Father, glorify thou me with thine own self with the glory which I had with thee before the world** was.

"It has been well said that a wise man will learn more from a fool's question than a fool will learn from a wise man's answer."

Unknown   **"See Proverbs 29:9"**

244. **He will be a righteous Servant** **Isaiah 53:11**
He shall see of the travail of his soul, and shall be satisfied: by his knowledge shall **my righteous servant justify many;** for he shall bear their iniquities.
Fulfillment: Romans 3:25-26
Whom God hath set forth *to be* a propitiation through faith in his blood, **to declare his righteousness** for the remission of sins that are past, through the forbearance of God; **To declare,** *I say***, at this time his righteousness:** that he might be just, and the justifier of him which believeth in Jesus.
Fulfillment: Hebrews 1:8-9
But unto the Son *he saith*, Thy throne, O God, *is* for ever and ever: a sceptre of righteousness *is* the sceptre of thy kingdom. **Thou hast loved righteousness,** and hated iniquity; therefore God, *even* thy God, hath anointed thee with the oil of gladness above thy fellows.
Fulfillment: 1 John 2:29
If ye know that **he is righteous,** ye know that every one that doeth righteousness is born of him.
Fulfillment: 1 John 3:7
Little children, let no man deceive you: he that doeth righteousness is righteous, even as **he is righteous.**

245. **God would be fully satisfied with His suffering** **Isaiah 53:11**
He shall see of the travail of his soul, and shall be satisfied: by his knowledge shall my righteous servant justify many; for he shall bear their iniquities.
Fulfillment: John 12:27
Now is my soul troubled; and what shall I say? Father, save me from this hour: **but for this cause came I unto this hour.**

246. **As God's servant He would justify man before God** **Isaiah 53:11**
He shall see of the travail of his soul, and shall be satisfied: **by his knowledge shall my righteous servant justify many; for he shall bear their iniquities.**
Fulfillment: Romans 5:8-9
But God commendeth his love toward us, in that, while we were yet sinners, Christ died for us. Much more then, **being now justified by his blood,** we shall be saved from wrath through him.
Fulfillment: Romans 5:18-19
Therefore as by the offence of one judgment came upon all men to condemnation; even so by the righteousness of one the free gift came upon all men unto justification of life. **For as by one man's disobedience many were made sinners, so by the obedience of one shall many be made righteous.**

"And he said to *them* all, If any *man* will come after me, let him deny himself, and take up his cross daily, and follow me."

Luke 9:22

247. **He would be the sin bearer for mankind** Isaiah 53:11
He shall see of the travail of his soul, and shall be satisfied: by his knowledge shall my righteous servant justify many; **for he shall bear their iniquities.**
Fulfillment: Hebrews 9:28
So **Christ was once offered to bear the sins of many;** and unto them that look for him shall he appear the second time without sin unto salvation.

248. **He would be exalted by God because of His sacrifice** Isaiah 53:12a
Therefore will I divide him a portion with the great, and he shall divide the spoil with the strong; because he hath poured out his soul unto death: and he was numbered with the transgressors; and he bare the sin of many, and made intercession for the transgressors.
Fulfillment: Matthew 28:18
And Jesus came and spake unto them, saying, **All power is given unto me in heaven and in earth.**

249. **His life and death would be a great example of self-denial** Isaiah 53:12
Therefore will I divide him a portion with the great, and he shall divide the spoil with the strong; because **he hath poured out his soul unto death:** and he was numbered with the transgressors; and **he bare the sin of many, and made intercession for the transgressors.**
Fulfillment: Mark 10:45
For even the Son of man came not to be ministered unto, but to minister, and to give his life a ransom for many.

250. **He would give up His life to save mankind** Isaiah 53:12
Therefore will I divide him a portion with the great, and he shall divide the spoil with the strong; **because he hath poured out his soul unto death:** and he was numbered with the transgressors; and he bare the sin of many, and made intercession for the transgressors.
Fulfillment: Luke 23:46
And when Jesus had cried with a loud voice, he said, **Father, into thy hands I commend my spirit: and having said thus, he gave up the ghost.**

"The study of the Book of Job and its comparison with the latest scientific discoveries has brought me to the matured conviction that the Bible is an inspired book and was written by the One who made the stars."

Charles Burckhalter, Chabot Observatory **"See Luke 4:40"**

185

251. **He was grouped with criminals to be the sin-bearer for all mankind**
                                                                    Isaiah 53:12
Therefore will I divide him a portion with the great, and he shall divide the spoil with the strong; because he hath poured out his soul unto death: **and he was numbered with the transgressors; and he bare the sin of many, and made intercession for the transgressors.**
   Fulfillment: Luke 23:32
And **there were also two other, malefactors, led with him** to be put to death.
   Fulfillment: 2 Corinthians 5:21
For he **hath made him to be sin for us, who knew no sin**; that we might be made the righteousness of God in him.

252. **He interceded to God in behalf of mankind**   **Isaiah 53:12**
Therefore will I divide him a portion with the great, and he shall divide the spoil with the strong; because he hath poured out his soul unto death: and he was numbered with the transgressors; and he bare the sin of many, and **made intercession for the transgressors.**
   Fulfillment: Luke 23:34
Then said Jesus, **Father, forgive them; for they know not what they do.** And they parted his raiment, and cast lots.

253. **He would be resurrected by God**   **Isaiah 55:3**
Incline your ear, and come unto me: hear, and **your soul shall live; and I will make an everlasting covenant with you, even the sure mercies of David.**
   Fulfillment: Acts 13:34
And as concerning **that he raised him up from the dead, now no more to return to corruption,** he said on this wise, I will give you the sure mercies of David.

254. **He would be a witness to the people**   **Isaiah 55:4**
Behold, **I have given him for a witness to the people,** a leader and commander to the people.
   Fulfillment: John 18:37
Pilate therefore said unto him, Art thou a king then? Jesus answered, Thou sayest that I am a king. **To this end was I born, and for this cause came I into the world, that I should bear witness unto the truth. Every one that is of the truth heareth my voice.**

"Oh my friends, we are loaded down with countless church activities, while the real work of the Church, that of evangelizing and winning the lost, is almost entirely neglected."

Oswald J. Smith   **"See 2 Timothy 4:5"**

255. **He would come to provide salvation** Isaiah 59:15-16a
Yea, truth faileth; and he that departeth from evil maketh himself a prey: and the LORD saw it, and it displeased him that there was no judgment. And he saw that there was no man, and wondered that there was no intercessor: **therefore his arm brought salvation unto him; and his righteousness, it sustained him.**
Fulfillment: John 6:40
And this is the will of him that sent me, that **every one which seeth the Son, and believeth on him, may have everlasting life:** and I will raise him up at the last day.

256. **Intercessor between man and God** Isaiah 59:15-16b
Yea, truth faileth; and he that departeth from evil maketh himself a prey: and the LORD saw it, and it displeased him that there was no judgment. And he saw that there was no man, and wondered that there **was no intercessor: therefore his arm brought salvation unto him; and his righteousness, it sustained him.**
Fulfillment: Matthew 10:32
Whosoever therefore shall confess me before men, him will I confess also before my Father which is in heaven.

257. **He would come to Zion as their Redeemer** Isaiah 59:20
And the Redeemer shall come to Zion, and unto them that turn from transgression in Jacob, saith the LORD.
Fulfillment: Luke 2:38
And she coming in that instant gave thanks likewise unto the Lord, and spake of him to all them that looked for **redemption in Jerusalem.**

"The fool hath said in his heart, *There is* no God. They are corrupt, they have done abominable works, *there is* none that doeth good. The LORD looked down from heaven upon the children of men, to see if there were any that did understand, *and* seek God. They are all gone aside, they are *all* together become filthy: *there is* none that doeth good, no, not one."

Psalm 14:1-3

258. **The Spirit of God is upon Him, He will preach the Gospel**   Isaiah 61:1-2a
The Spirit of the Lord GOD is upon me; because the LORD hath anointed me to preach good tidings unto the meek; he hath sent me to bind up the brokenhearted, to proclaim liberty to the captives, and the opening of the prison to them that are bound; **To proclaim the acceptable year of the LORD,** and the day of vengeance of our God; to comfort all that mourn.

Fulfillment: **Matthew 3:16-17**
And Jesus, when he was baptized, went up straightway out of the water: and, lo, the heavens were opened unto him, and **he saw the Spirit of God descending like a dove, and lighting upon him:** And lo a voice from heaven, saying, This is my beloved Son, in whom I am well pleased.

Fulfillment: **Luke 4:15-19**
And he taught in their synagogues, being glorified of all. And he came to Nazareth, where he had been brought up: and, **as his custom was, he went into the synagogue on the sabbath day, and stood up for to read.** And there was delivered unto him the book of the prophet Esaias. And when he had opened the book, he found the place where it was written, The Spirit of the Lord is upon me, because he hath anointed me **to preach the gospel** to the poor; he hath sent me to heal the broken-hearted, to preach deliverance to the captives, and recovering of sight to the blind, **to set at liberty** them that are bruised, **To preach the acceptable year of the Lord.**

259. **He would provide freedom from the bondage of sin and death and proclaim a period of grace**   Isaiah 61:1-2
The Spirit of the Lord GOD is upon me; because the LORD hath anointed me to preach good tidings unto the meek; he hath sent me to bind up the brokenhearted, **to proclaim liberty to the captives, and the opening of the prison to them that are bound; To proclaim the acceptable year of the LORD,** and the day of vengeance of our God; to comfort all that mourn.

Fulfillment: **Matthew 11:5**
The blind receive their sight, and the lame walk, the lepers are cleansed, and the deaf hear, the dead are raised up, and the poor have the gospel preached to them.

Fulfillment: **John 5:24**
Verily, verily, I say unto you, He that heareth my word, and believeth on him that sent me, hath everlasting life, and shall not come into condemnation; **but is passed from death unto life.**

Fulfillment: **John 8:31-32**
Then said Jesus to those Jews which believed on him, If ye continue in my word, then are ye my disciples indeed; And **ye shall know the truth, and the truth shall make you free.**

"A Christian man is the most free lord of all, subject to no one. A Christian man is the dutiful servant of all, subject to everyone."

Martin Luther   **"See Mark 10:44"**

JEREMIAH

This is the 24th book of the Bible, written approximately 640 B.C. **– 577** B.C. **Jeremiah covers from the earth being without form to about 539** B.C. **It was probably written in Jerusalem by Jeremiah and recorded by his scribe Baruch.
It has 52 chapters.**

260.   **The lord is True**   **Jeremiah 10:10**

But the LORD *is* **the true God,** he *is* the living God, and an everlasting king: at his wrath the earth shall tremble, and the nations shall not be able to abide his indignation.

   Fulfillment: Matthew 22:16

And they sent out unto him their disciples with the Herodians, saying, **Master, we know that thou art true, and teachest the way of God in truth,** neither carest thou for any *man*: for thou regardest not the person of men.

   Fulfillment: John 7:18

He that speaketh of himself seeketh his own glory: but he that seeketh his glory that sent him, **the same is true,** and no unrighteousness is in him.

   Fulfillment: 1 John 5:20

And we know that the Son of God is come, and hath given us an understanding, that **we may know him that is true, and we are in him that is true,** *even* in his Son Jesus Christ. This is the true God, and eternal life.

   Fulfillment: Revelations 19:11

And I saw heaven opened, and behold a white horse; and he that sat upon him *was* **called Faithful and True,** and in righteousness he doth judge and make war.

261.   **Descendant of David**   **Jeremiah 23:5-6**

Behold, the days come, saith the LORD, that I will raise unto David a righteous Branch, and a King shall reign and prosper, and shall execute judgment and justice in the earth. In his days Judah shall be saved, and Israel shall dwell safely: and this is his name whereby he shall be called, THE LORD OUR RIGHTEOUSNESS.

   Fulfillment: Luke 3:23-38

And Jesus himself began to be about thirty years of age, being (as was supposed) the son of Joseph, which was *the son* of Heli, 24Which was *the son* of Matthat, which was *the son* of Levi, which was *the son* of Melchi, which was *the son* of Janna, which was *the son* of Joseph, 25Which was *the son* of Mattathias, which was *the son* of Amos, which was *the son* of Naum, which was *the son* of Esli, which was *the son* of Nagge, 26Which was *the son* of Maath, which was *the son* of Mattathias, which was *the son* of Semei, which was *the son* of Joseph, which was *the son* of Juda, 27Which was *the son* of Joanna, which was *the son* of Rhesa, which was *the son* of Zorobabel, which was *the son* of Salathiel, which was *the son* of Neri, 28Which was *the son* of Melchi, which was *the son* of Addi, which was *the son* of Cosam, which was *the son* of Elmodam, which was *the son* of Er, 29Which was *the son* of Jose, which was *the son* of Eliezer, which was *the son* of Jorim, which was *the son* of Matthat, which was *the son* of Levi, 30Which was *the son* of Simeon, which was *the son* of Juda, which was *the son* of Joseph, which was *the son* of Jonan, which was *the son* of Eliakim, 31Which was *the son* of Melea, which was *the son* of Menan, which was *the son* of Mattatha, which

was *the son* of Nathan, which was ***the son* of David**, 32Which was *the son* of Jesse, which was *the son* of Obed, which was *the son* of Booz, which was *the son* of Salmon, which was *the son* of Naasson, 33Which was *the son* of Aminadab, which was *the son* of Aram, which was *the son* of Esrom, which was *the son* of Phares, which was *the son* of Juda, 34Which was *the son* of Jacob, which was *the son* of Isaac, which was *the son* of Abraham, which was *the son* of Thara, which was *the son* of Nachor, 35Which was *the son* of Saruch, which was *the son* of Ragau, which was *the son* of Phalec, which was *the son* of Heber, which was *the son* of Sala, 36Which was *the son* of Cainan, which was *the son* of Arphaxad, which was *the son* of Sem, which was *the son* of Noe, which was *the son* of Lamech, 37Which was *the son* of Mathusala, which was *the son* of Enoch, which was *the son* of Jared, which was *the son* of Maleleel, which was *the son* of Cainan, 38Which was *the son* of Enos, which was *the son* of Seth, which was *the son* of Adam, which was *the son* of God.

262. **The Messiah would be God**   **Jeremiah 23:5-6**

Behold, the days come, saith the LORD, that I will raise unto David a righteous Branch, and a King shall reign and prosper, and shall execute judgment and justice in the earth. In his days Judah shall be saved, and Israel shall dwell safely: **and this is his name whereby he shall be called, THE LORD OUR RIGHTEOUSNESS.**

         Fulfillment: John 13:13

Ye call me Master and Lord: and ye say well; for so I am.

263. **The Messiah would be God and man**   **Jeremiah 23:5-6**

Behold, the days come, saith the LORD, that **I will raise unto David a righteous Branch,** and a King shall reign and prosper, and shall execute judgment and justice in the earth. In his days Judah shall be saved, and Israel shall dwell safely: **and this is his name whereby he shall be called, THE LORD OUR RIGHTEOUSNESS.**

         Fulfillment: 1 Timothy 3:16

And without controversy great is the mystery of godliness: **God was manifest in the flesh,** justified in the Spirit, seen of angels, preached unto the Gentiles, believed on in the world, received up into glory.

264. **He shall govern His people as a Governor**   **Jeremiah 30:21**

And their nobles shall be of themselves, and **their governor shall proceed from the midst of them;** and I will cause him to draw near, and he shall approach unto me: for who *is* this that engaged his heart to approach unto me? saith the LORD.

         Fulfillment: Matthew 2:6

And thou Bethlehem, *in* the land of Juda, art not the least among the princes of Juda: **for out of thee shall come a Governor,** that shall rule my people Israel.

265. **His love would be everlasting and draw us to Him**   **Jeremiah 31:3**

The LORD hath appeared of old unto me, *saying*, Yea, **I have loved thee with an everlasting love: therefore with lovingkindness have I drawn thee.**

         Fulfillment: John 3:16

For God so loved the world, that he gave his only begotten Son, that whosoever believeth in him should not perish, but have everlasting life.

         Fulfillment: John 15:13

Greater love hath no man than this, that a man lay down his life for his friends.

         Fulfillment: 2 Corinthians 5:14-15

For the love of Christ constraineth us; because we thus judge, that if one died for all, then were all dead: **And *that* he died for all,** that they which live should not henceforth live unto themselves, but unto him which died for them, and rose again.

"It is wise to make fasting a way of life. Missing a meal on a regular basis will help you to keep your appetite in check. It will also put a joyful thanksgiving in your heart every time you sit down to a meal."

Ray Comfort   **"See Psalms 35:13"**

266.　　**His birth would trigger a massacre of infant boys**　　　　　**Jeremiah 31:15**
Thus saith the LORD; **A voice was heard in Ramah, lamentation, and bitter weeping; Rahel weeping for her children** refused to be comforted for her children, because they were not.
　　　　Fulfillment:　Matthew 2:16-18
Then Herod, when he saw that he was mocked of the wise men, was exceeding wroth, and **sent forth, and slew all the children that were in Bethlehem, and in all the coasts thereof, from two years old and under,** according to the time which he had diligently enquired of the wise men. Then was fulfilled that which was spoken by Jeremy the prophet, saying, In Rama was there a voice heard, **lamentation, and weeping, and great mourning, Rachel weeping for her children, and would not be comforted,** because they are not.

267.　　**He would be born of a virgin**　　　　　**Jeremiah 31:22**
How long wilt thou go about, O thou backsliding daughter? For the LORD hath created a new thing in the earth, **A woman shall compass a man.**
　　　　Fulfillment:　Matthew 1:18-20
Now the birth of Jesus Christ was on this wise: When as his mother Mary was espoused to Joseph, before they came together, **she was found with child of the Holy Ghost.** Then Joseph her husband, being a just man, and not willing to make her a publick example, was minded to put her away privily. But while he thought on these things, behold, the angel of the Lord appeared unto him in a dream, saying, Joseph, thou son of David, fear not to take unto thee Mary thy wife: **for that which is conceived in her is of the Holy Ghost.**

The average person dies at 70 years old.

If you are:　　　　　　　　You have:

20 years old	2,500 weekends left
30 years old	2,000 weekends left
40 years old	1,500 weekends left
50 years old	1,000 weekends left
60 years old	500 weekends left

According to the U.S. Census Bureau, 150,000 people die every 24 hours.

"For a thousand years in thy sight *are but* as yesterday when it is past, and *as* a watch in the night."

Psalms 90:4
191

268. **The Messiah would be the new covenant** Jeremiah 31:31

Behold, the days come, saith the LORD, that **I will make a new covenant with the house of Israel, and with the house of Judah.**

Fulfillment: Matthew 26:26-30

And as they were eating, Jesus took bread, and blessed it, and brake it, and gave it to the disciples, and said, Take, eat; this is my body. And he took the cup, and gave thanks, and gave it to them, saying, Drink ye all of it; **For this is my blood of the new testament, which is shed for many for the remission of sins.** But I say unto you, I will not drink henceforth of this fruit of the vine, until that day when I drink it new with you in my Father's kingdom. And when they had sung an hymn, they went out into the mount of Olives.

269. **Descendant of David** Jeremiah 33:14-15

Behold, the days come, saith the LORD, that I will perform that good thing which I have promised unto the house of Israel and to the house of Judah. In those days, and at that time, will **I cause the Branch of righteousness to grow up unto David;** and he shall execute judgment and righteousness in the land.

Fulfillment: Luke 3:23-38

And Jesus himself began to be about thirty years of age, being (as was supposed) the son of Joseph, which was *the son* of Heli, ^{24}Which was *the son* of Matthat, which was *the son* of Levi, which was *the son* of Melchi, which was *the son* of Janna, which was *the son* of Joseph, ^{25}Which was *the son* of Mattathias, which was *the son* of Amos, which was *the son* of Naum, which was *the son* of Esli, which was *the son* of Nagge, ^{26}Which was *the son* of Maath, which was *the son* of Mattathias, which was *the son* of Semei, which was *the son* of Joseph, which was *the son* of Juda, ^{27}Which was *the son* of Joanna, which was *the son* of Rhesa, which was *the son* of Zorobabel, which was *the son* of Salathiel, which was *the son* of Neri, ^{28}Which was *the son* of Melchi, which was *the son* of Addi, which was *the son* of Cosam, which was *the son* of Elmodam, which was *the son* of Er, ^{29}Which was *the son* of Jose, which was *the son* of Eliezer, which was *the son* of Jorim, which was *the son* of Matthat, which was *the son* of Levi, ^{30}Which was *the son* of Simeon, which was *the son* of Juda, which was *the son* of Joseph, which was *the son* of Jonan, which was *the son* of Eliakim, ^{31}Which was *the son* of Melea, which was *the son* of Menan, which was *the son* of Mattatha, which was *the son* of Nathan, which was *the son* of David, ^{32}Which was *the son* of Jesse, which was *the son* of Obed, which was *the son* of Booz, which was *the son* of Salmon, which was *the son* of Naasson, ^{33}Which was *the son* of Aminadab, which was *the son* of Aram, which was *the son* of Esrom, which was *the son* of Phares, which was *the son* of Juda, ^{34}Which was *the son* of Jacob, which was *the son* of Isaac, which was *the son* of Abraham, which was *the son* of Thara, which was *the son* of Nachor, ^{35}Which was *the son* of Saruch, which was *the son* of Ragau, which was *the son* of Phalec, which was *the son* of Heber, which was *the son* of Sala, ^{36}Which was *the son* of Cainan, which was *the son* of Arphaxad, which was *the son* of Sem, which was *the son* of Noe, which was *the son* of Lamech, ^{37}Which was *the son* of Mathusala, which was *the son* of Enoch, which was *the son* of Jared, which was *the son* of Maleleel, which was *the son* of Cainan, ^{38}Which was *the son* of Enos, which was *the son* of Seth, which was *the son* of Adam, which was *the son* of God.

"Remember that courage isn't the absence of fear, but the conquering of it. If we really care for the lost, each of us must learn to push aside fear and replace it with faith in God. You do your part, and God will do His."

Ray Comfort **"See Psalms 118:6"**

192

EZEKIAL

This is the 26th book of the Bible, written approximately 593 B.C. – 570 B.C. Ezekial covers from Eden to about 571 B.C. It was written in Babylon by Ezekial. It has 48 chapters

270. **He would speak in Parables**   **Ezekial 17:1-2**
And the word of the LORD came unto me, saying, Son of man, put forth a riddle, and **speak a parable unto the house of Israel.**
       Fulfillment: Matthew 13:3
And **he spake many things unto them in parables,** saying, Behold, a sower went forth to sow.
       Fulfillment: Mark 4:13
And he said unto them, **Know ye not this parable? and how then will ye know all parables?**
       Fulfillment: Luke 5:36-39
And he spake also a parable unto them; No man putteth a piece of a new garment upon an old; if otherwise, then both the new maketh a rent, and the piece that was *taken* out of the new agreeth not with the old. And no man putteth new wine into old bottles; else the new wine will burst the bottles, and be spilled, and the bottles shall perish. But new wine must be put into new bottles; and both are preserved. No man also having drunk old *wine* straightway desireth new: for he saith, The old is better.
       Fulfillment: Luke 8:10
And he said, **Unto you it is given to know the mysteries of the kingdom of God: but to others in parables;** that seeing they might not see, and hearing they might not understand.

271. **He would amaze the people**   **Ezekial 32:10**
Yea, I will make many people amazed at thee, and their kings shall be horribly afraid for thee, when I shall brandish my sword before them; and they shall tremble at *every* moment, every man for his own life, in the day of thy fall.
       Fulfillment: Mark 5:20
And he departed, and began to publish in Decapolis how great things Jesus had done for him: **and all *men* did marvel.**
       Fulfillment: Mark 14:33
And he taketh with him Peter and James and John, and began to be sore **amazed,** and to be very heavy.

"All the ways of a man *are* clean in his own eyes; but the LORD weigheth the spirits."

Proverbs 16:2

And I will set up one shepherd over them, and he shall feed them, even my servant David; he shall feed them, and he shall be their shepherd. And I the LORD will be their God, and **my servant David a prince among them;** I the LORD have spoken it.

Fulfillment: Matthew 1:1

The book of the generation of Jesus Christ, the **son of David,** the son of Abraham.

Fulfillment: Luke 3:23-31

And Jesus himself began to be about thirty years of age, being (as was supposed) the son of Joseph, which was *the son* of Heli, ^{24}Which was *the son* of Matthat, which was *the son* of Levi, which was *the son* of Melchi, which was *the son* of Janna, which was *the son* of Joseph, ^{25}Which was *the son* of Mattathias, which was *the son* of Amos, which was *the son* of Naum, which was *the son* of Esli, which was *the son* of Nagge, ^{26}Which was *the son* of Maath, which was *the son* of Mattathias, which was *the son* of Semei, which was *the son* of Joseph, which was *the son* of Juda, ^{27}Which was *the son* of Joanna, which was *the son* of Rhesa, which was *the son* of Zorobabel, which was *the son* of Salathiel, which was *the son* of Neri, ^{28}Which was *the son* of Melchi, which was *the son* of Addi, which was *the son* of Cosam, which was *the son* of Elmodam, which was *the son* of Er, ^{29}Which was *the son* of Jose, which was *the son* of Eliezer, which was *the son* of Jorim, which was *the son* of Matthat, which was *the son* of Levi, ^{30}Which was *the son* of Simeon, which was *the son* of Juda, which was *the son* of Joseph, which was *the son* of Jonan, which was *the son* of Eliakim, ^{31}Which was *the son* of Melea, which was *the son* of Menan, which was *the son* of Mattatha, which was *the son* of Nathan, which was ***the son* of David**, ^{32}Which was *the son* of Jesse, which was *the son* of Obed, which was *the son* of Booz, which was *the son* of Salmon, which was *the son* of Naasson, ^{33}Which was *the son* of Aminadab, which was *the son* of Aram, which was *the son* of Esrom, which was *the son* of Phares, which was *the son* of Juda, ^{34}Which was *the son* of Jacob, which was *the son* of Isaac, which was *the son* of Abraham, which was *the son* of Thara, which was *the son* of Nachor, ^{35}Which was *the son* of Saruch, which was *the son* of Ragau, which was *the son* of Phalec, which was *the son* of Heber, which was *the son* of Sala, ^{36}Which was *the son* of Cainan, which was *the son* of Arphaxad, which was *the son* of Sem, which was *the son* of Noe, which was *the son* of Lamech, ^{37}Which was *the son* of Mathusala, which was *the son* of Enoch, which was *the son* of Jared, which was *the son* of Maleleel, which was *the son* of Cainan, ^{38}Which was *the son* of Enos, which was *the son* of Seth, which was *the son* of Adam, which was *the son* of God.

Does This Remind You of How Your Church Views Witnessing?

This is a story about four people.   Their names were **Everybody, Somebody , Anybody, and Nobody**.   There was a very important job that needed to be done and **Everybody** was asked to do it. **Everybody** was sure **Somebody** would do it.   **Anybody** could have done it, but **Nobody** wound up doing it.   **Somebody** got really angry about that, because it was **Everybody**'s job.   **Everybody** thought **Anybody** could do it but **Nobody** realized that **Everybody** wouldn't do it. It ended up that **Everybody** blamed **Somebody** when **Nobody** did what **Anybody** could have done.

DANIEL

This is the 27th book of the Bible, written approximately 605 B.C. – 536 B.C. Daniel covers form about 605 B.C. to 537 B.C. It was written in Babylon by Daniel. It has 12 chapters.

273. **Jesus is the Stone made without hands**   **Daniel 2:34**

Thou sawest till that **a stone was cut out without hands, which smote the image** upon his feet *that were* of iron and clay, and brake them to pieces.

     Fulfillment: Matthew 21:44

And whosoever shall fall on this stone shall be broken: but on whomsoever it shall fall, it will grind him to powder.

274. **He would ascend into Heaven and in like manner come again**   **Daniel 7:13-14a**

I saw in the night visions, and, behold, one like the **Son of man came with the clouds of heaven, and came to the Ancient of days, and they brought him near before him.** And there was given him dominion, and glory, and a kingdom, that all people, nations, and languages, should serve him: his dominion is an everlasting dominion, which shall not pass away, and his kingdom that which shall not be destroyed.

     Fulfillment: Acts 1:9-11

And when he had spoken these things, while they beheld, he was taken up; and a cloud received him out of their sight. And while they looked stedfastly toward heaven as he went up, behold, two men stood by them in white apparel; Which also said, Ye men of Galilee, why stand ye gazing up into heaven? This same **Jesus, which is taken up from you into heaven, shall so come in like manner as ye have seen him go into heaven.**

275. **He would be highly exalted,**   **Daniel 7:13-14**

I saw in the night visions, and, behold, one like the Son of man came with the clouds of heaven, and came to the Ancient of days, and they brought him near before him. **And there was given him dominion, and glory, and a kingdom, that all people, nations, and languages, should serve him:** his dominion is an everlasting dominion, which shall not pass away, and his kingdom that which shall not be destroyed.

     Fulfillment: Ephesians 1:20-22

Which he wrought in Christ, when he raised **him from the dead, and set him at his own right hand in the heavenly places, Far above all principality, and power, and might, and dominion,** and every name that is named, not only in this world, but also in that which is to come: And hath put all things under his feet, and gave him to be the head over all things to the church.

"I believe the holier a man becomes, the more he mourns over the unholiness which remains in him."

Charles Spurgeon   **"See Romans 7"**

276.   **His dominion would be Everlasting**   **Daniel 7:13-14**
I saw in the night visions, and, behold, one like the Son of man came with the clouds of heaven, and came to the Ancient of days, and they brought him near before him. **And there was given him dominion, and glory, and a kingdom, that all people, nations, and languages, should serve him: his dominion is an everlasting dominion, which shall not pass away,** and his kingdom that which shall not be destroyed.
        Fulfillment: Luke 1:31-33
And, behold, thou shalt conceive in thy womb, and bring forth a son, and shalt call his name JESUS. He shall be great, and shall be called the Son of the Highest: and the Lord God shall give unto him the throne of his father David: **And he shall reign over the house of Jacob for ever; and of his kingdom there shall be no end.**

277.   **He would make an end to sins**   **Daniel 9:24**
Seventy weeks are determined upon thy people and upon thy holy city, to finish the transgression, and **to make an end of sins,** and to make reconciliation for iniquity, and **to bring in everlasting righteousness,** and to seal up the vision and prophecy, and to anoint the most Holy.
        Fulfillment: Galatians 1:3-5
Grace be to you and peace from God the Father, and from our Lord Jesus Christ, **Who gave himself for our sins, that he might deliver us from this present evil world,** according to the will of God and our Father: To whom be glory for ever and ever. Amen.
        Fulfillment: Romans 8:1-3
There is **therefore now no condemnation to them which are in Christ Jesus,** who walk not after the flesh, but after the Spirit. For the law of the Spirit of life in **Christ Jesus hath made me free from the law of sin and death.** For what the law could not do, in that it was weak through the flesh, **God sending his own Son in the likeness of sinful flesh, and for sin, condemned sin in the flesh.**

278.   **He would be Holy**   **Daniel 9:24**
Seventy weeks are determined upon thy people and upon thy holy city, to finish the transgression, and to make an end of sins, and to make reconciliation for iniquity, and to bring in everlasting righteousness, and to seal up the vision and prophecy, **and to anoint the most Holy.**
        Fulfillment: Luke 1:35
And the angel answered and said unto her, The Holy Ghost shall come upon thee, and the power of the Highest shall overshadow thee: therefore also **that holy thing which shall be born of thee shall be called the Son of God.**

"Scientists who go about teaching that evolution is a fact of life are great con – men, and the story they are telling may be the greatest hoax ever. In explaining evolution, we do not have one iota of fact."

Dr. T.N. Tahmisian, Atomic Energy Commission   **"See Mark 10:6"**

196

279.   Jesus Christ's baptism and anointing foretold   Daniel 9:24
Seventy weeks are determined upon thy people and upon thy holy city, to finish the transgression, and to make an end of sins, and to make reconciliation for iniquity, and to bring in everlasting righteousness, and to seal up the vision and prophecy, **and to anoint the most Holy.**
            Fulfillment: Matthew 3:13-17
Then cometh Jesus from Galilee to Jordan unto John, to be baptized of him. But John forbad him, saying, I have need to be baptized of thee, and comest thou to me? And Jesus answering said unto him, Suffer *it to be so* now: for thus it becometh us to fulfil all righteousness. Then he suffered him. **And Jesus, when he was baptized,** went up straightway out of the water: and, lo, the heavens were opened unto him, and **he saw the Spirit of God descending like a dove,** and lighting upon him: And lo a voice from heaven, saying, This is my beloved Son, in whom I am well pleased.

280.   Announcement of the Messiahs arrival 483 years from the decree to rebuild the city of Jerusalem   Daniel 9:25
Know therefore and understand, **that from the going forth of the commandment to restore and to build Jerusalem unto the Messiah the Prince shall be seven weeks, and threescore and two weeks:** the street shall be built again, and the wall, even in troublous times.
            Fulfillment: John 12:12-13
On the next day much people that were come to the feast, when they heard that Jesus was coming to Jerusalem, Took branches of palm trees, and went forth to meet him, and cried, Hosanna: **Blessed is the King of Israel that cometh in the name of the Lord.**

281.   The Messiah would be killed   Daniel 9:26
And after threescore and two weeks shall **Messiah be cut off,** but not for himself: and the people of the prince that shall come shall destroy the city and the sanctuary; and the end thereof shall be with a flood, and unto the end of the war desolations are determined.
            Fulfillment: Matthew 27:35
And they crucified him, and parted his garments, casting lots: that it might be fulfilled which was spoken by the prophet, They parted my garments among them, and upon my vesture did they cast lots.

"Believe what you believe, or else you will never persuade anybody else to believe it."

Charles Spurgeon   **"See Matthew 22:29"**

282. **He would be killed before the destruction of the temple** Daniel 9:26c

And after threescore and two weeks **shall Messiah be cut off, but not for himself: and the people of the prince that shall come shall destroy the city and the sanctuary;** and the end thereof shall be with a flood, and unto the end of the war desolations are determined.

Fulfillment: Matthew 27:50-51

Jesus, when he had cried again with a loud voice, yielded up the ghost. **And, behold, the veil of the temple was rent in twain from the top to the bottom;** and the earth did quake, and the rocks rent.

283. **He would cause the sacrifice and oblation to cease** Daniel 9:27

And he shall confirm the covenant with many for one week: and **in the midst of the week he shall cause the sacrifice and the oblation to cease,** and for the overspreading of abominations he shall make *it* desolate, even until the consummation, and that determined shall be poured upon the desolate.

Fulfillment: Hebrews 1010-12

By the which will **we are sanctified through the offering of the body of Jesus Christ nce *for all.*** And every priest standeth daily ministering and offering oftentimes the same sacrifices, which can never take away sins: But this man, after **he had offered one sacrifice for sins for ever,** sat down on the right hand of God.

284. **The Messiah in His glorified state** Daniel 10:5-6

Then I lifted up mine eyes, and looked, and behold a certain man clothed in linen, whose loins **were girded with fine gold of Uphaz: His body also was like the beryl, and his face as the appearance of lightning, and his eyes as lamps of fire, and his arms and his feet like in colour to polished brass, and the voice of his words like the voice of a multitude.**

Fulfillment: Revelations 1:13-16

And in the midst of the seven candlesticks one like unto the Son of man, clothed with a garment down to the foot, and girt about the paps with a golden girdle. **His head and his hairs were white like wool, as white as snow; and his eyes were as a flame of fire; And his feet like unto fine brass, as if they burned in a furnace; and his voice as the sound of many waters.** And he had in his right hand seven stars: and out of his mouth went a sharp twoedged sword: and his countenance was as the sun shineth in his strength.

"The heavens declare the glory of God; and the firmament sheweth his handiwork. Day unto day uttereth speech, and night unto night sheweth knowledge. *There is* no speech nor language, *where* their voice is not heard. Their line is gone out through all the earth, and their words to the end of the world. In them hath he set a tabernacle for the sun."

Psalms 19:1-4

HOSEA

This is the 28th book of the Bible, written approximately 760 B.C. – 715 B.C. Hosea covers from about 770 B.C. to 723 B.C. It was written in the Northern kingdom of Israel by Hosea. It has 14 chapters.

285. **He would come out of Egypt** **Hosea 11:1**
When Israel was a child, then I loved him, and **called my son out of Egypt.**
      Fulfillment: Matthew 2:14-15
When he arose, he took the young child and his mother by night, and departed into Egypt: And was there until the death of Herod: that it might be fulfilled which was spoken of the Lord by the prophet, saying, **Out of Egypt have I called my son.**

JOEL

This is the 29th book of the Bible, written approximately 839 B.C. – 795 B.C. Joel covers from 836 B.C. to about 828 B.C. It was written in the southern Kingdom of Israel by Joel. It has 3 chapters.

286. **He would offer salvation to all mankind** **Joel 2:32**
And it shall come to pass, that **whosoever shall call on the name of the LORD shall be delivered:** for in mount Zion and in Jerusalem shall be deliverance, as the LORD hath said, and in the remnant whom the LORD shall call.
      Fulfillment: Romans 10:12-13
For there is no difference between the Jew and the Greek: for the same Lord over all is rich unto all that call upon him. **For whosoever shall call upon the name of the Lord shall be saved.**

AMOS

This is the 30th book of the Bible, written approximately 765 B.C. – 750 B.C. Amos covers 764 B.C. It was written in new Jerusalem by Amos.
It has 9 chapters.

287. **God would darken the earth** **Amos 8:9**
And it shall come to pass in that day, saith the Lord GOD, that **I will cause the sun to go down at noon, and I will darken the earth in the clear day.**

      Fulfillment: Matthew 27:45
Now from the sixth hour **there was darkness over all the land** unto the ninth hour.

"What would life be if we had no courage to attempt anything?"

Vincent Van Gogh **"See Psalm 31:24"**

JONAH

This is the 32nd book of the Bible, written approximately 790 B.C. – 749 B.C. Jonah covers 767 B.C. It was written in Israel by Jonah. It has 4 chapters.

288.   Three days and three nights   Jonah 1:17

Now the LORD had prepared a great fish to swallow up Jonah. **And Jonah was in the belly of the fish three days and three nights.**
                    Fulfillment: Matthew 12:40
For as Jonas was three days and three nights in the whale's belly; so shall the Son of man be three days and three nights in the heart of the earth.

Do You Feel Discouraged By Negative Reactions To The Gospel?
(Paul wasn't received well, either.)

Acts 13:45 - But when the Jews…spake against those things which were spoken by Paul, contradicting and blaspheming.

Acts 13:50 - But the Jews stirred up…and raised persecution against Paul and Barnabas, and expelled them out of their coasts.

Acts 14:5 - And when there was an assault made both of the Gentiles, and also of the Jews with their rulers, to use *them* despitefully, and to stone them.

Acts 14:19 - Jews from Antioch and Iconium, who persuaded the people, and, having stoned Paul, drew *him* out of the city, supposing he had been dead.

Acts 16:23 - And when they had laid many stripes upon them, they cast *them* into prison.

Acts 18:6 - And when they opposed themselves, and blasphemed, he shook *his* raiment, and said unto them, Your blood *be* upon your own heads; I *am* clean.

Acts 19:28 - And when they heard *these sayings*, they were full of wrath.

Acts 20:23 - Save that the Holy Ghost witnesseth in every city, saying that bonds and afflictions abide me.

Acts 22:22 - And they gave him audience unto this word, and *then* lifted up their voices, and said, Away with such a *fellow* from the earth: for it is not fit that he should live.

Acts 23:2 - And the high priest Ananias commanded them that stood by him to smite him on the mouth.

Acts 23:10 - And when there arose a great dissension, the chief captain, fearing lest Paul should have been pulled in pieces of them, commanded the soldiers to go down, and to take him by force from among them, and to bring *him* into the castle.

Acts 23:13 - Certain of the Jews banded together, and bound themselves under a curse, saying that they would neither eat nor drink till they had killed Paul.

Acts 24:5 - For we have found this man *a* pestilent *fellow*, and a mover of sedition among all the Jews throughout the world, and a ringleader of the sect of the Nazarenes.

"I have given them thy word; and the world hath hated them, because they are not of the world, even as I am not of the world."
John 17:13

MICAH

This is the 33rd book of the Bible, written approximately 740 B.C. – 687 B.C. Micah covers from about 744 B.C. to 704 B.C. It was written in Judah by Micah. It has 7 chapters.

289. **He would be beaten with a rod**   Micah 5:1
Now gather thyself in troops, O daughter of troops: he hath laid siege against us: **they shall smite the judge of Israel with a rod upon thy cheek.**
      Fulfillment: Mark 15:19
And **they smote him on the head with a reed**, and did spit upon him, and bowing their knees worshipped him.

290. **He would be from everlasting**   Micah 5:2
But thou, Bethlehem Ephratah, though thou be little among the thousands of Judah, yet out of thee shall he come forth unto me that is to be ruler in Israel; **whose goings forth have been from of old, from everlasting.**
      Fulfillment: John 8:58
Jesus said unto them, Verily, verily, I say unto you, **Before Abraham was, I am.**

Evangelistic Survey

?   Where do people go when they die?

?   What do you think God is like?

?   If you could ask God one thing, what would it be?

?   Should God punish murderers? If so, how should He punish them?

?   What do you think a person has to do to go to Heaven?

?   Do you consider yourself to be a "good" person?

?   How many of the Ten Commandments can you name?

?   Do you think you have kept the Ten Commandments?

?   Where would you go if you died tonight?

?   Do you believe there is such a place as hell?

?   If there was a way to avoid death, would you be interested?

?   Do you think the Bible's claim that someone can know that they have everlasting life is true?

?   Who do you think Jesus is?

?   What is stopping you from asking God for forgiveness and being converted right now?"

"Do the work of an evangelist, make full proof of thy ministry."

2 Timothy 4:5

201

291. **He would be Born in Bethlehem**   Micah 5:2

But thou, **Bethlehem Ephratah,** though thou be little among the thousands of Judah, yet **out of thee shall he come forth unto me** that is to be ruler in Israel; whose goings forth have been from of old, from everlasting.

Fulfillment: Matthew 2:1-2

Now when **Jesus was born in Bethlehem** of Judaea in the days of Herod the king, behold, there came wise men from the east to Jerusalem, Saying, Where is he that is born King of the Jews? For we have seen his star in the east, and are come to worship him.

Fulfillment: John 7:42

Hath not the scripture said, **That Christ cometh of the seed of David, and out of the town of Bethlehem,** where David was?

Fulfillment: Luke 2:1-20

And it came to pass in those days, that there went out a decree from Caesar Augustus, that all the world should be taxed. (*And* this taxing was first made when Cyrenius was governor of Syria.) And all went to be taxed, every one into his own city. **And Joseph also went up from Galilee, out of the city of Nazareth, into Judaea, unto the city of David, which is called Bethlehem; (because he was of the house and lineage of David:) To be taxed with Mary his espoused wife, being great with child.** And so it was, that, while they were there, the days were accomplished that she should be delivered. **And she brought forth her firstborn son,** and wrapped him in swaddling clothes, and laid him in a manger; because there was no room for them in the inn. And there were in the same country shepherds abiding in the field, keeping watch over their flock by night. And, lo, the angel of the Lord came upon them, and the glory of the Lord shone round about them: and they were sore afraid. And the angel said unto them, Fear not: for, behold, I bring you good tidings of great joy, which shall be to all people. **For unto you is born this day in the city of David a Saviour, which is Christ the Lord.** And this *shall be* a sign unto you; Ye shall find the babe wrapped in swaddling clothes, lying in a manger. **And suddenly there was with the angel a multitude of the heavenly host praising God, and saying, Glory to God in the highest, and on earth peace, good will toward men.** And it came to pass, as the angels were gone away from them into heaven, the shepherds said one to another, **Let us now go even unto Bethlehem, and see this thing which is come to pass, which the Lord hath made known unto us.** And they came with haste, and found Mary, and Joseph, and the babe lying in a manger. And when they had seen *it*, they made known abroad the saying which was told them concerning this child. And all they that heard *it* wondered at those things which were told them by the shepherds. But Mary kept all these things, and pondered *them* in her heart. And the shepherds returned, glorifying and praising God for all the things that they had heard and seen, as it was told unto them.

"I have been driven many times upon my knees by the overwhelming conviction that I had nowhere else to go. My own wisdom, and that of all about me, seemed insufficient for that day."

Abraham Lincoln   **"See Mark 1:35"**

NAHUM

This is the 34th book of the Bible, written possibly before 612 B.C. It was written by Nahum. It has 3 chapters.

292.   **The Lord is Good**   **Nahum 1:7**
The LORD *is* **good,** a strong hold in the day of trouble; and he knoweth them that trust in him.
        Fulfillment: Matthew 19:16-17
And, behold, one came and said unto him, **Good Master**, what good thing shall I do, that I may have eternal life? And he said unto him, **Why callest thou me good?** *there is* **none good but one,** *that is,* **God:** but if thou wilt enter into life, keep the commandments.
        Fulfillment: Acts 10:38
How **God anointed Jesus of Nazareth** with the Holy Ghost and with power: **who went about doing good,** and healing all that were oppressed of the devil; for God was with him.

HABAKKUK

This is the 35th book of the Bible, It is unknown when it was written. It was written in Judah by Habakkuk. It has 3 chapters.

293.   **He would do marvelous things and amaze the people**   **Habakkuk 1:5**
Behold ye among the heathen, and regard, and **wonder marvellously:** for *I* **will work a work in your days,** *which* **ye will not believe,** though it be told *you*.
        Fulfillment: Matthew 12:22-24
Then was brought unto him one possessed with a devil, blind, and dumb: and he healed him, insomuch that the blind and dumb both spake and saw. **And all the people were amazed,** and said, Is not this the son of David? But when the Pharisees heard *it*, they said, This *fellow* doth not cast out devils, but by Beelzebub the prince of the devils.
        Fulfillment: Mark 2:11-12
I say unto thee, Arise, and take up thy bed, and go thy way into thine house. And immediately he arose, took up the bed, and went forth before them all; insomuch that **they were all amazed, and glorified God,** saying, We never saw it on this fashion.
        Fulfillment: Mark 5:20
And he departed, and began to publish in Decapolis how **great things Jesus had done for him: and all** *men* **did marvel.**
        Fulfillment: Mark 6:51
And he went up unto them into the ship; and the wind ceased: and **they were sore amazed in themselves beyond measure, and wondered.**

"Do I not destroy my enemies when I make them my friends?"

Abraham Lincoln   **"See Matthew 5:44-48"**

HAGGAI

This is the 37th book of the Bible, written 520 B.C. and covers 521 B.C. Haggai wrote this book in Jerusalem. It has 2 chapters.

294. **He would visit the temple** Haggai 2:6-9

For thus saith the LORD of hosts; Yet once, it is a little while, and I will shake the heavens, and the earth, and the sea, and the dry land; And I will shake all nations, and the desire of all nations shall come: and **I will fill this house with glory,** saith the LORD of hosts. The silver is mine, and the gold is mine, saith the LORD of hosts. **The glory of this latter house shall be greater than of the former, saith the LORD of hosts: and in this place will I give peace,** saith the LORD of hosts.

Fulfillment: Luke 2:27-32

And he came by the Spirit into the temple: and when the parents brought in the child Jesus, to do for him after the custom of the law, Then took he him up in his arms, and blessed God, and said, Lord, now lettest thou thy servant depart in peace, according to thy word: **For mine eyes have seen thy salvation, Which thou hast prepared before the face of all people; A light to lighten the Gentiles, and the glory of thy people Israel.**

295. **Descendant of Zerubbabel** Haggai 2:23

In that day, saith the LORD of hosts, will I take thee, O **Zerubbabel,** my servant, the son of Shealtiel, saith the LORD, **and will make thee as a signet: for I have chosen thee, saith the LORD of hosts.**

Fulfillment: Luke 3:23-38

And Jesus himself began to be about thirty years of age, being (as was supposed) the son of Joseph, which was *the son* of Heli, 24Which was *the son* of Matthat, which was *the son* of Levi, which was *the son* of Melchi, which was *the son* of Janna, which was *the son* of Joseph, 25Which was *the son* of Mattathias, which was *the son* of Amos, which was *the son* of Naum, which was *the son* of Esli, which was *the son* of Nagge, 26Which was *the son* of Maath, which was *the son* of Mattathias, which was *the son* of Semei, which was *the son* of Joseph, which was *the son* of Juda, 27Which was *the son* of Joanna, which was *the son* of Rhesa, which was *the son* of **Zorobabel,** which was *the son* of Salathiel, which was *the son* of Neri, 28Which was *the son* of Melchi, which was *the son* of Addi, which was *the son* of Cosam, which was *the son* of Elmodam, which was *the son* of Er, 29Which was *the son* of Jose, which was *the son* of Eliezer, which was *the son* of Jorim, which was *the son* of Matthat, which was *the son* of Levi, 30Which was *the son* of Simeon, which was *the son* of Juda, which was *the son* of Joseph, which was *the son* of Jonan, which was *the son* of Eliakim, 31Which was *the son* of Melea, which was *the son* of Menan, which was *the son* of Mattatha, which was *the son* of Nathan, which was *the son* of David, 32Which was *the son* of Jesse, which was *the son* of Obed, which was *the son* of Booz, which was *the son* of Salmon, which was *the son* of Naasson, 33Which was *the son* of Aminadab, which was *the son* of Aram, which was *the son* of Esrom, which was *the son* of Phares, which was *the son* of Juda, 34Which was *the son* of Jacob, which was *the son* of Isaac, which was *the son* of Abraham, which was *the son* of Thara, which was *the son* of Nachor, 35Which was *the son* of Saruch, which was *the son* of Ragau, which was *the son* of Phalec, which was *the son* of Heber, which was *the son* of Sala, 36Which was *the son* of Cainan, which was *the son* of Arphaxad, which was *the son* of Sem, which was *the son* of Noe, which was *the son* of Lamech, 37Which was *the son* of Mathusala, which was *the son* of Enoch, which was *the son* of Jared, which was *the son* of Maleleel, which was *the son* of Cainan, 38Which was *the son* of Enos, which was *the son* of Seth, which was *the son* of Adam, which was *the son* of God.

"Only the Bible has 100% accurate prophecy! No other person, book, or religion can make that claim, only God knows the future."

L.B.K **"See Isaiah 48:2-5"**

ZECHARIAH

This is the 38th book of the Bible, written approximately 520 B.C. – 487 B.C. Zechariah covers from about 521 B.C. to 494 B.C. It was written in Jerusalem by Zechariah. It has 14 chapters.

296. **He would be God's servant**   Zechariah 3:8

Hear now, O Joshua the high priest, thou, and thy fellows that sit before thee: for they are men wondered at: for, behold, **I will bring forth my servant** the BRANCH.

     Fulfillment: John 17:4

I have glorified thee on the earth: I have finished the work which thou gavest me to do.

297. **He would be a Priest and a King**   Zechariah 6:12-13

And speak unto him, saying, Thus speaketh the LORD of hosts, saying, Behold the man whose name is The BRANCH; and he shall grow up out of his place, and he shall build the temple of the LORD: Even he shall build the temple of the LORD; and he shall bear the glory, **and shall sit and rule upon his throne; and he shall be a priest upon his throne: and the counsel of peace shall be between them both.**

     Fulfillment: Hebrews 8:1

Now of the things which we have spoken this is the sum: **We have such an high priest, who is set on the right hand of the throne of the Majesty in the heavens.**

298. **He would govern Judah**   Zechariah 9:7

And I will take away his blood out of his mouth, and his abominations from between his teeth: but he that remaineth, even he, *shall be* for our God, and **he shall be as a governor in Judah,** and Ekron as a Jebusite.

     Fulfillment: Matthew 2:6

And thou Bethlehem, *in* the land of Juda, art not the least **among the princes of Juda: for out of thee shall come a Governor,** that shall rule my people Israel.

O Man, forgive thy mortal foe,
Nor ever strike him blow to blow;
For all the souls on earth that live
To be forgiven must forgive-
Forgive him seven times and seven!
For all the blessed souls in Heaven
Are both Forgivers and Forgiven.
Alfred Tennyson, poet

"If a man say, I love God, and hateth his brother, he is a liar: for he that loveth not his brother whom he hath seen, how can he love God whom he hath not seen? And this commandment have we from him, That he who loveth God love his brother also."

1 John 4:20

205

299. **He comes as a King greeted with rejoicing riding on a donkey** Zechariah 9:9
Rejoice greatly, O daughter of Zion; shout, O daughter of Jerusalem: **behold, thy King cometh unto thee:** he is just, and having salvation; **lowly, and riding upon an ass, and upon a colt the foal of an ass.**
Fulfillment: Matthew 21:1-11
And when they drew nigh unto Jerusalem, and were come to Bethphage, unto the mount of Olives, then sent Jesus two disciples, Saying unto them, Go into the village over against you, and straightway ye shall find an ass tied, and a colt with her: loose them, and bring them unto me. And if any man say ought unto you, ye shall say, The Lord hath need of them; and straightway he will send them. **All this was done, that it might be fulfilled which was spoken by the prophet, saying, Tell ye the daughter of Sion, Behold, thy King cometh unto thee, meek, and sitting upon an ass, and a colt the foal of an ass.** And the disciples went, and did as Jesus commanded them, And brought the ass, and the colt, and put on them their clothes, and they set him thereon. And a very great multitude spread their garments in the way; others cut down branches from the trees, and strawed them in the way. And the multitudes that went before, and that followed, cried, saying, Hosanna to the Son of David: Blessed is he that cometh in the name of the Lord; Hosanna in the highest. And when he was come into Jerusalem, all the city was moved, saying, Who is this? And the multitude said, This is Jesus the prophet, of Nazareth of Galilee.

300. **The Messiah would be just and bring salvation** Zechariah 9:9
Rejoice greatly, O daughter of Zion; shout, O daughter of Jerusalem: behold, thy King cometh unto thee: **he is just, and having salvation;** lowly, and riding upon an ass, and upon a colt the foal of an ass.
Fulfillment: John 5:30
I can of mine own self do nothing: as I hear, I judge: and my judgment is just; because **I seek not mine own will, but the will of the Father which hath sent me.**
Fulfillment: Luke 19:9-10
And Jesus said unto him, **this day is salvation come to this house,** forsomuch as he also is a son of Abraham. For the Son of man is come to seek and to save that which was lost.

"Who could draw a picture of a man not yet born? Surely God, and God alone. Nobody knew over 500 hundred years ago that Shakespeare was going to be born; or over 250 years ago that Napoleon was to be born. Yet here in the Bible we have the most striking and unmistakable likeness of a man portrayed, not by one, but by twenty or twenty-five artists, none of whom had ever seen the man they were painting."

Canon Dyson Hague **"See 2 Peter 1:19-21"**

301.　**He would speak Peace**　　　　　　　　　　　　　　　　　**Zechariah 9:10**

And I will cut off the chariot from Ephraim, and the horse from Jerusalem, and the battle bow shall be cut off: and **he shall speak peace unto the heathen:** and his dominion *shall be* from sea *even* to sea, and from the river *even* to the ends of the earth.

　　　Fulfillment:　Luke 2:11-14

For unto you is born this day in the city of David a Saviour, which is Christ the Lord. And this *shall be* a sign unto you; Ye shall find the babe wrapped in swaddling clothes, lying in a manger. **And suddenly there was with the angel a multitude of the heavenly host praising God,** and saying, Glory to God in the highest, **and on earth peace, good will toward men.**

　　　Fulfillment:　John 16:33

These things I have spoken unto you, that in me ye might have peace. In the world ye shall have tribulation: but be of good cheer; I have overcome the world.

　　　Fulfillment:　John 20:19, 21, 26

Then the same day at evening, being the first *day* of the week, when the doors were shut where the disciples were assembled for fear of the Jews, came Jesus and stood in the midst, and saith unto them, **Peace** *be* **unto you.** And when he had so said, he shewed unto them *his* hands and his side. Then were the disciples glad, when they saw the Lord. Then said Jesus to them again, **Peace** *be* **unto you:** as *my* Father hath sent me, even so send I you. And when he had said this, he breathed on *them,* and saith unto them, Receive ye the Holy Ghost: Whose soever sins ye remit, they are remitted unto them; *and* whose soever *sins* ye retain, they are retained. But Thomas, one of the twelve, called Didymus, was not with them when Jesus came. The other disciples therefore said unto him, We have seen the Lord. But he said unto them, Except I shall see in his hands the print of the nails, and put my finger into the print of the nails, and thrust my hand into his side, I will not believe. And after eight days again his disciples were within, and Thomas with them: *then* came Jesus, the doors being shut, and stood in the midst, and said, **Peace** *be* **unto you.**

302.　**The Messiah would be humble**　　　　　　　　　　　　　　　**Zechariah 9:9**

Rejoice greatly, O daughter of Zion; shout, O daughter of Jerusalem: behold, thy King cometh unto thee: he is just, and having salvation; **lowly, and riding upon an ass, and upon a colt the foal of an ass.**

　　　Fulfillment:　Matthew 11:29

Take my yoke upon you, and learn of me; **for I am meek and lowly in heart:** and ye shall find rest unto your souls.

303.　**He is the Cornerstone**　　　　　　　　　　　　　　　　　**Zechariah 10:4**

Out of him came forth the corner, out of him the nail, out of him the battle bow, out of him every oppressor together.

　　　Fulfillment:　Ephesians 2:20

And are built upon the foundation of the apostles and prophets, **Jesus Christ himself being the chief corner stone.**

"You cannot change the truth, but the truth can change you."

Unknown　　　　　　　　　　　　　　　　　　　　　　　　**"See Romans 12:2"**

207

304. **At His coming, Israel would have unfit leaders**   **Zechariah 11:4-6a**
Thus saith the LORD my God; Feed the flock of the slaughter; Whose possessors slay them, and hold themselves not guilty: and they that sell them say, Blessed be the LORD; for I am rich: and their own shepherds pity them not. **For I will no more pity the inhabitants of the land, saith the LORD: but, lo, I will deliver the men every one into his neighbour's hand, and into the hand of his king: and they shall smite the land, and out of their hand I will not deliver them.**
        Fulfillment: Matthew 23:1-4
Then spake Jesus to the multitude, and to his disciples, Saying, The scribes and the Pharisees sit in Moses' seat: All therefore whatsoever they bid you observe, that observe and do; **but do not ye after their works: for they say, and do not.** For they bind heavy burdens and grievous to be borne, and lay them on men's shoulders; but they themselves will not move them with one of their fingers.

305. **Rejection causes God to remove His protection**   **Zechariah 11:4-6a**
Thus saith the LORD my God; Feed the flock of the slaughter; Whose possessors slay them, and **hold themselves not guilty:** and they that sell them say, Blessed be the LORD; for I am rich: and their own shepherds pity them not. **For I will no more pity the inhabitants of the land,** saith the LORD: but, lo, I will deliver the men every one into his neighbour's hand, and into the hand of his king: and they shall smite the land, **and out of their hand I will not deliver them.**
        Fulfillment: Luke 19:41-44
And when he was come near, he beheld the city, and wept over it, Saying, If thou hadst known, even thou, at least in this thy day, the things which belong unto thy peace! But now they are hid from thine eyes. For the days shall come upon thee, that thine enemies shall cast a trench about thee, and compass thee round, and keep thee in on every side, And shall lay thee even with the ground, and thy children within thee; and they shall not leave in thee one stone upon another; **because thou knewest not the time of thy visitation.**

306. **Ministry to the poor**   **Zechariah 11:7**
And **I will feed the flock of slaughter,** even you, **O poor of the flock.** And I took unto me two staves; the one I called Beauty, and the other I called Bands; and **I fed the flock.**
        Fulfillment: Matthew 9:35, 36
And Jesus went about all the cities and villages, teaching in their synagogues, and preaching the gospel of the kingdom, and healing every sickness and every disease among the people. **But when he saw the multitudes, he was moved with compassion on them, because they fainted, and were scattered abroad, as sheep having no shepherd.**

"The gate of heaven, though it is so wide that the greatest sinner may enter, is nevertheless so low that pride can never pass through it."

Charles Spurgeon   **"See Matthew 19:24"**

307.   **He is despised and forced to reject them because of unbelief   Zechariah 11:8**
Three shepherds also I cut off in one month; and **my soul lothed them, and their soul also abhorred me.**
        Fulfillment: Matthew 23:23
Woe unto you, **scribes and Pharisees, hypocrites!** For ye pay tithe of mint and anise and cummin, and have **omitted the weightier matters of the law, judgment, mercy, and faith: these ought ye to have done, and not to leave the other undone.**
        Fulfillment: Matthew 27:20
But **the chief priests and elders persuaded the multitude that they should ask Barabbas, and destroy Jesus.**

308.   **He stops ministering to those who rejected Him   Zechariah 11:9**
Then said I, I will not feed you: that that dieth, let it die; and that that is to be cut off, let it be cut off; and let the rest eat every one the flesh of another.
        Fulfillment: Matthew 13:10-11
And the disciples came, and said unto him, Why speakest thou unto them in parables? He answered and said unto them, **Because it is given unto you to know the mysteries of the kingdom of heaven, but to them it is not given.**

309.   **Rejection cause God to remove His protection   Zechariah 11:10-11**
And I took my staff, even Beauty, and cut it asunder, **that I might break my covenant which I had made with all the people.** And it was broken in that day: and so the poor of the flock that waited upon me knew that it was the word of the LORD.
        Fulfillment: Luke 19:41-44
And when he was come near, **he beheld the city, and wept over it,** Saying, If thou hadst known, even thou, at least in this thy day, the things which belong unto thy peace! But now they are hid from thine eyes. **For the days shall come upon thee, that thine enemies shall cast a trench about thee, and compass thee round, and keep thee in on every side,** And shall lay thee even with the ground, and thy children within thee; and they shall not leave in thee one stone upon another; because thou knewest not the time of thy visitation.

"Even if I were utterly selfish and had no care for anything but my own happiness, I would choose, if God allowed, to be a soul winner, for never did I know perfect, overflowing, unutterable happiness of the purest and most ennobling order till I first heard of one who had sought and found a Savior through my means."

Charles Surgeon   **"See 1 Timothy 4:5"**

209

310. **He would be rejected and betrayed for thirty pieces of silver which would be thrown into the house of the Lord**   **Zechariah 11:11-12**

And it was broken in that day: and so the poor of the flock that waited upon me knew that it was the word of the LORD. And I said unto them, If ye think good, give me my price; and if not, forbear. **So they weighed for my price thirty pieces of silver.**

     Fulfillment: Matthew 26:14-15; 27:3-5

Then one of the twelve, called Judas Iscariot, went unto the chief priests, And said unto them, What will ye give me, and I will deliver him unto you? And they covenanted with him for **thirty pieces of silver...**Then Judas, which had betrayed him, when he saw that he was condemned, repented himself, and **brought again the thirty pieces of silver to the chief priests and elders,** Saying, I have sinned in that I have betrayed the innocent blood. And they said, What is that to us? See thou to that. And he **cast down the pieces of silver in the temple,** and departed, and went and hanged himself.

311. **Silver used to buy Potters field**   **Zechariah 11:12-13**

And I said unto them, If ye think good, give me my price; and if not, forbear. So they weighed for my price thirty pieces of silver. **And the LORD said unto me, Cast it unto the potter: a goodly price that I was prised at of them. And I took the thirty pieces of silver, and cast them to the potter in the house of the LORD.**

     Fulfillment: Matthew 27:3-10

Then Judas, which had betrayed him, when he saw that he was condemned, repented himself, and brought again the thirty pieces of silver to the chief priests and elders, Saying, I have sinned in that I have betrayed the innocent blood. And they said, What is that to us? See thou to that. And he cast down the pieces of silver in the temple, and departed, and went and hanged himself. And the chief priests took the silver pieces, and said, It is not lawful for to put them into the treasury, because it is the price of blood. **And they took counsel, and bought with them the potter's field, to bury strangers in.** Wherefore that field was called, The field of blood, unto this day. Then was fulfilled that which was spoken by Jeremy the prophet, saying, **And they took the thirty pieces of silver, the price of him that was valued, whom they of the children of Israel did value; And gave them for the potter's field, as the Lord appointed me.**

312. **The Messiah's body would be pierced**   **Zechariah 12:10**

And I will pour upon the house of David, and upon the inhabitants of Jerusalem, the spirit of grace and of supplications: and **they shall look upon me whom they have pierced,** and they shall mourn for him, as one mourneth for his only son, and shall be in bitterness for him, as one that is in bitterness for his firstborn.

     Fulfillment: John 19:34-37

But one of the soldiers with **a spear pierced his side,** and forthwith came there out blood and water. And he that saw it bare record, and his record is true: and he knoweth that he saith true, that ye might believe. For these things were done, that the scripture should be fulfilled, A bone of him shall not be broken. **And again another scripture saith, They shall look on him whom they pierced.**

"A man's heart deviseth his way; but the LORD directeth his steps."
Proverbs 16:9

313. **It was God's will that He die for mankind** Zechariah 13:7

Awake, **O sword, against my shepherd,** and against the man that is my fellow, saith the LORD of hosts: smite the shepherd, and the sheep shall be scattered: and I will turn mine hand upon the little ones.

Fulfillment: John 18:11

Then said Jesus unto Peter, **Put up thy sword into the sheath: the cup which my Father hath given me, shall I not drink it?**

314. **He would die a violent death** Zechariah 13:7

Awake, **O sword, against my shepherd, and against the man that is my fellow,** saith the LORD of hosts: **smite the shepherd,** and the sheep shall be scattered: and I will turn mine hand upon the little ones.

Fulfillment: Matthew 27:35

And they crucified him, and parted his garments, casting lots: that it might be fulfilled which was spoken by the prophet, They parted my garments among them, and upon my vesture did they cast lots.

When Jesus comes to gather His faithful followers everyone is going see Him, and to make sure He is going to shout. It is not going to be a secret!

"For as the lightning cometh out of the east, and shineth even unto the west; so shall also the coming of the Son of man be."

Matthew 24:27

What a Blessed Hope We Have In Our Lord!

"But I would not have you to be ignorant, brethren,concerning them which are asleep, that ye sorrow not, even as others which have no hope. For if we believe that Jesus died and rose again, even so them also which sleep in Jesus will God bring with him. For this we say unto you by the word of the Lord, that we which are alive *and* remain unto the coming of the Lord shall not prevent them which are asleep. For the Lord himself shall descend from heaven with a shout, with the voice of the archangel, and with the trump of God: and the dead in Christ shall rise first: Then we which are alive *and* remain shall be caught up together with them in the clouds, to meet the Lord in the air: and so shall we ever be with the Lord. Wherefore comfort one another with these words."

1 Thessalonians 4:13-18

211

315. **The disciples would forsake the Lord and be scattered**   **Zechariah 13:7**

Awake, O sword, against my shepherd, and **against the man that is my fellow,** saith the LORD of hosts: **smite the shepherd, and the sheep shall be scattered:** and I will turn mine hand upon the little ones.

Fulfillment: Matthew 26:31-56

Then saith Jesus unto them, All ye shall be offended because of me this night: for it is written, **I will smite the shepherd, and the sheep of the flock shall be scattered** abroad. [32]But after I am risen again, I will go before you into Galilee. [33]Peter answered and said unto him, Though all *men* thee, That this night, before the cock crow, thou shalt deny me thrice. [35]Peter said unto him, Though I should die with thee, yet will I not deny thee. Likewise also said all the disciples. [36]Then cometh Jesus with them unto a place called Gethsemane, and saith unto the disciples, Sit ye here, while I go and pray yonder. [37]And he took with him Peter and the two sons of Zebedee, and began to be sorrowful and very heavy. [38]Then saith he unto them, My soul is exceeding sorrowful, even unto death: tarry ye here, and watch with me. [39]And he went a little further, and fell on his face, and prayed, saying, O my Father, if it be possible, let this cup pass from me: nevertheless not as I will, but as thou *wilt*. [40]And he cometh unto the disciples, and findeth them asleep, and saith unto Peter, What, could ye not watch with me one hour? [41]Watch and pray, that ye enter not into temptation: the spirit indeed *is* willing, but the flesh *is* weak. [42]He went away again the second time, and prayed, saying, O my Father, if this cup may not pass away from me, except I drink it, thy will be done. [43]And he came and found them asleep again: for their eyes were heavy. [44]And he left them, and went away again, and prayed the third time, saying the same words. [45]Then cometh he to his disciples, and saith unto them, Sleep on now, and take *your* rest: behold, the hour is at hand, and the Son of man is betrayed into the hands of sinners. [46]Rise, let us be going: behold, he is at hand that doth betray me. **And while he yet spake, lo, Judas, one of the twelve, came, and with him a great multitude with swords and staves, from the chief priests and elders of the people. Now he that betrayed him gave them a sign, saying, Whomsoever I shall kiss, that same is he: hold him fast. And forthwith he came to Jesus, and said, Hail, master; and kissed him. And Jesus said unto him, Friend, wherefore art thou come? Then came they, and laid hands on Jesus, and took him. And, behold, one of them which were with Jesus stretched out *his* hand, and drew his sword, and struck a servant of the high priest's, and smote off his ear.** [52]Then said Jesus unto him, Put up again thy sword into his place: for all they that take the sword shall perish with the sword. [53] Thinkest thou that I cannot now pray to my Father, and he shall presently give me more than twelve legions of angels? [54]But how then shall the scriptures be fulfilled, that thus it must be? [55]In that same hour said Jesus to the multitudes, Are ye come out as against a thief with swords and staves for to take me? I sat daily with you teaching in the temple, and ye laid no hold on me. **But all this was done, that the scriptures of the prophets might be fulfilled. Then all the disciples forsook him, and fled.**

"Looking unto Jesus the author and finisher of our faith."

Hebrews 12:2

212

MALACHI

This is the 39th book of the Bible, written approximately 433 B.C. – 400 B.C. It is unknown what dates it covers. Malachi wrote this book in Judah. It has 4 chapters.

316.　**A messenger to prepare the way for the Messiah**　　　　**Malachi 3:1**
Behold, **I will send my messenger, and he shall prepare the way before me:** and the Lord, whom ye seek, shall suddenly come to his temple, even the messenger of the covenant, whom ye delight in: behold, he shall come, saith the LORD of hosts.
　　　　Fulfillment:　Matthew 11:10
For this is he, of whom it is written, **Behold, I send my messenger before thy face, which shall prepare thy way before thee.**

317.　**Sudden appearance at the temple**　　　　**Malachi 3:1**
Behold, I will send my messenger, and he shall prepare the way before me: and the Lord, whom ye seek, **shall suddenly come to his temple,** even the messenger of the covenant, whom ye delight in: behold, he shall come, saith the LORD of hosts.
　　　　Fulfillment:　Mark 11:15-16
And they come to Jerusalem: and **Jesus went into the temple,** and began to cast out them that sold and bought in the temple, and overthrew the tables of the moneychangers, and the seats of them that sold doves; And would not suffer that any man should carry any vessel through the temple.

318.　**Messenger of the new covenant**　　　　**Malachi 3:1c**
Behold, I will send my messenger, and he shall prepare the way before me: and the Lord, whom ye seek, shall suddenly come to his temple, even **the messenger of the covenant, whom ye delight in: behold, he shall come,** saith the LORD of hosts.
　　　　Fulfillment:　Luke 4:43
And he said unto them, **I must preach the kingdom of God to other cities also: for therefore am I sent.** And he preached in the synagogues of Galilee.

Summary of All Temples

Temples	Built Approx.	Destroyed
Solomon's temple	982 B.C.-975 B.C.	586 B.C
Zerubbabel's temple	539 B.C.-516 B.C	19 B.C
Herod's temple	19 B.C.	70 A.D

Your body is the temple.　　　　**"See 1 Corinthians 6:19"**

213

319. **A Forerunner will come in the spirit of Elijah** Malachi 4:5
Behold, I will send you Elijah the prophet before the coming of the great and dreadful day of the LORD.
Fulfillment: Matthew 3:1-2
In those days **came John the Baptist, preaching** in the wilderness of Judaea, And saying, Repent ye: for the kingdom of heaven is at hand.

320. **The forerunner would turn many to righteousness** Malachi 4:6
And he shall turn the heart of the fathers to the children, and the heart of the children to their fathers, lest I come and smite the earth with a curse.
Fulfillment: Luke 1:16-17
And many of the children of Israel shall he turn to the Lord their God. And he shall go before him in the spirit and power of Elias, to turn the hearts of the fathers to the children, and the disobedient to the wisdom of the just; to make ready a people prepared for the Lord.

"It is a terrible thing, I found, to be grateful and have no one to thank, to be awed and to have no one to worship."

Philip Yancey, *What's So Amazing About Grace* **"See Psalms 75:1"**

"Looking unto **Jesus,** the author and finisher of *our* faith!"
Hebrews 12:2

216

"The just shall live by his faith."

Habakkuk 2:4b

After reading Morris Venden's book *A Reason For The Season*, I was astonished. Mr. Venden is able to communicate in such a way as to help one understand what faith truly is. He has a way of creating an elevated understanding of whatever topic he explains. The book is out of print, but it has been reprinted under the title *It's Who You Know* and can be purchased through The Concerned Group, Inc. by calling 1-800-447-4332.

Morris Venden has written many books and has affected many people, including me, with his simple and effective way of communicating God's Word through his books. He was very gracious giving me permission to use his writings in this book. I thank God that there are men like Mr. Venden who commit their lives to sharing the Gospel, not for selfish gain but for the praise and glory of our Lord Jesus Christ.

This study is taken from *A Reason For The Season*. I have edited only where I thought to streamline the message, not to change it. I am not trying to reinvent the wheel. Mr. Venden has articulated my beliefs better than I ever could. I hope you receive as much of a blessing as I have from his message.

"The community desperately needed rain. The wells were dry and the crops were parched. So the preacher called a special prayer meeting. The church was packed that night. One little girl even brought an umbrella! The congregation smiled at the child's demonstration of faith. But when the rain came a few minutes later, the little girl was the only one who didn't get wet. What caused the rain? Was it the little girl and her umbrella? Or did she bring the umbrella because she knew it was going to rain? Your interpretation of the story will probably depend on your understanding of faith and how it operates.

There are many people who think that faith is simply positive thinking, and if you make yourself believe strongly enough that something is going to happen, it will happen. These people think of faith as something that is self-generated, something to work up. One of the most common understandings of faith in Christian circles is that "faith is believing." Other common definitions are that "faith is taking God at his word," or "faith is believing what God says." These concepts of faith are insufficient and intangible; we scarcely know what true faith really is!

"Commit thy works unto the LORD, and thy thoughts shall be established."

Proverbs 16:3

217

Let's consider a Bible experience found in **Matthew 15:21-28**, where Jesus commended a woman for her faith, and see how these definitions fit.

> **Then Jesus went thence, and departed into the coasts of Tyre and Sidon. And, behold, a woman of Canaan came out of the same coasts, and cried unto him, saying, Have mercy on me, O Lord, *thou* Son of David; my daughter is grievously vexed with a devil. But he answered her not a word.**

It was not uncommon for the Jews to ignore the Canaanites. But it is never pleasant to be ignored. It would seem that this woman would have given up and gone away. But she didn't.

> **And his disciples came and besought him, saying, Send her away; for she crieth after us.**

Jesus apparently agreed with them, for He replied,

> **But he answered and said, I am not sent but unto the lost sheep of the house of Israel.**

He might as well have said, "I didn't come to help her."

> **Then came she and worshipped him, saying, Lord, help me. But he answered and said, It is not meet to take the children's bread, and to cast *it* to dogs.**

Have you ever been ignored when you asked for help, and when you persisted in your request you were then insulted? Have you ever been called a dog? It seems surprising that this woman didn't give up long before Jesus got to the "dogs" part. But she found the opening she had been looking for. Jesus must have had a twinkle in His eye during the whole conversation and the Canaanite woman must have seen because she answered,

> **And she said, Truth, Lord: yet the dogs eat of the crumbs which fall from their masters' table.**

In other words, if I am a dog, then at least I am entitled to some dog food!

> **Then Jesus answered and said unto her, O woman, great *is* thy faith: be it unto thee even as thou wilt. And her daughter was made whole from that very hour.**

"Every man must do two things alone: he must do his own believing, and he must do his own dying."

Martin Luther   **"See Psalms 82:7"**

Now let me ask you: how is faith defined in this story? Is it taking God at His word? No! If the woman had taken God at His word, she would have given up. Do you define faith in terms of believing, or believing what God says? You can't; it doesn't fit. Faith in her case was disbelieving what Jesus said. Faith was not taking Him at His word.

Because of inadequate definitions of faith, there has developed a very subtle form of pseudo-faith. There was a motivational speaker, 35 years of age, who had retired on an income that would provide for him a comfortable living. His theme was that you must believe in yourself and your marvelous mind in order to be a success. He quoted a few Bible texts to support his view, and proposed that the only barrier to success was the failure to believe in one's own abilities. If his listeners would try his plan for 30 days, he promised they would be successful in anything they wanted to do. His logic almost made sense, except for a *Bible* verse, **Proverbs 28: 26,** that says, **"he that trusteth in his own heart (or mind) is a fool."**

The common denominator of counterfeit faith, regardless of what form it takes, is the idea that you can make yourself believe something; and that if you believe hard enough, this will cause God to move. It boils down to a type of mental gymnastics, or positive thinking, and perhaps its greatest danger is that it inevitably becomes self-centered, just as working hard on trying to overcome your sins makes you become self-centered.

With a false faith, a person's concept of God and understanding of God's will becomes confused. Some Christians believe that if you have enough faith, any promise you can find in God's Word is immediately in His will. This kind of person works hard to make himself believe that certain promises are going to be fulfilled, and he hinges his confidence and love for God on whether or not he gets adequate answers. He will often take scriptures out of context, and he begins to use God as a sort of Santa Claus or Aladdin's lamp. His primary purpose in prayer is to get answers.

The tragic thing about this is that a strong-minded person might be able to succeed in this to a certain extent, and then finds himself believing or having faith in himself, not God. And because he seems to have success, this self-generated faith can become a deadly escape from the personal relationship with Christ. He sees no need for God. That is why positive thinking is not faith. It has never been faith and never will be faith! Instead, it is a subtle form of "salvation by my own works," a "Glory Trip" in which I take the credit for having enough genius to cause things to happen. And when I do not succeed in getting the answers I want, my spiritual life can be devastated.

There are some people who believe that whatever you ask in prayer, believing, you shall receive. If this is true, what would you say to the mother who prays believing that her dying child will be spared, or the husband who prays and believes that his wife will be healed of cancer. They believe with all their heart, and yet her child dies and his wife is not healed. Then they think that either God let them down or that they are to blame because they didn't believe enough. This leads to anger with God or guilt with oneself.

"Nothing worse can happen to a church than to be conformed to this world."
Charles Spurgeon   **"See Romans 12:2"**

219

Do these people have faith? Maybe; the Bible makes it clear that everyone is given enough faith to get started. **Romans 12:3 says: For I say, through the grace given unto me, to every man that is among you, not to think *of himself* more highly than he ought to think; but to think soberly, according as <u>God hath dealt to every man the measure of faith.</u>**

Usually we think of faith in terms of quantity. So, we try to increase the amount we have. Jesus' disciples had the same idea, and one day they asked Jesus to increase their faith **Luke 17:5-6.**

> **And the apostles said unto the Lord, Increase our faith. And the Lord said, If ye had faith as a grain of mustard seed, ye might say unto this sycamine tree, Be thou plucked up by the root, and be thou planted in the sea; and it should obey you.**

What was He saying? He was saying that it wasn't the amount of faith that was so important; it was whether or not they had genuine faith. This looks at our faith in terms of quality, not quantity. If we had the real thing, then just the amount of a grain of mustard seed could work wonders.

Yet faith does grow as it is exercised. Have you ever wondered how to exercise faith? Is faith exercised by putting yourself in difficult places and then expecting God to bail you out? Is faith exercised by writing checks when your bank balance is zero, and then waiting for God to cover the checks? Do you exercise faith by claiming promises?

There was a family that had recently moved to the country. They bought a piece of land, and were ready to build their house, but there was no water on the land.

Then someone came to town to teach people how to claim promises. The family asked him to come out and help them claim a promise, and they gathered out at the farm. They claimed a promise: "seek and you shall find" – which, by the way, has nothing whatsoever to do with finding water in a well.

But water came! The family rejoiced, built their house, and moved to the new location. Then the well went dry. They became very confused. Was there something wrong with their faith? Was there something wrong with the promise? Or was something wrong with God?

A student was coming back to college after vacation. He was on a plane with a faculty member, and because of a dense fog, they couldn't land at the airport as planned. The student said to the faculty member beside him, "Watch this! I'm going to claim a promise and the fog will go away."

He did claim a promise, but the fog didn't go away. That was one discouraged student.

"The number one reason people don't share their faith is that their walk doesn't match their talk."
Mark Cahill   **"See Job 36:13-14"**

220

What he didn't realize was that it might not be necessary for him to land at that particular airport. Perhaps God's will was for him to land at some other location. In fact, there have been good people, godly people, who have gone down in plane crashes. It was neither because they were lacking in faith, nor because they didn't know how to claim the right promise.

Two men were burned at the stake. Their names were Huss and Jerome. And they are only two of thousands that perished during the Dark Ages. If claiming promises is the right way to cause God to act, then Huss and Jerome really missed it. For there is a beautiful promise in **Isaiah 43:2** that says,
> **When thou passest through the waters, I *will be* with thee; and through the rivers, they shall not overflow thee: <u>when thou walkest through the fire, thou shalt not be burned; neither shall the flame kindle upon thee.</u>**

But don't tell me that Huss and Jerome died because they didn't have the right kind of faith. If I understand correctly, Huss and Jerome died because they *did* have faith. And part of the promise was fulfilled for them, even without their claiming it, for its says, **"when thou walkest through the fire, thou shalt not be burned; neither shall the flame kindle upon thee."** Huss and Jerome died singing! Have you ever put your hand on a hot stove? Do you sing? Nobody dies at the stake with green wood and a slow burning fire singing, unless they've not been burned. But the last half of Scripture was not fulfilled. The singing martyrs were reduced to ashes and their ashes were thrown in the river.

John the Baptist was beheaded! Elisha died after a long lingering illness-Elisha, who had been given a double portion of Elijah's spirit! And these all died in faith, which tells us that faith is something far more than making yourself believe that God will answer prayer in the way you want Him to.

I do not believe that every promise you can find in God's word is God's will for you, at this time, and under the current circumstances John the Baptist, Elisha, Huss and Jerome, and a host of others have proved that.

There are some promises in God's Word, however, that are always God's will. Those are the promises that have to do with spiritual blessings. It is always God's will to forgive us from sin, to give us His grace and power, to give us the wisdom to do his work. These promises we may claim. For these blessings we are to ask, and believe that we will receive and give thanks when we do receive them. But it is obvious from the lives of godly people that when it comes to temporal blessings, including life and health, unless the person knows by special revelation what God's will is on a subject, he must pray **"Thy will be done."**

"By a Carpenter mankind was made, and only by that Carpenter can mankind be remade."

Deriderius Erasmus **"See Mark 6:3"**

What is genuine faith, then? It is more than taking God at His word. It's more than making yourself believe. Genuine faith is never worked at, and it is never worked up. When you study it, you come to the only definition of faith that will fit. It's just one word: **Trust.** Genuine faith is trusting God to perform that which He has promised.

The Greek word from which "faith" is translated in the New Testament is also translated in at least two other ways, "belief" and "trust." All come from the same Greek word. Therefore, you can take "belief" or "faith," whenever you find them, and without damaging the thought or the context, substitute the word "trust."

> For instance, **1 John 5:4 says: "For whatsoever is born of God overcometh the world: and this is the victory that overcometh the world, *even* our <u>faith</u>." Can be changed to, "this is the victory that overcometh the world, *even* our <u>trust</u>." Acts 16:31 says: "Believe in the lord Jesus Christ and thou shalt be saved," this can read, "<u>trust</u> in lord Jesus Christ." 1 Timothy 6:12. "Fight the good fight of trust."**

This is not the same as merely saying, "I believe." In our world today, there is a cheap kind of faith which only demands that you "believe in Christ" in order to be saved. No! Learning to trust God requires something deeper than that, it demands a personal, continuing relationship with a God who is completely trustworthy.

What is the genuine fight of faith? What is our part? Jesus said that our work is to trust. **John 6:28.**

> **Jesus answered and said unto them, This is the work of God, that ye believe (trust) on him whom he hath sent.**

We fight the good fight of learning to trust! That involves getting to know one who is trustworthy.

Unfortunately, most of us immediately confuse the good fight of faith, or trust, with the bad fight of sin. We think that fighting the good fight of faith consists of trying hard to live a good life. The problem is that a strong person who fights sin might outwardly succeed to some degree, but becomes proud of his success, and also fails to see his need of God. On the other hand, the weak person who tries to change his life by fighting sin doesn't even outwardly succeed, and he becomes discouraged. Neither understands what the fight of faith is all about.

When a person tries to fight the bad fight of sin, their relationship with Christ becomes toilsome, difficult, and gloomy. They are consumed with not doing this or not doing that. It becomes too hard to maintain and they see all their efforts to keep the law are to no avail; as a result they become "backsliders." They should have been fighting the good fight of faith instead. Once they understand that the power for victory comes only from knowing Jesus Christ, they become excited, renewing their relationship with God again.

"I would rather be fully understood by ten than admired by ten thousand."

Jonathan Edwards   **"See Acts 5:41-42"**

222

The truth is that you don't have to do bad things to be a sinner, and not doing bad things doesn't make you a Christian. In order to be a sinner, all you have to do is to be born, because all of us are born with inherent sinful natures.

The Bible tells us, in **1 John 5:17, All unrighteousness is sin.**

Romans 3:10, 23 As it is written, There is none righteous, no, not one... For all have sinned, and come short of the glory of God.

While some are better able to keep from doing bad things, they are actually no better off than the weak people who are obviously suffering defeat in their Christian experience.

So where should we direct our efforts in order to get genuine faith, or trust? Some people think we should work on trying to produce the faith, but I'd like to remind you that an apple tree bears apples because it is an apple tree, never in order to become an apple tree. If you want to have apples, then you get an apple tree. If you want genuine faith, pay attention to what causes faith.

Of course, that's a simplistic approach; it is nonetheless true. There is no point in trying to produce apples apart from an apple tree. The wax or plastic imitations might be very convincing from the outside but they certainly taste nothing like the real apples from an apple tree!

An imitation is always disappointing. An imitation of faith might be flattering to the ego in the beginning, but will be disappointing in the end.

If I want faith, I don't work on trying to produce faith. Why not? A genuine Christian has faith because he knows Jesus. Genuine faith cannot be self-generated; it comes only as the spontaneous result of fellowship with God.

There are at least two conditions to being able to trust anyone. First, you must find someone who is absolutely trustworthy. And second, you must get to know that person. Because a person can be ever so trustworthy, but if you don't know him, you won't trust him.

It works in the opposite way as well. A person can be absolutely untrustworthy, and you won't distrust him until you get to know him. But if you get to know him, you'll automatically distrust him!

"The Lord's righteous indignation at Israel's money changers in the Temple is equivalent to the money-hungry televangelists."

Ray Comfort   **"See John 2:15"**

You may have heard about the man who put his son upon a ladder, He told him to jump. The boy jumped, and the man stepped back and let him fall on his face. Then he said, "That will teach you never to trust anybody." That's the kind of world we live in. In the early days of our country, according to legends, everyone was trusted until he proved to be untrustworthy. If you owed someone some money, you'd put it in an envelope, and leave it fastened to your front gate. You could go on vacation knowing that no one would touch it except the person it was meant for. Even if he came by a week or so later he'd find his money still there. But today we live in an age when everyone tends to distrust until someone proves he can be trusted.

The Bible truth is that God is absolutely trustworthy. Although that's the truth about God, some people don't believe it. And the only reason they don't believe it is because they don't know Him. Anyone who is looking over his glasses at God is advertising the fact that he doesn't know Him. Because, to know God is to trust Him.

If you get to know someone who is absolutely trustworthy, you'll automatically, spontaneously trust him. You wont have to work at it, it will happen naturally. Trust in God is the first thing that happens when we get to know Him, and we don't have to work at it. Genuine faith trusts in God no matter what happens. Faith is trust in God when tragedy strikes, as well as when things are going smoothly. Genuine faith trust's God whether the airplane goes down, whether the well goes dry, in life, or in death. And this "Rich–Christian" idea, basing faith on whether or not we get answers to our prayers in the way we expect, is the devils counterfeit of faith.

Genuine faith is not an end in itself. It does not come to those who seek for it, but to those who seek it not and who seek only Jesus. **Faith always has an object**. But when faith itself becomes the object, it will destroy us.

Genuine faith can come only as a result of knowing God on a one-to-one, person-to-person basis. And how is this accomplished? In the same way you get to know anyone, by communication. We communicate with others by talking to them, by listening to them talk to us, and by going places and doing things together. In the Christian life, I can talk to God in prayer. I can listen to Him by reading His word. And I can go places and do things with Him by becoming involved in service and outreach.

The methods of becoming acquainted with God are the elements of a vital devotional life. And when I am in a meaningful relationship with God, day by day, I learn to trust Him, automatically, spontaneously, naturally. This is faith, trust, in its highest sense.

"If the world hate you, you know that it hated me before it hated you. If ye were of the world, the world would love his own:but because ye are not of the world, but I have chosen you out of the world, therefore the world hateth you."

John 15:18-19

224

Faith, or trust, is a gift from God. **Ephesians 2:8, 9** says,
> **"For by grace are ye saved through faith; and that not of yourselves: *it is* the gift of God: Not of works, lest any man should boast."**

There is only one way to receive the gift and that is to come into the presence of the giver of the gift. How do you come into God's presence to receive this gift of trust from him? **On your knees before His open word.**

The primary purpose of prayer is friendship and acquaintance with God - not to get answers. And the primary purpose of the Christian witness is to tell about the love of God - not to recount a list of all the answers you have received.

What is the good fight of faith? It is taking the measure of faith already given **(Romans 12:3)** and using it toward becoming personally acquainted with God each day, learning to know Jesus, so that we can trust Him as a spontaneous result of knowing Him. I never fight for faith, I fight to learn to know God. And it does not require effort to maintain that daily acquaintance with God, because the devil knows that you'll receive the power of God onto salvation if you learn to know God **(1 John 5:4)**. So satan does everything he can to distract you and keep you from spending time with God.

My appeal to you, my friend is that you become engaged in the effort that is involved in knowing God personally. As you become acquainted with Him, you'll receive His gift of faith as a spontaneous result.

What a wonderful privilege to become acquainted with the great God of the universe, to learn to know a God who can be trusted because He is trustworthy! I invite you to begin today to know Him as your personal friend."

This chapter is quoted from *It's Who You Know* by Morris Venden, published by The Concerned Group, Inc. 800-447-4332. Permission to use the chapter has been obtained by both author and publisher.

"Ignorance of the nature and design of the Law is at the bottom of most religious mistakes."

John Newton   **"See Psalms 119:18"**

"Death and life are in the power of the tongue: and they that love it shall eat the fruit thereof."

Proverbs 18:21

FACT: JESUS CHRIST IS THE WORD

John 1:1-14
In the beginning was the Word, and the Word was with God, and the Word was God.
The same was in the beginning with God.
All things were made by him;
and without him was not any thing made that was made.
In him was life; and the life was the light of men.
And the light shineth in darkness; and the darkness comprehended it not.
There was a man sent from God, whose name *was* John.
The same came for a witness, to bear witness of the Light, that all *men*
through him might believe.
He was not that Light, but *was sent* to bear witness of that Light.
That was the true Light, which lighteth every man that cometh into the world.
He was in the world, and the world was made by him, and the world knew him not.
He came unto his own, and his own received him not.
But as many as received him, to them gave he power to become the sons of God, *even* to
them that believe on his name:
Which were born, not of blood, nor of the will of the flesh, nor of the will of man,
but of God.
And the Word was made flesh, and dwelt among us,
(and we beheld his glory, the glory as of the only begotten of the Father,)
full of grace and truth.

The Word of God shows us Jesus in all His majesty and in all His humility, in all His power and in all His torment, in all His Godliness and in all His humanity.

The written Word reveals to us the Living Word, Jesus Christ.

"My soul, wait thou only upon God; for my expectation *is* from him. He only *is* my rock and my salvation: *he is* my defence; I shall not be moved. In God *is* my salvation and my glory: the rock of my strength, *and* my refuge, *is* in God. Trust in him at all times; *ye* people, pour out your heart before him: God *is* a refuge for us. Selah."

Psalm 62:5-8

227

I have come to know my Lord through His written Word. It is how I enjoy my relationship with Him. I pray to Him because He asks me, through His Word, and I listen to Him from the Words He gave me in His written Word. My relationship with my Lord is more important to me than the air I breathe. It is because of this relationship that I can trust Him to perform that which He has promised; salvation from sin, and His coming again to gather His church to spend eternity with Him.

I don't believe I ever realized how great a work God performed by preserving His Word until I came to understand that the King James Bible was His revealed perfect Word for English-speaking people. I had many different versions in my library, and although I preferred the KJB I thought the other versions were as good or better in helping me to understand God's Will.

It wasn't until I changed the scriptural text in this book from the King James Bible to the *New King James Version* that I began to look into the differences between the two. When I realized the truth and became aware of the errors in the other versions, I immediately changed the scriptural text back to the Authorized King James Bible.

I am including this chapter because I want to comfort and assure Bible readers and believers that the Word of God is still available through the written Word, and you don't have to be a Greek or Hebrew scholar to know God's pure truth. I want to expose the devilish deception, the manipulation of scripture, that has crept into the church regarding the *Holy Bible*. I pray the Holy Spirit reveals to you the truth regarding this matter.

When satan first approached man the first thing he did was attack God's Word.

A lot of people have been deceived. They have fallen for the same old line that Eve fell for many years ago: "Yea, hath God said?" **(Genesis 3:1.)** The Bible records this question as the first words spoken by the serpent. satan wants you to doubt God's word.

"Yea, hath God said?" Is the Bible really the word of God? Is the Bible really true? Can I really trust what it is saying? Wasn't the Bible mistranslated? Is the word of God really in English? Did God really raise Christ from the dead? Did Jesus really do all those miracles? Was Jesus really born of a virgin? What about Jonah and the whale? "Yea, hath God said?"
If satan can cause you to doubt the integrity of God's Word, he knows you will not submit to the authority of it.

Let's look to the scripture and let it reveal to us satan's cunningly deceptive practices.

"If any man shall add unto these things, God shall add unto him the plagues that are written in this book: And if any man shall take away from the words of the book of this prophecy, God shall take away his part out of the book of life, and out of the holy city, and *from* the things which are written in this book."

Revelation 22:18-19

Here is an example of what happened when satan first approached man and was allowed to question the integrity of God's Word.

Genesis 2:16-17

And the LORD God commanded the man, saying, Of every tree of the garden thou mayest freely eat: But of the tree of the knowledge of good and evil, thou shalt not eat of it: for in the day that thou eatest thereof thou shalt surely die.

Genesis 3:1-8

Now the serpent was more subtle than any beast of the field which the LORD God had made. And he said unto the woman, **Yea,** hath God said, Ye shall not eat of every tree of the garden?

Here are the methods satan uses:
1. he takes the positive approach, "Yea."
2. he casts a shadow of doubt. That's how he starts; he offered her doubt.
If he can get you to doubt God's Word you will never submit to the authority of it!

And the woman said unto the serpent, We may **(Eve omits "freely")** eat of the fruit of the trees of the garden:

But of the fruit of the tree which *is* in the midst of the garden, God hath said, Ye shall not eat of it, **neither shall ye touch it**, lest ye die.

Eve subtracts from the Word of God, God said "Ye may freely eat."
Eve adds to God's Word, God never said "neither shall ye touch it."

And the serpent said unto the woman, "Ye shall not surely die:"
3. satan calls God a liar.
4. satan changes God's Word (God said, "you will surely die!"). This bold-faced lie started out with a question:

"For God doth know that in the day ye eat thereof, then **your eyes shall be opened**, and **ye shall be as gods, knowing good and evil."**

5. satan trades (exchanges) faith in God's Word for carnal knowledge, intelligence, and intellect.

"And when the woman **saw** that the tree *was* good for food, and that it *was* **pleasant** to the **eyes**, and a tree to be **desired** to make *one* **wise,** she took of the fruit thereof, and did eat."

Rather than believing what God says, Eve reasons with her senses and ends up rejecting the truth and believing a lie, "and gave also unto her husband with her; and he did eat."

a) Adam eats willfully, thus rejecting the truth.
b) God entrusted Adam with His Word.
c) Either Adam did not explain it to her accurately, or Eve wasn't paying attention or changed it willfully.

Whatever happened, the result was the same.

"And the eyes of them both were opened, and they knew that they *were* naked; and they sewed fig leaves together, and made themselves aprons.
And they heard the voice of the LORD God walking in the garden in the cool of the day: and Adam and his wife hid themselves from the presence of the LORD God amongst the trees of the garden."

The immediate result is <u>they</u> hid themselves from the presence of the Lord God.

God gave us an example in His Word on how to resist temptation. This example shows what Jesus did when tempted by the devil.

Matthew 4:1-11

Then was Jesus led up of the Spirit into the wilderness to be tempted of the devil.
And when he had fasted forty days and forty nights, he was afterward an hungered.
And when the tempter came to him, he said, If thou be the Son of God, command that these stones be made bread.

But he answered and said, **It is written**, Man shall not live by bread alone, but by every word that proceedeth out of the mouth of God.
Then the devil taketh him up into the holy city, and setteth him on a pinnacle of the temple,
And saith unto him, If thou be the Son of God, cast thyself down: for it is written, He shall give his angels charge concerning thee: and in *their* hands they shall bear thee up, lest at any time thou dash thy foot against a stone.

Jesus said unto him, **It is written** again, Thou shalt not tempt the Lord thy God.
Again, the devil taketh him up into an exceeding high mountain, and sheweth him all the kingdoms of the world, and the glory of them;
And saith unto him, All these things will I give thee, if thou wilt fall down and worship me.

Then saith Jesus unto him, Get thee hence, Satan: for **It is written**, Thou shalt worship the Lord thy God, and him only shalt thou serve.
Then the devil leaveth him, and, behold, angels came and ministered unto him.

"The words of the LORD *are* pure words: *as* silver tried in a furnace of earth, purified seven times. Thou shalt keep them, O LORD, thou shalt preserve them from this generation *forever*."

Psalm 12:6-7

So what does all this mean?

1. When satan first approached man **the very first thing he did was question the Word of God and cause doubt of God's integrity.**

2. **He has not changed**! Doesn't it make sense that in these end times he would continue to cause people to doubt the integrity of God's Word?

3. **The only protection we have from being deceived is the Word of God.** satan knows the Word of God and quotes it. If we resist the devil he will flee from us. That's a promise!

4. **Having faith in God means that we believe what He says and trust His Word!** He says in His Word that every one of His Words is pure. We must either believe it or not! If it is pure, then there is no corruption at all. If it is not pure, then there are impurities, additions and/or subtractions, and we can know assuredly that it is not the Word of God.

5. God did a mighty work in making His Word available to man unto the end of time. God provided His Word for us, preserved His Word for us, and told us that **His Word would last forever!** I believe my God who created the Heavens and the Earth, who created life and shows His majesty in the complexity of a single cell, can preserve His perfect Word through imperfect man just as He promised.

6. **That is why God did not leave the preservation of His Word in man's hands.** We will look at scriptures which show that God took it upon Himself to preserve His Word.

"Behold, thou shalt call a nation *that* thou knowest not, and nations *that* knew not thee shall run unto thee because of the LORD thy God, and for the Holy One of Israel; for he hath glorified thee. Seek ye the LORD while he may be found, call ye upon him while he is near: Let the wicked forsake his way, and the unrighteous man his thoughts: and let him return unto the LORD, and he will have mercy upon him; and to our God, for he will abundantly pardon. For my thoughts *are* not your thoughts, neither *are* your ways my ways, saith the LORD. "

Isaiah 55:5-8

231

Why is the Word of God so important?

The Word of God is magnified above the name of our Lord and Savior Jesus Christ. That alone should tell us something about the importance He places on it.

I will praise thee with my whole heart: before the gods will I sing praise unto thee. I will worship toward thy holy temple, and praise thy name for thy loving kindness and for thy truth: for **thou hast magnified thy word above all thy name.**

Psalm 138:1-2

Jesus' name is so powerful that it will cause every knee to bow, in Heaven, on Earth, and below Earth. Yet He still places His Word above His own name!

Wherefore **God also hath highly exalted him**, and **given him a name which is above every name**: **That at the name of Jesus every knee should bow**, of *things* in heaven, and *things* in earth, and *things* under the earth.

Philippians 2:9-11

The Word of God will judge us. We will not be judged by the Lord in the last days, but by His Word. That is a sobering thought. Anyone who is thinking about calling on the compassion of the Lord on Judgement Day will be out of luck; even if Jesus wanted to have compassion on that person it is not His call, but God's Word.

Jesus cried and said, He that believeth on me, believeth not on me, but on him that sent me. And he that seeth me seeth him that sent me. I am come a light into the world, that whosoever believeth on me should not abide in darkness. And if any man **hear my words**, and believe not, <u>**I judge him not**</u>: for I came not to judge the world, but to save the world. He that rejecteth me, and receiveth not my words**, hath one that judgeth him: the word that I have spoken, the same shall judge him in the last day.**

John 12:44-48

And I saw a great white throne, and him that sat on it, from whose face the earth and the heaven fled away; and there was found no place for them. And I saw the dead, small and great, stand before God; and the books were opened: and another book was opened, which is *the book* of life: and **the dead were** <u>**judged out of those things which were written in the books,**</u> **according to their works.**

Revelation 20:11, 12

"Being born again, not of corruptible seed, but of incorruptible, by the word of God, which liveth and abideth forever."

1 Peter 1:23

This is why the Word of God has been preserved in all its purity and perfection. The written Word is our standard, our rule book for life. Everything that pertains to life and godliness is in it.

Grace and peace be multiplied unto you **through the knowledge of God, and of Jesus our Lord,** According as his divine power <u>**hath given unto us all things that**</u> ***pertain*** <u>**unto life and godliness, through the knowledge of him that hath called us to glory and virtue**</u>: Whereby are **given unto us exceeding great and precious promises**: that by these ye might be partakers of the divine nature, having escaped the corruption that is in the world through lust.

2 Peter 1:2-4

Even if we did not have all the evidence of the preservation of His Word, we could still take His Word for it. He tells us throughout His Word that He will preserve it.

The grass withereth, the flower fadeth: but **the word of our God shall stand for ever.** **Isaiah 40:8**
Heaven and earth shall pass away, but **my words shall not pass away.**
Matthew 24:35
And it is easier for heaven and earth to pass, than one tittle of the law to fail.
Luke 16:17

I am comforted by knowing that I can trust my *Bible* to be just as pure as when it was originally given to the writers, those holy men who were moved by the Holy Spirit.

Knowing this first, that no prophecy of the scripture is of any private interpretation. For the prophecy came not in old time by the will of man: **but holy men of God spake** *as they were* **moved by the Holy Ghost.**
2 Peter 1:20-21

The law of the LORD *is* **perfect**, converting the soul: the testimony of the LORD *is* sure, making wise the simple.
The statutes of the LORD *are* **right**, rejoicing the heart: the commandment of the LORD *is* pure, enlightening the eyes.
The fear of the LORD *is* **clean**, enduring for ever: the judgments of the LORD *are* true *and* righteous altogether.
More to be desired *are they* than gold, yea, than much fine gold: sweeter also than honey and the honeycomb.
Moreover by them is thy servant warned: *and* in keeping of them *there is* great reward. Who can understand *his* errors? cleanse thou me from secret *faults*.
Keep back thy servant also from presumptuous *sins*; let them not have dominion over me: then shall I be upright, and I shall be innocent from the great transgression.
Let the words of my mouth, and the meditation of my heart, be acceptable in thy sight, O LORD, my strength, and my redeemer.
Psalm 19:7-14

233

The foundations of mankind are philosophies and traditions.

Beware lest any man spoil you through **philosophy and vain deceit**, after the tradition of men, after the rudiments of the world, and not after Christ.

Colossians 2:8

O Timothy, keep that which is committed to thy trust, avoiding profane *and* vain babblings, and oppositions of **science falsely so called**.

1 Timothy 6:20

The reality, however, is that our very foundation for truth and the basis for our Hope rests in His Word.

Now faith is the substance of things hoped for, the evidence of things not seen. For by it the elders obtained a good report. **Through faith we understand that the worlds were framed by the word of God**, so that things which are seen were not made of things which do appear.

Hebrews 11:1-3

What and how we think is not as important as what God says. How we view our world is not how God views it.

For my thoughts *are* not your thoughts, neither *are* your ways my ways, saith the LORD.

Isaiah 55:8

Therefore, if we are to know the truth of a matter we must consider the words of God. Our duty, as pronounced by Christ, is to "search the scriptures." The believers of Berea searched the scriptures daily to see if what was told them was so.

These were more noble than those in Thessalonica, in that **they received the word with all readiness of mind, and searched the scriptures daily, whether those things were so.**

Acts 17:11

It is with this duty in mind that we study Biblical preservation and the Authorized Version. However, in the final conclusion it will not be us who judge the word of God but the Word of God which judges us.

For the word of God *is* quick, and powerful, and sharper than any two-edged sword, piercing even to the dividing asunder of soul and spirit, and of the joints and marrow, and *is* a discerner of the thoughts and intents of the heart. Neither is there any creature that is not manifest in his sight: but all things *are* naked and opened unto the eyes of him with whom we have to do.

Hebrews 4:12-13

The critics of the Bible **refuse to consider** that the Sovereign hand of Almighty God preserved His inerrant Word, or that the sinister influence of a literal Devil has been seeking to pervert the sacred Scripture. Without these considerations they are doomed to view the Word of God naturalistically, and thus remove Divine influence from the *Holy Bible*.

It is sad when Christians will take the word of an unbeliever over the Word of God. This is what is happening when Christians go to the skeptics and get lists of apparent contradictions in the *Bible* so as to show that God's Word is not pure, that it is corrupted. All this does is cause doubt in the unlearned or unstudied Christian who is not aware of the promise of scripture preservation given by God over 50 times in His Word.

These lists did not come from sincere Christians in study, but from unbelievers who want to destroy people's faith in God's Word. The people who hand them out do not even study these apparent contradictions, for if they did, they would see for themselves that they are NOT contradictions at all. Just misunderstood scriptures.

Psalm 12:6-7

The words of the LORD *are* pure words: *as* silver tried in a furnace of earth, purified seven times. Thou shalt keep them, **O LORD, thou shalt preserve them from this generation for ever.**

The Word is pure. If I find something wrong with something pure it is because I am not pure or there is something wrong with me - not the Word.

There are things I don't understand in the Bible, but I never think that my lack of understanding is reason to doubt the integrity of God's Word. If I don't understand something I still trust God to do what He promised.

How do we know which Bible is the pure Word of God that He promised to preserve and keep?

How to understand which Bible is the true Word and which one is a lie is very important. When you go to a Christian bookstore, to Barnes and Noble, or wherever there are Bibles available, you will find that there are many different versions. If you ask the sales people which one is God's Word, they will point to all of them. Are they telling the truth? They might think so, but the facts show us something far more sinister. The pure Word of God is nestled in the midst of a plethora of counterfeits. Most Christians do not know this! They think all bibles are God's Word. But, in order for that to be true, God would have to contradict Himself many times. And we know that God is perfect: one contradiction is too many. That is how we can find which one is the truth and which one is the lie. The true one will have no contradictions, but the fakes will have many. They are satan's fingerprint.

There are two kinds of manuscripts that make up the Bibles of today.

1.   **Accurate Copies** – The manuscripts that the "Tectus Receptus" came from, and from where we get the King James Bible. The "Tectus Receptus" is also referred to as the "Majority Text," because the majority of the manuscripts compared agreed with each other. We can know it is true by the vast number of copies that were collected over many regions and times. They were compared with each other, and the majority of them were found to be in harmony. This text has been accepted by Bible believing Christians for centuries and was translated into the King James Bible in 1611.
The majority text comes from manuscripts dating from the 2nd century down through the middle ages (A.D. 1500). It is also called the traditional text, the Syrian text, the Byzantine text, and the K (Kappa) or Common text. This text type is available today in English in the **Authorized Version,** or as it is called in the United States, The King James Version of the Bible.

2.   **Corrupted Copies** – These manuscripts were rejected because they did not agree with the majority text, and in most cases not even with each other. This is where we get the Greek texts for the newer versions, and where the Alexandrian manuscripts come from. The Vaticanus and Sinaiticus are part of these rejected texts. The new versions come from one region and reject the majority of manuscripts. The modern versions rely on these manuscripts to support their versions; Westcott and Hort also relied on these.

There are over 5,300 surviving manuscripts that contain all or part of our New Testament. These manuscripts agree with each other 95% of the time. The other 5% account for the differences between the King James and the modern versions.

The modern versions used Tectus Receptus, since it contains the majority of the surviving manuscripts. The problem is that when the Tectus Receptus disagreed with the Vaticanus or the Sinaiticus, they preferred these corrupted manuscripts over the Tectus Receptus.

This accounts for the 5% corruption in the modern versions. Even these two manuscripts agree with the Tectus Receptus much of the time. When they do not agree, it is because of the corruption of those manuscripts in 120-160 A.D. by Marcion or 184-254 A.D. by Origin. There are also others who corrupted manuscripts in the 5% that are inaccurate.

"For the grace of God that bringeth salvation hath appeared to all men,
Teaching us that, denying ungodliness and worldly lusts, we should live soberly, righteously, and godly, in this present world; Looking for that blessed hope, and the glorious appearing of the great God and our Saviour Jesus Christ; Who gave himself for us, that he might redeem us from all iniquity, and purify unto himself a peculiar people, zealous of good works. These things speak, and exhort, and rebuke with all authority. Let no man despise thee."

Titus 2:11-15

236

How do we know that the *King James Bible,* an English translation, is as good as the original languages of the Bible?

If we go to the Word of God and look up every time the word, "translate" occurs, we can begin to understand how God uses translations and what happens after something or someone is translated.

There are only **3 occurrences** of "translate" and they **all show improvement** from the prior state.

Colossians 1:12-14
Giving thanks unto the Father, which hath made us meet to be partakers of the inheritance of the saints in light: Who hath delivered us from the power of darkness, and hath **translated** *us* into the kingdom of his dear Son: In whom we have redemption through his blood, *even* the forgiveness of sins:

The *Bible* says the translation is superior to the original.

2 Samuel 3:9, 10
So do God to Abner, and more also, except, as the LORD hath sworn to David, even so I do to him...To **translate** the kingdom from the house of Saul, and to set up the throne of David over Israel and over Judah, from Dan even to Beersheba.

This translation is superior to the original (Saul).

Hebrews 11:5
By faith Enoch was **translated** that he should not see death; and was not found, because God had **translated** him: for before his translation he had this testimony, that he pleased God.

Enoch's translation is superior to his original state (from earth to Heaven).

If we look to the originals, we can assume they were in letter form, because God's Word was copied on many different types of manuscripts over the years. The Tectus Receptus is a collection of these:

Papyri   1-88   P66 is the oldest papyrus in the world and has predominately KJB readings
Uncials   1-274
Minuscule   1-2795
Lectionaries 1-2209

The majority of the surviving manuscripts were minuscules written without spaces or punctuation in all lower case. We now have verses, punctuation, chapters, etc., which make the *Bible* much easier to read, reference, and study. Are the manuscripts closest to the originals better? I believe my King James translation is much better than the earlier manuscripts, not in content (because the content is the same), but in format. It's easier to reference with chapters and verses. It makes studying and referencing easier.

237

Upon its publication, the King James or Authorized Version eclipsed all previous and subsequent *Bibles.* It is the best-selling book of all time.

We will use a quote from the Merit Student's Encyclopedia:

"The greatest English Bible is the Authorized, or *King James Version*...The King James Bible became the traditional Bible of English-speaking Protestants. Its dignified and beautiful style strongly influenced the development of literature in the English language. The influence can be seen in the works of John Bunyan, John Milton, Herman Melville and many other writers."

Although, it is now called the King James Version, when the translation was completed it was called, *The Holy Bible.* It was called the Holy Bible for about three hundred years! It wasn't until men started making their own versions that they labeled it "The King James Version.*" The King James Bible is **NOT** a version!* It is a translation. It is only a version because the version-makers labeled it one.

Satan knows that if he can succeed in planting even a small seed of doubt about the validity of God's Word, man will look someplace else. He will not take God's Word seriously. **Never in history has such doubt and confusion over the *Bible* existed as today!** And nothing has fueled the fire of confusion and doubt over the *Bible* more than that scores of different translations that have flooded the world. Most people believe the different versions are basically the same. They believe the newer versions are just harmless updating of the words, making the text easier to understand. Nothing could be further from the truth! We will compare some of these lies in a moment.

The King James Version has faithfully served the body of Christ for almost 400 years. Remember when I told you "The true one will have no contradictions and the fakes will." Let's see some of the counterfeits' contradictions.

"Every word of God is pure: he is a shield unto them that put their trust in him. Add thou not unto his words, lest he reprove thee, and thou be found a liar."

Proverbs 30:5
238

Contradictions in the Modern Versions

King James Bible (KJB)
Acts 13:21
> And afterward they desired a king: and God gave unto them Saul the son of Cis, a man of the tribe of Benjamin, **by the space of forty years**.

KJB
1 Samuel 13:1
> Saul reigned one year; and when he had reigned two years over Israel.
> **(No Contradiction)**

New International Version (NIV)
Acts 13:21
> Then the people asked for a king, and he gave them Saul of Kish, of the tribe of Benjamin, **who ruled forty years.**

NIV
1 Samuel 13:1
> Saul was thirty years old when he became king, and he reigned over Israel **forty two years. (Contradiction)**

New American Standard Bible (NASB)
Acts 13:21
> And then they asked for a king and God gave them Saul the son of Kish, a man of the tribe of Benjamin, **for forty years**.

NASB
1 Samuel 13:1
> Saul was forty years old when he began to reign, and he reigned **thirty-two years** over Israel. **(Contradiction)**

There is no contradiction in the KJB; the newer versions **not only contradict themselves, but also each other. The New International Version and the New American Standard Bible version come from the same manuscripts.**

"If any man shall add unto these things, *God shall add unto him the plagues* that are written in this book: *And if any man shall take away* from the words of the book of this prophecy, *God shall take away his part out of the book of life,* and out of the holy city, and *from* the things which are written in this book."

Revelation 22:18-19

239

Contradictions in the Modern Versions continued...

KJB
1 Corinthians 1:18-21

For the **preaching of the cross (the message)** is to them that perish foolishness; but **unto us which are saved it is the power of God.**

For it is written, I will destroy the wisdom of the wise, and will bring to nothing the understanding of the prudent.

Where *is* the wise? where *is* the scribe? where *is* the disputer of this world? hath not God made foolish the wisdom of this world?

For after that in the wisdom of God the world by wisdom knew not God, it pleased God by the foolishness of **preaching (the Act of)** to save them that believe.

(No Contradiction)

NIV
1 Corinthians 1:18-21

For the **message of the cross is foolishness** to those who are perishing, **but to us who are being saved it is the power of God.**

For it is written: "I will destroy the wisdom of the wise: the intelligence of the intelligent I will frustrate."

Where is the wise man? Where is the scholar? Where is the philosopher of this age? Has not God made foolish the wisdom of the world?

For since in the wisdom of God the world through its wisdom did not know him, **God was pleased through the foolishness of what was preached (the message) to save those who believe. (Contradiction)**

NASB
Vs. 21

The foolishness of the **message** preached to save those who believe. **(Contradiction)**

New Revised Standard Version (NRSV)
Vs. 21

The foolishness of our **proclamation**, to save those who believe. **(Contradiction)**

Notice the KJB distinguishes between the act of preaching and the message preached, yet the modern versions do not. The modern versions contradict themselves by saying the message of the Gospel is foolishness to them that perish as well as to those who believe.

"Remember the word that I said unto you, The servant is not greater than his Lord. If they have persecuted me, they will also persecute you; if they have kept my saying, they will keep yours also. But all these things will they do unto you for my name's sake, because they know not him that sent me."

John 15:20-21

240

While there are many places where phrases or words have been either changed or omitted, <u>here we see whole verses omitted or bracketed in modern versions compared to the KJV</u>. For example, both the **New American Standard Version** (NASV) and the **New International Version** (NIV) omit the following verses. I have chosen these verses because omissions from God's Word change the whole meaning of the scripture.

Check them out for yourself!

Matthew 17:21

Howbeit this kind goeth not out but by prayer and fasting.

Matthew 18:11

For the Son of man is come to save that which was lost.

Mark 7:16

If any man have ears to hear, let him hear.

Mark 9:44

Where their worm dieth not, and the fire is not quenched. (Also true of verse 46 which reads the same).

Mark 11:26

But if ye do not forgive, neither will your Father which is in heaven forgive your trespasses.

Mark 15:28

And the scripture was fulfilled, which saith, And he was numbered with the transgressors.

Luke 17:36

Two men shall be in the field; the one shall be taken, and the other left.

Luke 23:17

(For of necessity he must release one unto them at the feast.)

John 5:4

For an angel went down at a certain season into the pool, and troubled the water: whosoever then first after the troubling of the water stepped in was made whole of whatsoever disease he had.

John 7:53-8:11

And every man went unto his own house. Jesus went unto the mount of Olives. And early in the morning he came again into the temple, and all the people came unto him; and he sat down, and taught them. And the scribes and Pharisees brought unto him a woman taken in adultery; and when they had set her in the midst, They say unto him, Master, this woman was taken in adultery, in the very act. Now Moses in the law commanded us, that such should be stoned: but what sayest thou? This they said, tempting him, that they might have to accuse him. But Jesus stooped down, and with *his* finger wrote on the ground, *as though he heard them not*. So when they continued asking him, he lifted up himself, and said unto them, He that is without sin among you, let him first cast a stone at her. And again he stooped down, and wrote on the ground. And they which heard *it*, being convicted by *their own* conscience, went out one by one, beginning at the eldest, *even* unto the last: and Jesus was left alone, and the woman standing in the midst. When Jesus had lifted up himself, and saw none but the woman, he said unto her, Woman, where are those thine accusers? hath no man condemned thee? She said, No man, Lord. And Jesus said unto her, Neither do I condemn thee: go, and sin no more. (This may be in your Bible version but check the fine print and see what they have to say about it)

"A faith that cannot survive a collision with the truth is not worth many regrets."
Arthur C. Clarke   **"See 1 Timothy 6:11-12"**

Acts 8:37

I believe that Jesus Christ is the Son of God.

Acts 15:34

Notwithstanding it pleased Silas to abide there still.

Acts 24:7

But the chief captain Lysias came upon us, and with great violence took him away out of our hands.

Acts 28:29

And when he had said these words, the Jews departed, and had great reasoning among themselves.

Romans 11:6

But if *it be* of works, then is it no more grace

Romans 16:24

The grace of our Lord Jesus Christ be with you all. Amen.

1 John 5:7

For there are three that bear record in heaven, the Father, the Word, and the Holy Ghost: and these three are one.

1 John 5:13

and that ye may believe on the name of the Son of God.

The Revised Standard Version (RSV), **New Revised Standard Version** (NRSV), and **New English Version** (NEV) go further by not only omitting the above references from their text, but also omit the following verses:

Matthew 12:47

Then one said unto him, Behold, thy mother and thy brethren stand without, desiring to speak with thee.

Matthew18:11

For the Son of man is come to save that which was lost.

Matthew 21:44

And whosoever shall fall on this stone shall be broken: but on whomsoever it shall fall, it will grind him to powder.

Matthew 23:14

Woe unto you, scribes and Pharisees, hypocrites! for ye devour widows' houses, and for a pretence make long prayer.

Luke 22:20

Likewise also the cup after supper, saying, This cup is the new testament in my blood, which is shed for you.

Luke 24:12

Then arose Peter, and ran unto the sepulchre; and stooping down, he beheld the linen clothes laid by themselves, and departed, wondering in himself at that which was come to pass.

Luke 24: 40

And when he had thus spoken, he shewed them his hands and his feet.

By removing these verses or confining these verses to footnotes, these translations demonstrate...

The Greek texts from which they are translated **do not** contain these verses as part of their text. As Bible-believing Christians, this leaves us with a dilemma.

Three times the Bible warns against adding to or taking from the word of God:

Ye shall <u>not add</u> unto the word which I command you, <u>**neither shall ye diminish** *ought* **from it**</u>, that ye may keep the commandments of the LORD your God which I command you.

Deuteronomy 4:2

Every word of God *is* **pure**: he *is* a shield unto them that put their trust in him. <u>**Add thou not unto his words, lest he reprove thee, and thou be found a liar.**</u>

Proverbs 30:5-6

<u>**If any man shall add**</u> unto these things, God shall add unto him the <u>plagues</u> that are written in this book: <u>**And if any man shall take away**</u> from the words of the book of this prophecy, <u>**God shall take away**</u> his part out of the book of life, and out of the holy city, and *from* the things which are written in this book.

Revelation 22:18-19

Therefore, we must conclude that the Greek texts which <u>**underlie**</u> modern translations **are <u>corrupt in removing these verses</u>** from the text, or that the Greek text which <u>**underlies**</u> the *King James* Bible **is <u>corrupt for adding these verses</u>** to the text.

<u>**Either way, one cannot be Biblical**</u> and believe that the *<u>King James Bible</u>* **<u>and modern versions are both the word of God.</u>**

It is obvious that one of these *Bibles* have either **added to or taken from** the Word of God, either of **which is a violation of scripture**.

Any of these shown to be in error are corrupt and must be rejected by the Bible-believing Christian.

"Differences may be noted by comparing the **King James Bible** with the Modern versions. It doesn't take a Bible scholar to see the differences between the Truth and the counterfeits."

L.B.K.   **"See Malachi 3:18"**

243

Differences in Modern Versions

KJB

Psalm 138 1:1-2

I will praise thee with my whole heart: before the gods will I sing praise unto thee. I will worship toward thy holy temple, and praise thy name for thy lovingkindness and for thy truth: **for thou hast magnified thy word above all thy name.**

NIV

I will praise you, O Lord, with all my heart; before the "gods" I will sing your praise. I will bow down toward your holy temple and will praise your name for love and your faithfulness, **for you have exalted above all things your name and your word.**

Comment: Obviously, magnifying God's Word above His name is different from magnifying His Word and name above all things. This is one of many subtle deceptions found in the modern translations. It gets worse!

KJB

Mark 10:24

And the disciples were astonished at his words. But Jesus answereth again, and saith unto them, Children, how hard is it **for them that trust in riches** to enter into the kingdom of God!

Comment: NIV, NAS, RSV, NRSV, NCV, LB, etc…removed **"for them that trust in riches."** The modern versions say, "Children, how hard it is to enter the kingdom of God!" One of these is the truth and one is a lie! You decide.

Who Killed Goliath? If you have an elementary knowledge of the Bible you would know it was David.
The account is recorded in 1 Samuel 17.
Look at these differences and ask yourself if you still trust the so called Bible scholars who are responsible for the modern versions.

New International Version   **2 Samuel 21:19**
In another battle with the Philistines at Gob, *Elhanan son of Jaare-Oregim the Bethlehemite killed Goliath the Gittite,* who had a spear with a shaft like a weaver's rod.

King James Bible   **2 Samuel 21:19**
And there was again a battle in Gob with the Philistines, where **Elhanan *the son of Jaareoregim, a Bethlehemite slew* the brother** of *Goliath the Gittite*, the staff of whose spear *was* like a weaver's beam.

244

KJB

Luke 4:4

And Jesus answered him, saying, It is written, That man shall not live by bread alone, **but by every word of God.**

Comment: Here Jesus is quoting scripture from **Deuteronomy 8:3**...that he might make thee know that man doth not live by bread only, **but by every word that proceedeth out of the mouth of the LORD** doth man live.

The modern versions remove "but by every word of God," showing the corruption of their text by the removal of an obvious portion of Old Testament scripture that Jesus was quoting.

KJB

Luke 4:8

And Jesus answered and said unto him, <u>**Get thee behind me, Satan**</u>: for it is written, Thou shalt worship the Lord thy God, and him only shalt thou serve.

Comment: NIV, NAS, RSV, NRSV, NCV, LB, etc...Removed **"Get behind me satan"** One of these *Bibles* is right and one is wrong! God either said it or He didn't! They both cannot be God's Word. You decide!

KJB

Luke 11:2

And he said unto them, When ye pray, say, **Our** Father **which art in heaven,** Hallowed be thy name. Thy kingdom come. **Thy will be done, as in heaven, so in earth.** Give us day by day our daily bread. And forgive us our sins; for we also forgive every one that is indebted to us. And lead us not into temptation; **but deliver us from evil.**

Comment: Who gets to decide which words to take out of the Lord's prayer? The bolded words are those which have been removed. **There are 20 words missing!**

Father, hallowed be your name. Your kingdom come Give us each day our daily bread. And forgive us our sins, for we ourselves forgive everyone indebted to us. And do not bring us to the time of trial." **(NRSV)**

"Ye shall not add unto the word which I command you, neither shall ye diminish *ought* from it, that ye may keep the commandments of the LORD your God which I command you."

Deuteronomy 4:2

245

KJB

Luke 2:33

And **Joseph** and his mother marvelled at those things which were spoken of him.

NIV

Luke 2:33

The child's father and mother marveled at what was said about him.

Comment: It is explicitly stated that God was the Father of our Lord Jesus Christ! This is a blatant attempt to cause doubt in the Bible readers mind as to the position Jesus held with God. This verse alone should cause a Christian to see the devilish trend these modern versions have.

KJB

Matthew 20:23

And he saith unto them, Ye shall drink indeed of my cup, **and be baptized with the baptism that I am baptized with**: but to sit on my right hand, and on my left, is not mine to give, but it shall be given to them for whom it is prepared of my Father.

NIV

Matthew 20:23

Jesus said to them, You will indeed drink from my cup, but to sit at my right or left is not for me to grant. These places, belong to those for whom they have been prepared by my Father.

Comment: Removing the portion about being baptized changes the message. Notice the NIV mentions Jesus' Father; do you think they were talking about Joseph?

KJB

Ephesians 3:14

For this cause I bow my knees unto the Father **of our Lord Jesus Christ,**

Comment: NIV, NASB, RSV, NRSV, NAB, etc…Removed: **"of our lord Jesus Christ"** This is one of many instances where the modern versions attempt to remove the deity of Jesus Christ.

The grass withereth, the flower fadeth:
but the word of our God shall stand for ever.
Isaiah 40:8

Heaven and earth shall pass away, but my words shall not pass away.
Matthew 24:35

And it is easier for heaven and earth to pass, than one tittle of the law to fail.
Luke 16:17

KJB
Ephesians 3:9

And to make all *men* see what *is* the fellowship of the mystery, which from the beginning of the world hath been hid in God, who created all things **by Jesus Christ.**

Comment: NIV, NASB, RSV, NRSV, NAB, etc...Removed: **"by Jesus Christ."** All religions could rally around this verse when you remove "by Jesus Christ." The Muslims, Hindus, Jews, Catholics, etc...they all believe in God. It is the very words "by Jesus Christ" that removes the false gods and points men to the Way, the Truth, and the Life, which is in Jesus Christ alone and no other.

KJB
John 1:18

No man hath seen God at any time; **the only begotten Son,** which is in the bosom of the Father, he hath declared him.

NIV
John 1:18

No one has ever seen God, but God the **One and Only,** who is at the Father's side, has made him known.

Comment: Another subtle deception; removing "the only begotten Son" and replacing it with "One and Only" continues to show a trend of bias.

KJB
Matthew 6:13

And lead us not into temptation, but deliver us from evil: **For thine is the kingdom, and the power, and the glory, for ever. Amen.**

NIV
Matthew 6:13

And lead us not into temptation, but deliver us from the evil one.

Comment: Why would they remove this description of God's majesty? Because satan is jealous and envies God's position. It eats him up every time someone praises the true God; he hates it.

"People see God every day, they just don't recognize Him."

Pearl Bailey, American Singer   **"See Romans 1:20"**

KJB
Acts 2:30

Therefore being a prophet, and knowing that God had sworn with an oath to him, that **of the fruit of his loins, according to the flesh, he would raise up Christ** to sit on his throne.

NIV
Acts 2:30

But he was a prophet and knew that God had promised him an oath that he would place **one of his descendants** on his throne.

Comment: Here, the modern version removes the message that God would raise the Christ from David's lineage and downplays Christ as one of David's descendants. Can you see any difference in these two verses?

KJB
Matthew 9:13

But go ye and learn what that meaneth, I will have mercy, and not sacrifice: for I am not come to call the righteous, but sinners **to repentance.**

NIV
Matthew 9:13

But go and learn what this means: I desire mercy, not sacrifice. For I have not come to call the righteous, but sinners.

Comment: When Jesus came out of the wilderness after being tempted and fasting, He started His earthly ministry. The very first thing He is recorded preaching is to "*repent* for the Kingdom of God is at hand." Before we are brought into the family of God, we must repent of our sins. God brings us to repentance by showing us that we are sinners by the law of God. Then He brings us to knowledge of the truth. Without repentance there is no salvation! Can you see why satan removes repentance here?

"My soul, wait thou only upon God;
for my expectation *is* from him.
He only *is* my rock and my salvation: *he is* my defence;
I shall not be moved.
In God *is* my salvation and my glory:
the rock of my strength,
and my refuge, *is* in God. Trust in him at all times;
ye people, pour out your heart before him:
God *is* a refuge for us. Selah."

Psalm 62:5-8

KJB
Romans 1:16

For I am not ashamed of the gospel **of Christ**: for it is the power of God unto salvation to every one that believeth; to the Jew first, and also to the Greek.

NIV
Romans 1:16

I am not ashamed of the gospel, because it is the power of God for the salvation of every-one who believes: first for the Jew, then for the Gentile.

Comment: This is one of many example's of the modern versions removing Christ from the *Bible.*

KJB
Colossians 1:14

In whom we have redemption **through his blood**, even the forgiveness of sins:

NIV
Colossians 1:14

In whom we have redemption, the forgiveness of sins.

Comment: It is by the blood of Jesus that we are redeemed! It is His blood that covers our sins! Why remove "through his blood?" This is just one more devilish influence that shows a trend of deception that is in all modern versions.

KJB
1 Timothy 3:16

And without controversy great is the mystery of godliness: **God was manifest in the flesh,** justified in the Spirit, seen of angels, preached unto the **Gentiles,** believed on in the world, **received** up into glory.

NIV
1 Timothy 3:16

Beyond all question, the mystery of godliness is great: **He appeared in a body**, was vindicated by the Spirit, was seen by angels, was preached among the **nations**, was believed on in the world, was **taken** up in glory.

Comment: The bolded words are the ones that have been changed to the point of changing the meaning of the message. Are you able to discern between the two verses? I hope so.

"And take the helmet of salvation, and the sword of the Spirit, which is the word of God."

Ephesians 6:17

249

KJB
1 Timothy 6:5
Perverse disputings of men of corrupt minds, and destitute of the truth, supposing that gain is godliness: **from such withdraw thyself**.

Removed "from such withdraw thyself."

and wrangling among men who are depraved in mind and bereft of the truth, imagining that godliness is a means of gain. **(RSV)**

Comment: Not only is the King James translation easier to understand, but removing "from such withdraw thyself" changes the scripture once again. Don't be deceived!

KJB
Mark 6:11
And whosoever shall not receive you, nor hear you, when ye depart thence, shake off the dust under your feet for a testimony against them. **Verily I say unto you, It shall be more tolerable for Sodom and Gomorrah in the day of judgment, than for that city.**

NIV
Mark 6:11
And if any place will not welcome you or listen to you, shake the dust off your feet when you leave, as a testimony against them.

Comment: Jesus is emphasizing the severity of rejecting the Gospel. Removing the last sentence in the verse changes the scripture to a watered-down satanic lie.

KJB
Acts 9:6
And he trembling and astonished said, Lord, what wilt thou have me to do? And the Lord said unto him, Arise, and go into the city, and it shall be told thee what thou must do.

NIV
Acts 9:6
Now get up and go into the city, and you will be told what you must do.

Comment: The modern version enthusiasts will tell you that the new versions give you a fuller meaning of the scripture. I don't see how the newer versions give anything other than a lesser meaning of this scripture by removing the first half of it.

"The secret *things belong* unto the LORD our God: but those *things which are* revealed *belong* unto us and to our children for ever, that *we* may do all the words of this law."

Deuteronomy 29:29

250

KJB
Romans 8:1

There is therefore now no condemnation to them which are in Christ Jesus, <u>**who walk not after the flesh, but after the Spirit.**</u>

NIV
Romans 8:1

Therefore, there is now no condemnation for those who are in Christ Jesus.

Comment: God has written His Law in our hearts and our conscience bears witness. When I walk after the flesh my conscience condemns me and brings me to repentance. When we are being led by the Spirit there is no condemnation! Only peace, love, joy, patience, etc… This verse will cause a Christian who feels guilty about a transgression to think he is not in Christ. It is never good to remove any of God's Word!

KJB
Revelation 1:6

And hath made us **kings** and priests unto God and his Father; to him be glory and dominion for ever and ever. Amen.

NIV
Revelation 1:6

And has made us to **be a kingdom** and priests to serve his God and Father--to him be glory and power for ever and ever! Amen.

Comment: Is there a difference between "made us kings" and "made us to be a kingdom?" You decide.

KJB
Revelation 1:11

<u>**Saying, I am Alpha and Omega, the first and the last:**</u> and, What thou seest, write in a book, and send it unto the seven churches **which are in Asia**; unto Ephesus, and unto Smyrna, and unto Pergamos, and unto Thyatira, and unto Sardis, and unto Philadelphia, and unto Laodicea.

NIV
Revelation 1:11

Which said: Write on a scroll what you see and send it to the seven churches: to Ephesus, Smyrna, Pergamum, Thyatira, Sardis, Philadelphia and Laodicea.

Comment: These omissions are blatant and reprehensible! This is yet another example of the trend to remove the deity from our Lord Jesus Christ.

"He that turneth away his ear from hearing the law, even his prayer shall be an abomination."

Proverbs 28:9

251

KJB
2 Corinthians 2:17
> For we are not as many, which **corrupt** the word of God: but as of sincerity, but as of God, in the sight of God speak we in Christ.

NIV
2 Corinthians 2:17
> Unlike so many, we do not **peddle** the word of God for profit. On the contrary, in Christ we speak before God with sincerity, like men sent from God.

Comment: The *King James* Bible is very clear and understandable with its usage of "corrupt." The NIV changes the message of scripture by using "peddle." You decide.

KJB
Titus 2:11
> **For the grace of God that bringeth salvation** hath appeared to all men…

RSV
Titus 2:11
> **For the grace of God has appeared for the salvation** of all men…

Comment: I saved this for last because of its subtleness. At first it appears to be the same, but for the person who is searching for the truth the RSV tells them that "the grace of God has appeared for the salvation of all men," meaning all men are saved! Example; Buddhist, Muslim, any and all religions. The KJB states it correctly, saying "the grace of God that bringeth salvation has appeared to all men." The grace that brings salvation has appeared to all men, not salvation for all men. This is a very devilish deception which takes people's hope away from the truth.

The people who tell you, "All *Bibles* are corrupted and have mistakes" because man was in charge of translating and preserving them contradict themselves when they say the original manuscripts are the only pure Words of God, because the originals were written by man also.

They are also calling God a liar because His Word tells us that His Words are pure and that God is responsible to keep and preserve His Word. I believe that my God who created the universe and all it contains, my God who shows His majesty in the perfection and complexity of a single living cell, the Father of my Lord and Savior Jesus Christ, maker of Heaven and Earth, can preserve His Word through imperfect man as He has promised! I say this because I have faith in Him (I trust Him to perform that which He has promised) and that is good enough for me. I hope and pray that it might be good enough for you. Trust His Word!

If you doubt the Word of God you will not submit to it!

"I am the good shepherd: the good shepherd giveth his life for the sheep."

John 10:11

Is Jesus Your Lord?

"And it shall come to pass, *that* whosoever shall call on the name of the Lord shall be saved."
Acts 2:21

Would you like to receive Jesus as your Lord and Savior? Are you a professed Christian, but unsure you are truly saved? This chapter will help you to understand what God's Word says is needed to inherit eternal life. We will see what genuine conversion is and also discover what creates a false convert and how to recognize one. Knowing how to identify a false convert may help you to know if you are truly in the faith.

Where do we find the faith that leads to salvation?

Romans 10:17 says:
So then faith *cometh* by hearing, and hearing **by the word of God.**

The Word of God is where we learn about Jesus! If someone tells you about Jesus, it is only because they heard it from the Word or they heard it from someone who heard it from the Word. God's Word is vital in knowing Him and developing our personal and intimate relationship with Him. The Bible reveals the truth and promises of God - you can bet your life on it!

This is how you receive salvation.

Romans 10:9-13 says:
That if thou shalt confess with thy mouth the Lord Jesus, and shalt believe in thine heart that God hath raised him from the dead, thou shalt be saved. For with the heart man believeth unto righteousness; and with the mouth confession is made unto salvation. For the scripture saith, whosoever believeth on him shall not be ashamed. For there is no difference between the Jew and the Greek: for the same Lord over all is rich unto all that call upon him. **For whosoever shall call upon the name of the Lord shall be saved. (This means you!)**

"Jesus came to pay a debt He didn't owe because we owed a debt we couldn't pay."

Unknown   **"See 1 John 4:9"**

255

This gift is direct from God. No one can bring you to repentance and a knowledge of the truth but God! Christians can share the Gospel, but God provides the results.

2 Timothy 2:24-26 says:
And the servant of the Lord must not strive; but be gentle unto all *men*, apt to teach, patient, In meekness instructing those that oppose themselves; if **God peradventure will give them repentance to the acknowledging of the truth;** And *that* they may recover themselves out of the snare of the devil, who are taken captive by him at his will.

John 3:16 says:
For God so loved the world, that he gave his only begotten Son, that **whosoever believeth in him should not perish, but have everlasting life.** For God sent not his Son into the world to condemn the world; but that the world through him might be saved.

You might think you're a good person and don't need a Savior.

Proverbs 30:12 says:
There is a generation *that are* pure in their own eyes, and *yet* is not washed from their filthiness.

The truth is we all have broken the commandments of God! We all have lied, stolen, coveted, dishonored our parents, used the name of the Lord in vain, put something before God, etc. We were lost and without the ability to redeem ourselves. It was because of this that God made a way where there was no way. Jesus willingly submitted to the punishment we deserved, so that we would not have to.

Decide now what you will do! And know this: not to decide is to decide!

Let's assume God has given you the gift of repentance and knowledge of the truth and you have asked Jesus to be your Lord and Savior.

Congratulations!!!

You have made the best decision in your life; you have just joined the winning team! Your life is about to change and you have embarked on the greatest adventure ever known to man. Your life will never be the same now that you have accepted the free gift of salvation from the Lord. You are washed by the blood of Christ; your sins are forgiven. You are a new person.

"When we die we leave behind all that we have, and take with us all that we are."

Chapel of the Air   **"See Psalm 49:17"**

256

Three Things That Expose False Converts

1. **Tribulation** - Trials, problems, and difficulties when a man faces ridicule from friends or business associates because he won't lie, cheat, or give in to worldly behavior, because the *Bible* has taught him to live honestly and be like Christ. The false convert consistently falls away because he won't be honest or obedient if it means losing his friends or risking his business.
2. **Temptation** - Opportunities to sin, to do the wrong things that are pleasurable, or opportunities not to do the right things that are unpleasant. When faced with the temptation to pursue pornography on the Internet, or not use his money to help the poor, the false convert will consistently fall away and will consistently give in to the temptation of his flesh with little or no remorse. He will keep searching out pornography on the Internet and continuing to ignore the needs of the poor in order to sustain his own comfortable lifestyle.
3. **Persecution** - Insults, reproaches, and problems from others due to taking a stand for Biblical truth and Jesus Christ. When faced with the possibility of being ridiculed, fired from his job, or even physically harmed because of his faith in the *Bible* and Jesus Christ, a false convert will consistently fall away by not taking a stand for what he believes.

The difference between Christian discipline and Christian legalism is the Christian's motivation. A false Christian does good works to impress God and others. A true Christian is motivated to be obedient because of what Christ has already done for him. He is motivated by love.

Examine yourself and see if you're in the faith

The following parables teach us two outstanding truths: that in the professed Church good and evil are intermingled, and, that a time of separation has been set. Thus, the good may rejoice because of their bright, eternal future. The bad should mourn, for if they die in their sin, they are eternally doomed. I would like you to read these parables and see for yourself from God's Word how clearly it is defined. There should be no question in your mind whether you or anyone else is a false convert. You might think it's not a big deal to know if you are dealing with a true Christian or a fake one, but in the beginning of the church when they were under persecution, it meant life or death to everyone in their fellowship. You decide how important it is!

"The simplest and shortest ethical precept is to be served by others as little as possible, and to serve others as much as possible."

Leo Tolstoy   **"See John 13:3-15"**

259

When we understand this parable, then we can know all the other parables.
Notice what Jesus says in Mark 4:13

The Sower and the Seed

Mark 4:2-20

[2]And he taught them many things by parables, and said unto them in his doctrine,
[3]Hearken; Behold, there went out a sower to sow:
[4]And it came to pass, as he sowed, some fell by the way side, and the fowls of the air came and devoured it up.
[5]And some fell on stony ground, where it had not much earth; and immediately it sprang up, because it had no depth of earth:
[6]But when the sun was up, it was scorched; and because it had no root, it withered away.
[7]And some fell among thorns, and the thorns grew up, and choked it, and it yielded no fruit.
[8]And other fell on good ground, and did yield fruit that sprang up and increased; and brought forth, some thirty, and some sixty, and some an hundred.
[9]And he said unto them, He that hath ears to hear, let him hear.
[10]And when he was alone, they that were about him with the twelve asked of him the parable.
[11]And he said unto them, Unto you it is given to know the mystery of the kingdom of God: but unto them that are without, all *these* things are done in parables:
[12]That seeing they may see, and not perceive; and hearing they may hear, and not understand; lest at any time they should be converted, and *their* sins should be forgiven them.
[13]**And he said unto them, Know ye not this parable? And how then will ye know all parables?**
[14]The sower soweth the word.
[15]And these are they by the way side, where the word is sown; but when they have heard, Satan cometh immediately, and taketh away the word that was sown in their hearts.
[16]And these are they likewise which are sown on stony ground; who, when they have heard the word, immediately receive it with gladness;
[17]And have no root in themselves, and so endure but for a time: afterward, when affliction or persecution ariseth for the word's sake, immediately they are offended.
[18]And these are they which are sown among thorns; such as hear the word,
[19]And the cares of this world, and the deceitfulness of riches, and the lusts of other things entering in, choke the word, and it becometh unfruitful.
[20]And these are they which are sown on good ground; such as hear the word, and receive *it*, and bring forth fruit, some thirtyfold, some sixty, and some an hundred.

"A little science estranges men from God, but much science leads them back to Him."
Louis Pasteur   **"See Romans 1:20"**

Wise Virgins & Foolish Virgins
Matthew 25:1-13

Then shall the kingdom of heaven be likened unto **ten virgins**, which took their lamps, and went forth to meet the bridegroom.

[2]And five of them were wise **(true Christians)**, and five *were* foolish **(false Christians).**

[3]They that *were* foolish took their lamps, and took no oil with them:

[4]But the wise took oil in their vessels with their lamps.

[5]While the bridegroom tarried, they all slumbered and slept.

[6]And at midnight there was a cry made, Behold, the bridegroom cometh; go ye out to meet him.

[7]Then all those virgins arose, and trimmed their lamps.

[8]And the foolish said unto the wise, Give us of your oil; for our lamps are gone out.

[9]But the wise answered, saying, *Not so*; lest there be not enough for us and you: but go ye rather to them that sell, and buy for yourselves.

[10]And while they went to buy, the bridegroom came; and they that were ready went in with him to the marriage: and the door was shut.

[11]Afterward came also the other virgins, saying, Lord, Lord, open to us.

[12]But he answered and said, Verily I say unto you, I know you not.

[13]Watch therefore, for ye know neither the day nor the hour wherein the Son of man cometh.

The House Built On A Rock And On Sand
Matthew 7:24-27

Therefore whosoever heareth these sayings of mine, and doeth them, I will liken him unto a wise man, which built his house upon a rock:

[25]And the rain descended, and the floods came, and the winds blew, and beat upon that house; and it fell not: for it was founded upon a rock.

[26]And every one that heareth these sayings of mine, and doeth them not, shall be likened unto a foolish man, which built his house upon the sand:

[27]And the rain descended, and the floods came, and the winds blew, and beat upon that house; and it fell: and great was the fall of it.

"If a friend is in trouble, don't annoy him by asking if there is anything you can do. Think up something appropriate and do it."

Edgar Watson Howe   **"See James 2:15-17"**

The Wheat And The Tares
Matthew 13:24-30

The kingdom of heaven is likened unto a man which sowed good seed in his field:
[25]But while men slept, his enemy came and sowed tares among the wheat, and went his way.
[26]But when the blade was sprung up, and brought forth fruit, then appeared the tares also.
[27]So the servants of the householder came and said unto him, Sir, didst not thou sow good seed in thy field? from whence then hath it tares?
[28] He said unto them, An enemy hath done this. The servants said unto him, Wilt thou then that we go and gather them up?
[29]But he said, Nay; lest while ye gather up the tares, ye root up also the wheat with them.
[30]Let both grow together until the harvest: and in the time of harvest I will say to the reapers, Gather ye together first the tares, and bind them in bundles to burn them: but gather the wheat into my barn.

Matthew 13:37-43

He that soweth the good seed is the Son of man;
[38] The field is the world; the good seed are the children of the kingdom; but the tares are the children of the wicked *one*;
[39] The enemy that sowed them is the devil; the harvest is the end of the world; and the reapers are the angels.
[40]As therefore the tares are gathered and burned in the fire; so shall it be in the end of this world.
[41]The Son of man shall send forth his angels, and they shall gather out of his kingdom all things that offend, and them which do iniquity;
[42]And shall cast them into a furnace of fire: there shall be wailing and gnashing of teeth.
[43]Then shall the righteous shine forth as the sun in the kingdom of their Father. Who hath ears to hear, let him hear.

The Good and Bad Fish
Matthew 13:47-50

Again, the kingdom of heaven is like unto a net, that was cast into the sea, and gathered of every kind:
[48]Which, when it was full, they drew to shore, and sat down, and gathered the good into vessels, but cast the bad away.
[49]So shall it be at the end of the world: the angels shall come forth, and sever the wicked from among the just,
[50]And shall cast them into the furnace of fire: there shall be wailing and gnashing of teeth.

"Faith is trusting God to perform that which He has promised."

Anonymous   **"See Romans 4:20-21"**

262

Two Faithful Servants and a Slothful and Wicked Servant
Matthew 25:14-30

For *the kingdom of heaven is* as a man travelling into a far country, *who* called his own servants, and delivered unto them his goods.

[15]And unto one he gave five talents, to another two, and to another one; to every man according to his several ability; and straightway took his journey.

[16]Then he that had received the five talents went and traded with the same, and made *them* other five talents.

[17]And likewise he that *had received* two, he also gained other two.

[18]But he that had received one went and digged in the earth, and hid his lord's money.

[19]After a long time the lord of those servants cometh, and reckoneth with them.

[20]And so he that had received five talents came and brought other five talents, saying, Lord, thou deliveredst unto me five talents: behold, I have gained beside them five talents more.

[21] His lord said unto him, Well done, *thou* good and faithful servant: thou hast been faithful over a few things, I will make thee ruler over many things: enter thou into the joy of thy lord.

[22] He also that had received two talents came and said, Lord, thou deliveredst unto me two talents: behold, I have gained two other talents beside them.

[23]His lord said unto him, Well done, good and faithful servant; thou hast been faithful over a few things, I will make thee ruler over many things: enter thou into the joy of thy lord.

[24]Then he which had received the one talent came and said, Lord, I knew thee that thou art an hard man, reaping where thou hast not sown, and gathering where thou hast not strawed:

[25]And I was afraid, and went and hid thy talent in the earth: lo, *there* thou hast *that is* thine.

[26] His lord answered and said unto him, *Thou* wicked and slothful servant, thou knewest that I reap where I sowed not, and gather where I have not strawed:

[27]Thou oughtest therefore to have put my money to the exchangers, and *then* at my coming I should have received mine own with usury.

[28]Take therefore the talent from him, and give *it* unto him which hath ten talents.

[29]For unto every one that hath shall be given, and he shall have abundance: but from him that hath not shall be taken away even that which he hath.

[30]And cast ye the unprofitable servant into outer darkness: there shall be weeping and gnashing of teeth.

"Master, which *is* the great commandment in the law?

Jesus said unto him,
**Thou shalt love the Lord thy God with all thy heart,
and with all thy soul, and with all thy mind.**
This is the first and great commandment. And the second *is* like unto it,
Thou shalt love thy neighbour as thyself.
On these two commandments hang all the law and the prophets."

Matthew 22:36-40

263

What Do Christians Have that Makes Them Special?

Wherefore by their fruits ye shall know them.
Matthew 7:20

1. **Repentance** - A complete turn around from sinful behavior towards godly behavior.

2. **Thankfulness** - A thankful heart that is grateful for what God has done and manifests itself in a joyful disposition.

3. **Good Works** - Not self-centered (all free time consumed by personal hobbies and interests). A desire to keep God's Commandments and serve Him.

4. **Fruit of the Spirit** - An ever-growing capacity of Love, Joy, Peace, Patience, Gentleness, Goodness, Meekness, Faith and Self-Control in the life of the believer.

5. **Fruit of Righteousness** - Doing the right thing according to the way God defines it in His Word, not according to the way man defines it in his own mind.

As witnesses of the gospel, we do not want decisions for Christ. We want fruit Bearing Christians, followers of our Lord Jesus Christ. Not hearers only, but doers of the Word.

Finding God's Will for Your Life

1. God is always at work around you.
2. God pursues a continuing love relationship with you that is real and personal.
3. God invites you to become involved with Him in His work.
4. God speaks by the Holy Spirit through the *Bible*, prayer, circumstances, and the church to reveal Himself, His purposes, and His ways.
5. God's invitation for you to work with Him always leads you to a crisis of belief that requires faith and actions.
6. You must make major adjustments in your life to join God in what He is doing.
7. You come to know God by experience as you obey Him and He accomplishes His work through you.

Henry T. Blackaby, *Experiencing God*

What is a Genuine Conversion?

In order to be saved we must by experience know the meaning of true conversion. It is a terrible mistake for men or women to live their lives professing to be Christians when they have no right to the name. In God's sight profession is nothing; position is nothing. He wants our lives to be in harmony with His commandments.

There are many people who assume they are converted and fill the churches every week for their dose of religion. However, they are unable to bear the test of character presented in the Word of God. It will be a very sad day when every man is rewarded according to his works, for those who could not bear this test.

Genuine conversion is a change of heart, a turning from unrighteousness to righteousness. Relying on the merits of Christ, trusting Him to perform that which He has promised, the repentant sinner receives a pardon for sin. As they stop doing evil and learn to do good, they grow in grace and in the knowledge of God. They realize that in order to follow Jesus they must separate themselves from the world; counting the cost, they look upon all that they have as nothing if they may just receive Christ.

They join His side; they gladly join in the war and start fighting against natural inclinations and self-desires, and begin bringing their will into subjection to the will of Christ. Daily they seek the Lord for grace, and they are strengthened and helped. Selfishness once dominated them, and worldly pleasures were their motivation. Now they grow selfless, and God reigns supreme. The sins they once loved they now hate. Firmly and resolutely they follow in the path of holiness. This is genuine conversion.

Many church-goers have never had their lives changed; the truth has always been kept at a distance. There has never been a genuine conversion; no positive work of grace has been done in their hearts. If their desire to do God's will is based upon their own inclinations and not upon the deep conviction of the Holy Spirit, their conduct will not be brought into harmony with the Law of God. They profess to accept Christ as their Savior, but they do not believe that He will give them power to overcome their sins. They have no personal relationship with the living Savior and their character reveals many blemishes.

Many people who look in the mirror and see their spiritual condition become convinced that their life is not what it ought to be. Yet they fail to make changes. Once they leave the mirror, they forget their defects. They may profess to be a follower of Christ, but what does this benefit if their character hasn't changed, if the Holy Spirit hasn't convicted their heart? The effort has been superficial. They hold on to selfishness and their lives reveal it. They are not partakers of the divine nature. They may talk of God and pray to God, but their lives reveal that they are working against God.

"For I am persuaded, that neither death, nor life, nor angels, nor principalities, nor powers, nor things present, nor things to come, Nor height, nor depth, nor any other creature, shall be able to separate us from the love of God, which is in Christ Jesus our Lord."

Romans 8:38-39

265

Let's not forget that man's conversion and sanctification experience must be in harmony with God.

"Work out your own salvation with fear and trembling," the Word declares, "for it is God which worketh in you both to will and to do *his* good pleasure." Philippians 2:12-13

Man cannot transform himself by exercise of his will. He has no power to affect any change. The renewing power must come from God; the change can only be made by the Holy Spirit. Whosoever would be saved, high or low, rich or poor, must submit to the working power of God.

No mere outward change is sufficient to bring us into harmony with God. There are many who try to change by correcting bad habits, and they hope in this way to become Christians, but they are starting in the wrong place. Our first work is in the heart!

God's Word is the only way for this transformation of character. Christ prayed

"Sanctify them through thy truth: thy word is truth."   **John 17:17**

If studied and obeyed, the Word of God works in the heart, subduing every unholy attribute. The Holy Spirit comes convicting us of our sin, and then faith springs up in the heart working by love for Christ, conforming us body, soul, and spirit to His will. The conscience is awakened. The truth works secretly, silently, and steadily, to transform the soul. The natural inclinations are softened and subdued. New thoughts, new feelings, new motives, are implanted. The mind is changed; a new standard of character is established: the life of Christ.

The Spirit of God is working in him, and with fear and trembling he works on himself, seeking to find out his defects of character and to see what he can do to bring about the needed change in his life. His heart is humbled. By confession and repentance he shows the sincerity of his desire to reform. He confesses his sins to God, and if he has injured any one he confesses the wrong to the one he has injured. While God is working, the sinner-under the influence of the Holy Spirit works out that which God is working in mind and heart. He acts in harmony with the Spirit's working, and his conversion is genuine.

Those who choose to serve the Lord must give all and do all for Christ. Our Redeemer will not accept divided service. They must learn the meaning of self-surrender daily. They must study the Word of God, getting its meaning and obeying its precepts. There is no limit to the spiritual growth that can take place if they are a partaker of the divine nature. Day by day God works in them, perfecting their character. Each day of their life they minister to others. The light that is in them shines forth and dispels the darkness. Day by day they are working before men showing what the gospel can do for them.

"The gospel has not been clearly preached if the hearer doesn't know that not to make a decision is a decision."

Dan Arnold   **"See Luke 13:3"**

"I charge *thee* therefore before God, and the Lord Jesus Christ,

Who shall judge the quick and the dead at his appearing and his kingdom;

Preach the word;

Be instant in season, out of season;

Reprove, rebuke, exhort with all longsuffering and doctrine.

For the time will come when they will not endure sound doctrine;

But after their own lusts shall they heap to themselves teachers, having itching ears;

And they shall turn away *their* ears from the truth,

And shall be turned unto fables.

But watch thou in all things, Endure afflictions,

Do the work of an evangelist,

Make full proof of thy ministry."

2 Timothy 4:1-5

"Stand fast therefore in the liberty wherewith Christ hath made us free, and be not entangled again with the yoke of bondage."

Galatians 5:1

268

The Last Word

I hope you can now recognize that the facts do speak for themselves concerning our Lord Jesus Christ! You may have noticed the majority of this book directly quotes scripture taken from the King James Bible. My hope is that you will see the reality of Jesus through the truth of God's Word. Having almost all the scriptures regarding Jesus placed together gives no reason for anyone to say, "I don't understand what the Bible says regarding Jesus Christ."

If you are a Christian I hope this book has helped you draw closer to our Lord and Savior. This book can be used as a reference with your Bible, and will help you show those seeking the truth that Jesus is the Messiah the same way they did it in the first century, using the prophecy in God's Word. I went through the Old Testament in my Bible using a highlighter and marked all of the places where there were prophecies. I then wrote the fulfillment verse next to it so that I might have a ready reference to better show that Jesus is Lord. You might want to do the same.

We have learned who Jesus is all the descriptions, titles, and self proclamations shown in God's Word. We have examined almost all of the prophecies from the Old Testament concerning Him. We have come to understand and know what faith is, and how we receive it. We now understand what we must do to accept God's free gift of salvation, and how to be sure we are really saved.

This is all wonderful, but means nothing if you don't believe the source of these truths: the *Bible*, God's Holy inspired and preserved Word! We have revealed some of the deceptive works satan has used in perverting and counterfeiting God's Holy Word. We can see through history how satan has attacked the church, how he has debased mankind's morals and values. He has attacked the institution of the family and has sought to kill, steal and destroy man for thousands of years. If it *wasn't* for our God and Father of our Lord Jesus Christ he certainly would have succeeded. It amazes me that people think that satan would not attack God's Word. It also amazes me that some Christians can believe one part of the *Bible* and not another. The *Bible* says God preserved his (complete) Word; satan has been trying to alter it since the Garden of Eden. Trust God and His Word, for this is the first step in accepting the free gift of God.

Psalm 138:1-2

I will praise thee with my whole heart: before the gods will I sing praise unto thee. I will worship toward thy holy temple, and praise thy name for thy lovingkindness and for thy truth: **for thou hast magnified thy word above all thy name.**

God places great importance on his Word. We should also.

269

Jesus said, "I am the way, the truth, and the life: no man cometh to the Father, but by me." There are only two reasons why a person would not accept Jesus as their savior. The first is ignorance, a lack of knowledge. This can be overcome with instruction, using the *Bible* as the standard for truth. The second reason is willful rejection. They love the darkness, so they reject the light. It is no longer a "head" issue but a "heart" issue. The only way this can be overcome is to lovingly reveal to those rejecting the Lord the hardness of their heart and pray for them. This is best described in **2 Timothy 2:24-25**

> **And the servant of the Lord must not strive; but be gentle unto all *men*, apt to teach, patient, In meekness instructing those that oppose themselves; if God peradventure will give them repentance to the acknowledging of the truth; And *that* they may recover themselves out of the snare of the devil, who are taken captive by him at his will.**

God brings people to repentance and knowledge of the truth, not us. But He asks us to share the Gospel of Jesus Christ to the lost. Everyone can do something for the Lord; what can you do? Do not take God's gift for granted; let us express our love for Him through action. Let us keep His Commandments and share the Testimony of Jesus Christ to all who will hear.

"And he saith unto them, Follow me, and I will make you fishers of men."

Matthew 4:19

271

Index

A

Abhorred, 128, 208
Abomination, 141, 198, 205, 251
Abraham, 16, 44, 48, 51, 62, 70, 72, 83, 87, 96-103, 105, 108, 117, 155, 157, 160, 172, 189, 192, 194, 201, 204, 206
Acceptable, 34, 149, 158, 188, 233
Accurate copies, 236
Accurately, 229
Adam, 5, 52, 63, 102, 103, 157, 189, 192, 194, 204, 229, 230
Advocate, 27, 66, 98
Afflicted, 28, 128, 154, 176-179
Affliction, 19, 28, 84, 85, 128, 200, 260, 267
Alexandrian manuscripts, 236
Alien, an, 27, 136
Alive for Evermore, 27
All, and in All, the, 27
Alpha and Omega, 27, 29, 59, 168, 251
Altar, an, 27, 54, 78, 110, 111
Altogether lovely, 27, 150
Ambassador, 179, 286
Amen, the, 28, 29, 38
Amos, 96, 102, 157, 189, 192, 194, 199, 204
Ancestor, 96, 117
Ancient of days, 195, 196
Angel of God, the, 28
Angel of His Presence, the, 28
Angel of the Lord, the, 20, 28, 34, 70, 82, 95, 153, 191, 202
Angels, 15, 18, 24, 25, 38, 41, 42, 59, 73, 102, 118, 119, 123, 124, 133, 143, 154, 180, 181, 190, 202, 212, 230, 249, 262, 265
Angels testimony, 88
Anointed, the, 28, 38, 47, 48, 69, 71, 106, 117, 122, 129, 134, 141, 149, 157, 158, 184, 188, 203
Another king, 28
Anybody, 194, 197, 224
Apostle of our Profession, the, 28
Appeal, my, 225
Appearances, 116
Ark of the Covenant, the, 28
Arm of the Lord, the, 28, 65, 174
Armour, 76, 286
Arnold, Dan, 224, 266
Ascension, bodily, 119
Asher, 84, 85
Ass, an, 123, 200, 206, 207
Atonement, 109, 111, 173
Authority, 103, 120, 140, 179, 228, 229, 236
Authorized Version, 234, 236, 238
Author of Eternal Salvation, the, 28
Author of our Faith, the, 28, 121
Average person, 191

B

Babes, 123
Backsliders, 222
Balm of Gilead, the, 29
Banner to Them that Fear Thee, a, 29
Baptism, 33, 90, 197, 246
Baptized, 33, 82, 134, 157, 188, 197, 246
Barabbas, 99, 171, 173, 178, 181, 209
Bearer of Glory, the, 29
Bearer of Sin, the, 29
Bearing, 28, 43, 84, 100, 144, 264
Beaten, 171, 201
Beatitudes, 176
Before All Things, 29
Beginning, 27-29, 38, 39, 41, 45, 46, 55, 59, 62, 80, 87, 89, 90, 95, 97, 106, 112, 115, 142, 143, 145, 154, 168, 223, 227, 241, 247, 259
Beginning of the Creation of God, the, 28, 29, 38
Beginning and Ending, the, 29
Begotten Son, the only, 48, 59, 100, 113, 190, 247, 256
Believed, 15, 28, 42, 65, 87, 88, 88, 100, 111-113, 115, 120, 152, 154, 174, 188, 190, 249, 258
Believing, 22, 49, 64, 90, 123, 127, 217-219, 229, 236, 243
Beloved, the, 20, 27, 29, 31, 32, 33, 82, 84, 85, 94, 105, 123, 126, 150, 159, 165-167, 172, 188, 197
Beloved Son, my, 20, 29, 82, 105, 123, 172, 188, 197
Benjamin, 84, 85, 239
Bethlehem, 68, 92, 123, 139, 149, 190, 191, 201, 202, 205
Berea, believers, 234
Be strong, 163, 286
Betrayed, 48, 133-135, 137, 180, 181, 210, 210
Betrayer, 50, 135
Bible, 12, 17, 88, 91, 103, 117, 119, 122, 129, 147, 150, 151, 159, 161, 164, 167, 185, 189, 193, 195, 199-201, 203-206, 213, 218-220, 223, 224, 228, 233, 235, 236-239, 241, 243-246, 249, 252, 255, 257-259, 264, 269, 270
Bishop of Your Souls, the, 29
Blemish, without, 105
Blessed, 21, 29, 30, 34, 37, 40, 42, 43, 51, 55, 60, 62, 69, 73, 84, 96, 97, 101, 102, 105, 119, 122-124, 130, 132, 134-137, 140, 148, 163, 172, 176, 192, 197, 204-206, 208, 211, 236
Blessed and Only Potentate, the, 29, 55, 60
Blessed for Evermore, the, 30
Blessed Hope, the, 30, 43, 69, 211, 236
Blinded, 53, 151, 152
Blind eyes, 167
Blood Covenant, 83
Blood of the Lamb, 106

Blood, 38, 39, 43, 48, 50, 55, 57, 62, 80, 83, 95, 97, 105, 106, 107, 110-112, 126, 128, 131, 135, 142, 159, 173, 177, 181, 184, 192, 200, 205, 210, 227, 237, 242, 249, 256, 286
Boast, 225
Boldly, 45, 286
Book of Life, 52, 228, 232, 239, 243
Booth, Catherine, 10, 33, 109
Bone(s), 92, 107, 112, 113, 126, 127, 131, 144, 210
Bonaparte, Napoleon, 87
Bondage, 188, 268
Bonhoeffer, Dietrich, 114
Born, 18, 20, 21, 29, 32-34, 36, 39, 45-48, 51, 58, 62, 72, 80, 82, 84, 92, 95, 105, 113, 122, 123, 125, 128, 134, 139, 141, 147, 149, 152, 154-156, 160, 167, 184, 186, 188, 191, 196, 202, 206-208, 210, 223, 227, 228, 232, 247, 258
Bow, 22, 48, 56, 74, 104, 168, 170, 207, 232, 244, 246
Bradley, General Omar, 157
Branch, the, 17, 30, 31, 39, 40, 56, 66, 67, 71, 78, 157, 160, 189, 190, 192, 197, 205, 206
Branch of the Lord, the, 30, 40
Branch of Righteousness, the, 30, 192
Bread of God, the, 30
Bread of Life, the, 15, 18, 30
Breastplate of righteousness, 286
Bridegroom, the, 30, 261
Bright and Morning Star, the, 30, 59, 68, 118
Bright, Dr. Bill, 179
Brightness of His Glory, the, 30, 37, 78
Brightness of thy Rising, the, 30
Broken, 60, 62, 92, 104, 107, 112, 117, 126, 131, 134, 137, 149, 157, 158, 161, 172, 188, 195, 209, 210, 242, 256
Brother, 31, 40, 73, 136, 138, 205, 244
Bruised, 134, 149, 157-159, 165, 166, 176-178, 188
Buckler, a, 31, 40, 46
Burckhalter, Charles, 185
Buffeted, 171, 173, 180
Builder of the Temple, the, 31
Bundle of Myrrh, a, 31

C

Cahill, Mark, 17, 220
Canaan, a woman of, 218
Captain of the Host of the Lord, the, 31
Captain of Their Salvation, the, 31
Captives, 134, 149, 157, 158, 188
Captivity, 80, 135, 136, 171
Carpenter, the, 31, 73, 221
Carpenter's Son, the, 31
Centurion, 24, 66
Certain Nobleman, a, 31
Certain Samaritan, a, 31
Chambers, Oswald, 28, 98
Chapel of the Air, 256
Characteristics of a false convert, 258
Chastisement, 176-178
Chesterton, G.K., 144
Chief Cornerstone, the, 32
Chief Shepherd, the, 32

Chiefest among Ten Thousand, the, 32
Child, 21, 32, 34, 36, 37, 42, 47, 56, 58, 62, 72, 80-82, 92, 95, 106, 108, 109, 113, 122, 139, 152-156, 168, 170, 191, 199, 202, 204, 217, 219, 246
Child Born, a, 32
Children, 27, 37, 43, 43-45, 47, 56, 57, 66, 69, 70, 74, 82, 95, 96, 98, 101, 103, 105, 106, 110, 113, 117, 121, 123, 128, 134-136, 138, 140, 148, 155, 158, 163, 176, 179, 181, 184, 187, 191, 208-210, 214, 218, 244, 250, 262
Child of the Holy Ghost, a, 32, 95, 153, 168, 191
Child Jesus, the, 21, 32, 204
Chosen of God, the, 32, 127
Chosen out of the People, 32, 58
Christ a King, 19, 33
Christ Come in the Flesh, 33
Christ Crucified, 33, 76, 162
Christian(s), 2, 114, 132, 164, 167, 180, 219, 235, 236, 243, 256, 261, 264-266, 269
Christ Jesus, 22, 28, 33, 56, 57, 64, 66, 92, 162, 172, 196, 251
Christ Jesus our Lord, 265
Christ Jesus the Lord, 33
Christ of God, the, 22, 33
Christ the Lord, 21, 33
Christ the Son of God, 25
Christ our Passover, 33, 60, 106
Christ Risen from the Dead, 33, 39, 147
Christ's earthly ministry, 149, 248
Chronicles, 117, 119
Church views, 194
City of David, 21, 33
Clark, Arthur C., 177, 241
Cleft of the Rock, a, 33
Cluster of Camphire, a, 33
Cole, Dr. Edwin, 168
Comforter, the, 33, 137, 145, 150, 167
Comfort, Ray, 3, 49, 71, 104, 121, 133, 138, 146, 161, 164, 190, 192, 223
Commander to the People, a, 34, 52, 80, 186
Commandments, 53, 83, 101, 114, 129, 136, 141, 143, 160-162, 201, 203, 243-257, 263-265, 270
Commit thy works, 217
Common Sense, 111, 113
Compassion, 31, 120, 141, 146, 165, 208, 232
Conceive(d), 20, 34, 48, 84, 95, 109, 152, 153, 154, 168, 191, 196
Conceived of the Holy Ghost, 34
Concerned Group, 4, 217, 225
Confessing our sins, 172
Confidence, 73, 115, 134, 179, 219
Conformed, 39, 82, 105, 219
Confounded, 32, 104, 133, 162
Confusion, 121, 238
Consolation of Israel, the, 21, 34
Contradiction(s), 132, 235, 238-240
Coolidge, Calvin, 159
Corrupt, 187, 243, 250, 252
Corrupted Copies, 236
Corruption, 47, 76, 124, 186, 231, 233, 236, 245
Corner, the, 45, 55, 57, 61, 70, 74, 75, 104, 113, 148, 162, 207

273

Corn of Wheat, the, 34, 140
Counselor, 34, 36, 155, 170
Counterfeit, 91, 147, 219, 224, 235, 238, 243, 269
Covenant, new, 57, 192, 213
Covenant of the People, the, 34, 166
Covert from the Tempest, the, 34, 46, 66, 71, 163
Covert of Thy Wings, the, 34
Creator, the, 34, 38, 44, 104
Creator of the Ends of the Earth, the, 34
Creature, 34, 39, 48, 51, 75, 92, 128, 234, 265
Crown of Glory, a, 32, 35, 36
Crown of thorns, 56, 99, 100, 173, 178, 181
Crucified, 33, 55, 76, 88, 99, 100, 107, 110, 112, 122, 124-127, 131, 144, 147, 162, 171-174, 177, 178, 181-183, 197, 211
Crucifixion, 91, 92, 99, 126, 137
Crying, 25, 117, 121, 148, 155, 164
Cured, 163
Cursed, 116, 177

D

Dan, 84, 85, 224, 237, 266
Daniel, 51, 58, 62, 74, 103, 114, 195-198, 204
Dark Ages, 221
Darkness, 15, 35, 40, 43, 47, 53, 76, 92, 99, 105, 108, 125, 146, 154, 161, 163, 167, 170, 177, 199, 227, 232, 237, 263, 270
Darling, my, 35, 127, 128
Day, Dorothy, 18
Day, the, 35, 40, 64, 74, 75, 84, 90, 91, 115, 132, 144, 149, 188, 193, 203, 229, 230, 250, 261
Daysman, the, 35
Day Spring from on High, the, 35
Daystar to Arise, the, 35
Deaf, 73, 132, 151, 152, 163, 188
Dear Son, His, 35, 237
Death, 19, 21, 22, 27, 42-44, 55, 57, 77, 78, 82, 95, 100, 108, 110, 113, 114, 118, 120, 123, 126-131, 135, 137, 145, 147, 154, 160, 161, 165, 172-174, 180, 181, 183, 185, 186, 188, 196, 199, 201, 211, 212, 224, 226, 237, 258, 259, 265
Deceit(ful), 77, 115, 132, 145, 172, 183, 234, 260
Deceiver, that, 35
Decision(s), 133, 164, 224, 256, 264, 266
Defense, my, 35
Delight, 36, 58, 71, 125, 132, 166, 213
Deliverance, 46, 134, 149, 157, 158, 188, 199
Delivered, 18, 19, 25, 35, 56, 72, 99, 106, 108, 124, 137, 144, 147, 171, 173, 178, 181, 188, 199, 202, 237, 263
Deliverer, my, 35, 40, 46
Deny himself, 159, 184
Descendant of David, 189, 192, 194
Desire of all Nations, the, 35, 41, 204
Despised, 35, 56, 65, 80, 128, 162, 170, 174, 175, 209
Despised of the People, 35, 65, 80
Destitute of the truth, 250
Destruction, 45, 198
Deuteronomy, 36, 66, 67, 83, 84, 91, 114-116, 151, 243, 245, 250

Devil(s), 16, 24, 25, 27, 69, 83, 95, 105, 128, 129, 141, 147, 149, 151, 170, 175, 176, 181, 203, 218, 224, 225, 228, 230, 231, 235, 246, 249, 252, 256, 257, 262, 270, 286
Diadem of Beauty, a, 35, 36
Die, you will surely, 229
Diminish, 243, 245
Disciples, 21-23, 66, 81, 83, 88-90, 97, 112, 116, 121, 132, 133, 136, 137, 141, 145, 151, 156, 158, 167, 169, 175, 176, 180, 182, 188, 189, 192, 206-209, 212, 218, 220, 244
Discipline, 259
Discouraged, 164, 166, 200, 220, 222
Disobedience, 184
Disputings of men, 250
Doctrine, 19, 130, 135, 162, 163, 180, 182, 260, 267
Dominion, 124, 128, 139, 172, 195, 196, 207, 233, 251
Door of the Sheep, the, 16, 36
Doubt, 58, 88, 91, 111, 228, 229, 231, 235, 238, 246, 252
Doud, Guy Rice, 131
Dove, 20, 109, 134, 137, 148, 157, 188, 197, 213
Drout, Tom, 48
Dwelling Place, 36

E

Ear(s), 19, 46, 48, 63, 71, 76, 89, 132, 133, 140, 144, 151, 152, 160, 163, 170, 171, 180, 186, 212, 241, 251, 260, 262, 267
Edwards, Jonathan, 222
Egypt, 82, 83, 101, 106, 112, 113, 115, 199
Einstein, Albert, 125, 169
Eisenhower, Dwight, 88
Elect, mine, 36, 71, 166
Elijah, 36, 119, 151, 214, 221
Eliot, T.S., 64
Emerson, Ralph Waldo, 44
Emmanuel, 36, 42, 141, 152, 153
Empty Tomb, 88
Encircled, 126
End of the Law, the, 36
End of the World, 153, 166, 198, 262
Enemy's Response, 89
Ensign of the People, the, 36, 68, 159, 160
Epp, Theodore, 150
Equal with God, 22, 36, 172
Erasmus, Deriderius, 180, 221
Established Forever, 118
Eternal God, the, 36
Eternal life, 16, 22, 36, 43, 86, 113, 129, 141, 143, 183, 189, 203, 255, 257
Evangelistic Survey, 201
Evans, Lewis H., 23
Eve, 228, 229
Everlasting, 68, 143, 189, 190, 196, 201, 202
Everlasting Arms, 36
Everlasting Covenant, 43, 76, 98, 186
Everlasting Dominion, 195, 196
Everlasting Doors, 51
Everlasting Father, the, 32, 34, 36, 58, 62, 72, 80, 154-156

274

Everlasting Hills, 70
Everlasting Kingdom, 54, 156
Everlasting life, 15, 59, 79, 100, 113, 120, 158, 187, 188, 190, 201, 256
Everlasting light, an, 37
Everlasting name, an, 37
Everlasting Righteousness, 196, 197
Everybody, 194
Evidence, 87, 88, 91, 104, 132, 138, 233, 234
Evil, 27, 99, 110, 115, 118, 120, 129, 133, 163, 174, 176, 178, 181, 187, 196, 229, 245, 247, 259, 265
Evil day, 286
Exalted, 22, 32, 42, 58, 59, 62, 113, 129, 140, 143, 164, 172, 185, 195, 232, 244
Examine yourself, 259
Exceeding Great Reward, thy, 37
Excellency, His, 37, 77
Excellency of Our God, the, 37
Excellent, 30, 37, 40, 57, 59
Exhort, 19, 115, 236, 267
Exodus, 33, 57, 82, 83, 105-108
Expose false converts, 259
Express Image of His Person, the, 30, 37, 78
Ezekial, 48, 61, 151, 193, 194

F

Fables, 19, 267
Face of the Lord, the, 37, 108
Fairer than the Children of Men, 37, 134
Faith, 4, 17, 28, 38, 48, 55, 63, 95, 104, 116, 121, 125, 135, 145, 159, 161, 164, 169, 170, 173, 177, 179, 184, 192, 209, 212, 216, 217-225, 229, 234, 235, 237, 241, 252, 255, 257-259, 262, 264-266, 269, 272, 286
Faithful, 28, 29, 37, 38, 51, 71, 159, 166, 170
Faithful and True, 28, 29, 38, 54, 189
Faithful and True Witness, the, 38
Faithful Creator, a, 38
Faithful Follower, 211
Faithful High Priest, a, 38, 57
Faithful Priest, a, 28, 38
Faithful Servant, 114, 263
Faithful Witness, the, 38, 39, 62, 142, 159, 173
Faithful Witness Between Us, a, 38
Faithful Witness in Heaven, a, 38, 142
Faith, genuine, 220, 222-224
Faith, great is thy, 218
Faith, measure of, 220, 225
Faith, pseudo, 219
Fakes, 235, 238
False Converts, 54, 257-259
False Faith, 219
False Witnesses, 131, 145, 180
Familiar, 133, 175
Fear of the Lord, 63, 140, 157, 158, 160, 233
Feet, 16, 71, 74, 92, 101, 103, 104, 108, 124, 126, 127, 132, 168, 170, 171, 172, 195, 198, 242, 250
Feet, under His, 124, 172, 195
Fellow, my, 38, 211, 212
Fiery darts, 286
Filthiness, their, 256
Finally, 286

Find, 14, 16, 35, 49, 56, 57, 72, 81, 92, 93, 98, 108, 117, 123, 137, 169-171, 183, 202, 206, 207, 212, 219-224, 235, 255, 264, 266
Finding God's Will for your life, 264
Finished, It is, 128, 138, 144
Finisher of our Faith, the, 28, 38, 212, 216
Fire, 40, 55, 64, 79, 100, 110, 111, 115, 119, 156, 182, 198, 221, 238, 241, 259, 262
First, 29, 33, 38, 39, 45, 48, 51, 52, 54, 55, 57, 59, 62, 63, 82, 88, 90, 92, 96-98, 105, 107, 112, 131, 135, 138, 141, 142, 147, 154, 159, 161, 168, 169, 173, 182, 202, 207, 209, 211, 223, 224, 228, 229, 231, 233, 241, 248-252, 258, 262, 263, 266, 269, 270
First and the last, 59, 168, 251
First Begotten, the, 38, 39, 62
First Begotten of the Dead, the, 38, 39, 142, 159, 173
Firstborn, the, 29, 39, 45, 48, 62, 82, 141, 210
Firstborn among Many Brethren, the, 39, 82, 105
Firstborn from the Dead, the, 29, 39, 45, 62
Firstborn of Every Creature, the, 39, 48
Firstborn Son, her, 39, 125, 154, 174
First Fruit, the, 33, 39, 14
First fruits of Them That Slept, the, 33, 39, 147
Fishless Fishermen, 108
Flavel, John, 154
Fled, 75, 130, 133, 175, 180, 212, 232
Flesh, 15, 18, 33, 39, 41, 42, 49, 54, 60, 68, 70, 78, 95, 101, 107, 110, 111, 120, 124, 128, 137, 150, 154, 162, 183, 190, 196, 209, 212, 227, 248, 249, 251, 259, 286
Flock, 71, 165, 202, 208-210, 212
Follow up, 121
Fool, 16, 145, 183, 187, 219
Foolish, 162, 240, 261
Foolishness, 33, 76, 79, 162, 240
Footnotes, 243
Foreordained before the Foundation of the World, 39
Forever, 42, 46, 49, 50, 62, 69, 118, 120, 129, 142, 230-232
Forerunner, the, 39, 46, 97, 146, 214
Forsaken, 40, 125, 126, 177
Forsook, 67, 130, 133, 175, 180, 212
Fortress, 40, 46
Foundation, 32, 39, 40, 52, 62, 76, 77, 79, 91, 137, 142, 156, 196, 222
Foundation which is Laid, the, 40
Fountain of Life, the, 40
Fountain of Living Waters, the, 40
Free, 12, 27, 73, 184, 188, 196, 256, 264, 268, 269
Friend of Publicans and Sinners, the, 40, 56
Friend that Sticketh Closer than a Brother, a, 40
Fruit, 17, 20, 30, 33, 34, 39, 40, 57, 78, 140, 147, 148, 192, 226, 229, 248, 260, 262, 264
Fruit of the Earth, the, 30, 40
Fruit of Righteousness, 264
Fruit of the Spirit, 264
Fruit of Thy Womb, the, 40
Fullers' Soap, 40, 64
Function of the Law, 81, 95

275

G

Gad, 84, 85
Galilee, 49, 63, 88, 89, 111, 112, 114, 124, 129, 131, 136, 141, 143, 147, 154, 159, 171, 175, 195, 197, 202, 206, 212, 213
Garden, the, 229, 230, 269
Garments, my, 110, 127, 182, 197, 211
Gather the people, 104
Generation, a, 36, 41, 44, 46, 72, 98, 107, 112, 115, 117, 140, 143, 147, 160, 174, 180, 182, 194, 230, 235, 240, 256
Genesis, 28, 37, 50, 57, 70, 71, 74, 82, 84, 95-104, 151, 228, 229
Gentiles, 15, 19, 21, 30, 34, 36, 42, 47, 53, 58, 68, 71, 106, 122, 152, 154, 159, 160, 165-167, 169, 173, 190, 200, 204, 249
Gentle, 57, 63, 256, 270
Genuine Conversion, 255, 265
German Proverb, 92
Gift, free, 184, 256, 269
Gift of God, the, 40, 158, 225, 269
Gifts to men, 135, 171
Gin (A trap for Birds), 41, 69, 72, 153
Gladness, 134, 184, 258, 260
Glorified state, 198
Glorious High Throne from the Beginning, a, 41
Glorious name, a, 41, 140
Glory, 15, 17, 18, 21, 22, 24, 25, 29-33, 35-37, 39, 41, 42, 47, 50-53, 55, 60, 65, 78-80, 103, 112, 121, 123, 124, 140, 142, 149, 151, 154, 162, 166, 169, 183, 189, 190, 195, 196, 198, 202, 204, 205, 207, 217, 219, 223, 227, 230, 233, 247-249, 251
Glory as of the Only Begotten of the Father, the, 39, 41, 60, 154, 227
Glory of God, the, 22, 41, 53, 198, 223
Glory of His Father, the, 41
God Blessed Forever, 42
God For Ever and Ever, our, 42, 44
God in the midst of her, 42
God manifest in the Flesh, 42
God, my, 23, 35, 40, 46, 54, 67, 78, 115, 125, 126, 128, 130, 132, 168, 177, 208, 231, 252
God of Glory, the, 42
God of My Life, the, 42
God of My Righteousness, 42
God of My Salvation, 42
God of My Strength, 42
God the Father, 20, 22, 73, 196
God Who Avengeth Me, 41
God Who Forgavest Them, 42
God with Us, 36, 42, 15, 153
God, your, 28, 111, 128, 153, 163, 164, 165, 243, 245
Gold, 63, 74, 79, 81, 139, 140, 151, 170, 198, 204, 233, 258
Gomorrah, 250
Good and bad fish, 262
Good Fruits, 57
Good Man, a, 43
Good Master, 43, 129, 141, 143, 203
Good Shepherd, the, 16, 43, 129, 165, 254
Good works, 175, 236, 259, 264

Gospel, the, 51, 79, 92, 97, 99, 107, 128, 134, 149, 154, 157, 158, 161, 163, 164, 169, 188, 200, 208, 217, 224, 240, 249, 250, 256, 258, 264, 266, 270, 286
Gospel of peace, the, 286
Government, 32, 34, 36, 58, 62, 72, 80, 136, 154, 155, 156, 159
Governor, 43, 89, 128, 132, 139, 149, 173, 174, 178, 181, 190, 202, 205
Governor among Nations, the, 43, 128
Grace, 29, 37, 39, 41, 60, 61, 67, 73, 79, 81, 90, 123, 134, 135, 150, 154, 169, 171, 172, 181, 188, 196, 210, 214, 220, 221, 225, 227, 233, 236, 242, 252, 265
Grave, 120, 124, 129, 150, 161, 183
Graven, 90, 120, 122, 128, 143, 156, 178
Great God, the, 30, 43, 69, 74, 225, 236
Great High Priest, a, 43
Great Light, a, 43, 154
Great prophet, a, 43
Great Shepherd of the Sheep, that, 43
Greater, a, 44, 258
Greater and More Perfect Tabernacle, a, 44
Greater Than Our Father Abraham, 44
Greater Than Our Father Jacob, 44, 158
Greater Than Jonas, 44
Greater Than Solomon, 44
Greater Than the Temple, 44
Greek Texts, 236, 243
Grief, 56, 138, 174-178, 183
Guest, 44
Guide Even Unto Death, our, 42, 44
Guiltless, the, 44
Guinness, Os, 110

H

Habitation of Justice, the, 44, 48
Haggai, 35, 41, 204
Hanged, on a tree, 89, 116
Harmless, 45, 70, 77, 262
Harvest, 55, 66, 250
Hated, 82, 84, 134, 136, 170, 184, 200
He Goat, an, 18, 45, 105, 110
Head, 29, 39, 41, 45, 52, 55, 57, 61, 62, 69, 70, 74, 75, 88, 95, 99, 100, 104, 106, 118, 120, 122, 125, 128, 129, 135, 136, 138, 144, 148, 162, 171-173, 178, 181, 195, 198, 201, 270
Head of all Principality and Power, the, 45
Head of Every Man, the, 45
Head of the Body, the Church, the, 29, 39, 45, 62
Head of the Corner, the, 45, 55, 57, 61, 74, 75, 104, 148, 162
Healed, 92, 130, 148, 151, 152, 176, 177, 178, 203, 219
Healing, 76, 129, 141, 149, 163, 176, 203, 208
Hearing, 63, 152, 160, 193, 251, 255, 260
Heart, 28, 30, 35, 38, 41, 43, 46, 47, 53, 55-57, 59, 62, 67, 81, 90-93, 97, 99, 101, 114, 115, 123, 124, 126, 128, 132-134, 137, 138, 140, 144, 145, 149, 151, 152, 154, 157, 158, 161-164, 169, 170, 172, 176, 187, 188, 190, 200, 202, 207, 210, 214, 219, 227, 232-234, 244, 248, 251, 255, 258, 260, 263-266, 269, 270

276

Heaven, 17-20, 22, 28-31, 37-39, 43, 45, 47, 48, 51, 54, 55, 58, 70, 72, 73, 76-79, 82, 97, 98, 101, 102, 104, 105, 117, 119, 123, 124, 128, 129, 133-137, 139, 142, 143, 145-147, 153, 154, 156, 157, 161, 162, 164, 166, 167, 170, 172, 173, 176, 177, 183, 185, 187-189, 195-198, 201, 202, 204, 205, 207-209, 211, 214, 231-233, 237, 241, 242, 245, 246, 252, 257, 261-263

Heir, 45, 73

Heir of All Things, 45

Hell, 16, 27, 47, 66, 98, 124, 130, 135, 141, 161, 179, 201

Helmet of Salvation, 249, 286

Helper, my, 45

Helper of the Fatherless, the, 45

Hen, a, 45, 163

Henry, Matthew, 181, 258

Hidden Manna, the, 46

Hiding Place, 34, 46, 66, 71, 163

Hiding Place from the Wind, a, 34, 46, 66, 71

High and Lofty One Who Inhabiteth Eternity, the, 46, 47

High Priest, an, 19, 28, 30, 38, 39, 43-46, 57, 58, 69-71, 73, 77, 97, 103, 110, 133, 146, 180, 182, 200, 205, 212

High Priest after the Order of Melchisedec, an, 39, 46, 62, 97, 146

High Tower, my, 40, 46

Highest Himself, the, 46

Holy, 18, 20, 21, 24, 25, 29, 31, 32, 34, 39, 41, 45-48, 54, 55, 58, 65, 70, 71, 77, 88-92, 97, 106, 108-111, 115, 122, 124, 129, 134, 135, 141, 149, 150, 152, 153, 156, 161, 166, 168-170, 172, 180, 191, 196, 197, 200, 203, 207, 228, 230, 231-133, 235, 238, 239, 242-244, 258, 264-266, 269

Holy Bible, 12, 228, 235, 238

Holy Child, thy, 47, 106, 122

Holy Ghost, 20, 21, 32, 34, 47, 89, 90, 95, 115, 129, 135, 141, 149, 150, 152, 153, 156, 166, 168. 169, 191, 196, 200, 203, 207, 233, 242

Holy men, 90, 233

Holy One, Thine, 47, 124

Holy One and just, the, 47

Holy One of God, the, 25

Holy One of Israel, the, 47, 71, 168, 170, 231

Holy Thing which shall be born of Thee, 21, 47, 95, 152, 196

Holy to the Lord, 47

Honey, 140, 233

Hope, our, 47, 234

Hope of Glory, the, 47

Hope of His People, the, 47

Hope of Israel, the, 40, 47

Hope of Their Fathers, the, 44, 48

Horn of David, the, 48

Horn of the House of Israel, the, 48

Horn of Salvation, an, 48

Horns, 100, 110, 127, 128

Hort, 236

Hosea, 82, 199

House, 20, 28, 35, 38, 41, 48, 59, 61, 63, 73, 74, 81, 106, 107, 114, 117, 118, 122, 129, 134, 137, 139, 141, 142, 144, 148, 156, 160, 167, 170, 176, 192, 193, 196, 202-204, 206, 210, 218, 220, 237, 241, 261

House built on rock and sand, 261

House of Defense, an, 48

Householder, an, 48, 262

Humility, 101, 227

Husband, her, 48, 98, 153, 191, 229

Huss, 221

Howe, Edgar Watson, 261

Hovind, Kent, 24, 162

Hypocrisy, 57

Hypocrites, 162, 209, 242

I

Incorruption, 78, 160

Image of the Invisible God, the, 39, 48

Immanuel, 48, 152, 153

Infirmities, 163, 176

Iniquity, 43, 54, 66, 117, 130, 134, 135, 141, 160, 164, 178, 184, 196, 197, 236, 157, 262

Innocent Blood, 48, 135, 181, 210

Instructing, 63, 121, 256, 270

Integrity of God's Word, 228, 229, 231, 235

Intercessor, 187

Interpretation, private, 90, 223

Isaac, 48, 96, 98-103, 157, 160, 189, 192, 194, 204

Isaiah, 28, 30, 32, 34-37, 40, 41, 43, 46-48, 50, 52, 53, 56, 58-63, 65-69, 71-77, 79-81, 83, 90, 147, 151, 152-188, 231, 233, 234, 246

Is Jesus your Lord, 255

Israel, 21, 23, 30, 34, 40, 41, 47, 48, 51-53, 56, 57, 61, 62, 67-75, 82, 83, 85, 90, 104-107, 110, 113, 117, 122, 125, 126, 128, 133, 139, 148, 149, 151, 153, 166, 168, 169, 170, 171, 177, 181, 189, 190, 192, 193, 197, 199-202, 204, 205, 208, 210, 214, 218, 223, 231, 237, 239

Issachar, 84, 85

Itching Ears, 19, 267

It's Who You Know, 4, 217, 225

J

Jacob, 20, 32, 44, 53, 58, 61, 70, 74, 82-84, 96, 98, 101-104, 113, 118, 128, 139, 141, 142, 156-158, 160, 168, 169, 187, 189, 192, 194, 196, 204

Jasper Stone, the, 49

Jeremiah, 29, 30, 38, 40, 41, 43, 44, 48, 49, 61, 65, 66, 68, 93, 119, 189, 190-192

Jerome, 221

Jesse, 36, 67, 68, 96, 102, 103, 157, 159, 160, 189, 192, 194, 204

Jesus Christ, 19, 22, 27, 29, 30, 32, 33, 38-40, 43, 47, 49, 53-55, 58, 61, 62, 66, 69, 70, 72, 73, 78, 87, 88, 91, 92, 95, 98, 103, 104, 110, 117, 122, 124, 142, 150, 153, 154, 159-161, 164, 168, 169, 173, 179, 183, 189, 191, 194, 196-198, 207, 217, 222, 227, 232, 236, 242, 246, 247, 251, 252, 259, 264, 267, 269, 270

Jesus of Galilee, 49

Jesus of Nazareth, the King of the Jews, 25, 49, 56, 63, 72, 102, 129, 133, 141, 144, 149, 203

Jews, 18, 19, 33, 44, 49, 51, 61, 69, 76, 79, 89, 97, 99, 100, 107, 111-113, 120, 122, 131, 136, 137, 139, 144, 149, 152, 158, 162, 164, 165, 170, 173, 175, 178, 181-183, 188, 200, 202, 207, 218, 242, 247
Job, 35, 37, 64, 79, 120, 121, 138, 185, 194, 259
Joel, 47, 199
John, an apostle, 22
John the Baptist, 21, 36, 49, 63, 97, 164, 214, 221
Jonah, 151, 200, 228
Joseph, 20, 32, 34, 49, 70-72, 82, 84, 85, 95, 96, 102, 103, 117, 121, 123, 134, 148, 153, 155, 157, 158, 160, 168, 189, 191, 192, 194, 202, 204, 246
Joseph's Son, 49, 121, 134, 148, 155
Joy, 17, 21, 28, 30, 37, 38, 67, 79, 95, 121, 124, 127, 131, 132, 139, 202, 251, 258, 263, 264
Judah, 31, 68, 71, 84, 85, 103, 104, 151, 153, 165, 189, 189, 190, 192, 201-203, 205, 213, 237
Judas, 31, 98, 133, 135, 160, 180, 181, 210, 212
Judge, 19, 38, 39, 50, 55, 57, 63, 66, 98, 117, 156, 159, 160, 168, 189, 190, 201, 206, 232, 234, 267
Judge of All the Earth, the, 50
Judge of the Quick and the Dead, the, 19, 50
Judgement, 44, 140, 232
Just One, the, 50
Just Person, this, 50, 181

K

Keeper, thy, 50
Kennedy, Dr. D. James, 95, 132, 175
Kill, 16, 45, 106, 110, 111, 136, 165, 175, 269
Killed, 62, 89, 91, 182, 197, 198, 200, 244
Kindness, 42 43, 50, 73-75, 133, 232
Kindness and Love of God, the, 50
King, a, 18, 19, 31, 33, 45, 66 97, 149, 186, 189, 190, 195, 196, 205, 206, 239
King David, 92, 117
Kingdom, 18-20, 24, 25, 31, 35, 43, 48, 54, 55, 70, 90, 92, 113, 117-119, 128, 133, 134, 139, 141, 142, 148, 151, 152, 154, 156, 161, 164, 164, 176, 184, 192, 193, 195, 196, 199, 208, 209, 213, 214, 230, 233, 244, 245, 247, 248, 251, 257, 260-263, 267
King Eternal, the, 50, 60
Kingdom of God, 90, 92, 148, 151, 152, 161, 193, 213, 244, 248, 260
King Forever and Ever, the, 50
King Immortal, the, 50
King in His Beauty, the, 50
King Invisible, the, 50
King James Bible, 4, 147, 228, 236, 237, 239, 243, 244, 252, 269
King Jr., Martin Luther, 76
King of All the Earth, the, 50
King of Glory, the, 51
King of Heaven, the, 51
King of Israel, the, 23, 51, 52, 72, 125, 126, 177, 197
King of Kings, 29, 51, 55, 60, 113, 122
King of Peace, the, 51, 97
King of Righteousness, the, 51, 97
King of Saints, 51
King of Salem, the, 51, 57, 62, 97

King of the Jews, 19, 49, 51, 99, 100, 113, 122, 139, 144, 149, 173, 178, 181, 202
Kings, 28-30, 38, 39, 51, 55, 58, 60, 62, 71, 97, 113, 119, 122, 139, 141, 142, 149, 151, 170, 173, 193, 251
King Who Cometh in the Name of the Lord, the, 51
Kinsman, the, 51
Knee should bow, 22, 232
Knees, 99, 173, 201, 202, 225, 246
Knowledge, 53, 66, 80, 81, 92, 97, 108, 121, 135, 148, 157, 158, 160, 164, 171, 184, 185, 198, 229, 233, 244, 248, 256, 265, 270

L

Lamb, 21, 51, 52, 53, 80, 100, 105-107, 109, 165, 178, 179
Lamb of God, the, 21. 52. 100, 165, 178
Lamb Slain from the Foundation of the World, 52
Lamb that was slain, the, 52, 80
Lamb Who Is in the Midst of the Throne, the, 52
Last, the, 15, 23, 52, 55, 59, 63, 97, 111, 119, 131, 145, 168, 180, 187, 221, 232, 241, 250, 251, 269
Last Adam, the, 52, 63
Last days, 45, 150, 232
Last Supper, 97
Last Word, the, 269
Laurie, Greg, 129
Law, 21, 28, 32, 36, 43, 47, 49, 56, 67, 72, 73, 81, 83, 87, 88, 95, 97, 103, 107, 109, 113, 116, 120, 131, 132, 136, 140, 147, 150, 152, 161, 164, 166, 170, 182, 196, 204, 209, 222, 225, 233, 241, 246, 248, 250, 251, 263, 265
Lawgiver, 52, 71, 103, 104
Leader(s), 34, 52, 80, 92, 186, 208
Lectionaries, 237
Legalism, 259
Leper, 109, 163, 188
Levi, 63, 84, 85, 96, 102, 103, 157, 189, 192, 194, 204
Leviticus, 62, 69, 79, 109-111
Lewis, C.S., 16, 60, 130
Liar, 11, 161, 205, 229, 238, 243, 252, 257
Liberty, 134, 149, 157, 158, 188, 268
Liederbach, Mark, 34
Life, the, 17, 18, 23, 26, 36, 52, 54, 65, 77, 79, 105, 111, 143, 153, 159, 227, 247, 258, 264-266, 270
Lifter-Up of Mine Head, the, 52
Light, the, 15, 18, 43, 52, 53, 56, 99, 105, 143, 154, 166, 169, 227, 266, 270
Light of Men, the, 52, 143, 227
Light of the City, the, 53
Light of the Glorious Gospel of Christ, the, 53
Light of the Knowledge of the Glory of God, the, 53
Light of the Morning, the, 53
Light of the World, the, 15, 53
Light to Lighten the Gentiles, a, 21, 53, 166, 169, 204
Light to the Gentiles, a, 53, 169
Lily among Thorns, the, 53
Lily of the Valleys, the, 53, 68
Lincoln, Abraham, 89, 172, 202, 203
Lion of the Tribe of Juda, the, 53, 67
Living Bread, the, 18, 54

Living God, the, 22, 54, 69, 73, 115, 180, 189
Livingstone, David, 41
Loins, 159, 160, 198, 248, 286
Loins, fruit of his, 248
Lord also of the Sabbath, 54
Lord and My God, my, 23, 54
Lord and Saviour, the, 54, 232, 252, 255, 256, 269,
Lord both of the Dead and the Living, 54
Lord from Heaven, the, 54
Lord God Almighty, 51, 54
Lord God of the Holy Prophets, the, 54
Lord God of Truth, 54
Lord God Omnipotent, 54
Lord God Who Judgeth Her, the, 55
Lord, Holy and True, the, 55
Lord Jesus Christ, 19, 30, 47, 55, 61, 73, 78, 92, 122, 124, 159, 164, 169, 179, 196, 217, 222, 242, 246, 251, 264, 267, 269
Lord of Glory, the, 55
Lord of the Harvest, the, 55, 66
Lord of Lords, 29, 51, 55, 60, 113, 122
Lord of Peace, 55
Lord of the Vineyard, the, 55
Lord of the Whole Earth, the, 55
Lord, my, 23, 31, 54, 146, 228, 252
Lord's Christ, the, 21, 55
Lord's Doing, the, 55, 57, 74, 148
Lothed, 209
Love, 15, 16, 18, 35, 48, 50, 53, 56, 59, 60, 66, 68, 73, 74, 76, 84, 87, 94, 106, 117, 135, 138, 142, 145, 161, 165, 170, 178, 184, 190, 204, 205, 219, 225, 226, 244, 251, 257, 259, 263, 264-266, 270
Lovely, 27, 150
Love of God, 50, 225, 257, 265
Lowly in Heart, 56, 57, 81, 123, 170, 207
Lusts, 19, 236, 260, 267
Luther, Martin, 81, 112, 218

M

Macarthur, John, 101
Madison, James, 136, 137
Magnified, 56, 149, 232, 244, 269
Majority Text, 236
Maker, our, 56
Malachi, 40, 58, 63, 64, 76, 213, 214
Malefactor, a, 56, 177, 186
Manasseh, 85
Man, the, 23, 25, 30, 31, 38, 45, 56, 57, 67, 109, 116, 130, 153, 167, 205, 206, 211, 212, 224, 229, 237
Man Approved of God, a, 56
Man Child, a, 56
Man Christ Jesus, the, 56, 57
Man Gluttonous, a, 56
Manifest in the flesh, 15, 42, 154, 190, 249
Mankind, 136, 177, 178, 183, 185, 186, 199, 211, 221, 234, 269
Man Whose Name is the Branch, the, 30, 31, 56, 205
Man of Sorrows, the, 56, 174, 175
Man whom He hath Ordained, the, 57
Manna, 18, 46, 57
Manuscripts, 236, 237, 239, 252

Marcion, 236
Marred, 173
Martha, 23
Marvelous in Our Eyes, 57
Masters, two, 114
Master, your, 57
McDowell, Josh, 46
Measure of Faith, 220, 225
Mediator, the, 57
Mediator of a Better Covenant, the, 57
Mediator of the New Covenant, the, 57
Mediator of the New Testament, the, 57
Meek, 56, 57, 81, 123, 128, 149, 159, 160, 170, 176, 188, 206, 207
Meekness, 63, 256, 264, 270
Melanchthon, 96
Melchizedek, 57, 62, 97, 146
Merciful and Faithful High Priest, a, 38, 57
Mercy, 35, 42, 44, 57, 58, 65, 73, 77, 108, 110, 117, 118, 129, 143, 160, 172, 176, 209, 218, 231, 248
Mercy, full of, 57
Mercy and His Truth, His, 58
Merit Student Encyclopedia, 238
Message, 85, 95, 217, 240, 246, 249, 252, 258
Messenger, 8, 9, 58, 213
Messenger of the Covenant, the, 58
Messiah, 58, 87, 88, 91, 92, 111, 123, 137, 145, 147, 158, 162, 190, 192, 197, 198, 206, 207, 210, 213, 269
Messiah the Prince, 58, 197
Micah, 67, 68, 201, 202
Mighty, 27, 29, 32, 34, 36, 43, 51, 54, 58, 62, 63, 71, 72, 74, 80, 104, 136, 154-156, 162, 172, 231
Mighty God, the, 32, 34, 36, 43, 58, 62, 72, 74, 80, 104, 154, 155, 156, 235
Mighty One of Jacob, the, 58
Minuscule, 237
Ministering, 198, 209
Minister of Sin, the, 58
Minister of the Circumcision, a, 58
Minister of the Sanctuary, the, 58
Ministry, 19, 57, 97, 112, 135, 149, 154, 163, 176, 208, 248, 267
Miracles, 56, 64, 76, 92, 103, 112, 120, 163, 168, 169, 174, 228
Mocked, 19, 99, 100, 126, 173, 178, 181, 191
Mocking, 125, 126, 177
Modern Versions, 236, 239, 240, 241, 243, 244-246, 249
Moody, D.L., 148
More Excellent Name, a, 59
Morning Star, the, 30, 59, 68
Moses, 37, 49, 51, 57, 70, 72, 77, 82, 83, 87, 95, 105-107, 109, 112-115, 120, 122, 150-152, 167, 208, 241
Mother's belly, 125
Mouth, 24, 27, 48, 49, 55, 59, 61, 83, 87, 90, 91, 114, 115, 121-123, 126-128, 130, 132, 134, 135, 137, 138, 140, 144, 145, 148-150, 155, 159-162, 168, 169, 173, 178, 179, 183, 198, 200, 205, 230, 233, 245, 255, 286
Mouth of God, the, 24, 59, 83, 230
Mystery, the, 15, 42, 59, 88, 154, 157, 190, 247, 249, 260, 286
The Mystery of the Gospel, 286

279

N

Nail Fastened in a Sure Place, a, 59
Naked, 175, 230, 234
Name above Every Name, a, 59
Name of the Lord, 51, 75, 91, 108, 148, 197, 199, 206, 255, 256
Naphtali, 84, 154
Nations, 18, 35, 41, 43, 56, 89, 96, 101, 113, 128, 139, 153, 154, 166, 172, 173, 189, 195, 196, 204, 231, 249
Nazarene, a, 59, 157
Nehemiah, 119
New Covenant, 57, 192, 213
New American Standard Version, 239, 241
New International Version, 239, 241, 244
Newton, John, 225
Niebuhr, Reinhold, 72
Nobody, 194, 206, 221
Numbers, 70, 74, 112, 113, 151, 172
Numerous Witnesses, 89

O

Obedience, 80, 162, 171, 179, 184, 258
Obvious, 221, 223, 243, 244, 245
Offering and a Sacrifice to God, an, 59, 68, 76
Offspring of David, the, 30, 59, 68, 118
Ointment Poured Forth, 59
Omega, the, 27, 29, 59, 168, 251
Omissions, 241, 251
Only Begotten Son, His, 48, 59, 100, 113, 190, 247, 256
Only Begotten of the Father, the, 39, 41, 60, 154, 227
Only Potentate, 29, 55, 60
Only Wise God, the, 50, 60
Oppose themselves, 63, 256, 270
Oppressed, 64, 65, 129, 141, 149, 178, 179, 203
Original language, 237
Origin, 236
Owl of the Desert, an, 60, 144

P

Packer, J. I., 56
Papyri, 237
Parable(s), 10, 91, 92, 108, 140, 151, 193, 209, 259, 260
Pass away, 137, 147, 156, 195, 196, 212, 233, 246
Passover, our, 33, 60, 106
Pasteur, Louis, 260
Paul, an apostle, 22, 47, 169, 200
Patience of the saints, 257
Patient, 63, 166, 256, 270
Pavilion, a, 60, 70
Peaceable, 57
Peace, made, 177
Peace, our, 60, 176, 177, 178
Pelican of the Wilderness, a, 60, 144
Penalty, 177
Penn, William, 75

People, my, 29, 65, 111, 116, 136, 140, 149, 164, 180, 182, 190
Perfect Man, a, 60, 135
Perfection, 233, 252
Perfect, the Lord is, 230
Perish, 16, 50, 59, 69, 100, 103, 113, 123, 133, 145, 162, 164, 180, 190, 193, 212, 221, 240, 256
Persecute(d), 50, 130, 138, 176, 180
Persecution, 10, 200, 258-260
Perseverance, 286
Person of Christ, the, 60, 102
Persuaded, 181, 200, 209, 265
Perverse, 250
Peter, an apostle, 22
Peter, Laurence J., 70
Pharisees, 103, 112, 159, 175, 203, 208, 209, 241, 242
Philosophies, 234
Physician, 29, 61, 81
Pierced, 92, 107, 112, 126, 127, 131, 210
Piercing, 234
Pink, A.W., 97
Piper, John, 134
Pity, 28, 137, 208
Place of Refuge, a, 61, 76
Plagues, 55, 163, 228, 239, 243
Plant of Renown, a, 61
Polished Staff, a, 61
Poor, 27, 35, 45, 61, 65, 71, 75, 109, 134, 149, 157-160, 163, 174, 176, 188, 208-210, 259, 266
Portion, my, 61
Portion of Jacob, the, 61
Portion of Mine Inheritance, the, 61
Potter, the, 61, 181, 210
Potters field, 210
Power, all, 12, 117, 153, 156, 166, 179, 185
Power of God, the, 19, 61, 79, 162, 172, 225, 240, 249, 258, 266
Powerful, 232, 234
Praying, 286
Prayer, 22, 42, 112, 121, 134, 144, 145, 148, 164, 172, 217, 219, 221, 224, 225, 241, 242, 245, 251, 264
Preach, 19, 21, 33, 50, 51, 76, 87, 107, 128, 133-135, 149, 154, 157, 158, 162, 188, 213, 267
Preached, 15, 42, 89, 96, 133, 154, 163, 188, 190, 213, 224, 240, 249, 266
Preaching, 44, 52, 107, 162, 164, 208, 214, 240, 248
Precious, 20, 32, 45, 61, 62, 64, 76, 77, 104, 105, 162, 233
Precious Corner Stone, 62, 76, 77, 162
Preeminence, 29, 39, 45, 62
Pre-existence of Jesus, 142
Prepar(d), 21, 37, 48, 58, 65, 97, 108, 118, 129, 161, 164, 169, 200, 204, 213, 214, 246
Preservation, 231, 233-235
Preserve, 34, 46, 147, 174, 230, 231, 233, 235, 240, 252
Preserved, 53, 78, 147, 159, 169, 172, 193, 231, 233, 235, 269
Price, a, 10, 62, 181, 210
Price of His Redemption, the, 62
Priest for sin, 110
Priest Forever, a, 46, 62

Priest, 19, 28, 29, 31, 38, 39, 44-46, 57, 58, 62, 69, 70, 73, 77, 97, 103, 109, 110, 146, 180, 182, 198, 200, 205
Priest of the Most High God, the, 57, 62, 97
Prince and Saviour, a, 62
Prince of Life, the, 62, 89
Prince of Peace, the, 32, 34, 36, 58, 62, 72, 80, 154-156
Prince of Princes, 62
Prince of the Kings of the Earth, the, 38, 39, 62, 142, 159, 173
Principalities, 128, 265, 286
Prison, 154, 167, 180-182, 188, 200
Proof(s), 19, 64, 90, 100, 104, 132, 150, 267
Promised, 10, 100, 106, 108, 119, 147, 151, 192, 219, 222, 228, 231, 235, 248, 252, 262, 265
Promises, 48, 53, 57, 58, 70, 83, 101, 219-221, 233, 255
Prophecy, 35, 87, 90, 91, 95, 123, 152, 196, 197, 228, 233, 239, 243, 269
Prophet, that, 91, 114, 164
Prophet, the, 19, 36, 37, 44, 45, 49, 50, 59, 63, 72, 82, 87, 91, 96, 108, 110, 113, 114, 133, 139, 140, 149, 152-154, 157, 163, 164, 167, 169, 173, 174, 176, 180-182, 188, 191, 197, 199, 206, 210-212, 214, 263
Prophet Mighty in Deed and Word, a, 63
Prophet of Nazareth, the, 63
Prophet without Honour, a, 63
Prophets, one of the, 36, 49, 63
Propitiation for Our Sins, the, 63, 178, 182, 184
Prosper, 62, 66, 103, 172, 183, 189, 190
Protection, 208, 209, 231
Proverb(s), 23, 40, 45, 47, 56, 61, 75, 77, 78, 149, 150, 172, 183, 193, 210, 217, 219, 226, 238, 243, 251, 256, 276
Prudent, 162, 172, 240
Psalms, 27-29, 31, 32, 34-38, 40-58, 60-75, 78, 80, 81, 87, 103, 122, 129, 136, 159, 161, 190-192, 198, 204, 214, 218, 225
Pure, 57, 63, 147, 174, 176, 209, 228, 230, 231, 233, 235, 238, 240, 243, 252, 256
Purifier of Silver, a, 63
Purity, 223

Q

Questions, 121, 257
Quick and the Dead, 19, 50, 267
Quick Understanding, of, 63, 160
Quickening Spirit, a, 52, 63
Quotes, 15, 231, 238, 269

R

Rabbi, 23, 51, 64, 72, 76, 112, 120, 168
Rabboni, 64
Rain Upon the Mown Grass, 64
Raise up Christ, 248
Raise up, a prophet, 114, 115
Ransom for All, a, 64
Ransom for Many, a, 64, 111, 183, 185
Ravenhill, Leonard, 52

Reason for the Season, the, 217
Rebuke, 19, 145, 160, 236, 267
Redeemer, 52, 58, 64, 71, 101, 120, 128, 166, 168, 170, 187, 233, 266
Redeemer, my, 64, 120, 233
Redemption, 57, 62, 64-66, 157, 181, 225, 237
Redemption of Their Soul, the, 64
Redpath, Alan, 119
Reed, a, 99, 100, 126, 173, 178, 181, 201
Refiner's Fire, a, 40, 64
Refuge, my, 35, 67, 227, 248
Refuge, our, 64, 78
Refuge in Times of Trouble, a, 64, 65
Refuge for the Oppressed, a, 64, 65
Refuge from the Storm, a, 65, 71, 75
Reid, Paris, 107
Rejected, 17, 55-57, 74, 92, 136, 148, 157, 174, 175, 209, 210, 236, 243
Rejected Stone, 148
Rejected Texts, 236
Rejection, 151, 208, 209, 270
Relationship, my, 228
Remission of sins, 83, 89, 97, 111, 184, 192
Repent(ed), 33, 44, 62, 75, 133, 135, 146, 154, 161, 164, 181, 210, 214, 248
Repentance, 33, 62, 63, 89, 96, 97, 156, 164, 172, 248, 251, 256, 264, 266, 270
Report, our, 28, 65, 174
Reproach of Men, a, 35, 65, 80
Reprove, 19, 63, 99, 150, 159, 160, 238, 243, 267
Resting Place, their, 65
Resurrected, 186
Resurrection, 17, 23, 65, 88, 90, 105, 116, 120, 124, 128, 129, 132, 147, 151, 160, 161
Resurrection, appearances, 116
Resurrection and the Life, the, 17, 65, 105
Revealed, 21, 28, 65, 85, 174, 228, 250, 269
Reverend, 65
Reviled Him, 125, 146, 167
Reward for the Righteous, a, 65
Rich, 27, 61, 65, 183, 199, 208, 224, 255, 266
Riches, 47, 52, 59, 65, 80, 244, 260
Riches of His Glory, the, 65
Riddle, the, 65
Riding upon an ass, 206, 207
Right, 19, 27, 28, 30, 37, 38, 42, 50, 58, 62, 66, 68, 70, 78, 91, 98, 100, 105, 123, 124, 134, 143, 146, 151, 168, 172, 173, 175, 177, 178, 180, 181, 183, 195, 198, 201, 205, 221, 233, 245, 246, 259, 264, 265
Righteous, 27, 50, 54, 65, 66, 75, 98, 139, 140, 145, 184, 185, 189, 190, 223, 233, 248, 262
Righteous Branch, a, 66, 189, 190
Righteous Servant, my, 66, 184, 185
Righteous Judge, the, 66
Righteous man, a, 66, 231
Righteousness, 30, 34, 36, 38, 42, 51, 57, 63, 64, 66, 72, 76, 78, 92, 97, 107, 108, 118, 124, 125, 128, 129, 130, 133, 134, 139, 150, 159, 160, 162, 166, 168, 176, 177, 184, 186, 187, 189, 190, 192, 196, 197, 214, 223, 255, 264, 265, 286
Righteousness of God, the, 66, 72, 107, 125, 186

Right hand, 19, 28, 30, 37, 38, 50, 58, 62, 68, 78, 100, 105, 124, 143, 146, 168, 172, 173, 177, 178, 180, 181, 183, 195, 198, 205, 246
Rise again, 19, 23, 35, 88, 124, 147, 173
River of Water in a Dry Place, a, 66
Robinson, Darrell, 141
Rock, a, 41, 67, 69, 72, 74, 119, 132, 153, 258, 261
Rock, my, 40, 42, 46, 78, 227, 248
Rock, the, 33, 35, 53, 66, 67, 107, 119, 120, 198, 227, 248, 258, 273
Rock that is Higher than I, the, 67
Rock of Israel, the, 53, 67, 107
Rock of Offence, a, 41, 67, 69, 72, 74, 153
Rock of My Refuge, the, 35, 67
Rock of His Salvation, the, 67
Rock of Our Salvation, the, 67
Rock of Thy Strength, the, 67
Rod, the, 61, 67, 117, 159, 160
Rod out of the Stem of Jesse, a, 67, 157, 160
Roosevelt, Franklin D., 111
Roosevelt, Theodore, 38
Root of David, the, 53, 67
Root of Jesse, a, 36, 68, 159, 160
Root out of Dry Ground, a, 68
Root and Offspring of David, the, 68
Rose of Sharon, the, 53, 68
Ruben, 84, 85
Ruler, a, 68

S

Sacrifice, his, 177, 185
Sacrifice for Sins, the, 68
Sacrifice to God, a, 59, 68, 76
Sacrificial Lamb, 179
Salvation, 20, 21, 28, 29, 31, 34, 40, 42, 46, 48, 49, 53, 54, 56, 67, 68, 73, 75, 79, 104, 107, 108, 121, 133, 139, 152, 158, 161, 162, 164, 166, 167, 169, 171, 185, 187, 199, 204, 206, 207, 219, 225, 227, 228, 236, 248, 249, 252, 255, 256, 257, 266, 269, 286
Salvation, my, 40, 42, 46, 53, 68, 73, 75, 169, 227, 248
Salvation of God, the, 68, 152
Salvation of Israel, the, 68
Samaritan, a, 31, 49, 69, 158, 170
Same Yesterday, Today, and Forever, the, 49, 69
Samuel, 28, 68, 53, 67, 75, 117, 118, 237, 239, 244
Sanctify, 78, 110, 159, 266
Sanctuary, a, 41, 58, 69, 72, 110, 153, 197, 198
Sardine Stone, a, 49, 69
satan, 24, 25, 91, 95, 128, 225, 228, 229, 230, 231, 235, 238, 245, 247, 248, 250, 260, 269
Satisfied, 66, 124, 128, 184, 185
Saul, 117, 237, 239
Save, 18, 20, 48, 49, 52, 58, 63, 72, 78, 98 , 114, 125, 126-129, 145, 153, 162, 163, 177, 184, 185, 200, 206, 232, 240-242
Saved, 16, 28, 37, 55, 80, 97, 100, 104, 106, 107, 113, 121, 125-127, 161, 162, 164, 167, 169, 177, 184, 189, 190, 199, 222, 225, 240, 252, 255-257, 265, 266, 269
Saving Strength of His Anointed, the, 69
Saviour, 21, 30, 33, 43, 47, 50, 54, 58, 62, 69, 125, 138, 167, 202, 207, 236

Saviour of All Men, the, 69
Saviour of the Body, the, 69
Saviour of the World, the, 69
Scapegoat, the, 69
Scattered, 38, 69, 103, 141, 146, 165, 208, 211, 212
Scepter of Israel, the, 70
Scepter of Thy Kingdom, the, 70
Schaff, Philip, 102
Schweitzer, Albert, 171
Science, 92, 102, 234, 260
Scourge, 19, 137, 173
Scripture preservation, 235
Scripture(s), 55, 57, 74, 85-87, 91, 130, 133, 148, 172, 180, 204, 212, 219, 231, 234, 235, 269
Search, 86, 93, 139, 234
Secret, 60, 70, 71, 91, 120, 131, 136, 140, 175, 182, 211, 233, 250
Secret of Thy Presence, the, 60, 70
Seed of Abraham, the, 70, 83, 98
Seed of David, the, 70, 148, 202
Seed of Judah, 103
Seed of the Woman, the, 70
Seek, 14, 36, 56, 58, 68, 88, 92, 93, 128, 132, 133, 147, 156, 159, 160, 162, 164, 169, 187, 206, 213, 220, 224, 231, 265
Self Test, 257
Sent, 15, 17, 20, 24, 30, 39, 45, 54, 59, 65, 68, 69, 70, 72, 95, 96, 100, 103, 105, 113, 115, 118, 120, 132, 134, 139, 142, 149, 152, 156-158, 163, 164, 178, 181, 183, 187-189, 191, 206, 207, 213, 218, 222, 227, 232, 252, 256
Sent by the Father, 115
Sent One, the, 70
Separate from His Brethern, 70
Separate from Sinners, 45, 70, 77
Serpent on a pole, 113
Serpent in the Wilderness, the, 70, 113
Servant, 21, 22, 30, 31, 36, 48, 51, 53, 63, 66, 71, 83, 96, 101, 107, 114, 122, 133, 137, 153, 159, 165-172, 174, 180, 184, 185, 194, 204, 205, 212, 233, 256, 263, 270
Servant, my, 18, 30, 36, 53, 71, 83, 150, 153, 159, 165-167, 169, 172, 194, 204, 205
Servant of Rulers, a, 71, 170
Servant the Branch, my, 30, 71, 205
Shadow from the Heat, a, 65, 71, 75
Shadow of the Almighty, the, 71
Shadow of a Great Rock, the, 34, 46, 66, 71, 163
Shakespeare, William, 105, 206
Shake the head, 125
Sharper, 234
Sheep, 16, 18, 29, 36, 38, 43, 65, 104, 105, 120, 129, 137, 141, 146, 165, 178, 179, 208, 211, 212, 218, 254
Shelter, a, 71. 75
Shem, 96
Shepherd, 16, 18, 29, 32, 32, 38, 43, 65, 71, 74, 104, 118, 120, 129, 141, 146, 165, 194, 202, 208, 203, 211, 212, 254
Shepherd, my, 38, 71, 118, 129, 211, 212
Shepherd of Israel, the, 71
Shield of Faith, 286
Shield, our, 71

282

Shiloh, 71, 103, 104
Shocked, 173
Sign of the Lord, a, 72
Silent, 125, 178
Siloam, 72
Silver, 63, 74, 92, 135, 147, 174, 181, 204, 210, 230, 235, 240, 258
Simean, 84, 85
Simon Peter, 22, 73, 88, 182
Sin, 21, 27, 29, 39, 45, 49, 52, 54, 56, 58, 65, 66, 72, 81, 95-98, 100, 109, 110, 115, 125, 130, 132, 136, 143, 150, 151, 160, 164, 165, 170, 178, 179, 183, 185, 186, 188, 196, 221-223, 228, 241, 259, 265, 266
Sinaiticus, 236
Sinned, all have, 41, 223
Skeptics, 235
Slaughter, 62, 97, 178, 179, 208
Smite, 38, 70, 74, 106, 107, 113, 159, 160, 171, 200, 201, 208, 211, 212, 214
Smith, Oswald J., 186
Smitten, of God, 138, 176-178
Smote, 74, 99, 106, 133, 171, 173, 178, 180, 181, 195, 201, 212
Snare to the Inhabitants of Jerusalem, a, 41, 69, 72, 153
Sodom, 98, 250
Somebody, 194
Song of Solomon, 27, 31-33, 53, 59, 68, 150
Son, His, 39, 42, 45, 70, 72, 80, 82, 84, 88, 95, 96, 99, 100, 103, 105, 113, 146, 158, 178, 189, 224, 256, 257
Son, the, 15, 25, 31, 40, 41, 43, 47, 49, 51, 54, 56, 63, 64, 69, 70, 72-74, 82, 87, 94-98, 102, 103, 105, 111, 113, 115, 117-121, 123-126, 130, 134, 135, 137, 139, 141, 142, 146-148, 152-157, 160, 166-168, 173, 177, 180, 183-185, 187, 189, 192, 194-196, 198, 200, 203, 204, 206, 212, 227, 230, 239, 241, 242, 244, 257, 261, 262
Son from Heaven, His, 72
Son Given, a, 72, 154
Son of Abraham, the, 72, 96, 98, 102, 103, 157, 160, 189, 192, 194, 204
Son of David, the, 72, 96, 98, 102, 103, 117, 121, 146, 148, 155, 157, 160, 189, 192, 194, 203, 204, 206
Son of God, the, 16, 17, 19, 21-25, 43, 47, 49, 51, 72, 87, 95-97, 102, 103, 118-120, 123, 125, 126, 130, 135, 152, 154, 157, 167, 177, 180, 189, 192, 194, 196, 204, 230, 242, 257
Son of Joseph, the, 49, 72, 96, 102, 103, 117, 157, 189, 192, 194, 204
Son of Man, the, 15, 18, 19, 40, 41, 54, 56, 64, 70, 73, 74, 105, 111, 113, 115, 120, 124, 137, 147, 173, 180, 183, 185, 195, 196, 198, 200, 206, 212, 241, 242, 261, 262
Son of Mary, the, 31, 73
Son of the Blessed, the, 19, 73
Son of the Father, the, 73
Son of the Free Woman, the, 73
Son of the Highest, the, 20, 73, 118, 141, 142, 148, 154, 156, 196
Son of the Living God, the, 22, 73
Son of the Most High God, the, 25, 73
Son over His own House, a, 73

Son who is consecrated for evermore, the, 73
Song, my, 73, 75
Sorrows, 56, 174-178
Soul, 15, 29, 35, 36, 38, 45, 47, 52, 54, 56, 57, 63, 64, 66, 71, 76, 77, 78, 81, 111, 118, 123, 124, 126-129, 133, 137, 139, 140, 148, 149, 154, 159, 164-167, 170, 173, 183-186, 205, 207, 209, 212, 227, 233, 234, 248, 258, 263, 266
Sovereign hand, 235
Sower, a, 10, 74, 193, 260
Sower and the seed, 10, 260
Spalding, John L., 117
Spanish Proverb, 47
Sparrow alone upon the Housetop, a, 74, 144
Speak, 15, 25, 30, 31, 47, 56, 91, 96, 98, 108, 115, 132-134, 140, 150, 158, 164, 167, 170, 193, 205, 207, 236, 242, 252, 269, 286
Speak Boldly, 286
Speaking, 90, 108, 135, 228, 238
Special, 92, 108, 134, 217, 221, 264
Spirit, 15, 17, 21, 25, 30, 32, 33, 36, 41, 42, 46, 47, 52, 54, 62, 63, 71, 78, 83, 88, 92, 121, 127, 130, 134, 135, 137, 139, 145, 146, 149, 150, 154, 157-161, 163, 165-167, 170, 171, 176, 185, 188, 190, 196, 197, 204, 210, 212, 214, 221, 228, 230, 233, 234, 249, 251, 258, 264, 265, 266, 286
Spiritual Rock, that, 74, 107
Spiritual Wickedness, 286
Spitefully entreated, 19, 173
Spitted on, 19, 173
Spot, without, 105, 122
Sprung up, 10, 154, 258, 262
Spurgeon, Charles, 21, 30, 32, 37, 42, 65, 126, 135, 139, 143, 165, 173, 182, 195, 197, 208, 219
Stand, 23, 36, 40, 62, 64, 68, 107, 114, 120, 129, 131, 136, 143, 147, 152, 159, 160, 195, 232, 233, 242, 246, 259, 268, 286
Star, a, 70, 74, 113
Star out of Jacob, a, 70, 74, 113
Stay, my, 74
Stone, 24, 25, 32, 41, 45, 46, 49, 55, 57, 61, 62, 67, 69, 72, 74-77, 83, 88, 104, 143, 148, 153, 162, 175, 195, 200, 207-209, 230, 241, 242
Stone, corner, 32. 62, 76, 77, 104, 162, 207
Stone Cut out of the Mountain, a, 74
Stone Cut without Hands, a, 74
Stone, rejected, 148
Stone of Israel, the, 74
Stone of Stumbling, 41, 69, 72, 74, 153
Stone which the Builders Refused, the, 74, 148
Stone which the Builders Rejected, the, 55, 57, 74, 148
Stone which was set at Nought, the, 75, 104, 162
Stony ground, 258, 260
Stood afar off, 131, 141
Stranger, a, 27, 75, 107, 136
Strength, my, 40, 42, 46, 73, 75, 126, 127, 168, 227, 233, 248
Strength of Israel, the, 75
Strength of My Life, the, 68, 75
Strength to the Needy in Distress, a, 65, 71, 75
Strength to the Poor, a, 65, 71, 75

283

Stricken, 176-178, 180, 182
Stripes, 117, 130, 176, 177, 178, 200
Stripped, 127, 173, 178, 181
Strong Consolation, a, 75
Stronghold in the Day of Trouble, a, 75
Strong Tower, a, 71, 75
Strong Tower from the Enemy, a, 71, 75
Stronger than He, a, 76
Studd, C.T., 29
Study, 91, 108, 151, 185, 217, 222, 234, 235, 237, 266
Stumbling Block, a, 76, 162
Stupidity, 69
Submit, 228, 229, 252, 266
Suffering, 19, 31, 40, 110, 126, 126, 144, 175, 184, 223, 267
Sun of Righteousness, the, 76
Sunday, Billy, 122
Sure Foundation, a, 62, 76, 77, 162
Sure Mercies of David, the, 76, 186
Surety of a Better Testament, a, 76
Sweet Smelling Savour, a, 59, 68, 76
Sword, 35, 38, 61, 120, 127, 128, 130, 133, 138, 180, 183, 193, 198, 211, 212, 234
Sword of the Spirit, 30, 249, 286

T

Tabernacle for a Shadow, a, 61, 76
Tabernacle of David, 160, 169
Tabernacle of God, the, 76
Tahmisian, Dr. T.N., 196
Taylor, J. Hudson, 68
Teach, 12, 63, 83, 120, 129, 140, 153, 166, 167, 220, 224, 256, 259, 270
Teacher(s), 16, 19, 64, 76, 92, 112, 120, 135, 168, 267
Teacher Come from God, a, 64, 76, 112, 120, 168
Teaching us, 236
Tectus Receptus, 236, 237
Televangelists, 223
Temple, the, 21, 24, 25, 29, 30-32, 44, 56, 76, 111, 120, 121, 124, 125, 130, 133, 135, 137, 148, 151, 155, 170, 180-182, 198, 204, 205, 210, 212, 213, 223, 230, 241
Temptation, 11, 25, 40, 83, 115, 137, 212, 230, 245, 247, 258, 259
Tempted, 83, 112, 115, 230, 248
Tender Plant, a, 68, 77, 174
Tender Mercy of God, the, 77
Testator, the, 77
Testimony of God, the, 77
Thankfulness, 77
Thicket, 100
Thieves, 125, 126, 148, 177, 183
Third day, 19, 89, 99, 124, 147, 173
Thirst, 7, 15, 30, 54, 75, 79, 105, 111, 114, 119, 127, 138, 144, 158, 167, 176
Thirty pieces of Silver, 135, 181, 210
Thomas, an apostle, 23
Thoughts, 43, 106, 132, 204, 217, 231, 234, 266
Thousand years, 191
Three days and three nights, 200
Throne, Thy, 70, 117, 118, 134, 139, 148, 184

Tidings, good, 21, 165, 171, 188, 202
Timberlake, Mack, 61
Tittle, 147, 233, 246
Tolstoy, Leo, 259
Tongue, 22, 60, 70, 126, 127, 135, 145, 150, 163, 168, 170, 180, 226
Tradition of men, 234
Transgressors, 185, 186, 241
Transgressions, 57, 110, 172, 176-178
Translate(ed), 35, 222, 236, 243
Translation, 237, 238, 250
Treasure(s), 77, 81, 139, 170
Trembling, 250, 266
Tribulation, 10, 11, 18, 155, 207, 259
Tried Stone, a, 62, 76, 77, 162
True Bread from Heaven, the, 77
True Light, the, 77, 227
True Vine, the, 17, 77, 83
True Witness, the, 28, 29, 38, 77
Trust, 10, 31, 34, 40, 44, 46, 49, 68, 69, 73, 75, 115, 123, 132, 159, 160, 165, 166, 179, 203, 222-225, 227, 228, 231, 233-235, 238, 243, 244, 248, 252, 269
Trust in riches, 244
Trusted, 76, 125, 126, 130, 133, 177, 224, 225, 229
Trustworthy, 222-225
Truth, in, 73, 148, 158, 160, 189
Truth, the, 3, 11, 12, 17-19, 26, 29, 34, 52, 58, 63, 77, 79, 92, 135, 145, 150, 153, 159, 163, 167, 171, 177, 186, 188, 207, 223, 224, 228, 229, 234, 235, 238, 241, 243, 244, 247, 248, 250, 252, 255-258, 265-267, 269, 270
Truth, the acknowledging of the, 63, 256, 270
Truth, Thy Word is, 266
Twain, Mark, 36, 55, 58, 155, 174, 181, 198

U

Unbelief, 115, 209
Unbelievers, 235
Uncials, 237
Unclean Spirits, 25, 176
Undefiled, 45, 70, 77
Understanding, 3, 4, 9, 10, 34, 50, 59, 63, 78, 92, 107, 151, 157, 158, 160, 162, 189, 217, 219, 235, 240
Unknown, 20, 50, 54, 62, 69, 73, 78, 117, 119, 120, 122, 183, 203, 213, 255
Unknown God, the, 78
Unspeakable Gift, the, 78
Upholder of All things, the, 78
Upright, 78, 146, 233

V

Van Gogh, Vincent, 199
Vaticanus, 236
Veil, the, 78, 170, 198
Venden, Morris, 4, 217, 225
Very God of Peace, the, 78
Very Great, 78, 206
Very Present Help in Trouble, a, 64, 78
Victory, the, 78, 222

Vinegar, 110, 126, 128, 138, 144
Vine, true, 17, 77, 83
Vine, the, 78, 192
Vineyard, the, 33, 55
Violation, 243
Violent death, 211
Virgin Birth, 95
Virtue, 144, 172, 176, 233
Visage, 173
Voice, the, 28, 42, 54, 79, 115, 120, 144, 164, 198, 211, 230
Voltaire, 113

W

Wall of Fire, a, 79
Walk, who, 196, 251
Washed, 38, 39, 50, 62, 72, 142, 159, 173, 181, 256
Water, 7, 8, 9, 28, 34, 37, 40, 42, 46, 50, 52, 54, 64, 66, 71, 79, 82, 107, 111-113, 118, 119, 126, 129, 131, 134, 137, 156-158, 163, 167, 181, 188, 197, 198, 210, 220, 221, 241, 250, 258
Wave Offering, the, 79
Way, the, 9, 10, 12, 17, 26, 28, 52, 58, 74, 77, 79, 108, 114, 123, 129, 141, 149, 153, 154, 159, 164, 168, 189, 193, 206, 213, 220, 221, 224, 247, 260, 264, 270
Weakness of God, the, 79, 162
Weary, 34, 46, 66, 71, 163, 170
Webster, Daniel, 103, 204
Wedding Garment, a, 79
Weeping, 144, 191, 263
Weiss, Daniel, 114
Well of Living Waters, the, 79
Well of Salvation, the, 79
Wept, 174, 208, 209
Wesley, John, 40
Whale's belly, 200
Wheat and the tares, 262
Whipped, 178
Whole Armour of God, 286
Wicked, 10, 50, 98, 126, 127, 145, 149, 159, 160, 183, 231, 262, 263, 286
Wickedness, 81, 134, 135, 181, 286
Wilderness, 18, 28, 60, 70, 83, 95, 105, 109, 112-115, 121, 144, 151, 163, 164, 214, 230, 248
Wilkerson, David, 128
Wiser, 79, 162
Wisdom, 44, 52, 56, 57, 61, 64, 66, 67, 72, 77-80, 140, 155, 157, 158, 160, 162, 172, 179, 202, 214, 221, 240
Wisdom of God, the, 61, 79, 140, 162, 240
Wise and foolish virgins, 261
Wise Master Builder, a, 79
Withdraw thyself, from such, 250
Witness, 18, 20, 24, 28, 29, 34, 36, 38, 39, 43, 49, 52, 62, 77, 79, 80, 90, 111, 121, 131, 132, 134, 142, 145, 148, 155, 159, 164, 169, 173, 178, 180, 181, 186, 225, 227, 251
Witnesses, 62, 89, 129, 131, 145, 180, 264
Witnessing, 3, 161, 164, 179, 194
Witness, my, 79
Witness of God, a, 80
Witness to the People, a, 34, 52, 80, 186

Woman of Canaan, a, 218
Womb, 20, 40, 47, 109, 125, 154, 168, 196
Wonderful, 32, 34, 36, 58, 62, 72, 80, 121, 132, 140, 148, 154-156, 225, 257, 269
Wood, 99, 100, 221
Word, His, 3, 11, 87, 91, 92, 115, 147, 152, 162, 176, 182, 198, 200, 217, 219, 222, 224, 228-235, 238, 243, 244, 252, 257, 264, 269
Word, the, 10, 19, 30, 31, 37, 39, 41, 60, 73, 74, 78, 80, 87, 91, 121, 125, 131, 136, 140, 143, 147, 149, 152-154, 162, 163, 168-170, 174, 179, 188, 193, 209-211, 222, 227-235, 237-240, 242, 243, 245-247, 249, 250, 252, 255, 258, 260, 264-267, 286
Word, thy, 21, 61, 149, 169, 200, 204, 232, 244, 266, 269
Word of God, every, 25, 238, 243, 245
Word of God, the, 80, 136, 147, 188, 227-229, 231-235, 237, 243, 247, 249, 252, 255, 265, 266, 286
Word of Life, the, 80
Words, pure, 147, 174, 230, 235, 240, 252
Works, 11, 24, 41, 51, 70, 102, 104, 106, 111, 115, 116, 124, 132, 136, 140, 145, 147, 149, 155, 156, 169, 170, 175, 179, 182, 187, 208, 217, 219, 223, 225, 232, 236, 238, 242, 257, 259, 264-266, 269
Worm and No Man, a, 80
Worshipped, 10, 16, 23, 25, 34, 81, 99, 106, 124, 139, 158, 167, 170, 173, 201, 218
Worthy, 52, 80, 121, 156
Worthy Name, that, 80
Worthy to be praised, 80
Wounded, 138, 176-178
Wrestle, 286
Written, it is, 24, 25, 47, 52, 59, 63, 67, 83, 89, 109, 116, 132, 139, 143, 148, 148, 149, 162, 168, 169, 212, 213, 223, 230, 240, 245
Written Word, 225, 228, 233
Wurmbrand, Richard, 45, 149

Y

Yancey, Philip, 214
Yokefellow, the, 81
Young Child, the, 81, 82, 113, 139, 170, 199

Z

Zacharias, Ravi, 39
Zeal of the Lord of Hosts, the, 81, 156
Zeal of thine House, the, 81, 137
Zechariah, 29-31, 38, 56, 71, 79, 205-212
Zebulun, 84, 85, 154
Zerubbabel, 204, 213

"Finally,

My brethren, be strong in the Lord, and in the power of his might. Put on the whole armour of God, that ye may be able to stand against the wiles of the devil. For we wrestle not against flesh and blood, but against principalities, against powers, against the rulers of the darkness of this world, against spiritual wickedness in high places. Wherefore take unto you the whole armour of God, that ye may be able to withstand in the evil day, and having done all, to stand. Stand therefore, having your loins girt about with truth, and having on the breastplate of righteousness; And your feet shod with the preparation of the gospel of peace; Above all, taking the shield of faith, wherewith ye shall be able to quench all the fiery darts of the wicked. And take the helmet of salvation, and the sword of the Spirit, which is the word of God: Praying always with all prayer and supplication in the Spirit, and watching thereunto with all perseverance and supplication for all saints.

And for me, that utterance may be given unto me, that I may open my mouth boldly, to make known the mystery of the gospel, for which I am an ambassador in bonds: that therein I may speak boldly, as I ought to speak."

Paul, an apostle of our Lord Jesus Christ   **"See Ephesians 6:11-20"**